INTRODUCTION TO
LANGUAGE DEVELOPMENT

SECOND EDITION

INTRODUCTION TO LANGUAGE DEVELOPMENT

SECOND EDITION

SANDRA LEVEY, PhD

PLURAL
PUBLISHING
INC.

PLURAL PUBLISHING
INC.

5521 Ruffin Road
San Diego, CA 92123

e-mail: information@pluralpublishing.com
Website: https://www.pluralpublishing.com

Library of Congress Cataloging-in-Publication Data

Names: Levey, Sandra, author.
Title: Introduction to language development / Sandra Levey.
Description: Second edition. | San Diego, CA : Plural Publishing, Inc.,
   [2019] | Includes bibliographical references and index.
Identifiers: LCCN 2017041445| ISBN 9781944883430 (alk. paper) | ISBN
   1944883436 (alk. paper)
Subjects: | MESH: Language Development | Infant | Child | Adolescent
Classification: LCC P118 | NLM WS 105.5.C8 | DDC 616.85/5--dc23
LC record available at https://lccn.loc.gov/2017041445

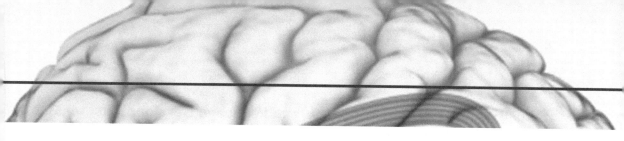

CONTENTS

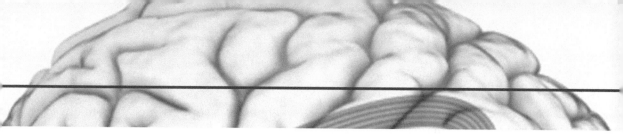

PREFACE

The inspiration for this text began when I was teaching undergraduate language acquisition courses. The goal was to ensure that complex concepts were at the appropriate level for students' understanding. An additional goal was to prepare students for future practice. To address these goals, these are the features of the second edition:

◆ Updated to reflect current research
◆ Expanded focus on evidence-based practice
◆ Improved readability through the use of boxes, explanations, and definitions
◆ A greater number of figures and tables for deeper comprehension

To help students better understand the process of language acquisition, this text presents an integrated view of the various factors that play an important role in children's acquisition of language: articulation, syntax, semantics, phonology, morphology, pragmatics, hearing, cognition, and literacy. To prepare students for what follows, an introductory chapter presents them with terminology and concepts that they will encounter in the following chapters. To support students' learning, each chapter begins with a case study and learning objectives. Case studies allow

instructors to involve students more fully in classroom discussion while developing critical thinking and using problem-solving skills. Learning objectives are provided to guide students' learning. Within each chapter, boxes, tables, figures, and examples elaborate and clarify the information presented. Study questions appear at the end of each chapter to ensure that students understand and retain the information presented in the text and classroom lectures. A comprehensive glossary of the key words in each chapter is included to help students locate and grasp the definitions of key terms. On the PluralPlus companion website, multiple-choice questions that address the material in each chapter are available, along with PowerPoint lecture slides for all chapters.

Highlights of the second edition include:

◆ A chapter that introduces theories of language development. Understanding the theoretical foundations of language development is an essential prerequisite for future evidence-based practice. This chapter concludes with practical strategies that are drawn from these theories.
◆ Several chapters include information on the *differences* that can appear when children are learning a new

language. The goal is for students to be able to distinguish differences from disorders. This information is essential, given that 5 million or more school-age children in the United States alone are English-language learners.

◆ A chapter on the brain in relation to speech, language, and cognitive development is an important contribution to students' knowledge, given the frequent interaction between speech-language pathologists and other practitioners (e.g., neurologists, psychologists, doctors, occupational therapists, physical therapists).

◆ A chapter on literacy development offers strategies for the support of children's literacy skills. The importance of literacy goes beyond reading and writing. Literacy skills are intertwined with oral language and are used to support success in mathematics skills and other academic subjects in later grades.

◆ A chapter on bilingualism introduces students to an important area of knowledge, given the growing number of children in schools who are learning a new language. This chapter describes socio-cultural factors related to bilingual language acquisition, summarizes bilingual language development, applies best practice principles for assessment, and describes cross-linguistic and bilingual approaches to intervention.

◆ A chapter on hearing loss introduces students to the impact of hearing loss on language development. While students do enroll in an audiology course within their study program, this chapter focuses on the consequences of hearing loss for speech and language.

ACKNOWLEDGMENTS

Thanks to David Munro for his help in developing the glossary and careful review of citations and references. Thanks to Marissa and David for their edits. Thanks to Celeste Roseberry-McKibbin, Susan Hocker, and Deborah Rhein for their feedback on the chapters that fell within the areas of their expertise.

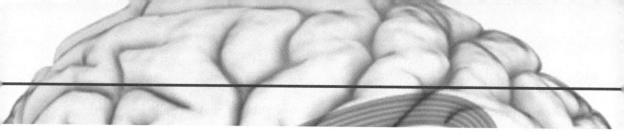

CONTRIBUTORS

Diana Almodovar, PhD, CCC-SLP received her doctorate from The Graduate Center, City University of New York. She is an Assistant Professor in the Department of Speech, Language, Hearing Sciences, at Lehman College, CUNY, where she teaches, serves as a clinical educator, and conducts research in childhood language impairments. The focus of her research centers on phonological and semantic processing during word retrieval in monolingual and English- Spanish bilingual children with language impairments.

María R. Brea-Spahn, PhD, CCC-SLP received her doctorate in Psychology from the University of South Florida. She is a Clinical Associate Professor and Director of the Bilingual Extension Program in the Department of Communicative Sciences and Disorders at New York University–Steinhardt. Her research has focused on the interaction between working memory, semantic knowledge, and language-specific phonological patterns in bilingual children. Clinical areas of practice and investigation include research on syntactic complexity in narrative discourse, strategic writing instructional approaches, and family-centered biliteracy instruction.

Denise Cruz is a bilingual speech-language pathologist and the Director of Clinical Education and Clinical Services at The Ruth Smadbeck Communication & Learning Center, Marymount Manhattan College. She has published and presented on topics that addressed bilingual language acquisition/speech perception. Clinical areas of practice and research interest include head and neck cancer, swallowing disorders, voice disorders, care of the professional voice, transgender voice, and clinical supervision.

Sylvia F. Diehl, PhD, CCC-SLP is recently retired from the University of South Florida (USF) Department of Communication Sciences in Tampa, Florida. Dr. Diehl was team leader in the language/phonology clinic and member of the USF Interdisciplinary Center for Evaluation and Intervention Team, which offers guidance to Florida Public School Systems regarding children with complex needs. She is the founder of *Friends with Sylvia* at USF, which provides social communication intervention along with parent training to children with autism spectrum disorder (ASD). She is currently the president of *Knowledge Counts,* which has supported children with ASD and their families for over 30 years.

Brian J. Fligor, ScD., PASC is Chief Development Officer at Lantos Technologies, Inc. in Wakefield, MA, and President of Boston Audiology Consultants, Inc. in Mansfield, MA. Dr. Fligor is the chair of the World Health Organization working group on standards for the Make Listening Safe™ initiative to provide consumers, health professionals, and manufacturers of portable audio systems (headphones/ MP3 players) guidance for lessening the risk for noise-induced hearing loss from improper use. He has published peer-reviewed scientific papers and academic book chapters, given invited presentations, and is author of *Understanding Childhood Hearing Loss* (Rowman and Littlefield Publishers, Baltimore, MD).

Brian A. Goldstein, PhD, CCC-SLP is Provost/VP of Academic Affairs and Professor of Communication Sciences and Disorders at La Salle University in Philadelphia, PA. Dr. Goldstein is well-published in communication development and disorders in Latino children focusing on language development and disorders in monolingual Spanish and Spanish-English bilingual children. He is a Fellow of the American Speech-Language-Hearing Association.

Sandra Levey, PhD is Professor Emerita in the City University of New York (CUNY), Lehman College. She is the chair of the Multilingual and Multicultural Affairs Committee of the *International Association of Logopedics and Phoniatrics* (IALP). Dr. Levey has published and presented on bilingual/ multilingual children's and adult's perception, language acquisition, and reading skills, along with the multicultural aspects of noise-induced hearing loss. She has received recognition from the American Speech-Language-Hearing Association as a Board Certified Specialist in Child Language.

To Aaron, who has an active interest in learning the definitions of new words; to Micah, who loves to use words to make jokes and riddles; to Marissa, the wordsmith, who creates beautiful and lyrical words and phrases; to Tania, the researcher and writer, who has written a book of her own that examines the impact of words on others; to Daniel, the musician, who loves the language of music; and to David, my husband, for his many years of companionship.

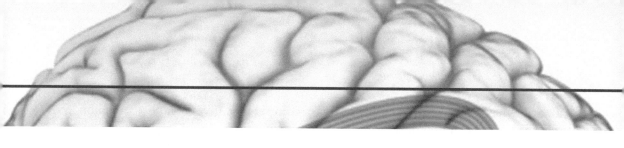

1

An Introduction to Language Acquisition

Sandra Levey

Case Study

Casey is a kindergartner who has communication difficulties. Casey does not initiate conversations with other children in the class, and friends sometimes do not understand her because of her difficulty in producing some sounds and her habit of leaving some sounds out of words (e.g., "top" instead of stop, "tay" instead of stay, and "pay" instead of play). She also has difficulty understanding directions when the teacher is asking the children to complete a task within the classroom. Identify the areas of difficulty by whether they involve communication, speech, or language.*

CHAPTER OBJECTIVES

This chapter presents an overview of children's language development, with a focus on the terminology and concepts that you will encounter in the chapters that follow. This chapter also presents a discussion of *differences*. This is a term that refers to the language factors associated with children who are learning a second language. There are a growing number of new language learners in classrooms across the world. For example, in one classroom of 30 students, 14 different languages were spoken. The ability to distinguish between a true communication disorder versus a language difference (due to learning a new language) is essential to provide evidence-based assessment and intervention. After reading this chapter, you should understand:

◆ The distinction between communication (the process of information exchange), speech (the production of sounds), and language (meaning conveyed by words, sentences, and longer utterances)
◆ The five components of language (syntax, semantics, morphology, phonology, and pragmatics)
◆ The role of cognition in language
◆ Terminology found in later chapters in this text
◆ The differences that may appear when children are learning a new language

We begin this introduction to children's speech and language development with a discussion of **communication**, followed by a discussion of **speech** and **language**. This chapter also presents a brief review of **cognition** and a discussion of the connection between cognition and language.

COMMUNICATION, SPEECH, AND LANGUAGE

Communication

Communication is the process of exchanging information through a speaker's ideas, thoughts, feelings, needs, or desires. We possess the ability to communicate using various modalities: verbal, written, gesture, pantomime, drawing, or through sign language. The ability to communicate a message successfully and to understand the concepts being communicated reflects **communicative competence**. Communicative competence involves the appropriate use of language in interaction, while **linguistic**

competence involves the acquisition and use of morphology, phonology, syntax, and semantics (Gleason & Ratner, 2017).

Morphology: In what way words and smaller units can be combined to form other words (*go + ing = going*)

Phonology: In what way sounds are combined to form words (*c + a + t = cat*)

Syntax: The word combinations used to express meaning in sentence structures (*I + see + a + bird*)

Semantics: In what way words correspond to things and events in the world (*It's raining*), how language reflects a speaker's intent (*I want to tell you a story*), or feelings (*I'm feeling good today*).

Communicative interaction involves the exchange of information between a sender (speaker) and a receiver (listener). In the exchange of information, the sender transmits information (**encodes**) that the receiver comprehends or understands (**decodes**).

Encoder/speaker	*I have a new toy!*
Decoder/listener	*Can I play with it?*

Receptive language is the ability to understand others, and *expressive language* is the ability to express and share thoughts, ideas, and feelings. Receptive language is the understanding of spoken language, sometimes referred to as auditory comprehension. It is the ability to understand language (the meanings of words, sentences, stories, and conversation); concepts (e.g., size, color, emotions, and time); and directions (e.g., *Put your books away and open your crayon box*). *Expressive language* is the ability to convey meaning and thoughts through the production of words and sentences, retelling of events and stories, and engaging in conversation.

In addition to the verbal or spoken features of communication, a listener must learn to interpret the **paralinguistic** cues that accompany spoken language (Table 1–1). Paralinguistic cues accompany spoken language and often help the listener better understand a speaker's meaning. For example, a speaker can use facial expressions to convey feelings. A speaker can also use intonation to express a question (rising intonation across a spoken utterance) or a statement (falling intonation across an utterance to confirm a fact). Produce each of the sentences that follow to demonstrate the differences in intonation in the productions of a question, a statement, or to confirm that it is Jason who is coming, and not someone else.

Jason is COMING? Asking a question to determine if Jason is coming

Jason IS coming. Making a statement to confirm that Jason is coming

JASON is coming? Asking if *Jason* is the person who is coming

Prosody is a communicative tool that involves duration (length), intensity (loudness), and frequency (pitch) when producing words or longer utterances. For example, notice that you can express sarcasm by producing the first syllable in the word with greater duration or length than the second syllable (i.e., *REAlly?*). In other words, we can change the meaning of an utterance using paralinguistic cues.

Table 1–1. *Paralinguistic Cues*

Affect	Facial expressions
Gestures	Head nods that indicate agreement or disagreement
Posture	Body position
Physical	Distance or proximity between a speaker and a listener
Intonation	Voice or vocal pitch that marks the difference between a statement (falling intonation) and a question (rising intonation)
Word stress	Emphasis on a single syllable word or on syllables in a multisyllabic word (e.g., *baNAna*)
Speech rate and rhythm	Fast, moderate, or slow, and pause or hesitation
Volume or intensity	Louder speech indicates anger or assertiveness
Pitch	High or low pitch used by different speakers
Inflection	Differences related to the context (exaggerated inflection when reading to a child versus natural inflection in conversation with an adult)

Prosody allows us to communicate different attitudes, such as sarcasm or sympathy, by changing the duration, intensity, and frequency of our spoken language.

Another factor in communication is the rhythm of speech. This involves the rising and falling patterns across the production of an utterance. For example, a sentence may consist of the following rhythm pattern (with rising patterns shown in bolded syllables or words):

I **know** you **prefer** the **bigger** cookie.

At times, the rhythm of speech is broken by hesitation as a speaker tries to think of a word. Hesitation is not always the sign of a disorder, as children learning a new language often hesitate while searching for a word in the language being learned. Examples follow of these patterns found in children learning English as a new language (Hlavac, 2011, p. 3798):

Filled pauses: *Like, you know*

Paralinguistic markers: Laughter, nervous coughing, gestures, facial expressions

Silent pauses: Lasting for a few seconds, which may occur when a new language learner is searching for a particular word

Speech and Articulation

Speech is defined as the verbal means of communicating through articulation. Articulation involves the production of speech sounds by movement of the lips, tongue, and soft palate or velum (Figure 1–1). The

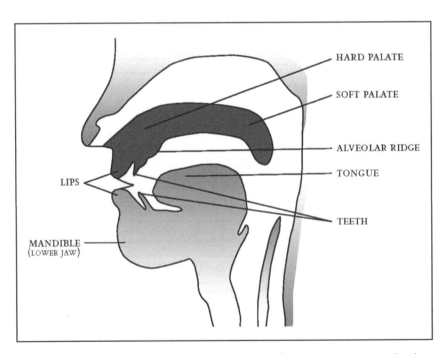

Figure 1–1. *The movable articulators consist of the lips, tongue, and velum (soft palate). Reproduced with permission from* Language Development: Understanding Language Diversity in the Classroom *(p. 85), by S. Levey & S. Polirstok (Eds.), 2011, Los Angeles, CA: Sage.*

velum plays a role in the production of certain sounds. The larynx is a muscular organ that contains the vocal cords or folds (Figure 1–2). The vocal cords are stimulated by respiration (air from the lungs). The vocal folds vibrate to produce **phonation** or voice (sound produced by the vibration of the vocal folds). The respiratory system provides the support for phonation (Figure 1–3).

Phonemes

Notice that you bring your lips together to produce the sounds "p" and "b" when producing the initial sounds in the words *pat* and *bat*. The sounds "p" and "b," along with many other sounds in English, are termed **phonemes**. Phonemes are the smallest units of sound that create a difference in meaning (e.g., /p/ vs. /b/ to distinguish *pea* vs. *bee*). Note that the change of the initial phoneme in a word results in a change in word meaning in the following examples.

Sue-two	/su/-/tu/
Tip-dip	/tɪp/-/dɪp/
Bat-cat	/bæt/-/kæt/

Phonemes are the abstract representation of speech sounds (phones), with phonemes indicated by slashes (e.g., /p/ and /b/), as found in the words *pat* /pæt/ and *bat* /bæt/. Consonant phonemes (Table 1–2) and vowel phonemes (Table 1–3) are types of English phonemes that compose words.

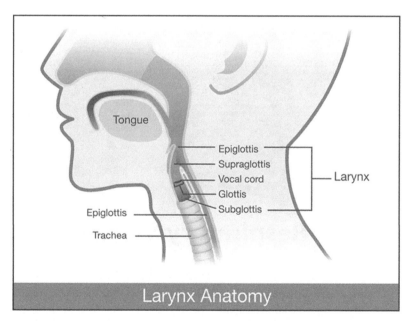

Figure 1–2. *The larynx. The vocal cords, also called the vocal folds, are shown. The glottis is the space between the vocal folds. The epiglottis is attached to the entrance of the larynx and is open for breathing and closed during swallowing. The supraglottis is the area above the glottis, and the subglottis is the area below. The trachea is a tube that extends from the larynx to the bronchial tubes in the lungs, allowing air to flow to and from the lungs. Reproduced with permission from Getty Images.*

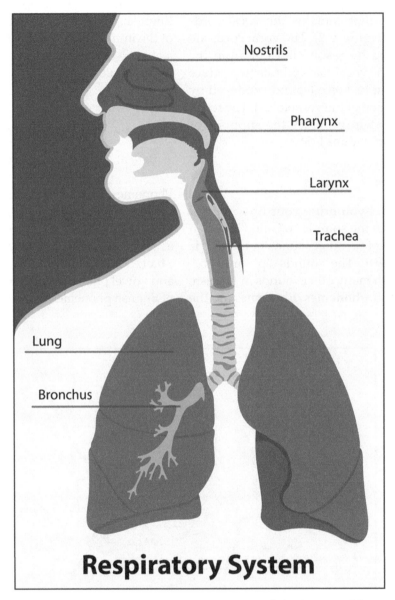

Respiratory System

Figure 1–3. The respiratory system consists of the lungs and bronchus, which is one of the two tubes (bronchi) that carry air from throat to lungs and air into the lungs. The pharynx is the place in the mouth where the nasal passages connect to the mouth and throat. Reproduced with permission from Getty Images.

Table 1–2. *Consonant Phonemes of English*

Phoneme	Initial	Medial	Final
/p/	pot	apple	lap
/b/	boy	table	cab
/t/	tea	attic	cot
/d/	dot	ladder	sad
/k/	cap	actor	sick
/g/	go	tiger	leg
/m/	mop	summer	gum
/n/	nap	tunnel	fun
/ŋ/		hanger	sang
/f/	fat	taffy	half
/v/	vest	silver	sleeve
/s/	sit	passing	bus
/z/	zoo	buzzard	fuzz
/θ/	threw	bathtub	bath
/ð/	they	mother	bathe
/ʃ/	shell	pressure	push
/ʒ/		measure	beige
/l/	leave	balloon	tall
/r/	road	farmer	car
/j/	yet	tri( )al	
/w/	wet		
/tʃ/	chin	teacher	teach
/dʒ/	jam	badger	lodge

Note: The consonant phoneme /ʒ/ occurs only in medial and final position, while the phoneme /w/ occurs only in initial position. The consonant phoneme /j/ is the sound produced in the word trial, i.e., tri /j/al). The /r/ in farmer and car (i.e., "er" and "ar") can be classified as rhotic diphthongs.

Table 1–3. *Vowel Phonemes of English*

Phoneme	Word	Phonetic Transcription
/i/	feet, eat, ski	/fit/, /it/, /ski/
/ɛ/	bet, met, friend	/bɛt/, /mɛt/, /frɛnd/
/e/	date, train, beige	/det/, /tren/, /beʒ/
/ɪ/	hit, bit, sit	/hɪt/, /bɪt/, /sɪt/
/æ/	hat, ladder, mad	/hæt/, /lædɚ/, /mæd/
/u/	you, tune, soon	/ju/, /tun/, /sun/
/ʊ/	took, should, cook	/tʊk/, /ʃʊd/, /kʊk/
/o/	go, shoulder, load	/go/, /ʃoldɚ/, /lod/
/ɑ/	on, cot, father	/ɑn/, /kɑt/, faðɚ/
/ɔ/	paw, bought, taught	/pɔ/, /bɔt/, /tɔt/
/ʌ/	sun, love, uncle	/sʌn/, /lʌv/, /ʌnkl/
/ə/	about, cannon, undo	/əbaʊt/, /kænən/, /əndu/
/ɝ/	fur, sir, burn	/fɝ/, /sɝ/, /bɝn/
/ɚ/	father, bother, burner	/faðɚ/, /baðɚ/, /bɝnɚ/

There are also vowels that are classified as **rhotic diphthongs**. These are phonemes that occur in words such as *ear, air, door,* and *car.* These phonemes are a combination of a vowel and the vowel /ɚ/. Although these sounds are combined, a rhotic diphthong is considered a single sound. Examples of these words and their phonetic form appear below.

/iɚ/   ear, deer, hear, near, appear

/eɚ/   air, hair, care, pair, stair

/oɚ/   door, floor, more, wore

/ɑɚ/   car, cart, sorry, jar, far

Orthography describes the symbols or alphabet letters (**graphemes**) of written language. Note that there is not a one-to-one correlation between graphemes and phonemes. For example, the phoneme /f/ is the last sound in the word *laugh,* while the word *laugh* is spelled with the graphemes -*gh.* It is also the first sound in the word ***physician,*** while the word *physician* is spelled with two graphemes *ph-.* Children must learn to recognize the variations between written and spoken language to develop basic reading skills.

Words are composed of one syllable (e.g., *bug, dog, cat, see, run*), two syllables (e.g., *cartoon, monkey, daytime, many*), or three or more (e.g., *gorilla, summertime, watermelon, elementary*).

A syllable is composed of the onset, which is the initial consonant or consonants (e.g., **c**at, and **st**ar). In these examples, the onset consists of the consonants "c" and "st." A syllable is also composed of the rime, which consists of the vowel and any final consonant or consonants (e.g., c**at**, and st**ar**). In these examples, the rime consists of the vowel and consonants "at" and "ar."

Speech Production

Speech production involves drawing air into the lungs. Voice is produced through the vibration of the vocal folds when this airflow is directed upward from the lungs. The air flow from the lungs sets the vocal folds into vibration (opening and closing). Vocal fold vibration results in voice production. Voiced sounds are produced when the vocal folds are brought together (adducted) to produce these sounds (e.g., /b, d, g, v, z, m, n/). The vocal folds are open (abducted) to produce unvoiced sounds (e.g., /p, t, k, f, s, h/). An unvoiced sound is produced when the vocal folds are in abducted (open) position and vocal fold vibration does not occur. A voiced sound is produced when the vocal folds are adducted (closed) for vocal fold vibration to occur (Figure 1–4).

Another factor in speech production involves the movement of the **velum** (soft palate), shown in Figure 1–5. Nasal consonants are produced when sounds exit through the nasal cavity. The presence of sound passing through the nasal cavity can be observed by placing your fingers gently on the side of your nose while producing the nasal consonant /m/, as in the word *me*. The consonant sounds that are produced with the airstream exiting through the nose are found in the words *man* /m/, *nose* /n/, and the last two sounds (ng) in the word *hang* /ŋ/. To produce these sounds, the velum is lowered so that air exits through the nose. All other consonants are produced with the velum raised, so that air exits the mouth or oral cavity.

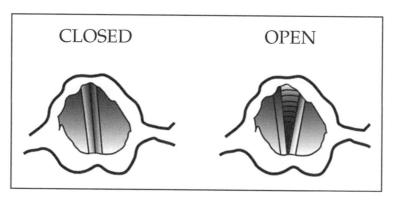

CLOSED   OPEN

Figure 1–4. *The vocal folds in adducted (closed) and abducted (open) position. Voicing occurs when the vocal folds are adducted. Unvoiced sounds are produced when the vocal folds are abducted. Reproduced with permission from* Language Development: Understanding Language Diversity in the Classroom *(p. 83), by S. Levey & S. Polirstok (Eds.), 2011, Los Angeles, CA: Sage.*

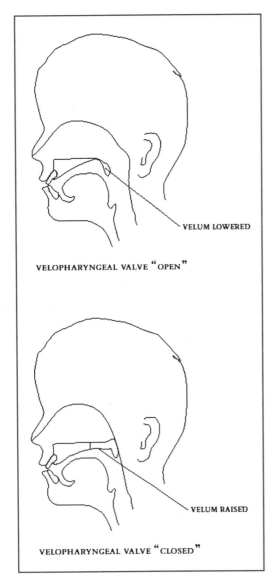

VELUM LOWERED

VELOPHARYNGEAL VALVE "OPEN"

VELUM RAISED

VELOPHARYNGEAL VALVE "CLOSED"

Figure 1–5. *The velum is lowered to allow air to flow from the nasal cavity to produce the nasal sounds, such as /m/ and /n/ and "ng" (e.g., hang). The velum is raised for all other sounds. This closes the passage between the oral cavity (mouth) and the nasal cavity (nose). Reproduced with permission from* Language Development: Understanding Language Diversity in the Classroom *(p. 88), by S. Levey & S. Polirstok (Eds.), 2011, Los Angeles, CA: Sage.*

It is important to understand that phonemes differ across languages. For example, there are English vowels that are absent in Spanish, while there are consonants in Spanish that are absent in English. The following words demonstrate some of the English vowels absent in Spanish: *cot* /ɑ/, *paw* /ɔ/, *fit* /ɪ/, and *bet* /ɛ/. Children learning a new language may not have a concept or understanding of the phonemes in the language being learned. This indicates a *difference* when a child is learning a new language that contains new sounds (or words) absent from his or her native language.

Phonology

Phonology is the part of language that is concerned with the combination of speech sounds for word formation. For example, we can combine the sounds or phonemes associated with "c" /k/, "a" /æ/, and "t" /t/ to form the word *cat* /kæt/. A different combination would result in *act* /ækt/. Over time, children understand the contrasts between sounds, such as the differences between the sounds /p/ and /b/. Children learn that these sound contrasts signal differences in meaning, as shown in the following examples:

/p/ versus /b/	*pin-bin*
/t/ versus /d/	*tip-dip*
/f/ versus /v/	*fairy-very*
/k/ versus /g/	*Kate-gate*

Phonological rules govern the distribution and sequencing of sounds in words. Distributional rules govern the position of sounds in words. For instance, the sequence *ng* can occur in word final (*sing*) or medial position (*singer*) in English. However, this sequence does appear in initial position in other languages, such as the language *Grebo*, spoken in the African country of Liberia.

Morphophonology

Another interesting aspect of phonology is that certain phonemes change because of the effect of one sound on another. These changes reflect the interaction between phonology and morphemes (**morphophonology**). For example, the unvoiced phoneme /s/ changes to a voiced phoneme /z/ when it follows a voiced consonant (e.g., /g/). However, the unvoiced phoneme /s/ does not change when it follows an unvoiced consonant (e.g., /t/). The following examples show that the plural -*s* changes to the phoneme /z/ when it follows the voiced phoneme /g/.

Dog + s = dogs /dɔgz/

Cat + s = cats /kæts/

Produce the following words and note the differences that occur when the plural /s/ follows a voiced sound (e.g., /g, d, b/) versus an unvoiced sound (e.g., k, t, p).

cups	cabs
bats	dads
cakes	bags

Phonological Processes

Phonological processes describe children's early productions of words. Phonological processes label a child's production that differs from a target word produced by adults. These productions may reflect their **perception** (auditory interpretation) of target words that are produced by adults or older language users. Phonological processes are described in Chapter 5, with examples of children's early word productions shown below.

"Nana" produced in place of *banana*

"Dada" produced in place of *daddy*

"Gogi" produced in place of *doggy*

Language

Language is defined as the means for human communication through the use of spoken words, written symbols, or sign language. Note that symbols label things, actions, thoughts, and activities. Language is also defined as a shared code that represents concepts through the use of arbitrary symbols. A shared code means that speakers and listeners can understand one another, based on a common or shared language. Language also represents concepts or ideas through the use of arbitrary symbols. The term *arbitrary* is used to label symbols that identify words, because there is no direct relationship between a word and its meaning. For example, English speakers label the entity *apple* as "apple," whereas this entity has a different name across many other languages: *pomme* (French), *manzana* (Spanish), and *æble* (Danish).

The term **generative** is also used to describe the nature of language. This describes a speaker's ability to generate many types of sentences, including novel sentences produced by children when they lack a word to identify a thing or an action (*I'm crackering my soup*). **Grammar** is the description of a language with respect to its components. The components of language consist of **form, content,** and **use** (Table 1–4). We begin with a discussion of the component *form*, which includes **syntax, morphology,** and **phonology**.

FORM

Syntax

Syntax is the component of language that involves rules for combining words to form sentences. A basic sentence is composed of subject + verb (e.g., *Tania ran*). The subject of a sentence contains nouns or pronouns. Common nouns label a person, place, or thing, while proper nouns label specific persons, places, and things. Note that proper nouns are marked with capital letters.

Nouns: *mother, dog, home, book*

Proper nouns: *Sue, New York, Sesame Street*

Pronouns: *he, she, you, it, we, they*

The basic syntactic structure (sentence) consists of a *noun phrase* (which must contain a noun) and a *verb phrase* (which must contain a verb). Children expand the length and increase the complexity of their sentences by adding modifiers. Noun modifiers include determiners and adjectives. Examples of determiners include articles (*a, an, the*); cardinal and ordinal numbers (*one, two, three* and *first, second, third*); demonstratives (*that, these, those*); quantifiers (*some of, every, each, most, all*); and possessives (*my, your, his, her, its, our, their*). Adjectives include colors; sizes (*big, thin, large*); shapes (*round, square*); qualities; and other descriptions (*happy, new, loud, sweet*).

Determiners: **the** *girl,* **a** *book,* **an** *apple*

Demonstratives: **that** *book,* **one** *book,* **some** *books are yours,* **my** *book*

Adjectives: **big** *boys,* **new** *books,* **red** *apples,* **happy** *children are playing*

Table 1–4. *The Components of Language*

Form	Syntax	Rules for sentence structure
	Morphology	Rules for forming word structure
	Phonology	Rules for combining sounds to form words
Content	Semantics	Word, sentence, or longer language meaning
Use	Pragmatics	Rules for the appropriate use of language in social interaction

Verbs label actions, and there are two classes of verbs: main verbs and auxiliary verbs. Main verbs describe an action (*run, cry, eat, sleep, read, drink, fly*), while auxiliary verbs provide information that clarifies meaning (*am, is, are, was, were, be, been, have, has, had*). There are also modal auxiliary verbs that express mood (*can, could, shall, should, will, would, do, did, may, might*). These verbs clarify speakers' attitudes when they produce utterances: a fact (*I **did** eat the cookies*) or a desire (*I **could** eat the cookies when no one is looking*).

Main verbs: *They **eat, drink, run, fell***

Auxiliary verbs: *They **are** reading, **were** reading, **have** read*

Modal auxiliary verbs: *They **can** come, **could** come, **should** come*

Syntactic structure can also be expanded by adding adverbs that modify verbs. Adverbs supply information on how, when, where, quantity (how much or how long), and time (*before, now*).

How	*The girl ran **quickly***
When	*We are going to the park **tomorrow***
Where	*Put the book **there***
Quantity	*He ate so **much** that he fell asleep*
Time	*They went to school **before** they watched TV*

Prepositional phrases indicate place (***on** the table, **in** the bowl, **next to** the chair*). The sentence *The boy threw a ball* is represented in a syntactic tree in Figure 1–6.

Children begin to produce single words at about 12 months of age, while

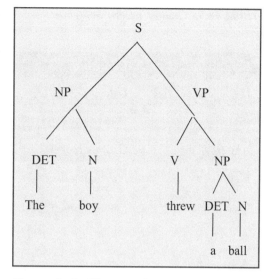

Figure 1–6. *This sample syntactic tree shows a sentence (S) that consists of a noun phrase (NP) and a verb phrase (VP). The noun phrase contains a determiner (DET), such as* the, a, *or* an, *and a noun (N). The VP contains a verb (V) and another NP. This noun phrase contains another DET and an N. There are many kinds of sentences, and this is only one example of a tree diagram.*

syntax emerges with the combination of two words at about 18 months of age. Syntactic development begins with sentences that express a request (*More cookie*), notification (*That doggy*), and negation (*No bed*). Syntactic development is demonstrated when children produce sentences with increased length and complexity. This occurs with the development of vocabulary skills and the inclusion of grammatical morphemes that indicate continued action (e.g., *going*) and plurals (e.g., *toys*). Children's early sentence productions (Table 1–5) show the development of a variety of different structures that appear at about 3 years of age (Bernstein, 2011).

Table 1–5. *Children's Early Sentence Production*

Sentence	Example
Declaratives	*I sleepy.*
Interrogatives	*Where mommy?*
Imperatives	*Gimme cookie.*
Negatives	*No more milk.*
Quantity use	*I have **two** cars.*
Adjective use	*Gimme the **big** ball.*
Adverb use	*Run **fast**.*

Morphology

Morphology is concerned with the structure of words and the parts that compose words. For example, the word *cats* is composed of two morphemes: the root morpheme *cat* and the plural morpheme *-s*. **Morphemes** are the minimal distinctive units of words that determine meaning. For example, the word *cat* cannot be broken down into smaller units (*c* or *at*) or the meaning of the word *cat* would be lost.

Free morphemes are those that have meaning by themselves (*nouns, verbs, adjectives, adverbs,* and *prepositions*). Bound morphemes occur only in combination with free morphemes (e.g., the past tense form *-ed*, the plural form *-s*, and the ongoing activity form *-ing*). Bound morphemes can be divided into two types: inflectional morphemes (e.g., *-s, -est, -ing*) and derivational morphemes (e.g., *-ful, -like, -ly, un-, dis-*).

Inflectional morphemes modify verb tense (*walk + ed*) or indicate noun number

(*dog + s*). Inflectional morphemes include the plural *-s* attached to nouns to indicate plurality, the possessive *'s* to indicate possession (*mommy's*), the present progressive *-ing* attached to verb stems to indicate present and ongoing action (*running*), and the past tense marker *-ed* to indicate a previous activity (*walked*).

Cat → cat**s**

Big → *biggest*

Run → *running*

Derivational morphemes involve a prefix (un-) or suffix (-ness). These morphemes can change the meaning of a word (e.g., *kind* becoming **un** + *kind*). This class of morphemes can also change a verb to a noun (e.g., *farm* becomes *farm + er*), as shown in the examples that follow.

Lucky → **un**lucky

He farms → He is a farm**er**

Happy → happi**ness**

Examples of free and bound morphemes are presented in Table 1–6.

Grammatical morphemes consist of conjunctions (*and, but*), articles (*the, an, a*), and prepositions (*in, under*). These morphemes have a grammatical function: to show the difference between one (one cup) and more than one (two cups), to show possession (Jason**'s** computer), or to show something that is exceptional (the bigg**est** dog I have ever seen). The role of grammatical morphemes in word formation can be found in Table 1–7. Note that these morphemes mark number (plurality), time (past and progressive action), and other areas that clarify and expand the meaning of spoken and written language.

Table 1–6. Free and Bound Morphemes

Morpheme	Example
Free	
Nouns	*car, boy, tree, book, girl*
Verbs	*run, walk, eat, drink*
Adverbs	*slowly, quickly, faster, fastest, late*
Adjectives	*good, better, best; rich, richer; dirty*
Bound	
Derivational	
Prefix: *un-, non-, in-, pre-, trans-*	*unlucky, nonstick, inappropriate, preview, insufficient, transatlantic*
Suffix: *-ly, -ist, -er, -ness, -ment*	*slowly, bicyclist, farmer, happiness, contentment*
Inflectional	
Plural	*cats, dogs, horses*
Possessive	*cat's, mommy's*
Third person singular	*eats, drinks*
Past tense	*walked* (regular) and *ate* (irregular)
Past participle	*eaten*
Present participle (present progressive)	*eating*
Comparative	*bigger*
Superlative	*biggest*

Table 1–7. *The Role of Grammatical Morphemes*

Morphemes	Grammatical Function	Example
Plural	Marks more than one of a noun	
Regular		dog**s**, chair**s**
Irregular		child/children
Possessive	Marks possession or ownership	mommy**'s**
Comparative	Marks a comparison	bigg**er**, clos**er**
Superlative	Marks something as exceptional	bigg**est**, quick**est**
Third person singular	Marks agreement with singular third person (i.e., *he, she, it*)	eat**s**, walk**s**, bark**s**
Past tense	Marks past action	
Regular		walk**ed**, bark**ed**
Irregular		ate, threw, swam
Past participle	Verb form used as an action; follows *be* or *have*	
Regular		chos**en**, prov**en**
Irregular		drunk, sung
Present progressive	Marks present action	eat**ing**, sing**ing**, bark**ing**
Uncontractible auxiliary	The *be* verb preceding other verbs; examples are *am, is, are, was, were, been*	The dog **is** barking
Contractible copula	The main copular verb is the verb *to be*	I**'m** happy, he**'s** big (from *I **am** happy* and *he **is** big*)
Contractible auxiliary	The *be* verb contracted	Baby**'s** crying (*baby **is** crying*)

Irregular Verbs

To form the past tense of certain verbs, we can add *-ed* (e.g., *walked,* and, *talked*), whereas other verbs require changes in consonants and vowels (*eat/ate, throw/threw,* and *catch/caught*). Young children often **overgeneralize** the regular past-tense inflectional morpheme *-ed* (e.g., *walk + ed*) to form the past tense of irregular verbs. In a game that involved hide and seek, 3½-year-old Micah was asked if he had left the house. He answered, *Yes, I leaved.* Aaron, age 4, was asked if he would like to see a movie. He said, *I sawed that movie.* Examples of young children's irregular verb productions are shown in the following examples.

I eated the cookie.

I throwed the ball.

I catched the ball.

Over time, children learn the irregular verbs and can say, *I ate, threw, and caught.* The irregular past-tense changes are difficult for children until the early elementary grade years (Proctor-Williams & Fey, 2007). Greater difficulty with the correct production of irregular verbs is found for children learning a second language, with greater accuracy over time with greater exposure and experience in learning a new language (de Zeeuw, Schreuder, & Verhoeven, 2013).

There is a connection between irregular past-tense verb learning and phonology (the rules for forming words). Difficulty appears in the change from /d/ to /t/ in final word position when forming irregular past-tense verbs, such as the change in the present-tense verb (*build*) to the irregular past-tense verb (*built*) (Shipley, Maddox, & Driver, 1991). Difficulty also appears with verbs that involve an internal vowel change (*ride* to *rode*).

CONTENT

Semantics

Semantics is the component of language that describes *meaning* that is conveyed by words, sentences, narratives, and conversations. Meaning is attached to entities (e.g., things and people) and to events or activities that children encounter in the world (walking, throwing, rain falling). Semantics also refers to the relationship between entities and events, as shown in the following example that illustrates the semantic relationship between *children*, *ball*, and *dog* (entities) and *throwing* (event or action).

*The **children** are **throwing** a **ball** to the **dog**.*

Semantic knowledge combines knowledge of *words* with *knowledge of the world.* Word knowledge involves learning that there are names for entities, such as people, animals, and things (*boy, dog, tree*); actions and events (*throw, drive, birthday party*); and concepts that label feelings (*happy, sad, surprised*), space (*in, on, under*), and time (*soon, late, next*). Young children observe the connection between spoken language and the entities or events/actions they label. These experiences within the environment result in their development of concepts (ideas or theories) about the things they see, hear, and experience. Conceptual knowledge is the basis for children learning the words/labels for entities, actions, feelings, space, and time.

Conceptual knowledge is what a child knows and understands about ideas, entities (people, animals, and things), and actions (events that take place in the environment) (Alt, Meyers, & Alt, 2013). Children's conceptual learning depends on two factors: information from others in the environment and innate cognitive learning skills (Gelman, 2009). Bracken and Panter (2011) describe the basic concepts understood by young children (pp. 467–468), as shown in Table 1–8.

Table 1–8. Concepts Developed by Young Children

Colors	Primary and basic color terms
Letters recognition	Upper and lowercase letters
Counting recognition	Numbers and the number of objects in a set
Size/dimension comparisons	Big/little, tall/short, long/short, same/different
Shape recognition	Circle, square, triangle
Direction/position	Under, over, near, far, in front of, behind
Self/social awareness	Happy, sad, old, young, right, wrong
Quantity	Lots, few, full, empty
Temporal/sequence	First, last, morning, night, almost

Source: Reproduced with permission from Bracken, B. A. & Panter, J. E. (2011). Basic Concepts Considered Part of the Bracken Basic Concept Scale Development (Table 1, pp. 467–468). *Psychology in the Schools, 48*(5), 464–475. John Wiley & Sons Ltd.

Conceptual knowledge begins with an understanding of spatial concepts at about 1 to 3 years of age (*in, on, under*); understanding dimensional concepts at about 2 to 3 years of age (*big/little*); colors at 3 to 4 years of age; understanding temporal (time) concepts (*yesterday, today, tomorrow*), understanding spatial/positional concepts (*first, middle, last*), and understanding concepts of *difference* or *similarity* at 4 to 5 years of age (Lanza & Flahive, 2009).

Overextension and Underextension

While children are developing their semantic knowledge, they may identify entities with similar **semantic features** as having the same label. For example, it is not uncommon to hear very young children call all four-legged animals *doggie*, produced to label a cow, cat, or tiger. Young children frequently use the perceptual characteristics of entities to extend the meaning beyond that entity (**overextension**). Over time, children acquire a more refined set of features and word meanings. Children also may have a limited representation of an entity or a thing (**underextension**), viewing a word to have a very restricted meaning. For example, Daniel, age 4, was amazed when he was told that the dog pictured on the front cover of a dog-training book was his dog's grandfather. He asked, *Shanti's grandfather was a DOG?* This represents restricted meaning, given that Daniel believed that the word *grandfather* could only refer to a person (not an animal). Over time, children learn that words can have multiple meanings. For example, the word *block* is first learned as the label for a toy (*toy **block***), then as a place (*going around the **block***), then as a verb (***block**ing the door*), and later as a metaphor (*mental **block***).

Semantic Roles and Semantic Relations

Children's early semantic development consists of semantic roles, used to convey meaning at the one-word stage of development. Some examples of semantic roles are agent, action, and affected.

Agent	Initiator (doer) of an action	*daddy, mommy, doggie*
Action	Event	*throw, kiss, drink*
Affected	Entity influenced by an action	*ball, baby, water*

At around 2 to 3 years of age, children begin to combine words to form some **semantic relations** (Bloom, Lahey, Hood, Lifter, & Fiess, 1980), with better learning of these relations occurring after age 5 (Deák & Wagner, 2013). Examples of the semantic relations acquired early are presented below.

Agent + Action	initiator + event	*Daddy throw*
Action + Affected	event/act + entity acted upon	*Drink water*
Entity + Location	entity + place	*Doggy bed* (dog in bed)

USE

Pragmatics

Pragmatics refers to the appropriate use of language in social interaction, along with the rules that govern interaction with others. Pragmatic language rules are defined as the effective and appropriate use of language to accomplish social goals, manage turns and topics in conversation, and express appropriate degrees of politeness, awareness of social roles, and recognition of others' conversational needs (American Speech-Language-Hearing Association, 2014). The behaviors that involve appropriate pragmatic interaction include *eye contact* when someone is talking to you and *turn-taking* as sender and receiver when involved in a conversation.

Pragmatics encompasses a wide range of communicative functions. These functions include the reasons for communicating; the frequency of speaking (turn-taking, maintaining the topic under discussion, and making appropriate topic changes); and the ability to modify the style of communication to adapt to different listeners (e.g., adults vs. children) and different contexts (e.g., formal vs. informal social situations). Children learn pragmatic rules through observation of others' behaviors in their environment and through insight into others' feelings and needs. Children must possess a **theory of mind** (TOM) that allows them to understand others' internal thoughts and emotions. TOM describes children's ability to understand other individuals' mental states (thoughts and feelings), a crucial skill to support pragmatic interaction (Abdelal, 2009). For example, a TOM allows a child to recognize the mental states of happiness, sadness, or other internal states. In these cases, appropriate interaction requires that we take these mental states into account.

Appropriate pragmatics are culturally determined, with differing pragmatic rules existing across cultures (Tannen, 1984). For example, some cultures consider it inappropriate to use the term *why,* while other cultures consider it inappropriate to speak to a stranger. One of the areas of pragmatic differences may appear in the relationship between a speech-language pathologist and a family, given that there are cultural differences in individuals' beliefs regarding parent–child interaction patterns (Trembath, Balandin, & Rossi, 2005). Some parents believe in structured learning and might have doubts regarding a more naturalistic or informal approach. Other parents may feel uncomfortable when asked to collaborate in a child's intervention program, given that this role differs from their cultural experiences or beliefs. Consequently, it is important to become aware of cultural differences when working with parents from different cultural backgrounds, along with being sensitive to these differences.

Speech Acts

A **speech act** labels a speaker's intent or meaning when she or he produces a sentence in social interaction (Searle, 1983). These utterances are termed "acts" because they frequently have an effect or result in an action. Notice that the following examples, produced by Sara at age 3½, frequently request or result in some sort of action.

Greeting: *Hi*

Promise: *I promise I eat my beans*

Request: *I need chocolate ice cream*

Indirect request: *Can I have a snack?*

Complaint: *Why I can't have snack?*

Invitation: *Come play with me?*

Refusal: *Don't want lunch*

The speech act *request* occurs when someone produces a question, such as *Can I have some juice?* Note that the request for juice takes the syntactic form of a question (*Can I . . . ?*) while requesting an action on the part of the listener (*Give me juice*). This is an **indirect speech act** that has the *syntactic form* of a question but has the *meaning* of a request. The understanding of the word *can* is acquired early (e.g., *Can I have a cookie?*), although the understanding of most indirect speech acts is acquired later (Evans, Stolzenberg, Lee, & Lyon, 2014), Over time, children learn to make requests in a more pragmatic or appropriate manner by using the word *please* and through the use of indirect requests (*Can you, could you, would you mind . . . ?*). Children's pragmatic/social interaction skills become more appropriate over time through observation and better understanding of others' minds in terms of how they might feel or react to a request or a comment.

Children are able to make requests in a more appropriate manner when their language skills develop to include **modal auxiliary verbs** (e.g., *can, could, shall, should, will, would, may,* and *might*) to produce indirect speech acts (e.g., *Can I have a snack?*). The use of modal auxiliaries leads to more polite requests. Children begin to use modal auxiliaries around age 5. Note that the older child's approach to making a request for a cookie is *very* indirect in the following examples. Note that the younger children's requests are more direct.

2-year-old	COOKIE!
3-year-old	*Gimme cookie*
5-year-old	*Can I have a cookie?*
7-year-old	*Those cookies sure smell good!*

WRITTEN LANGUAGE

Written language is also a method of communication, with a strong connection between writing skills and literacy (the ability to read and understand written text). Engaging children in writing games also prepares them for reading tasks in early grades, as children's early writing skills are associated with the development of literacy (Graham, Harris, & Fink, 2000). Children begin their writing with scribbles and drawing, advance to writing letters, and progress to writing their names. Children's written development follows the following examples (Bernstein & Levey, 2002). Children first represent syllables, frequently without vowels (*girl* written as GRL). Next, simple and frequently seen words are spelled correctly (e.g., *cat*). However, less frequently seen words are not spelled correctly (e.g., *knife* or *night*). The development of writing is shown in the attempt to spell the word *dragon* at different stages of writing development.

Kindergarten	MPRMRHM
First grade	GAGIN
Second grade	DRAGUN

COGNITION

Cognition involves knowledge and intellectual capacity (Levey, 2011). Cognition is a mental mechanism that allows a child to achieve the cognitive skills shown in Table 1–9 (Ferry, Hespos, & Gentner, 2015; Gentner, 2003). Cognitive skills involve

Table 1–9. Cognitive Abilities

Adapt to the environment	Adjusting to different elements, situations, and events
Draw abstractions	Forming ideas or concepts by extracting information from experiences
Plan	Thinking ahead to arrange a method for achieving a goal
Generalize experiences	Forming conclusions for experiences and drawing on information from prior experiences
Thought about objects/events	Making sense of the things that one has experienced
Compare/contrast objects/events	Evaluating differences and/or similarities
Use symbols (words)	Representing the label and meaning for objects and events
Language learning	Acquisition of syntax, semantics, phonology, morphology, and pragmatics
Store information	Allowing later retrieval through working and long-term memory for entities, objects, actions, and events

the ability to plan, adapt to new situations, draw on previous experience, and to store information in memory.

There are two important factors associated with cognition: attention and working memory. Attention consists of the ability to focus on the essential factors in a specific context or task, along with the ability to ignore distractions and irrelevant information. Working memory, also sometimes termed *short-term memory*, provides children with the ability to store information encountered in a current experience (Galotti, 2017). Working memory is essential for a child to be able to store, internalize, and retrieve or remember information. An example of working memory is when we are asked to remember a series of spoken directions (e.g., first . . . next . . . finally). Limited short-term memory skills may influence the acquisition of language skills (Gathercole & Baddeley, 1990; Montgomery, Magimairaj, & Finney, 2010). Children with poor working memory skills have difficulty with classroom tasks, such as the recall of spoken directions and spoken sentences and the identification of rhyming words in a lengthy verbal task (Gathercole, Durling, Evans, Jeffcock, & Stone, 2008).

Working Memory

Working memory is defined as the holding of information in mind, along with updating this information when necessary to revise or add new information. For example, if an adult gives the child a multi-step set of directions to follow (e.g., put on your shoes, go into my room, and get my purse), a child with poor working memory will have difficulty keeping the series of directions in mind. Storage of information allows children to save this information in memory. Internalizing information consists of the child adopting information and making it part of his or her knowledge. Retrieving information is the ability to recall the information that has been stored.

Social Cognition

Social cognition allows us to determine what information is already known by a listener, what information is needed, and what possible misunderstandings might occur. It is the development of a TOM (understanding others' thoughts, desires, goals, motives, and emotions or feelings) that allows children to acquire social cognition. Social cognition allows children to interact appropriately with others and to see things from others' point of view, given the knowledge of others' mental states.

Social cognition is a cognitive process that enables a child to recognize and understand social signals (Frith, 2008). Examples of social signals include facial expressions (fear or anxiety) that may warn the presence of danger and eye gaze direction that may indicate the presence of an interesting object or event. Social cognition is an important skill in infants' cognitive development. It allows infants to refer to mothers' facial expressions to determine whether it is safe (or not safe) to approach a novel object.

In one study of social cognition, infants were exposed to a situation in which an object was caused to fall. In this study, infants were shown two conditions when an object fell: there were adults who had not seen the object fall and there were adults who had seen the object fall. Infants as young as 12 months of age understood who needed help finding the object versus who did not need help (Liszkowski, Carpenter, & Tomasello, 2008). They pointed more often for the adults who did not see where it fell to show them the location of the fallen object. Social cognitive skills were demonstrated when infants pointed more frequently to the fallen object to assist the adults who did not see where it fell.

Executive Function

Executive function refers to the cognitive abilities used to control and to coordinate information for planning goals, controlling responses (inhibition), shifting between tasks (cognitive task or set shifting), and keeping information in mind to guide future actions (working memory) (Carlson, Zelazo, & Faja, 2013). Executive functions also play a role in regulating lower order cognitive processes (Key-DeLyria & Altmann, 2016), such as initiation, planning, working memory, attention, problem solving, and verbal reasoning (Table 1–10). Executive functions also play a role in the control and regulation of cognitive flexibility (shifting between ideas or tasks) and the inhibition of inappropriate actions. Children's executive function abilities have been shown to develop between 3 and 4 years of age (Willoughby, Wirth, & Blair, 2012).

Executive functions allow children to accomplish the following tasks, essential

Table 1–10. *Cognitive Functions*

Cognitive Function	Examples
Executive Functions	
Inhibition	The conscious or unconscious restraint of a behavior or an impulse to act
Initiation	Beginning an activity or thought process
Planning	The ability to list steps needed to attain a goal or complete a task
Working memory	The capacity to hold and process information
Attention	Sustained focus on a task and the ability to disregard distractions
Discrimination	The recognition of differences
Problem solving	The ability to define and solve a problem in an efficient manner
Verbal reasoning	The ability to understand facts and concepts or ideas expressed in words and to manipulate this information to solve a problem
Theory of mind	The ability to understand others' thoughts, feelings, and ideas

as children become older and enter academic contexts:

Keep track of time

Plan

Accomplish tasks within time limits

Apply previously learned information to solve current problems

Analyze information

Request help when needed

Theory of Mind

Another aspect of cognitive development is the **theory of mind**. TOM describes the ability to understand the mental states of others (Baron-Cohen, 1993, 1996; Peterson, 2014), along with understanding and predicting how someone else will act and explaining why a person acted in a certain manner. Mental states consist of our thoughts, feelings, emotions, reactions to events, and ideas. TOM allows a child to appreciate others' mental states (Baillargeon, Scott, & He, 2010; Miller, 2006). Children's TOM can develop through exposure to conversations that contain **mental state verbs** (Astington, 1990; Ruffman, Slade, & Crowe, 2002), such as *thinks, knows,* and *believes.*

He thinks he will get a new bike.

He knows where I put the car.

He believes that I will share my candy.

Failure to develop a theory of mind is a factor in certain disorders, such as autism (Baron-Cohen, 1996; Laing Gillam, Hartzheim, Studenka, Simonsmeir, & Gillam, 2015; Whyte, Nelson, & Scherf, 2014).

The ability to understand someone else's mind does not emerge until around 4 years of age (Baillargeon et al., 2010; Hale & Tager-Flusberg, 2003; Miller, 2006). However, 3- to 4-year-old children possess the understanding that others' desires and beliefs are associated with certain emotions, such as happiness, sadness, surprise, and other emotional reactions (Lane, Wellman, Olson, LaBounty, & Kerr, 2010). The true understanding of the mental state verbs that are associated with the human mind appears around 31 months (Bartsch & Wellman, 1995), with the production of *think* and *know.* The mental state verbs that emerge at 36 months are *think, remember, forgot, thought,* and *pretend* (Nielson & Dissanayake, 2000). The following mental terms were produced by Micah, at age 3, when he heard his baby brother crying.

*I **think** his feelings are hurt. I **know** what to do. I can fix it.*

A TOM marks the cognitive abilities of typically developing children, shown in the ability to take another person's perspective or point of view into consideration (Paul, Landa, & Simmons, 2014).

Narratives play a role in learning mental state verbs (Laing Gillam et al., 2015). Narratives require that children understand characters' feelings and actions, which can be described with mental state verbs such as *thinks, worries,* and *feels* (de Villiers & de Villiers, 2003). Narratives introduce children to characters' feelings, beliefs, and thoughts, along with the language associated with these concepts. For example, in a story such as "Goldilocks and the Three Bears," children must understand the motivations that guide the characters' behavior, along with understanding the characters' feelings that result from the problematic situations (e.g., the broken chair, the missing porridge, and someone sleeping in the baby bear's bed).

Metacognition and Metalinguistic Abilities

Metacognition consists of a child's self-knowledge of his or her own language and thought processes. Metacognition refers to the mental processes used to plan, monitor, and analyze one's thinking and behaviors. Metacognitive strategies consist of processes used to regulate and self-monitor cognitive abilities, such as planning and checking outcomes of a task. This allows children to determine what they need to do to complete a goal and how successful they are at completing this goal. This skill provides children with the skills needed for successful academic progress, such as preparing for class and completing class assignments. Metacognition allows children to be aware of their learning abilities, what strategies may help to remember details from directions or a lecture, and what strategies are most successful in solving problems or making decisions.

Metalinguistic abilities involve the ability to think overtly about language; manipulate the structural features of language at the phoneme, word, or sentence level; and focus on the language form (Finestack, 2014). Metalinguistic abilities allow a child to think and talk about language, along with the ability to use language to talk about language (Bernstein & Levey, 2002). Metalinguistic awareness allows a child to become aware of syllables and phonemes in words, rhymes, and ambiguous words (e.g., *cut* as using

a knife, *cut* as sharing profits, *cut* as moving ahead of someone in a line); to become aware of antonyms (add-subtract), synonyms (afraid-scared), and homonyms (ate-eight); and to become aware of syntax (e.g., the awareness to rewrite a task to make it more understandable).

Verbal Reasoning

Verbal reasoning consists of the ability to make inferences about new experiences, transfer what has been learned across different experiences, and identify relevant information when making comparisons. Children's development of analogical reasoning allows them to notice correspondences and make inferences about similar facts or experiences across contexts (Morrison, Doumas, & Richland, 2010). A typical analogical reasoning task is presenting a child with the items *cat*, *kitten*, and *dog* ("Cat is to kitten as dog is to?"). A successful response to this analogy task requires the production of a relational similarity, such as *puppy*. Children's analogical reasoning plays a role in problem solving (Richland, Chan, Morrison, & Au, 2010). For example, when a child notes that a *stool* can be the tool to reach a toy, the child can understand that a *ladder* is a tool to reach something high. This reflects analogical reasoning through drawing the connection between approaches to solving a problem.

LANGUAGE DIFFERENCES

There has been a growing awareness of bilingual cultural and language differences over the last decade (Beverly-Ducker & Polovoy, 2009). Over this period, there have been efforts to improve the quality of speech, language, and hearing services for diverse language speakers. Given the increased diversity in classrooms across the world, speech-language pathologists must become aware that "differences" (i.e., dialect or language differences from a speaker's dialect or language) do not imply "disorders" or "deficiencies."

> A **dialect** is a variation of a particular language that is distinguished by phonology, grammar, or vocabulary. Each dialect spoken is considered a legitimate rule-governed language system. In the United States, examples of dialects include African American English, Appalachian English, and Standard American English. Variations in the use of language are an important reflection of an individual's cultural identity, which derives from sociocultural, sociolinguistic, and historical roots (DeJarnette, Rivers, & Hyter, 2015; Rickford & Rickford, 2000; Rickford & Rickford, 1976; Smitherman, 2000).

Practitioners must also be aware of the positive aspects of bilingual or multilingual learning. For example, children from bilingual homes who become proficient in both their native and second languages have improved educational outcomes in terms of school completion rates, grades, achievement test scores, educational aspiration, and personal adjustment (Bedore, 2010). Research also shows that typically developing children draw on the correspondence between their native language and the language being learned to support learning a new language (Siu & Ho, 2015). It is essential to acquire the knowledge of bilingual differences, given that so many children whose primary language is not English are currently enrolled in kindergarten to twelfth-grade programs in the United States and other countries across the globe.

> One of the language productions that may be seen with children learning a new language is the use of the word "do" as a general all-purpose (GAP) verb, when the correct verb is absent in a child's language ability (Paradis, 2016). In this case, a child may produce the sentence *I do baseball* instead of *I played baseball*. The use of the GAP verb disappears as the language skills of new language learners develop over time.

SUMMARY

In this chapter, we have reviewed the following components of language:

◆ We reviewed the components of speech and language and the relationship between language and cognition.
◆ We learned that there is a close relationship between the components of language: A speaker's meaning (semantics) must be conveyed in the appropriate sentence form (syntax), with the correct morphemes assigned to indicate past tense (morphology), with the correct phonetic patterns assigned (phonology), and the appropriate manner of interaction between a speaker and a listener (pragmatics).
◆ We also learned that children form hypotheses or theories of how language works, as when children produce the word *eated*. This shows that children have acquired grammar

but have not yet learned the correct application of the rules.
◆ We discussed the distinction between a disorder and a linguistic difference.

Chapter 2 explores the theories that account for children's language acquisition and development to aid in the understanding of how children acquire and develop language.

KEY WORDS

Cognition

Communication

Communicative competence

Content

Decode

Dialect

Encode

Executive function

Form

Generative

Grammar

Graphemes

Indirect speech act

Language

Linguistic competence

Metacognition

Metalinguistic abilities

Modal auxiliary verbs

Morphemes

Morphology

Morphophonology

Orthography

Overextension

Overgeneralize

Paralinguistic

Perception

Phonation

Phonemes

Phonological processes

Phonology

Pragmatics

Prosody

Rhotic diphthongs

Semantic features

Semantic relations

Semantics

Social cognition

Speech

Speech act

Syntax

Theory of mind

Underextension

Use

STUDY QUESTIONS

1. What is the difference between communication, speech, and language?

2. Describe the importance of metalinguistic abilities in a child's language development.

3. Explain why morphology is an important part of sentence development.

4. Describe and give an example of the connection between morphology and phonology.

5. Explain why a child may say *I eated a cookie*.

REFERENCES

Abdelal, A. M. (2009). Assessment and treatment of pragmatic disorders: Integrating linguisticand neurocognitive perspectives. *Perspective on Language Learning and Education, 16(2)*, 70–78.

Alt, M., Meyers, C., & Alt, P. M. (2013). Using ratings to gain insight into conceptual development. *Journal of Speech, Language, and Hearing Research, 56(5)*, 1650–1661.

American Psychiatric Association. (2013). *Diagnostic and statistical manual of mental disorders* (5th ed.). Washington, DC: Author.

American Speech-Language-Hearing Association. (2012). *ASHA's recommended revisions to the DSM-5*. Retrieved from http://www.asha.org/uploadedFiles/DSM-5-Final-Comments.pdf

American Speech-Language-Hearing Association. (2014). *Social language use (pragmatics)*. Retrieved from http://www.asha.org/public/speech/development/Pragmatics

American Speech-Language-Hearing Association. (2016). *Speech and language disorders and diseases*. Retrieved from http://www.asha.org/public/speech/disorders/

Astington, J. W. (1990). Narrative and the child's theory of mind. In B. K. Britton & A. D. Pellegrini (Eds.), *Narrative thought and narrative language* (pp. 151–171). Hillsdale, NJ: Erlbaum.

Baillargeon, R., Scott, R. M., & & He, Z. (2010). False-belief understanding in infants. *Trends in Cognitive Science, 14(3)*, 110–118.

Baron-Cohen, S. (1993). From attention-goal psychology to belief-desire psychology: The development of a theory of mind, and its dysfunction. In S. Baron-Cohen, H. Tager-Flusberg, & D. J. Cohen (Eds.), *Understanding other minds: Perspectives from autism* (pp. 59–82). New York, NY: Oxford University Press.

Baron-Cohen, S. (1996). *Mind blindness: An essay on autism and theory of mind*. Cambridge, MA: MIT Press.

Bartsch, K., & Wellman, H. M. (1995). *Children talk about the mind*. Oxford, UK: Oxford University Press.

Bedore, L. M. (2010). Choosing the language of intervention for Spanish-English bilingual preschoolers with language impairment. *Evidence-Based Practice Briefs, 5(1)*, 1–13.

Bernstein, D. K. (2011). Language development form age 3 to 5. In S. Levey & S. Polirstok (Eds.), *Language development: Understanding language diversity in the classroom* (pp. 139–160). Los Angeles, CA: Sage.

Bernstein, D. K., & Levey, S. (2002). Language development: A review. In D. K. Bernstein & E. Tiegerman-Farber (Eds.), *Language and Communication Disorders in Children* (5th ed., pp. 27–94). Boston, MA: Allyn & Bacon.

Beverly-Drucker, K., & Polovoy, C. (2009, June 16). ASHA multiculturalism expands as 20th century closes. *The ASHA Leader*.

Bloom, L., Lahey, M., Hood, L., Lifter, K., & Fiess, K. (1980). Complex sentences: Acquisition of syntactic connectives and the semantic relations they encode. *Journal of Child Language, 7*, 235–261.

Bracken, B. E., & Panter, J. E. (2011). Using the Bracken basic concept scale and Bracken concept development program in the assessment and remediation of young children's concept development. *Psychology in the Schools, 48(5)*, 464–475.

Carlson, S. M., Zelazo, P. D., & Faja, S. (2013). Executive function. In P. D. Zelazo (Ed.), *The Oxford handbook of developmental psychology* (1), *Body and mind* (pp. 706–743). Oxford, UK: Oxford University Press.

Cavallo, S. A. (2011). The production of speech sounds. In S. Levey & S. Polirstok (Eds.), *Language development: Understanding language diversity in the classroom* (pp. 79–100). Los Angeles, CA: Sage.

Cavallo, S. A., & Levey, S. (2014). Speech production. In S. Levey (Ed.), *Introduction to language development* (pp. 59–72). San Diego, CA: Plural.

Deák, G. O., & Wagner, J. H. (2013). "Slow mapping" in learning of semantic relations. *Proceedings of the Annual Conference of the Cognitive Science Society, 25*, 318–323.

DeJarnette, G., Rivers, K. O., & Hyter, Y. D. (2015). Ways of examining speech acts in young African American children. *Topics in Language Disorders, 35*(1), 61–75.

de Villiers, J. G., & de Villiers, P. A. (2003). Language for thought: Coming to understand false beliefs. In D. Gentner & S. Goldin-Meadow (Eds.), *Language in mind: Advances in the study of language and thought* (pp. 335–384). Cambridge, MA: MIT Press.

de Zeeuw, M., Schreuder, R., & Verhoeven, L. (2013). Processing of regular and irregular past-tense verb forms in first and second language reading acquisition. *Language Learning, 63*(4), 740–765.

Evans, A. D., Stolzenberg, S. N., Lee, K., & Lyon, T. D. (2014). Young children's difficulty with indirect speech acts: Implications for questioning child witnesses. *Behavioral Sciences and the Law, 32*, 775–788.

Ferry, A. L., Hespos, S. J., & Gentner, D. (2015). Prelinguistic relational concepts: investigation analogical processing in infants. *Child Development, 86*(3), 1386–1405.

Finestack, L. H. (2014). Language learning of children with typical development using a deductive metalinguistic procedure. *Journal of Speech, Language, and Hearing Research, 57*, 509–523.

Frith, C. D. (2008). Social cognition. *Philosophical Transactions of the Royal Society B: Biological Sciences.* Retrieved from http://rstb.royalsocietypublishing.org/content/363/1499/2033

Galotti, K. M. (2017). *Cognitive development: Infancy through adolescence* (5th ed.). Los Angeles, CA: Sage.

Gathercole, S. E., & Baddeley, A. (1990). Phonological memory deficits in language disordered children: Is there a causal connection? *Journal of Memory and Language, 29*, 336–360.

Gathercole, S. E., Durling, E., Evans, M., Jeffcock, S., & Stone, S. (2008). Working memory abilities and children's performance in laboratory analogues of classroom activities. *Applied Cognitive Psychology, 22*, 1019–1037.

Gelman, S. A. (2009). Learning from others: Children's construction of concepts. *Annual Review of Psychology, 60*, 115–140.

Gentner, D. (2003). Why we're so smart. In D. Gentner & S. Goldin-Meadow (Eds.), *Language in mind: Advances in the study of language and thought* (pp. 195–235). Cambridge, MA: MIT Press.

Gleason, J. B., & Ratner, N. B. (2017). *The development of language* (9th ed.). Boston, MA: Pearson.

Graham, S., Harris, K. R., & Fink, B. (2000). Extra handwriting instruction: Prevent writing difficulties right from the start. *Teaching Exceptional Children, 33*, 88–92.

Hale, C. M., & Tager-Flusberg, H. (2003). The influence of language on theory of mind: A training study. *Developmental Science, 6*(3), 346–359.

Hlavac, J. (2011). Hesitation and monitoring phenomena in bilingual speech: A consequence of code-switching or a strategy to facilitate its incorporation? *Journal of Pragmatics, 43*(15), 3793–3806.

Key-DeLyria, S. E., & Altmann, L. J. P. (2016). Executive function and ambiguous sentence comprehension. *American Journal of Speech-Language Pathology, 25*, 252–267.

Laing Gillam, S., Hartzheim, D., Studenka, B., Simonsmeir, V., & Gillam, R. (2015). Narrative intervention for children with autism spectrum disorder. *Journal of Speech-Language-Hearing Research, 58*, 920–933.

Lane, J. D., Wellman, H. M. Olson, S. L., LaBounty, J., & Kerr, C. R. (2010). Theory of mind and emotion understanding predict moral development in early childhood. *British Journal of Developmental Psychology, 28*(4), 871–889.

Lanza, J. R., & Flahive, L. K. (2009). *LinguiSystems guide to communication milestones.* East Moline, IL: LinguiSystems.

Levey, S. (2011). Theories and explanations of language development. In S. Levey & S. Polirstok (Eds.), *Language development:*

Understanding language diversity in the classroom (pp. 17–36). Los Angeles, CA: Sage.

Liszkowski, U., Carpenter, M., & Tomasello, M. (2008). Twelve-month-olds communicate helpfully and appropriately for knowledgeable and ignorant partners. *Cognition, 108*(3), 732–739.

Miller, C. A. (2006). Developmental relationships between language and theory of mind. *American Journal of Speech-Language Pathology, 15,* 142–154.

Montgomery, J., Magimairaj, B., & Finney, M. (2010). Working memory and specific language impairment: An update on the relation and perspectives on assessment and treatment. *American Journal of Speech-Language Pathology, 19,* 78–94.

Morrison, R. G., Doumas, L. A. A., & Richland, L. E. (2010). A computational account of children's analogical reasoning: Balancing inhibitory control in working memory and relational representation. *Developmental Science,* 1–14.

Murray, E., McCabe, P., Heard, R., & Ballard, K. J. (2015). Differential diagnosis of children with suspected childhood apraxia of speech. *Journal of Speech, Language, and Hearing Research, 58,* 43–60.

National Institute on Deafness and Other Communication Disorders. (2011). *Specific language impairment.* Retrieved from http://www.nidcd.nih.gov/health/voice/pages/specific-languageimpairment.aspx

National Institute on Deafness and Other Communication Disorders. (2015). *Specific language impairment.* Retrieved from https://www.nidcd.nih.gov/health/specific-language-impairment

Nielson, M., & Dissanayake, C. (2000). An investigation of pretend play, mental state terms and false belief understanding: In search of a metarepresentational link. *British Journal of Developmental Psychology, 18,* 609–624.

Paradis, J. (2016). The development of English as a second language with and without specific language impairment: Clinical implications. *Journal of Speech, Language, and Hearing Research, 59,* 171–182.

Paul, R., Landa, R., & Simmons, E. (2014). Assessing and treating communication. In J. McPartland, A. Klin, & F. Volkmar (Eds.), *Asperger syndrome: Assessing and treating high functioning autism spectrum disorder* (2nd ed., pp. 103–142). New York, NY: Guilford Press.

Peterson, C. (2014). Theory of mind understanding and empathic behavior in children with autism spectrum disorders. *International Journal of Developmental Neuroscience, 39,* 16–21.

Proctor-Williams, K., & Fey, M. E. (2007). Recast density and acquisition of novel irregular past tense verbs. *Journal of Speech, Language, and Hearing Research, 50,* 1029–1047.

Redmond, S. (2016). Language impairment in the attention deficit/hyperactivity disorder context. *Journal of Speech, Language, and Hearing Research, 59,* 133–142.

Richland, L. E., Chan, T.-K., Morrison, R. G., & Au, T. K. (2010). Young children's analogical reasoning across cultures: Similarities and differences. *Journal of Experimental Child Psychology, 105,* 146–153.

Rickford, J., R., & Rickford, A. E. (1976). Cut eye and suck teeth: African words and gestures in New World guise. *Journal of American Folklore, 89*(353), 294–309.

Rickford, J. R., & Rickford, R. J. (2000). *Spoken soul: The story of Black English.* New York, NY: Wiley & Sons.

Roseberry-McKibbin, C., & O'Hanlon, L. (2005). Nonbiased assessment of English language learners: A tutorial. *Communication Disorders Quarterly, 26*(3), 178–185.

Ruffman, T., Slade, L., & Crowe, E. (2002). The relationship between children's and mothers' mental state language and theory-or-mind understanding. *Child Development, 73*(3), 734–751.

Searle, J. (1983). *Intentionality: An essay in the philosophy of mind.* New York, NY: Cambridge University Press.

Shipley, K. G., Maddox, M. A., & Driver, J. E. (1991). Children's development or irregular past tense verb forms. *Language, Speech, and Hearing Services in Schools, 22,* 115–122.

Siu, C. T.-S., & Ho, C. S.-H. (2015). Cross-language transfer of syntactic skills and reading comprehension among young Cantonese-

English bilingual students. *Reading Research Quarterly, 50,* 313–336.

Smitherman, G. (2000). *Talkin that talk.* New York, NY: Routledge.

Tannen, D. (1984). The pragmatics of cross-cultural communication. *Applied Linguistics, 5*(3), 190–195.

Trembath, D., Balandin, S., & Rossi, C. (2005). Cross-cultural practice and autism. *Journal of Intellectual and Developmental Disability, 30*(4), 240–242.

Whyte, E. M., Nelson, K. E., & Scherf, K. S. (2014). Idiom, syntax, and advanced theory of mind abilities in children with autism spectrum disorders. *Journal of Speech, Language, and Hearing Research, 57,* 120–130.

Willoughby, M. T., Wirth, R. J., & Blair, C. B. (2012). Executive function in early childhood: Longitudinal measurement and developmental change. *Psychological Assessment, 24*(2), 418–431.

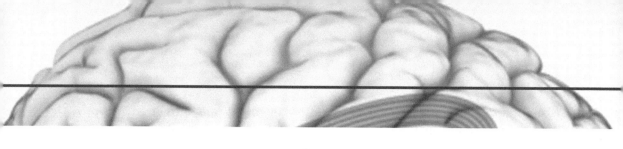

2

An Introduction to Theories of Language Development

Sandra Levey

Case Study

A child is part of a family that has moved to a new country. The first language spoken by this child is Japanese, but now the child must enter a school where English *is spoken. Based on one of the theories presented in this chapter, what are some of the methods that can be used to support this child's learning a new language?*

The theories we review in this chapter offer explanations of children's language development. These theories also offer insights into how practitioners might best provide support for children with language disorders. After you have read this chapter, you should understand the following topics:

◆ The role of innate skills in language acquisition
◆ The role of the environment in language acquisition
◆ The interaction between innate skills and the environment in language development

◆ The factors that best support children's language development

CHAPTER OBJECTIVES

The theories of language acquisition presented in this chapter can be placed into four main categories: **principles and parameters theory**, **social interaction theory**, **cognitive theory**, and **emergentism**. Understanding these theories is essential, as language development theories offer approaches that can be used to support children with language difficulties.

A summary of the main points of these theories is presented in Table 2–1.

PRINCIPLES AND PARAMETERS THEORY

Chomsky (Berwick & Chomsky, 2016; Chomsky, 1957, 1965) argues that language acquisition is based on an **innate** (inborn) structure in the human brain, with the brain prewired to provide children with the capacity to learn language. The term *prewired* means that human infants are born with a brain equipped with the ability to learn language. This innate brain mechanism is termed the **language acquisition device (LAD)** (Namy, 2001). The LAD is the part of the human mind that provides children with the ability to grasp the basic structure of a language's syntax (sentence forms). The LAD contains **principles** and

Table 2–1. Language Development Theories

Theory	Description
Principles and Parameters	An innate language acquisition device (LAD) allows children to establish grammatical information from spoken language. The LAD consists of innate language principles that are common to all languages (e.g., a noun occurs in all sentences across all languages) and parameters that can be set for the grammatical rules for a particular language. Through hypothesis testing, children use information from spoken language in the child's environment. Thus, parameter setting is the process that allows children to produce the correct grammatical forms for different languages.
Social Interaction	Social interaction within the environment provides the essential information for language development. Language develops through experience with language as it is used in the environment. Language information is gained from interaction with peers and adults with more advanced language skills.
Cognitive	Language acquisition emerges through cognitive skills, such as object permanence (the ability to produce words for entities or things that are absent). Play is viewed an essential vehicle for language development. Children form *schemas*, consisting of psychological structures that allow children to attach meaning to entities (e.g., living things), objects, and actions or events in their environment.
Emergentism	Language learning is based on the "emergent" effect of cognitive, social, pragmatic, and attentional factors. Language develops through pattern-finding for language used across different situations. Patterns involve regularities, such as the use of the word "more" to obtain additional items. Children are also viewed as sensitive and alert to the frequency of words that are used in spoken language. For example, they become aware of the frequent use of *wh*-words (e.g., *what, where, why*) to form questions.

parameters that facilitate a child's language development.

- ◆ **Principles** are innate language general rules that include the general principles that apply to all languages, such as the principle that a sentence must contain a subject (e.g., *The **dog** ate my cookie*) and a verb (e.g., *The dog **ate** my cookie*).
- ◆ Parameters are language-specific rules that apply to the specific syntactic structure for different languages, such as the word-order rules that differ across languages. For example, subject-verb-object (SVO) word order is a rule for English but not for other languages, which use different word orders to form sentences.

> SVO is the word order used in English, Swahili, and romance languages (e.g., Spanish, Portuguese, French, Italian, and Romanian); SOV is the word order used in Korean, Persian, and Turkish; VSO is the word order used in Arabic and Hawaiian; VOS is the word order used in Fijian and Malagasy; and OSV is the word order used in Warao (spoken in Venezuela, Guyana, and Suriname).

Parameters can be viewed as *switches* that can be turned "on" or "off," with the language spoken in the environment acting as a trigger for these switches. Exposure to the language spoken in the environment will allow the child to set the correct parameter (structure) for a specific language (e.g., SVO or OVS). Both English and Japanese involve different settings for this parameter: English is an SVO language, while Japanese is a subject-object-verb (SOV) language. The word-order difference between these languages is shown below (Smith, 2012).

John put the book on the table.

John-gahon-woteiburu-niokimashi.ta [John book table put].

Parameter setting provides the language learner with the ability to set the correct parameters for that language spoken in the environment (e.g., SVO or SOV).

In this theory, the basic mechanism for syntactic development is based on an operation termed *merge* (Berwick & Chomsky, 2016). *Merge* combines two syntactic objects (e.g., noun and verb) to create a new object (noun + verb), as in the following example.

Noun: *Dogs*

Verb: *Bark*

Noun + verb: *Dogs bark*

The process continues with the combination of additional objects to form longer utterances, as shown in the following examples. This process is presented to explain children's development of more lengthy and complex sentence structures.

Read books: verb + noun

I read books: noun + verb + direct object noun

I read new books: noun + verb + adjective + noun

In summary, children are born with an innate mechanism that provides them with the ability to learn the structure (syntax) of a language. There are innate principles that apply to rules that govern all languages across the world. Parameters are set by exposure to the sentence structure of the language spoken in the child's environment.

SOCIAL INTERACTION THEORY

Social interaction theory is based on the hypothesis that children's language acquisition emerges through interaction with others and through experience with the language used in the external environment (Bates, 1976; Bates & MacWhinney, 1982; Piaget, 1954; Vygotsky, 1935). Children possess the desire to interact with others, and language acquisition and development emerge from these social interactions. Within social interaction, adults and children with greater knowledge provide guidance for children's language acquisition and development. Language learning takes place with exposure to language as more experienced language users label, describe, and discuss entities (e.g., people, things, and animals); actions (swimming, drinking, and cutting); events (parties, football games, and parades); and others' states of mind (feelings, beliefs, and knowledge).

Language emerges within the environment through play, conversation, observation, and experience with the use of language in daily activities, such as shopping, school, cooking, and play. Children also use these daily activities to develop play schemes that require language used by more advanced users (e.g., a pretend birthday party, visit to the doctor, or grocery shopping). Learning the *meaning* of spoken language emerges as children learn how words/sentences are used to represent entities, actions,

and events. One example is learning the word "cut." At first, a child perceives the word *cut* when someone is talking about *cutting* paper, bread, cake, or hair. Later, the word *cut* is heard when someone says, *He cut class today* or *They cut jobs in our department.* Thus, the environment contains actions and events that allow children to expand their vocabulary knowledge.

Social interaction theory is based on the idea that more experienced language users play a role in developing higher-order functions. Vygotsky (1935) used the term **zone of proximal development** to describe the distance between a child's actual developmental level (determined by independent problem solving) and his or her level of potential development. The zone of proximal development is the distance between what children can do by themselves (**retrospective mental development**) and the concepts or skills that they can learn with assistance from adults or children with more advanced language skills (**prospective mental development**). In this theory, social interaction is the vehicle that facilitates the development of language skills for children to reach prospective mental and language development goals. Communicative interaction in a social context activates children's internal developmental processes, especially through tasks that demand conscious reflection or problem solving (Vygotsky, 1988). **Scaffolding** is the approach frequently used by adults to support learning language (Table 2–2). Examples of **scaffolds** are conversational recasts, used to add new information to a child's utterance while preserving the child's meaning. In the examples shown below, note that the adult provides the correct irregular verb form (*ate*), the auxiliary verb (*are*),

Table 2–2. *Scaffolds*

Expansions to extend the length of an utterance	Child: *Baby run* Adult: *That's right. The baby is running.*
Extensions to extend the length of an utterance while adding information	Child: *The boy cry* Adult: *The boy is crying because he fell down.*
Recasts are models of the correct target forms of a child's incorrect production.	
Syntactic recasts	Child: *That doggie* Adult: *Yes, that **is a** doggie.*
Semantic recasts	Child: *That **apple*** Adult: *That's a **peach.***
Phonological recasts	Child: *Wanna**nana*** Adult: *You want a **banana.***
Cloze procedures (sentence completion) use an open-ended phrase that stimulates a child's language skills, with the goal to elicit the target word (*play*).	Adult: *You said, "I want to____."*
Models are used when a child requires an example of an appropriate response.	Adult: *You could say, I want milk.*

the inflectional morpheme (-*ing*), and the preposition (*to*).

Child	*I eated*
Adult	*You ate*
Child	*I go play*
Adult	*Yes, you are going to play*

Scaffolds provide an effective approach to developing children's language skills (Cleave, Becker, Curran, Owen Van Horne, & Fey, 2015). With scaffolds, children can learn the correct target form of words and more complex language structures. Many studies have shown that the use of scaffolds, such as recasts, play a positive role in children's language development (Cleave et al., 2015). As shown in Table 2–2, a scaffold may provide syntactic, semantic, and/or phonological information.

In summary, language develops through social interaction. Within the context of social interaction, children gain information from adults and children with greater knowledge. Scaffolds play a role in language development, with more experienced speakers providing correct models of the child's intended language goal.

COGNITIVE THEORY

Cognitive theory is based on the idea that language acquisition and **cognition** are connected (Piaget, 1954). A cognitive approach to learning and human development places greater emphasis on mental or internal factors than on environmental or external factors (Heo, Han, Koch, & Aydin, 2011).

In children's early cognitive development, **schemas** (psychological structures) allow children to understand, attach meaning, and organize knowledge about entities they are exposed to in the environment. A schema can be defined as a mental representation of a child's experiences in the environment, allowing the child to develop the word or words to describe these experiences. These mental representations are internalized or stored in memory for future events.

Schemas develop when a child is first exposed to a particular entity, such as the word *dog* used to describe this animal. The child then forms a schema for the label *dog* that includes a description (e.g., tail, four-legged, and furry). Frequently, children use the schema that identifies a dog to label other entities that share similar characteristics. For example, young children frequently identify cows, cats, and other furry and four-legged animals as *doggy*. Over time, children learn the correct labels for these animals, along with other labels that share similar characteristics.

In Piaget's (1954) theory, certain cognitive abilities are viewed to play a role as prerequisites for language development. For example, **object permanence** is the ability to produce words for entities or events that are *out of sight*. Once children achieve this cognitive ability, at around 10 months of age, they understand that entities (e.g., *mommy*) and objects (e.g., *ball*) exist even when they cannot be seen or heard. Piaget also emphasized the role of play as essential in learning language (Mooney, 2013). Play represents the imitation and the use of language that identifies

activities and experiences in a child's environment (e.g., taking care of a baby, shopping, cooking, going to school, or going to the doctor). Children learn the language that is used to label these experiences (e.g., *diapering*, paying at *checkout*, putting your coat in the *cubby*). Children's play also supports the development of the language aspects of social skills, such as turn-taking, cooperation with other children in developing and interacting in a play scheme, and learning how to initiate and terminate this interaction (Galotti, 2017).

In summary, innate cognitive abilities allow children to learn language gained through interaction and experience within the external environment. Certain cognitive skills support language development, such as the ability to form schemas or concepts (ideas) about how things look and how things work. Schemas provide children with the language used to label things, actions, and events that they are exposed to in their environment.

EMERGENTISM

Emergentism posits that language development *emerges* from the "emergent" effects of social, pragmatic, and cognitive factors (Bates & MacWhinney, 1982, 1988; Behrens, 2009; Hirsh-Pasek, Golinkoff, & Hollich, 1999; Poll, 2011; Seidenberg & Elman, 1999).

- ◆ Social skills emerge from children's innate desires to interact with others.
- ◆ Pragmatic skills involve interaction, such as eye contact and appropriate communication.
- ◆ Cognitive skills involve the ability to remember information, maintain attention to tasks, understand

language, and understand others' feelings and thoughts.

Language development also emerges from children's **pattern finding**. Pattern finding describes children's sensitivity to regularities in the patterns of adults' utterances (Tomasello, 2003), such as spoken language patterns across different situations. One example is the pattern used with the word *more*, associated with the meaning of additional items or amounts (e.g., *more milk*, *cookies*, or *blocks*). Children are sensitive to these repeated patterns, with the word *more* shown in early language production. Children also acquire the patterns associated with forming questions, as speakers use *Wh*-words (e.g., *what, where,* and *why*) to form questions. This is an example of another pattern that contributes to children's language development, while early productions do not follow the structure of adults' productions:

What you do?

Where you go?

Why he cry?

Children's pattern sensitivity is also seen in their early production of the past-tense form of the words *eat* and *throw* (e.g., *eated* and *throwed*). This is because the regular past-tense verb form of *-ed* (*walked, talked, baked*) is produced far more frequently than the irregular past-tense forms of *ate* and *threw*. Subsequently, children's active **language processing** leads to later production of the correct irregular past-tense forms, given greater experience and longer exposure to spoken language (Poll, 2011).

In summary, emergentism proposes that language learning is based on the "emergent" effect of cognitive, social, and pragmatic factors, while pattern finding allows children to find similarities in the way words, phrases, and sentences are used and combined across different utterances and different situations. Patterns are based on the consistent use of language to label certain actions. These patterns are stored in children's memory for later language use, such as the use of *Wh*-words to form questions.

> Language processing refers to the way we use words to communicate ideas and feelings, and how communication is understood. This is a process of the brain that allows individuals to create and understand language.

SUMMARY

The theories presented in this chapter have provided explanations of language acquisition and development. As presented in the introduction to this chapter, there is a connection between language development theories and practice, as practitioners may employ the factors presented in theories to address children's needs. The following section presents the factors and approaches drawn from the theories presented in this chapter.

FACTORS AND APPROACHES DRAWN FROM LANGUAGE DEVELOPMENT THEORIES

The application of principles and parameters involves the following approaches (Wilson, 2008).

◆ Complete grammatical sentence models: children require complete correct grammatical models, i.e., sentences that contain all elements. These elements could consist of determiners (e.g., *the, a, an*), pronouns (e.g., *she, he, we, they, him, her, our, their*), auxiliary verbs (e.g., *is, am, are, was, were*), and locative terms (e.g., *in, on, under, between, behind*).

◆ Syntax structure: the use of subject-verb-object order for English-speaking children is essential to provide a model of the use of nouns and verbs to construct sentences.

◆ *Wh*-questions: these questions can be used to elicit utterances (e.g., *Who is sitting on the chair/What is he doing?*). In contrast, yes/no questions (e.g., *Is that a dog?*) will only elicit the single word *yes* or *no*. The use of *Wh*-questions will encourage the child to produce a longer and more complex utterance.

Social interaction theory offers the following approaches to support children's language development.

◆ Language emerges from a child's desire to communicate with others in the environment. Thus, language emerges from the innate desire for social interaction and to engage in communication. Learning occurs when adults provide labels for objects, actions, and events (e.g., *apple, running, parade*).

◆ It is important to create situations that engage a child in social interaction. This can be developed in a play scheme, in explaining a game, a conversation that addresses a child's interest, and other types of social schemes.

◆ More experienced language users play a role in developing children's language, as interaction between these language users and children activates children's internal learning skills (Vygotsky, 1935, 1988). Communicative interaction with others is an essential factor in children's language development. Children must be engaged in problem solving with adult guidance to stimulate the development of thought. Scaffolding is the process to guide this development.

◆ Recasts: the use of scaffolds includes recasts, used to ensure that a child produces a full grammatical utterance. For example, if the child omits the auxiliary verb (e.g., *I going*), an adult can recast the utterance to provide a model of the inclusion of this element (e.g., *I **am** going*).

The application of cognitive theory offers the following methods for developing language abilities, along with the development of the social use of language in play.

◆ Piaget (1954) proposed that play supports children's language development, as play involves the imitation of daily and familiar activities in a child's environment. Thus, the language used in these activities can be used in the children's pretend play schemes, with the use of more sophisticated language skills than in ordinary contexts (e.g., playing the role of an adult or another entity that differs from the child's actual identity).

◆ Play and language: children learn to use objects in a symbolic manner in pretend play, allowing them to function at a higher cognitive level than in ordinary contexts. For example, cognitive skills are activated when children use objects to represent other entities, such as the use of a doll to represent a real baby with the feelings and needs of a living entity (e.g., crying, hungry, sick).

◆ Pretend play and active engagement: play schemes frequently consist of reconstructing familiar activities (e.g., going to school, going on a doctor visit, or shopping) with the use of language used by more advanced language users in these actual activities. The familiar context ensures that the child will be able to understand the context and increases the likelihood of producing utterances.

Emergentism has provided approaches that play a role in children's language acquisition and development (Poll, 2011).

◆ Input: there is a need for frequent and abundant input to activate and strengthen language learning. The quantity of input is the crucial element, consisting of the amount and the number of inputs. For example, if a child lacks the use of plurals (e.g., cats), frequent and abundant examples of plurals are necessary for learning. If a child requires models of the correct sentence structure, greater input can be achieved using storybooks that contain the sentence structures that will support their learning. Book reading can be followed by conversational exchanges about the storybook (e.g., *What do you think will happen . . . why do you think she . . . what would you do if . . . ?*). Research shows that shared book reading may provide support for

progress in children with delayed language development (Poll, 2011).

◆ Active engagement: active engagement can be achieved through activities that are based on a child's interests. This approach is most successful in eliciting children's production of sentences. In these activities, scaffolds can be used to provide a model of the correct language target, with some examples of scaffolds shown in Table 2–2. Conversational recasts are an example of this approach, with the adult providing the correct language form in a positive manner while maintaining the child's meaning.

In summary, there are similar factors that appear across the theories discussed in this chapter, which are suggested to play a role in children's language development.

◆ The use of scaffolds to provide a positive model of the correct language target
◆ Play as a vehicle to develop language skills
◆ Focus on children's interests to attain engagement in all tasks
◆ Interactive tasks that include frequent and abundant input to target children's communicative interaction, such as interactive book reading, discussion of readings, and the elicitation of children's interpretation of characters' behaviors and feelings to encourage the use of mental state verbs (e.g., *think, believe, feel*).

The goal of this chapter was to provide an understanding of the theories that offer explanations of language acquisition, along with the methods that may play a role in children's language learning.

KEY WORDS

Cognition

Cognitive theory

Emergentism

Innate

Language acquisition device (LAD)

Language processing

Main verb

Object permanence

Parameters

Pattern finding

Principles

Principles and parameters theory

Prospective mental development

Retrospective mental development

Scaffolding

Scaffolds

Schemas

Social interaction

Social interaction theory

Zone of proximal development

STUDY QUESTIONS

1. What is one main difference between these theories of language acquisition?

2. Explain why more frequent input leads to language learning.

3. Explain why scaffolds, such as conversational recasts, are important in supporting children's language development.

4. Explain the role of play in children's language development.

REFERENCES

Bates, E. (1976). *Language and context: The acquisition of pragmatics.* San Diego, CA: Academic Press.

Bates, E., & MacWhinney, B. (1982). Functionalist approaches to grammar. In E. Wanner & L. R. Gleitman (Eds.), *Language acquisition: The state of the art* (pp. 173–218). Cambridge, UK: Cambridge University Press.

Bates, E., & MacWhinney, B. (1988). What is functionalism? *Papers and Reports on Child Language Development, 27,* 137–152.

Behrens, H. (2009). Usage-based and emergentist approaches to language acquisition. *Linguistics, 47*(2), 383–411.

Berwick, R. C., & Chomsky, N. (2016). *Why only us: Language and evolution.* Cambridge, MA: MIT Press.

Chomsky, N. (1957). *Syntactic structures.* The Hague, Netherlands: Mouton.

Chomsky, N. (1965). *Aspects of the theory of syntax.* Cambridge, MA: MIT Press.

Cleave, P. L., Becker, S. D., Curran, M. K., Owen Van Horne, A. J., & Fey, M. E. (2015). The efficacy of recasts in language intervention: A systematic review and meta-analysis. *American Journal of Speech-Language Pathology, 24,* 237–255.

Galotti, K. M. (2017). *Cognitive development: Infancy through adolescence* (2nd ed.). Los Angeles, CA: Sage.

Heo, J. C., Han, S., Koch, C., & Aydin, H. (2011). Piaget's egocentrism and language learning: Language egocentrism (LE) and language differentiation (LD). *Journal of Language Teaching and Research, 2*(4), 733–739.

Hirsh-Pasek, K., Golinkoff, R. M., & Hollich, G. (1999). Trends and transitions in language development: looking for the missing piece. *Developmental Neuropsychology, 16*(2), 139–162.

Mooney, C. G. (2013). *An introduction to Dewey, Montessori, Erikson, Piaget, & Vygotsky* (2nd ed.). St. Paul, MN: Redleaf Press.

Namy, L. L. (2001). Language acquisition device. In A. J. Salkind (Ed.), *Child development: The Macmillan psychology reference series* (p. 227). New York, NY: Macmillan.

Piaget, J. (1954). *The construction of reality in the child.* New York, NY: Basic Books.

Poll, G. H. (2011). Increasing the odds: Applying emergentist theory in language intervention. *Language, Speech, and Hearing Services in Schools, 42,* 580–591.

Seidenberg, M. S., & Elman, J. (1999). Do infants learn grammar with algebra or statistics? *Science, 284,* 5413.

Smith, M. (2012). *Testing the head directionality parameter in L2 Japanese.* Retrieved from https://ttu-ir.tdl.org/ttu-ir/handle/2346/45201

Tomasello, M. (2003). *Constructing a language: A usage-based theory of language acquisition.* Cambridge, MA: Harvard University Press.

Vygotsky, L. S. (1935). *Mind in society: The development of higher psychological processes.* Cambridge, MA: Harvard University Press.

Vygotsky, L. S. (1988). Inner speech. In M. B. Franklin & S. S. Barten (Eds.), *Child language: A reader* (pp. 181–187). New York, NY: Oxford University Press. (Original work published 1962)

Wilson, M. S. (2008). Chomsky's minimalist program: A linguistic primer. *Perspectives,* 69–77.

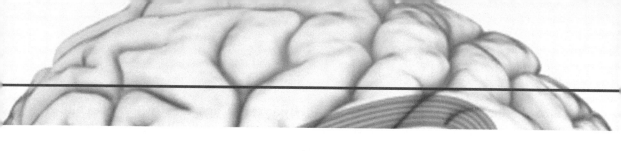

3

The Brain and Cognitive, Speech, and Language Development

Denise Cruz and Sandra Levey

Case Study

Sammy is a 3-year-old child who engages in communicative interaction with other children in his preschool class. He follows multiple-step directions (e.g., put away your toys, find your place on the rug, and choose a book). He can also understand and respond to feedback from his teacher and when he has difficulty sharing toys with other children. He is also able to understand other children's emotions when they are *upset. He pays attention when the classroom teacher is reading a story and does not interrupt her storytelling. The other children enjoy playing with him, as he is able to think of new play activities. After reading this chapter, you will understand the role of the brain in communication, in the ability to understand and follow verbal directions, and in the ability to understand others' feelings, thoughts, and emotions.*

CHAPTER OBJECTIVES

A speech-language pathologist (SLP) must develop an understanding of the functions of the brain, given that there is often interaction between an SLP and other practitioners (e.g., neurologists, psychologists, doctors, occupational therapists, physical therapists). Knowledge of the brain and the terminology used to describe the brain provide an SLP with the ability to appropriately interact with these other professionals. The SLP must also have a good understanding of the neurological systems that relate to speech, language, and cognitive abilities. This knowledge provides an SLP with a better understanding of the nervous system and the role of the brain in language development, along with understanding the language difficulties associated with disorders. Given that the brain represents the path to the acquisition and development of speech and language abilities, engaging children's interest and participation in tasks is essential so that their brains are activated for learning. After reading this chapter, you should have a basic understanding and appreciation of:

◆ The components and divisions of the human nervous system
◆ The role of the brain in speech and language abilities
◆ The role of the brain in cognitive and executive functions

SKILLS ASSOCIATED WITH THE BRAIN

Early language development is influenced by a child's environmental experiences and the stimulation that comes from interaction with language and events in the environment (Levey & West, 2011). Based on a child's experiences, specific neural pathways develop. Neural pathways associated with behaviors that are repeated more frequently will be strengthened and reinforced. Consequently, rich and frequent interaction plays a positive role in children's language development.

By 5 years of age, the structure of a child's brain approximates that of an adult (Mildner, 2008).

We have gained a better understanding of the skills of the brain through technological advances that allow investigators to view the activity of the brain while an individual is processing information or engaged in different tasks (Booth, Wood, Lu, Houk, & Bitan, 2007; Brownsett & Wise, 2010; Buccino et al., 2001; Mottonen, Jarvelainen, Sams, & Hari, 2004; Watkins & Paus, 2004; Watkins, Strafella, & Paus, 2003). The electrophysiological tests that examine language and cognitive processing are presented in Table 3–1. Through these methods, we have learned that the brain is organized into networks that support speech, language, and cognitive abilities.

One of the methods to measure brain function is **real-time functional magnetic resonance imaging (rtfMRI)**. This method examines changes in regional cerebral blood flow to measure oxygen levels in the brain. This reveals which areas of the brain are active in certain cognitive or language tasks. For example, there was increased activity and blood flow to the frontal regions of the brain when children were asked questions about a story character's state of mind (e.g., what the character *thought, felt, desired,* or *believed*) (Baron-Cohen et al., 1994). This increased activity appeared when children were asked to think about someone else's state of mind (e.g., *What is she thinking?*), while this activity did not appear when asked to answer questions regarding simple physical actions (e.g., *What is he doing?*).

The frontal areas of the brain are involved in cognitive tasks that require making decisions, solving problems, and making judgments about others' men-

Table 3–1. Electrophysiological Tests that Examine Language and Cognitive Processing

Event Related Potentials (ERPs)	Measures a brain response during a sensory, cognitive, or motor task
Magnetoencephalography (MEG)	Provides information regarding brain activity during perceptual or cognitive processing tasks (Eysenck & Keane, 2015; Kemmerer, 2015)
Positron Emission Tomography (PET)	Allows the visualization of brain function by monitoring blood flow and glucose metabolism. Active brain regions will metabolize more glucose. This technique is used to examine mental functions during cognitive and language tasks (Webb, 2017).
Functional Magnetic Resonance Imaging (fMRI)	Detects changes in neural activity by tracking changes in blood oxygenation (Beeson, 2010; Eysenck & Keane, 2015). Functional MRI images allow for mapping increased neural activity during tests that examine language and cognitive processing.

tal states (e.g., what others are thinking, feeling, or expecting). A **theory of mind (TOM)** provides children with the ability to understand others' mental states. This allows the child to interact appropriately with others through an understanding of their internal thoughts, feelings, needs, and intentions. The findings of the rtfMRI study show that children's brains are more active when they are asked to consider others' mental states.

The human brain makes it possible for a child to develop the ability to plan, organize, and learn. Exposure to new information and events leads to the ability of the brain to reorganize its structure in response to these experiences. Brain plasticity, also known as **neuroplasticity**, describes the ability of the brain to change and adapt when an individual is exposed to new experiences (Cherry, 2016). Neuroplasticity is the lifelong ability of the brain to alter or make changes in its structure when exposed to new information or new experiences. The brain possesses the ability to reorganize pathways, create new connections, and in some cases even create new neurons in response to these experiences. The development of the brain continues through adolescence and early adulthood. The changes that occur during puberty and adolescence support the essential skills for executive functions (e.g., attention, memory, reasoning, logic, and problem solving).

Neuro refers to neurons (nerve cells that are the building blocks of the brain and nervous system) and *plasticity* refers to the brain's malleability, defined as the ability to change in response to new experiences and new information.

THE STRUCTURE OF THE NEURON

We begin with a discussion of the function of the **neuron**, the basic functional unit of the nervous system (Webb, 2017). Neurons underlie all neural behavior that play a role in speech, language, and hearing abilities (Figure 3–1). A neuron is a nerve cell that receives and sends electrical signals within the body, consisting of **sensory neurons** and **motor neurons**.

◆ Sensory neurons are nerve cells that transmit information to the central nervous system (the spinal cord or brain) that includes sensations: sight, hearing, taste, smell, and touch.
◆ Motor neurons transmit "directions" to muscles for movement.

Sensory neurons provide the ability of children to see, hear, taste, smell, and touch things in the environment. When they are provided with the labels for these experiences (e.g., *doggie, music, sweet, perfume, soft*), their vocabulary skills develop. Their motor skills allow them to engage in actions, along with learning the labels for these experiences (e.g., *throw, break, roll*).

Interneurons are a third type of neurons, located in the CNS (brain and spinal cord). Interneurons act as a link between sensory (sensation) and motor (movement) neurons. They transmit signals through the use of **neurotransmitters**. Neurotransmitters are the chemicals that allow the transmission of signals from one neuron to the next across a **synaptic cleft** (the space between two neurons).

Neurons have three structural components: the **soma** (cell body), an **axon**, and a branching complex of **dendrites** (see Figure 3–1).

◆ **The soma**, or cell body, maintains the function of the neuron. The cell body

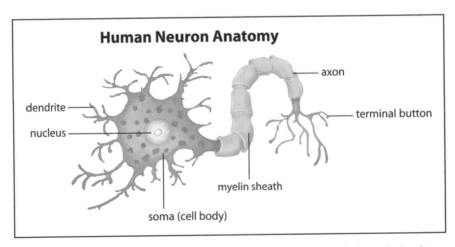

Figure 3–1. *The structure of the neuron, including the cell body (soma), dendrites, axon, myelin sheath, and axon (terminal buttons). Reproduced with permission from Getty Images.*

also integrates and transmits information to other cells.

◆ An axon is the projection of a nerve cell that conducts impulses *from* the neuron.

◆ A dendrite is a projection of the neuron that gathers information from other neurons and directs that information *to* the cell body.

Dendrites bring information to the cell body and axons take information away from the cell body. Information from one neuron moves to another neuron across a **synapse** or synaptic cleft (Figure 3–2). The synapse is the structure that allows a neuron to transmit a signal to other neurons. The signal moves across the synaptic cleft, which is the region between two communicating neurons. The process of nerve transmission moves from neuron to neuron across the synaptic cleft, leading to the contraction of a muscle fiber, the secretion of a gland, or the response of specialized

structures in the brain that perceive sensations (e.g., pain, pressure, sounds, temperature). Connections between nerve cells transmit sensory and motor information.

Some nerve fibers are covered with a white sheath or cover called **myelin**, shown in Figure 3–1. Myelin sheaths are critical to neural transmission. Myelin sheaths allow the rapid transmission of an electrical impulse along the myelinated nerve fiber. For example, transmission of the electrical impulse along a myelinated fiber is 50 times faster than along an unmyelinated fiber (Webb, 2017).

THE CENTRAL NERVOUS SYSTEM AND THE PERIPHERAL NERVOUS SYSTEM

The human **nervous system** consists of the **central nervous system (CNS)** and the

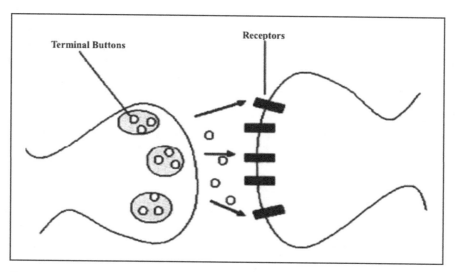

Figure 3–2. *A schematic of a synapse illustrating the transmission of a signal from the terminal buttons of one neuron to the receptors on the dendrites of a second neuron. Reproduced with permission from* Language Development: Understanding Language Diversity in the Classroom, *by S. Levey & S. Polirstok (Eds.), 2011, Los Angeles, CA: Sage.*

peripheral nervous system (PNS). The CNS consists of the brain and the spinal cord. The function of the CNS is to process information and determine appropriate responses. The PNS consists of nerve fibers that branch off the spinal cord and extend throughout the body. The PNS is composed of sensory and motor neurons that gather sensory information (sensations such as touch and temperature) and to control motor (movement) actions of the human body.

The Central Nervous System

The CNS consists of the brain and the spinal cord, as shown in Figure 3–3. The nerves that exit the brain transmit sensory or motor information that controls our speech, language, and hearing abilities. The spinal cord consists of nerves that innervate (stimulate or send nerve impulses to) parts of the body and send sensory information (sensations) from

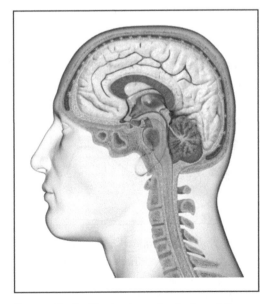

Figure 3–3. The brain and spinal cord. Reproduced with permission from Getty Images.

the body parts to the brain. The brain processes and interprets the sensory information that is received from the spinal cord.

The Peripheral Nervous System

The PNS comprises portions of the nervous system found outside the brain and spinal cord. The PNS consists of spinal nerves and cranial nerves. **Cranial nerves** play an important role in speech, language, and hearing processes. Cranial nerves relay information between the brain and body. Spinal nerves transmit motor and sensory information to and from the CNS. Sensory nerves transmit sensory information (e.g., pain, touch, temperature) and motor information that control accurate voluntary movements.

The PNS consists of two parts: the **somatic nervous system** and the **autonomic nervous system**. The somatic nervous system carries motor (movement) and sensory (e.g., hearing, touch, sight) information to and from the CNS. The autonomic nervous system innervates muscles and glands for involuntary actions (e.g., gland secretions) and is responsible for the control of visceral functions (e.g., heart, digestion, respiration).

Some cranial nerves have motor functions, some have sensory functions, and others have both sensory and motor functions. Cranial nerves II, III, IV, and VI are related to vision. The cranial nerves involved in speech, language, hearing, and swallowing functions are presented in Table 3–2. As shown in Table 3–2, the cranial nerves that are involved in speech production consist of tongue movement, lip closure, and movement of the velum

Table 3–2. *Cranial Nerves Associated with Speech and Language Processes*

V.	Trigeminal nerve	Innervation of speech production muscles.
		Flattening and tensing of the soft palate (velum) and tongue retraction.
VII.	Facial nerve	Facial expression.
		Lip closure.
VIII.	Vestibulocochlear nerve	Sound sensitivity: information from internal ear to the nervous system.
		Sensitivity to changes in equilibrium (balance).
IX.	Glossopharyngeal nerve	Functions related to the tongue and the pharynx.
		Sensory information relative to swallowing.
X.	Vagus nerve	Innervation to muscles of velum (soft palate).
		Innervation to intrinsic laryngeal muscles (attachments inside the larynx).
		Sensory information from larynx.
XI.	Spinal accessory nerve	Body posture.
XII.	Hypoglossal nerve	Innervation of the intrinsic (internal) and extrinsic (external) muscles of the tongue.

(soft palate), described in Chapter 1. This table also shows the cranial nerves that are involved in hearing.

> The cerebrum is the largest part of the brain and is covered by the cerebral cortex. The cerebral cortex is the outer layer of neural tissue that surrounds the brain.

THE TWO HEMISPHERES OF THE CEREBRUM: RIGHT AND LEFT LOBES

The **cerebrum** is the largest part of the brain. The cerebrum consists of two cerebral hemispheres that consist of the right and the left lobes of the brain. The two cerebral hemispheres are connected by the **corpus callosum** that connects the right and left cerebral hemispheres (Figure 3–4). The role of the corpus callosum is to allow the transfer of sensory, motor, and cognitive information between hemispheres.

The right side of the brain contributes to attention, memory, reasoning, and problem solving, areas essential to communication (American Speech Language Hearing Association, 2007). The role of the right hemisphere consists of the following functions (Webb, 2017, p. 196):

◆ Visual processing allows individuals to see and to understand objects, space, and entities (e.g., people,

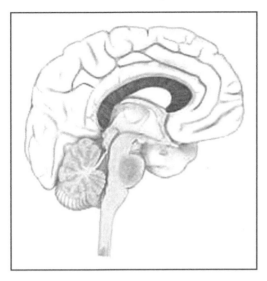

Figure 3–4. *The corpus callosum. Reproduced with permission from Getty Images.*

The functions of the left hemisphere of the brain contribute to logical thought, critical thinking skills, reasoning, understanding and producing language, and memory for spoken and written language (Cherry, 2017). In addition, the left hemisphere appears to be responsible for **categorical perception** (Kemmerer, 2015; Liebenthal et al., 2010). Categorical perception refers to the ability to discriminate (tell the difference) between similar sounds (e.g., f-v, s-z, t-d).

> Behaviors that appear in left brain disorders consist of communication difficulties that affect receptive language (understanding of spoken language). The signs of left brain damage may show problems with speech, writing, and memory.

animals, insects, and other living things).

◆ Visual perception is what you see and understand by using your eyes and brain.
◆ The ability to understand and produce facial and vocal emotions (e.g., a happy or sad voice or facial expression).
◆ The ability to pay attention and shift attention to a new event or activity or a different speaker in a conversation.

> Behaviors that appear in right brain hemisphere disorders consist of difficulty picking up on contextual cues (what is happening in the environment), inhibiting impulsive responses (difficulty with urges in behaviors or communication), and understanding more abstract language (e.g., figurative language, such as jokes and riddles; and implied meaning) and emotional responses (Webb, 2017, p. 221).

THE FOUR LOBES OF THE CEREBRUM AND SPEECH, LANGUAGE, AND COGNITIVE FUNCTIONS

Each hemisphere of the cerebrum is divided into four lobes: frontal, temporal, parietal, and occipital (Figure 3–5). These four lobes provide motor and sensory functions. The sensory functions consist of vision, hearing, touch, and olfaction (smell). The frontal lobe contributes to conscious thought, the parietal lobe to spatial reasoning, the occipital lobe to visual processing, and the temporal lobe to language processing and facial recognition.

> It is important to consider the sensory functions of the brain in relation to language. As children

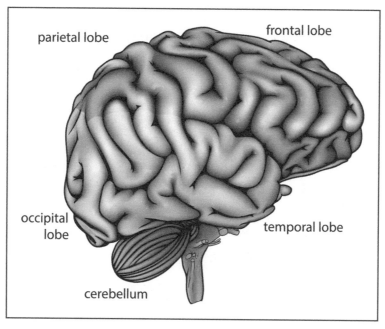

Figure 3–5. *Locations and functions of the four primary lobes of the brain: frontal, temporal, parietal, and occipital. Reproduced with permission from Getty Images.*

learn language, they are exposed to the words that describe the things they see, along with the things they smell (e.g., *smoke, flowers, burnt toast,* and *perfume*).

The Frontal Lobe

The frontal lobe is involved in motor (movement) and cognitive functions (planning, reasoning, and memory). **Broca's area** is located in the left frontal lobe of the brain (Figure 3–6). Early information on the role of the brain in language was found in the behaviors associated with language disorders. In 1861, Pierre Paul Broca (1824–1880) found that loss of the ability to produce words was associated with damage to the left front side of the brain (Berker,

Berker, & Smith, 1986). This area became known as Broca's area. Broca's area activates the articulators for speech production (e.g., lips, and tongue). Broca's area plays a role in fluent and well-articulated speech (Webb, 2017, p. 20). The following language functions are associated with this area of the brain (Webb, 2017):

◆ Semantic processing: Understanding the meaning of words, sentences, or conversations
◆ Syntactic processing: Understanding the structure of sentences (e.g., question versus request)
◆ Phonological processing: Understanding the phonological structure or the sound structure of words
◆ Motor control: Movements that allow the production of speech and language

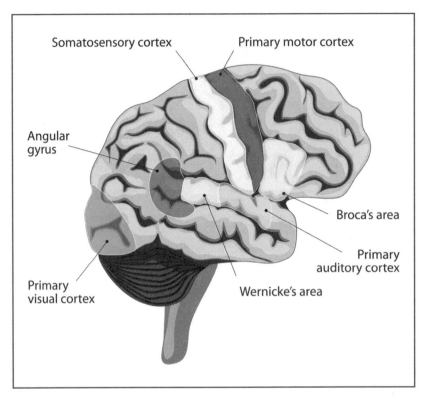

Figure 3–6. *Broca's and Wernicke's areas of the brain are shown, along with the primary auditory cortex, also known as Heschl's gyrus. Reproduced with permission from Getty Images.*

The frontal lobe has three divisions, with each responsible for a particular function:

◆ Prefrontal: The prefrontal cortex covers the front part of the frontal lobe. It is responsible for the cognitive functions of working memory and decision making, the executive functions for generating and carrying out action plans, and the modification of plans when considering potential outcomes and past experiences
◆ Premotor: Responsible for planning and executing movements
◆ Motor: Responsible for voluntary (deliberate) movement

The Parietal Lobe

Positron emission tomography (PET) was used to examine the language abilities associated with the parietal lobe. Functional neuroimaging results indicated extensive parietal activity associated with the sensorimotor control of writing. This involved the planning, execution, and monitoring of writing, even if only the forming of a single letter (Brownsett & Wise, 2010). The ability to grasp the visual and spatial aspects of writing (e.g., the formation of letters that create words) is provided by the parietal lobe (Glass, 2016).

The Temporal Lobe

The temporal lobe is the center of auditory processing in the brain. Auditory processing refers to the ability of the brain to recognize and understand sounds. In 1876, Karl Wernicke (1848–1905) found that the temporal lobe of the brain plays a role in the comprehension (understanding) of spoken language. This area became known as **Wernicke's area** (shown in Figure 3–6). The language functions of this area of the brain are speech reception and the comprehension or understanding of spoken language (Webb, 2017).

Heschl's gyrus, named for Richard L. Heschl, 1824–1881, is labeled as the primary auditory area in Figure 3–6. Heschl's gyrus plays a role in processing linguistic information. Auditory information is relayed to Heschl's gyrus in the auditory cortex. Here, linguistic information is filtered from nonessential sounds and sent to Wernicke's area, where the linguistic analysis of auditory information takes place (linguistic analysis of the spoken language that is heard). Heschl's gyrus plays an important role in understanding speech by decoding phonetic differences (Skipper & Small, 2006). The ability to decode phonetic differences is essential in determining the distinctions among speech sounds (e.g., /p/ vs. /b/).

The Occipital Lobe

The occipital lobe is critical to the interpretation of visual **sensory information**. The occipital lobe makes sense of visual information so that we are able to understand what we see. The primary visual cortex is located here. Visual stimuli (visual-spatial processing, discrimination of movement and color) are interpreted in the occipital lobe. The importance of this area of the brain is shown when young children are exposed to novel objects or actions. More experienced language users provide labels or names for the novel events, contributing to children's vocabulary development.

THE ARCUATE FASCICULUS

The **arcuate fasciculus** is a bundle of nerve fibers that connects Broca's and Wernicke's areas, linking the speech and language areas in the brain (Figure 3–7). The arcuate fasciculus connects Wernicke's area (speech and language comprehension) to Broca's area (speech and language production) to create a connection between the recognition of words and

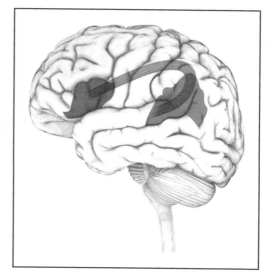

Figure 3–7. *The arcuate fasciculus connects Wernicke's area in the temporal lobe with Broca's area in the frontal lobe. Reproduced with permission from Getty Images.*

the production of words. Communication consists of the following pattern:

The concept of an intended message is formed in the brain.

This message to be conveyed is constructed in Wernicke's area.

The intended message is transmitted through the arcuate fasciculus.

Broca's area programs the verbal output of the message.

SUBCORTICAL STRUCTURES AND FUNCTIONS

Subcortical areas of the brain are those areas below the cerebral cortex (the outer layer of the brain). These subcortical areas include the **thalamus** and **hypothalamus** (Figure 3–8), along with the **basal ganglia** (Figure 3–9) and **limbic system** (Figure 3–10). These areas play a role in motor control, memory, and basic functions of the human body. Their function is described in Table 3–3.

The basal ganglia and cerebellum have been found to play a role in reading and language processing, with abnormal cerebellar activity in patients with developmental **dyslexia** and language impairment (Booth et al., 2007). The limbic system plays a role in memory. The memory function of the brain is essential for language development, given that memory plays a role in learning and storing new words in memory. Memory also plays an important role in academic success.

The **cerebellum** is located at the base of the cerebrum (shown in Figure 3–8).

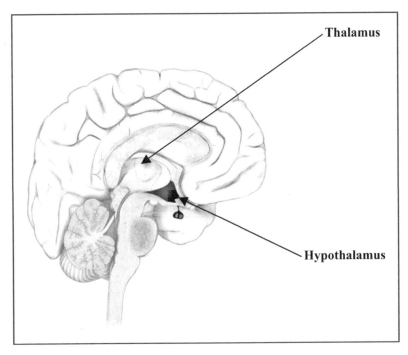

Figure 3–8. *The thalamus and hypothalamus. Reproduced with permission from Getty Images.*

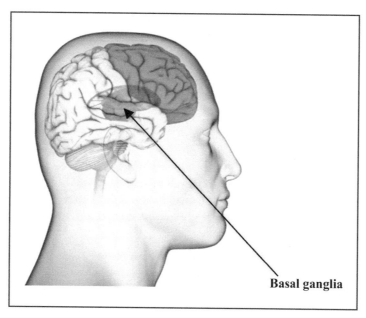

Figure 3–9. *The basal ganglia. Reproduced with permission from Getty Images.*

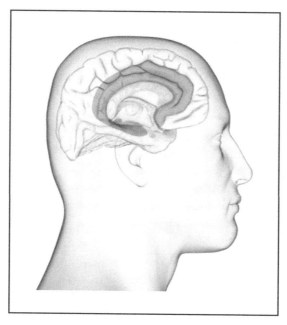

Figure 3–10. *The limbic system. Reproduced with permission from Getty Images.*

Table 3–3. *Subcortical Structures of the Brain*

Basal ganglia	Motor control of muscle tone and posture; organization and guidance of complex motor functions
Limbic system	Self-preservation, emotions, memory, olfaction (the sensory function associated with smell or scents)
Thalamus	The chief sensory integrator in the brain and can be considered a relay station, conveying sensory and motor information to and from the cerebral cortex. All information (traveling to the brain), with the exception of olfaction (sense of smell), is routed through the thalamus. The thalamus also regulates sleep, emotion, and arousal.
Hypothalamus	Associated with basic functions, such as eating and temperature

The cerebellum plays a role in the performance of voluntary actions (actions based on purpose and intent), such as writing and speech production. The cerebellum is associated with motor control for connected speech efforts (Webb, 2017). For example, the cerebellum is responsible for the coordination of respiration, articulation, and the muscles involved with phonation (voice production).

Linguistic disorders were found to result from impaired cerebellar function (De Smet et al., 2007). These disorders consist of fluency, naming and word-finding difficulties, reading difficulties, writing problems, and higher-level language deficits.

THE BRAINSTEM

The role of the **brainstem** is to control messages between the brain and the rest of the body (Figure 3–11). The brainstem plays a role in respiration that supports phonation for speech production. The brainstem is also involved in basic functions of the body (e.g., breathing, swallowing, heart rate, blood pressure, and consciousness). The brainstem consists of the medulla oblongata (also called the myelencephalon), the pons, and the midbrain (called the mesencephalon). The roles of these areas in speech and language are shown below.

Medulla oblongata: Respiration (breathing) to support vocal production

Pons: Swallowing, hearing, facial expression, and sensation

Midbrain: Relay station for auditory and visual information, control of respiratory muscles and the speech and articulation functions (vocal folds, palate, tongue, lips, and mandible or jaw)

While respiration and hearing are essential components of speech and language abilities, children must also learn

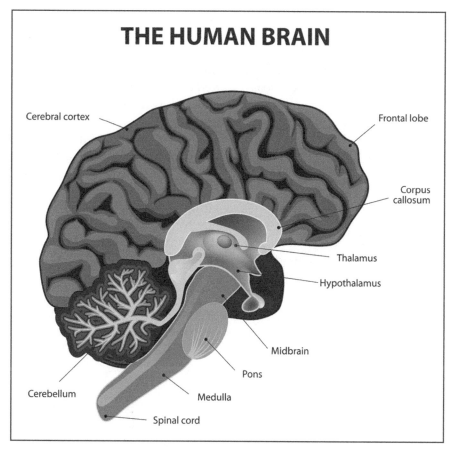

THE HUMAN BRAIN

Cerebral cortex

Frontal lobe

Corpus callosum

Thalamus

Hypothalamus

Midbrain

Pons

Cerebellum

Medulla

Spinal cord

Figure 3–11. The brainstem. Reproduced with permission from Getty Images.

the meaning of others' facial expressions (e.g., happy, or sad). The interpretation of facial expression is essential in interactions with others.

COGNITIVE FUNCTIONS AND THE BRAIN

Cognition includes the cognitive skills that distinguish humans from other living entities (Gentner, 2003, p. 195).

◆ The ability to create abstractions (e.g., inner language used to create thoughts about experiences) and to generalize experiences and store common experiences and results across varied outcomes (e.g., use of prior or past experiences to predict consequences)

◆ The ability to maintain hierarchies of abstraction to store information (e.g., thoughts about your pet dog, dogs in general, and other living things)

◆ The ability to arrive at a conclusion, given certain facts or pieces of information

◆ The ability to compare and contrast objects and entities for similarities and differences

◆ The ability to learn that symbols represent numerical, spatial, and conceptual information (e.g., numbers, locations in space, concepts about time, and other abstract ideas)

The cognitive and communicative factors that are associated with the brain can be found in Table 3–4.

Embodied Cognition

Embodied cognition views children's cognitive development as depending on two innate or inborn neurological abilities (Wilson & Foglia, 2011): sensory skills and motor skills. The sensory skill of visual perception allows infants to perceive objects and events in the environment. The motor skills allow infants to explore these objects and events as they interact in activities within the environment. This is a dynamic and active process in which infants organize and develop their cognitive skills over time, given greater experience with adults, peers, objects, and events in the environment. These experiences contain the language used to label the object and actions that are present in the environment

Table 3–4. Cognitive Factors in Communication and Associated Areas of the Brain

Attention and information processing	Requires arousal (alertness) and perception of sensory input
	Attentional capacity: the amount of information that can be held
	Selective engagement
	Prefrontal cortex, which is also involved in planning and other executive functions
Memory	Retention and recall of experience changes over time
	Visual and auditory storage:
	Short-term memory (temporary storage)
	Long-term memory (permanent storage)
	Hippocampus and amygdala
Reasoning and problem solving	Problem solving: evaluation based on reasoning to produce a conclusion
	Prefrontal and subcortical areas (areas below the cortex)
Metacognition and executive functions	Metacognition involves the ability to recognize when to use reason and problem-solving skills to solve problems with cognitive strategies.
	Executive functions involve anticipation, goal direction, planning, monitoring of events, and feedback interpretation.
	The frontal lobes carry out metacognitive and executive function processes.

Source: Reproduced with permission from *Neurology for the Speech-Language Pathologist* (p. 199), by W. G. Webb, 2017, St. Louis, MO: Elsevier.

(e.g., *spill, drink, throw, run,* and *wipe*). The interaction between sensory and motor skills provides the essential support for language development.

Mirror Neurons

At 1 to 3 days after birth, infants' innate or inborn sensorimotor skills are demonstrated by their perception and physical imitation of adults' tongue protrusion and mouth opening (Meltzoff & Moore, 1983). What is most interesting is that imitation of the adult's movements occurs even though infants are totally unaware of their own facial structure or physical movement. Cognitive neuroscience explains these early behaviors through the role of **mirror neurons** (Jackson, Brunet, Meltzoff, & Decety, 2006; Lamm & Majdandžić, 2015).

Mirror neurons are a type of neuron in the brain that fires when individuals perceive the facial expressions or actions of others (e.g., sadness, or yawning). These neurons provide an inner simulation or mirror of the actions that we observe, allowing the brain to symbolize and understand the actions of others (Rizzolatti & Craighero, 2004). Mirror neurons may play a role in interpreting another person's emotions or feelings, laying the foundation for such higher-order social processes as empathy (sympathy, compassion, and understanding) and a theory of mind. Theory of mind describes the ability to understand someone else's mind and mental state (e.g., happy, sad, worried). Theory of mind is expressed in language by the use of mental state verbs that describe the human mind (e.g., what someone thinks, knows, or believes). Mirror neurons also play an important role in speech perception (Eysenck & Keane, 2015).

Executive Functions

Executive functions consist of attention and memory, along with the ability to plan, organize, and learn from prior experiences. For example, children with intact executive functions can learn from prior errors and can correct these errors when reviewing their work or when given new assignments within the classroom. Executive functions are involved in the development of academic skills, such as **abstract thought** (drawing conclusions from written text), the ability to revise plans (to correct errors), to initiate action (to prepare for exams and assignments), to reject inappropriate actions (to interact appropriately with peers), and to learn from past mistakes. Executive functions also consist of critical thinking skills. Examples of executive functions are described in Table 3–5.

> Children who have executive function difficulties may be disorganized and forgetful and have poor critical thinking skills. Children with executive function difficulties may also be **disinhibited** (lack the ability to restrain from impulsive actions), resulting in inappropriate social behaviors (e.g., interrupting; or aggressive behavior toward other children).

SUMMARY

The case study presented at the beginning of this chapter describes a typically developing 3-year-old whose behaviors suggest intact brain structures and typical development.

Table 3–5. *Examples of Executive Functions*

Attention	Active and alert processing of a situation
Discrimination	Identification of differences based on some feature or features
Reasoning	Forming conclusions, inferences, or judgments
Logic	Reasoning or drawing conclusions from facts or evidence
Organization	Mentally classifying/categorizing thoughts, tasks, or objects
Memory	Recall of information
Transfer	Generalization of knowledge to apply to new situations
Metacognition	Knowledge and awareness of language and thought
Problem solving	The thought processes involved in solving a problem
Planning	Monitoring, evaluating, and updating actions
Mental flexibility	The ability to shift to a different thought or action in response to situational changes
Response inhibition	The ability to suppress irrelevant or interfering information (not relevant to the situation) and impulses
Generativity	The ability to generate novel ideas and behaviors
Self-monitoring	The ability to monitor one's thoughts and actions

◆ Sammy is able to understand and follow directions, showing intact auditory comprehension. This ability is provided by the left temporal lobe.

◆ The ability to form memories is provided by the participation of two subcortical regions: the hippocampus and the amygdala (Webb, 2017), shown in Figure 3–12.

◆ The ability to maintain attention to spoken language is correlated with activity in the temporal parietal junction (TPJ) (Hasenkamp, 2014). This is the area in which the temporal and parietal lobes of the brain meet (Figure 3–13).

◆ Sammy's ability to understand other children's emotions and mental states shows the presence of a theory of mind (TOM) (Rhodes & Brandone, 2014), an ability that is basically established in the human brain (Otti, Wohlschlaeger, & Noll-Hussong, 2015). **Functional magnetic resonance imaging (fMRI)** shows activity in two areas of the brain when individuals are presented with TOM tasks: the area where the temporal and parietal lobes meet and the right frontal gyrus.

◆ The ability to understand other children's emotions is associated with the identification of facial expressions (e.g., happiness, sadness). This ability is provided by the medial temporal gyrus (Cheng, Rolls, Gu, Zhang, & Feng, 2015), shown in Figure 3–14.

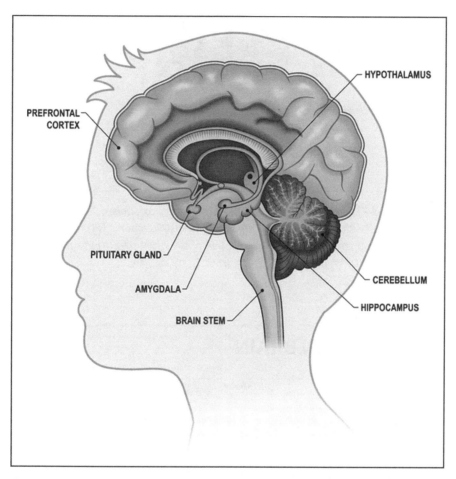

Figure 3–12. *The hippocampus and the amygdala are also indicated. The amygdala plays a role in the processing of emotions. The hippocampus is located in the temporal lobe and is associated with memory. Reproduced with permission from Getty Images.*

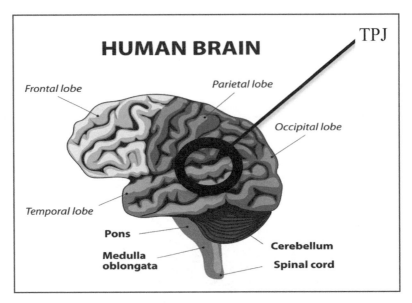

Figure 3–13. *The ability to maintain attention to spoken language is correlated with activity in the temporal parietal junction (TPJ), the area in which the temporal and parietal lobes of the brain meet (Hasenkamp, 2014). Reproduced with permission from Getty Images.*

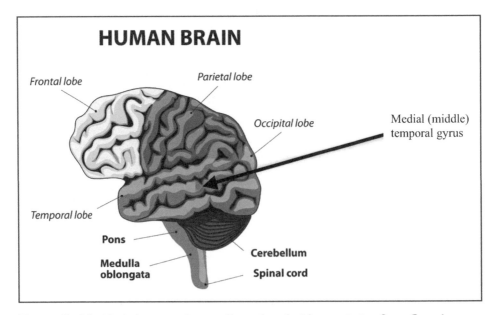

Figure 3–14. *Medial temporal gyrus. Reproduced with permission from Getty Images.*

Sammy possesses the ability to take advantage of the sensory information in the environment. For example, he is sensitive to what he sees and hears (e.g., spoken language, facial expressions, and other input that provides him with information on others' meaning and feelings). His cognitive skills allow him to engage in appropriate interaction with his teacher and peers. In summary, many behaviors are learned through interaction with others in the environment. However, the brain provides the basic ability to develop these behaviors.

To further explain the role of the brain, the functions of the brain can be found in Figure 3–15. A review of the speech, cognitive, and language functions of the brain can be found in Table 3–6.

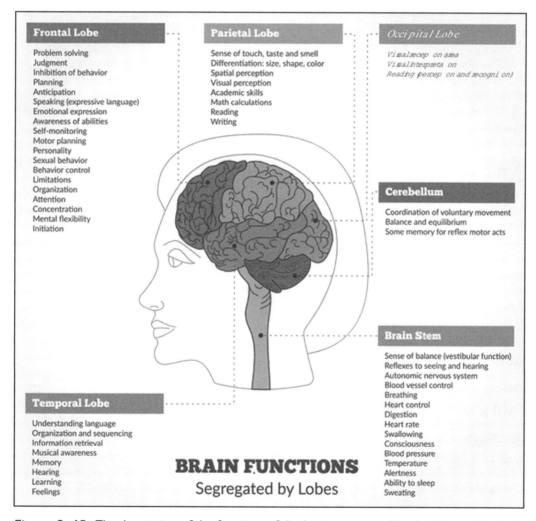

Frontal Lobe

Problem solving
Judgment
Inhibition of behavior
Planning
Anticipation
Speaking (expressive language)
Emotional expression
Awareness of abilities
Self-monitoring
Motor planning
Personality
Sexual behavior
Behavior control
Limitations
Organization
Attention
Concentration
Mental flexibility
Initiation

Parietal Lobe

Sense of touch, taste and smell
Differentiation: size, shape, color
Spatial perception
Visual perception
Academic skills
Math calculations
Reading
Writing

Occipital Lobe

Visual percep on area
Visual interpreta on
Reading percep on and recogni on)

Cerebellum

Coordination of voluntary movement
Balance and equilibrium
Some memory for reflex motor acts

Temporal Lobe

Understanding language
Organization and sequencing
Information retrieval
Musical awareness
Memory
Hearing
Learning
Feelings

Brain Stem

Sense of balance (vestibular function)
Reflexes to seeing and hearing
Autonomic nervous system
Blood vessel control
Breathing
Heart control
Digestion
Heart rate
Swallowing
Consciousness
Blood pressure
Temperature
Alertness
Ability to sleep
Sweating

BRAIN FUNCTIONS
Segregated by Lobes

Figure 3–15. *The description of the functions of the brain, segregated by the lobes of the brain. Reproduced with permission from Getty Images.*

Table 3–6. *Brain and Language Functions*

Frontal lobe	Planning and execution of motor activities (movement); cognitive functions (planning, reasoning, working memory; decision making); semantic processing (understanding the meaning of words, sentences, or conversations); syntactic processing (understanding the structure of sentences); phonological processing (understanding the phonological structure or the sound structures of words); and motor control (movements that allow the production of speech and language)
Parietal lobe	Planning, execution, and monitoring writing
Temporal lobe	Speech reception and the comprehension or understanding of spoken language
Occipital lobe	Visual sensory information; makes sense of visual information
Brainstem	Consists of the medulla oblongata (respiration for breathing and support for vocal production); pons (swallowing, hearing, facial expression, and sensation); and midbrain (relay station for auditory and visual information, control of respiratory muscles and the speech and articulation functions of the vocal folds, palate, tongue, lips, and mandible or jaw
Cerebellum	Motor control for connected speech efforts; important for the performance of voluntary actions (actions based on purpose and intent)

KEY WORDS

Abstract thought

Arcuate fasciculus

Autonomic nervous system

Axon

Basal ganglia

Brainstem

Broca's area

Categorical perception

Central nervous system (CNS)

Cerebellum

Cerebrum

Cognition

Corpus callosum

Cranial nerves

Dendrites

Disinhibited

Dyslexia

Embodied cognition

Functional magnetic resonance imaging (fMRI)

Heschl's gyrus

Hypothalamus

Interneurons

Limbic system

Mirror neurons

Motor

Motor neurons

Myelin

Neuron

Nervous system

Neuroplasticity

Neurotransmitters

Peripheral nervous system (PNS)

Positron emission tomography (PET)

Real-time functional magnetic resonance imaging (rtfMRI)

Sensory information

Sensory neurons

Soma

Somatic nervous system

Synapse

Synaptic cleft

Thalamus

Theory of mind (TOM)

Wernicke's area

STUDY QUESTIONS

1. Describe the role of the cranial nerves in speech and language.

2. Describe the role of the brain in language production and language comprehension.

3. Explain the importance of the knowledge of the human neurological system when working with individuals with speech or language difficulties.

4. Describe the role of the brain related to cognitive abilities.

5. Explain the importance of executive functions in children's academic progress.

REFERENCES

American Speech-Language-Hearing Association. (2007). *Childhood apraxia of speech* [Position statement]. Retrieved from http://www.ASHA.org/policy

American Speech-Language-Hearing Association. (2017). *Right hemisphere brain damage.* Retrieved from http://www.asha.org/public/speech/disorders/RightBrainDamage/

Baron-Cohen, S., Ring, H., Moriarty, J., Schmitz, B., Costa, D., & Ell, P. (1994). Recognition of mental state terms. Clinical findings in children with autism and a functional neuroimaging study of normal adults. *British Journal of Psychiatry, 165*(5), 640–649.

Beeson, M. P. (2010). Neuroimaging research: Brain-behavior relationships and language. *The ASHA Leader, 15*, 18–21.

Berker, E. A., Berker, A. H., & Smith, S. (1986). Translation of Broca's 1865 report. Localization of speech in the third left frontal convolution. *Archives of Neurology, 43*(10), 1065–1072.

Booth, J. R., Wood, L., Lu, D., Houk, J. C., & Bitan, T. (2007). The role of the basal ganglia and cerebellum in language processing. *Brain Research, 1133*(1), 136–144.

Brownsett, S. L. E., & Wise, R. J. S. (2010). The contribution of the parietal lobes to speaking and writing. *Cerebral Cortex, 20*, 517–523.

Buccino, G., Binkofski, F., Fink, G. R., Fadiga, L., Fogassi, L., Gallese, V., . . . Freund, H. J.

(2001). Action observation activates premotor and parietal areas in a somatotopic manner: An fMRI study. *European Journal of Neuroscience, 13*, 400–404.

Cheng, W., Rolls, E. T., Gu, H., Zhang, J., & Feng, J. (2015). Autism: Reduced connectivity between cortical areas involved in face expression, theory of mind, and the sense of self. *Brain, 13*, 1382–1393.

Cherry, K. (2016). *What is brain plasticity?* Retrieved from https://www.verywell.com/what-is-brain-plasticity-2794886?print

Cherry, K. (2017). *Left brain vs right brain dominance: The surprising truth.* Retrieved from https://www.verywell.com/left-brain-vs-right-brain-2795005

De Smet, H. J., Baillieux, H., De Deyn, P. P., Merien, P., & Paquier, P. (2007). The cerebellum and language: The story so far. *Folia Phoniatrica et Lagopaedica, 59*, 165–170.

Eysenck, M. W., & Keane, M. T. (2015) *Cognitive psychology: A student's handbook.* New York, NY: Psychology Press.

Gentner, D. (2003). Why we're so smart. In D. Gentner & S. Goldin-Meadow (Eds.), *Language in mind: Advances in the study of language and thought* (pp. 195–235). Cambridge, MA: MIT Press.

Glass, A. L. (2016). *Cognition: A neuroscience approach.* Cambridge, UK: University Printing House.

Hasenkamp, W. (2014). *Theory of mind: Contemplative science begins to unpack the critical elements of caring.* Retrieved from https://www.mindandlife.org/theory-mind/

Jackson, P. L., Brunet, E., Meltzoff, A. N., & Decety, J. (2006). Empathy examined through the neural mechanisms involved in how I feel versus how you feel pain. *Neuropsychologia, 44*, 752–761.

Kemmerer, D. (2015). *Cognitive neuroscience of language.* New York, NY: Psychological Press.

Lamm, C., & Majdandžić, J. (2015). The role of shared neural activations, mirror neurons, and morality in empathy—a critical comment. *Neuroscience Research, 90*, 15–24.

Levey, S., & West, J. F. (2011).The role of the brain in speech and language. In S. Levey & S. Polirstok (Eds.), *Language development: Understanding language diversity in the classroom* (pp. 101–114). Los Angeles, CA: Sage.

Liebenthal, E., Desai, R., Ellingson, M. M., Ramachandran, B., Desai, A., & Binder, J. R. (2010). Specialization along the left superior temporal sulcus for auditory categorization. *Cerebral Cortex 20*, 2958–2970.

Meltzoff, A. N., & Moore, K. (1983). Newborn infants imitate adult facial gestures. *Child Development, 54*(3), 702–709.

Mildner, V. (2008). *The cognitive neuroscience of human communication.* New York, NY: Erlbaum.

Mottonen, R., Jarvelainen, J., Sams, M., & Hari, R. (2004). Viewing speech modulates activity in the left SI mouth cortex. *NeuroImage, 24*, 731–737.

Otti, A., Wohlschlaeger, A. M., & Noll-Hussong, M. (2015). *Is the prefrontal cortex necessary for theory of mind?* Retrieved from https://www.scienceexchange.com/publications/9227

Rhodes, M., & Brandone, A. C. (2014). Three-year-olds' theories of mind in action and words. *Original Frontiers in Psychology, 5*, 1–8.

Rizzolatti, G., & Craighero, L. (2004). The mirror-neuron system. *Annual Review of Neuroscience, 27*, 169–192.

Skipper, J. I., & Small, S. L. (2006). FMRI studies of language. *Encyclopedia of Language and Linguistics.* Retrieved from http://www.sciencedirect.com/science/article/pii/B0080448542023993

Watkins, K. E., & Paus, T. (2004). Modulation of motor excitability during speech perception: The role of Broca's area. *Journal of Cognitive Neuroscience, 16*(6), 978–987.

Watkins, K. E., Strafella, A. P., & Paus, T. (2003). Seeing and hearing speech excites the motor system involved in speech production. *Neuropsychologia, 41*, 989–994.

Webb, W. G. (2017). *Neurology for the speech-language pathologist.* St. Louis, MO: Elsevier.

Wilson, R. A., & Foglia, L. (2011). Embodied cognition. *Stanford Encyclopedia of Philosophy.* Retrieved from http://philosophysother.blogspot.com/2011/08/wilson-robert-and-lucia-foglia-embodied.html

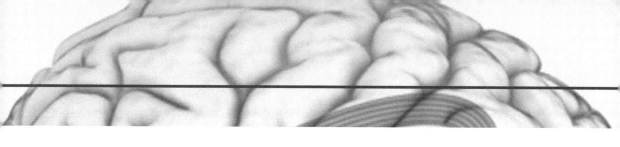

4

Infant and Toddler Language Development

Sandra Levey

Case Study

*Aaron is a 4-year-old who produces the past tense of some verbs in the following manner: "Mommy comed home yesterday" (rather than the correct production of "He **came** home yesterday") and "I standed* in the puddle" (rather than the correct production of "I **stood** in the puddle"). Provide an explanation of why phonology plays a role in these productions of irregular past tense verbs.*

CHAPTER OBJECTIVES

This chapter describes children's language development from birth to 3 years of age. After reading this chapter, you should understand:

◆ Language development from birth to 3 years of age
◆ The factors that play a role in children's language development
◆ Differences associated with second-language learners of English

AN OVERVIEW OF INFANT AND TODDLER LANGUAGE DEVELOPMENT

Newborn infants possess a powerful **innate** learning mechanism that equips them for language acquisition (Berwick & Chomsky, 2016; Chomsky, 1957, 1965; Gopnik, Meltzoff, & Kuhl, 1999). Infants possess innate **perceptual** abilities that prepare them for interaction with people and the task of learning language, while language development progresses as children are exposed to spoken language in the environment (Barna & Legerstee, 2005). Infants are equipped with the ability to process information. **Processing** is the mental ability that allows the infant to be aware of, to perceive, and to understand spoken language, along with understanding speakers' ideas and feelings. Highlights of children's language development, from birth through age 3, are described in Table 4–1.

> The term *innate* refers to abilities present in the human brain at birth. Innate abilities are not acquired or learned through experience after birth. *Perceptual abilities* refer to the mechanisms that allow the infant to process and interpret sensory information (i.e., what is seen, smelled, touched, taste, and heard).

Soon after birth, infants show a preference for animate (living) entities, an ability that allows them to detect and recognize human faces versus objects that do not resemble human faces (Simion & Di Giorgio, 2015). Newborn infants have been shown to process their mother's faces and to store this information in memory for later recognition (Bushnell, 2001). Infants focus on a speaker's eyes as early as 2

months of age, showing recognition that this part of the human face conveys social information (Carter, Davis, Klin, & Volkmar, 2005). At 2 months of age, infants are able to imitate human facial gestures (Legerstee, 2000) while not truly aware of their own faces. At 9 weeks of age, infants fixate more consistently on an adult's eyes when the adult is speaking than when the adult is silent (Beier & Spelke, 2012).

Infants possess the ability to use gestures to communicate with others before they are able to produce meaningful words. Further language development is based on experience and interaction with people, things, and actions in the environment. Communication begins to emerge in infancy, when 3-month-olds produce speech-like sounds in response to adults' vocalizations (Gleason & Ratner, 2017). Between 9 and 12 months, children follow the direction of an adult's gaze, imitate others' actions and movements, and use gestures to gain adults' attention and interest (Tomasello, Carpenter, & Liszkowski, 2007). These early behaviors precede language production while demonstrating the early ability to communicate through gesture and sound production.

By the end of the first year of life, infants understand many spoken words and produce their first words. By 18 to 24 months, children begin to produce simple two-word utterances. This marks the emergence of syntax or sentence formation. By age 3, children produce sentences that express questions and comments. Children's language skills mirror those of adults by 4 years of age, with the production of adult sentence forms (Owens, 2016). The process of language acquisition is unique to humans because only human beings can generate or create new words (*texting*) and novel utterances, such as

Table 4–1. *Infants' Innate Perceptual Skills*

Visual perception	Sight
Auditory perception	Hearing
Gustatory perception	Taste
Olfactory perception	Smell
Somatosensory perception	Touch

nexterday, produced by 2½-year-old Guy when lacking the term *tomorrow*.

In summary, language develops over time, given more experience with and exposure to it. Children learn language through exposure to that used in the environment, with more experienced speakers using language to identify objects, living entities, and actions in the children's environment. Although children possess the innate ability to learn language, language develops through experience with language as it used. Children also possess the unique ability to construct methods of communication when they lack the word to communicate meaning, such as the use of the word *nexterday* to express the concept of *tomorrow*. This reflects the creative abilities of the human mind.

INFANT PERCEPTION AND PRODUCTION

Infant Perception

The examination of infants' **perception** tells us a great deal about the human mind. Within minutes after birth, infants exhibit sensitivity to face-like objects, suggesting an innate ability to recognize other human individuals (Wilkinson et al., 2014). In addition, 4-day-old infants show a preference for looking at their mothers' faces, rather than at less familiar faces (Bushnell, Sai, & Mullin, 1989). Infants' **auditory perception** also reflects their early learning skills. For example, the infant's mother's voice plays a role in the recognition of her face (Sai, 2005). At 1 to 4 months, infants can detect intonational changes in speech patterns (Jusczyk, 1992). By 8 months, infants can distinguish rising from falling intonations, providing the early ability to understand the difference between statements (falling intonation) and questions (rising intonation). This provides children with the ability to recognize the difference between a statement and a question. As early as 3 months of age, infants engage in vocal turn-taking in response to sounds produced by adults (Owens, 2016). These are the early abilities that precede more advanced language abilities.

Auditory perception involves the ability to perceive and understand sounds that are associated with spoken language. In spoken language, *intonation* is the use of fluctuating or changing vocal pitch (rising and falling), such as the production of a question with rising intonation (I want to know where you are GOING?) or a statement (He is REALLY nice).

By 5 months of age, infants begin to imitate some sounds. Although infants respond to their names by 5 months of age (Mandel, Jusczyk, & Pisoni, 1995), they often confuse their names with words that have the same number of syllables (e.g., *mommy* and *monkey*). Between 5 and 8 months, infants recognize the difference between a human voice and nonsocial or nonhuman stimuli (e.g., whistles, and horns) (Legerstee, Anderson, & Schaffer, 1998). At about 6 months of age, infants become more sensitive to changes between sounds. For example, they react to the change when a series of stop-plosive sounds, such as /b-b-b-b-b-b/, is followed by a series of unvoiced stop-plosive sounds, such as /p-p-p-p-p-p/) (Hillenbrand, 1983). Their reaction to the differences in sounds shows that language-relevant abilities are present at an early age, providing the later ability to understand that sounds mark differences in words (e.g., *bad* vs. *pad*).

Children also begin to understand differences in adults' facial expressions. Between 6 and 12 months, infants choose an object based on an adult's positive or negative facial expression (Moses, Baldwin, Rosicky, & Tidball, 2002), choosing the object that matches the adult's positive facial expression. A **theory of mind (TOM)**, described in Chapter 1, provides children with the ability to interpret others' facial expressions that reflect their feelings or thoughts.

A TOM is the ability to interpret or understand another person's mental state (e.g., happiness, sadness, fear), intent (the goal of carrying out an action or a plan), beliefs (attitudes or ideas), desires (goals), or knowledge (information). It is the ability to *step into someone else's shoes* to understand this person's mind, thoughts, and feelings. The early ability to recognize facial expressions is the sign of a developing, but still primitive, TOM.

Infants have been shown to imitate adults' facial movements, such as sticking out their tongues. This imitation behavior is interesting, given that infants are not aware of their own faces or tongues. Examination of the role of the brain in infants' perception has provided an explanation of infants' responses to adults' facial expressions. The discovery of **mirror neurons** in the brain has led to the theory that these neurons play a role in perception. Mirror neurons "mirror" the behavior of others, as though the observer

were acting her/himself. Mirror neurons also allow us to receive and interpret facial expressions. Mirror neurons "mirror" the things that are sensed or perceived in the environment, allowing infants to mirror the things they observe (Gruber, 2016). This is found in infants' imitation of adults' facial expressions (e.g., frowning, smiling) and facial movements (e.g., sticking out their tongues). Understanding the inner mental state of others is proposed to depend on the activation of these mirror neurons, allowing the infant to perceive the inner mental states of others (Acharya & Shukla, 2012; Keysers, Kaas, & Gazzola, 2010; Lamm & Majdandžić, 2015). These inner states can consist of surprise, happiness, fear, or other emotional states that may be reflected in an individual's face. These mirror neurons may also facilitate emergence of a TOM, allowing the development of the ability to interpret or understand another's feelings or thoughts.

An interesting aspect of development appears after 7 months of age, when infants exhibit sustained and voluntary focus, rather than passive responses to things in the environment (Columbo, Kapa, & Curtindale, 2011). At about 7 months of age, infants spend a greater amount of time looking at things that capture their interest (Galotti, 2017). This sustained attention pattern reflects goal-directed attention, an essential skill for learning language (Oakes, Kannass, & Shaddy, 2002). For example, the ability to maintain attention allows the infant to follow longer examples of spoken language, such as a story. By the end of the first year, infants understand many words. Between 7 and 12 months, children recognize words for common objects and can understand and respond to simple requests for actions (e.g., *Find your bunny. Give mommy your cup. Don't spill your milk*).

In summary, infants possess innate learning abilities that prepare them for the acquisition of language. These abilities consist of the early ability to perceive sounds, to understand some familiar words, and to recognize differences in facial expressions. Infants are able to interpret a speaker's intent or meaning by the recognition of facial expression, indicating the early emergence of a TOM (understanding the inner thoughts or feelings of other individuals). Next, we examine infants' sound production.

Infant Production

Newborn infants' productions move through various stages of development (Oller, 1980; Patten et al., 2014), as presented in Table 4–2. At 5 to 10 months, infants begin to babble, producing basic canonical syllables. These productions consist of a series of the same consonant-vowel (CV) syllables (e.g., ba-ba-ba-ba-ba) and are termed **reduplicated babbling**. The next stage consists of nonreduplicated or **variegated babbling**, with the production

Table 4–2. Infants' Productions: Stages of Development

Reflexive stage (0–2 months)	Vegetative sounds such as burping and coughing
	Cooing and gooing
	Crying, fussing
	Syllable shapes may be produced, such as consonant-vowel-consonant vowel (CVCV) forms and vowels (e.g., *wawa, ah*).
	Quasi-resonant nuclei (partial vowel production)
Control of phonation (1–4 months)	Fully resonant nuclei (true vowel production)
	Vocalizations with a vowel-like segment are combined with a consonant-like segment
	Laughter
Expansion (3–8 months)	Isolated vowel production or a series of two or more vowels
	Marginal babbling (a series of consonants and vowels or isolated consonants and vowels)
Basic canonical syllables (5–10 months)	Reduplicated babbling consists of a series of the same consonant-vowel (CV) syllables, such as ba-ba-ba-ba.
	Nonreduplicated or variegated babbling consists of a series of different CV sequences, such as ba-bi-bu-bu.
Advanced forms (10–18 months)	Complex syllables such as CV (*up*), CVC (*cat*), and CVCC (*milk*)
	Multisyllabic strings with variations in stress or intonation (emphasis on a syllable or changing emphasis on an utterance)
	Jargon: a syllable series with two different consonants and vowels with changes in stress and intonation, syllables that have the intonational patterns of adult language, such as the pattern of questions or statements

of varied CV syllables (e.g., ba-bi-ba-bi-bu). The onset of canonical babbling has been found to develop no later than 10 months of age in typically developing infants (Patten et al., 2014). A delay in canonical babbling after 10 months of age may be a predictor of language delay or a developmental disability.

Beginning at about 9 months of age, infants produce consistent vocal patterns that function as words. These vocalizations are called protowords or **phonetically consistent forms** (PCFs), which are often accompanied by gestures. PCFs are used by infants to convey consistent meaning; for instance, *doggy* is used only to label dogs, *uh* to request a food item (such as a drink), or *mama* to only label the child's mother.

> Resonance is the quality of speech that is shaped as it passes through the oral cavity (mouth) and nasal cavity (nose). Infants produce speech sounds with a less open oral cavity posture than adults. Thus, the resonance of each of these productions is termed a quasi-resonant nucleus. These early sound productions are not well formed, but productions become more similar to the resonance patterns of adults over time.

Words appear at 12 months, starting with the production of words that identify familiar entities in the child's environment: animate (alive) and inanimate (not alive).

Animate entities: *mommy, doggie, birdie, cow, kitty*

Inanimate entities: *cookie, car, shoe, ball, cup*

Jargon may also appear in children's productions when they begin to produce real words, with a combination of a jargon word and a real word (e.g., *Dawa go?*). Jargon is a child's speech production that is very similar to adults' speech production in intonation and rhythm.

PARENT AND CHILD INTERACTION

Parent-to-child or adult-to-child interaction plays a significant role in children's language development. This interaction is characterized by the adult's production of shorter sentences, simplified syntactic structures, slowed speech rate, pauses between separate utterances, and a greater number of prompts (questions and commands) (Bernstein & Levey, 2009). This style of interaction ensures that children can better comprehend spoken language. Adults also provide children with scaffolds (discussed in Chapter 2), when children produce a word that differs from the adult target or from a word that a child has not yet learned.

Child: *I eated*
Adult: *That's right, you ate*

Child: *Nana*
Adult: *That's a banana*

Child: *Where he go*
Adult: *Where did he go?*

Two factors that have been found to play a role in children's vocabulary development are more frequent input (more communication more often) and the diversity of words used in interaction (a greater number of different words or different topics) (Ruston & Schwanenflugel, 2010). The amount of talk that children hear from speakers in their environments is a predictor of vocabulary size (Shneidman, Arroyo, Levine, & Goldin-Meadow, 2012), while vocabulary growth is related to the diversity of words produced by caregivers (Pan, Rowe, Singer, & Snow, 2005). A study of Spanish-speaking children's vocabulary development found that more spoken language input at 18 months resulted in larger receptive and expressive vocabulary at 24 months (Hurtado, Marchman, & Fernald, 2008), providing evidence that more frequent and abundant input acts to activate and strengthen language learning (Poll, 2011).

Children rely on contextual information (language produced in the environment in specific situations) to learn the meaning and use of new words. For example, a child may listen to a conversation about a broken piece of furniture and the methods required for repair (e.g., *broken, fix, hammer*). In this encounter, the child may learn the vocabulary terms as they apply to this context. Later, the child will use these words to apply to new contexts, such as conversation about a broken toy (e.g., *broken, fix*). Children acquire many new words through **incidental learning** (Akhtar, Jipson, & Callanan, 2001). In incidental learning, children learn new words through exposure to communicative events, such as conversation. This is the opposite of *deliberate learning*, where children are purposefully taught new words.

EARLY LANGUAGE DEVELOPMENT

At about 12 months, children begin to produce words that represent inanimate entities (e.g., *ball*), animate entities (*mommy*, and *doggie*), and actions (*go* and *throw*). One of the characteristics of vocabulary development is that early words are remarkably similar for children across all languages (e.g., the words for *book, cookie, ball, dog, cat, eye, nose, bed, mommy,* and *shoes*) (Rescorla, Alley, & Christine, 2001, p. 605). These early productions take the form of consonant-vowel (CV) and vowel-consonant (VC) productions with later production of consonant-vowel-consonant (CVC) forms.

CV   go

VC   up

CVC   cup

Children's early words are not always accurate **phonemic representations**, a production that corresponds to the form consistent with a target word produced by adults. For example, one young child attempted to produce the target word *baby* with attempts consisting of *bih* and *bihbi*, along with the correct phonemic representation of the target word *baby* during these repeated attempts to produce the target word (Sosa & Stoel-Gammon, 2006). Phonemic representation is variable when children begin to combine words to produce two-word utterances, as in the example of a child's production *I waai* for the target utterance *I want ice cream*. Phonemic representation accuracy increases when children acquire 150 to 200 words (Maekawa & Storkel, 2006).

Two-word utterances, such as *push it* and *more cookie*, appear at about 18 months. By 24 to 36 months, children can produce longer utterances as their vocabulary increases (e.g., *I want more cookies and milk*). By age 3, greater phonemic accuracy appears when children use language to communicate feelings, observations, and needs. Children's productions are now more intelligible or understandable.

JOINT ATTENTION AND JOINT ACTION

Joint attention (the infant and another person sharing the same direction of eye gaze) and **joint action** (two individuals sharing action on the same object or task) are essential components of early word learning (Tomasello, 1998). In these interactive contexts, infants are supplied with the language associated with the adults' actions and the labels of objects. The most significant feature of joint attention and joint action is that children's first words are produced in these contexts. There is also a high correlation (connection) between the amount of time spent in joint attention tasks and the infant's vocabulary development (Tomasello & Todd, 1983). During joint attention tasks, infants' visual attention to objects and activities increases between birth and 10 weeks of age, with infants spending a greater amount of time engaged in activities (Columbo, Kapa, & Curtindale, 2011). The following is an example of an infant's joint interaction with an adult who is demonstrating how to manipulate a toy. Notice that the adult produces the words and the phrases *look, push,* and *it's your turn* to elicit the infant's interest and to encourage participation in the task.

Look—produced to draw the infant's attention and visual gaze toward the toy (joint attention results)

Push—produced to demonstrate how to open a slot in the toy

It's your turn—produced to engage the infant in turn-taking (joint action results)

Between 9 and 12 months, children notice where adults are looking (gaze following), use adults as social reference points (social referencing), and model adults' actions and language productions (imitation) (Tomasello, 2003, p. 21). At this point of development, children begin to understand that adults have inner thoughts and goals (Gleason & Bernstein Ratner, 2017). These early social skills are presented in Table 4–3.

Infants are able to interpret an adult's attitude toward an object by viewing the adult's facial expressions of pleasure or displeasure (Barna

Table 4–3. *Infants' Early Social Skills*

Gaze following	Occurs when an infant follows the direction and focus of the adult's eye gaze
Social referencing	Occurs when an infant identifies the feelings of the adult toward an object or an event and later uses this information for his or her own feelings toward the object or event
Imitation	Occurs when an infant uses an adult's actions or words for his or her own productions or actions

& Legerstee, 2005), along with awareness of the adult's direction of eye gaze. One study found that 12-month-old infants chose a specific toy by noting the adults' direction of eye gaze (Phillips, Wellman, & Spelke, 2002).

PHONOLOGICAL DEVELOPMENT

Phonological development describes children's acquisition of the sounds that form words. Phonological processes or patterns describe the manner in which young children first produce certain words. The most common phonological patterns found for younger children are syllable omission, reduplication, and final consonant deletion.

Banana	*nana*	Syllable omission
Daddy	*dada*	Reduplication
Bus	*bu*	Final consonant deletion

Most phonological patterns generally disappear by 3 years of age. Unstressed syllable omission or deletion (e.g., *nana* produced for the target word *banana*) reflects children's bias toward a strong or stressed syllable in the initial position of words (e.g., baNAna, MONkey, MAma, BUnny) (Levey & Schwartz, 2002). Notice that the word *banana* is produced with stronger emphasis on the second syllable (e.g., baNAna). In this example, the first syllable is weak (receives no stress or emphasis) and the second syllable is strong (receives main or primary stress or emphasis). Consequently, children omit

the initial weak syllable (*ba-*) and produce the second strong syllable (e.g., *-NAna*). It is important that all children receive audiological assessment to rule out hearing loss, which may affect their perception of the sounds in words.

Phonological awareness is a factor in children's literacy development. This is defined as a child's awareness of the sounds in words, along with the structure of words (e.g., sounds and syllables). Children first become aware of words, followed by syllable awareness. The awareness that spoken words consist of syllables appears at 3 to 4 years of age. Later, children recognize rhyme, a skill that indicates the awareness of sounds that compose words. For example, children are able to recognize that the words *key* and *bee* rhyme when they are able to perceive the similarity between the sounds that occur in these words. Later skills show the development of phoneme awareness, emerging about 6 to 7 years of age (e.g., the ability to recognize the sounds that compose a word).

◆ Word awareness begins with the ability to identify and isolate the individual words in a sentence, through pointing to the individual words that compose the sentence (e.g., *the boy ran* = three words).
◆ Syllable awareness consists of recognition of the syllables that compose words (e.g., *hot + dog = hotdog*).

COGNITIVE DEVELOPMENT

Cognition refers to mental abilities and includes perception, attention, memory, thought, categorization skills, and reasoning (Galotti, 2017).

◆ Perception involves awareness of sensory stimuli (smell, touch, taste, sounds, and vision).

◆ Attention involves mental focus on a task or on an activity.

◆ Memory involves the ability to retain and to recall information.

◆ Thought involves using our minds to consider or reason about something.

◆ Categorization skills involve placing things or ideas into classes or groups.

◆ Reasoning involves a logical manner of thinking about something

At 9 months of age, infants develop the understanding that others have thoughts, goals, and feelings (Gleason & Bernstein Ratner, 2017). When infants begin to understand that they can influence an adult's responses to their needs or requests, they begin to use pointing to draw the adult's attention. The infant's goal could be a question (*What is that over there? I don't know its name*), a request (*Let's go that way, I see another baby*), or an attempt to gain the adult's attention (*Look, it's a doggie*). The cognitive factors that play an essential role are presented in Table 4–4.

A cognitive mechanism for the ability to assign meaning to auditory information is termed *language processing*. Language processing involves attaching meaning to the sounds that form words, sentences, conversation, and stories. A child with a language processing disorder cannot assign meaning to auditory information.

Some of the specific cognitive skills that are essential for language development include **working memory** (Bates & Elman, 1996; Osman & Sullivan, 2014; Seidenberg & Elman, 1999), attentional skills, language processing skills, and a TOM.

◆ Working memory is a system that allows encoding, storing, processing, and rehearsal of information (Baddeley, 2003; Baddeley & Larsen, 2007), essential for language learning and academic success and progress.

◆ Attentional skills involve the ability to focus on a conversation or a task.

◆ Language processing applies to the functions performed in the brain that allow children to understand spoken

Table 4–4. Cognitive Skills

Perception involves the ability to interpret or understand sensory information through taste, smell, sight, hearing, or touch.

Attention involves mental focus on a specific task, with selective attention marking the absence of distraction.

Memory involves the ability to store information, along with the ability to retrieve or to recall the stored information.

Thought involves the mental manipulation or management of information.

Reasoning involves the process of thinking about a fact, event, or an idea in a logical way to formulate a conclusion or a judgment to make a choice of different possibilities or options.

language, along with a speaker's ideas and feelings.

♦ Theory of mind is defined as a child's understanding of others' thoughts, feelings, and intentions.

Working memory stores the active information that has occurred in a current experience (Galotti, 2017), such as a birthday party or watching a movie. Verbal working memory is the amount of memory a child has when given verbal language information or directions (Newbury, Klee, Stokes, & Moran, 2016). Working memory allows children to think or talk about these experiences at a later time. Preschool-aged children might be able to store three or four pieces of information (Galotti, 2017), such as *go to your cubby, take out your blanket, and come to the rug*. Children's working memory provides them with the ability to be successful in learning.

> Working memory allows the child to temporarily hold, process, and manipulate information (e.g., hold or keep this information in mind, think about and understand the information that has been given, and think about how to manipulate this information or use it in the future).

As discussed earlier, a TOM involves understanding a speaker's meaning, thoughts, feelings, and emotions, or what a speaker intends to do. Children learn the words that identify a speaker's inner mental state through conversation, when speakers describe their lives and feelings using **mental state verbs**, such as *think, know,* and *believe* (Harris, de Rosnay, & Pons, 2005). Often, facial expressions give children a clue about what these men-

tal state verbs mean (e.g., happy, upset, puzzled). Children learn to understand a speaker's intent (meaning) when observing the use of these mental state verbs in different contexts (Mazzone, 2009). At age 2, children begin to use terms that label physiological states, emotional states, and desires with terms such as *happy* and *sad*. The earliest psychological state words that appear in children's speech are the following (Bartsch & Wellman, 1995; Lee & Rescorla, 2008).

Physiological words: *sleepy* and *hungry*

Desire words: *want* and *need*

Emotional words: *happy* and *sad*

Children's use of mental state verbs increases during the third year of language learning, with the use of terms such as *think* and *know. Know* is an early occurring term, followed by the words *think, believe,* and *mean* (Shatz, Wellman, & Silber, 1983).

THE DEVELOPMENT OF HUMOR

The social environment plays a role in the development of humor (Hoicka, 2014). Infants begin to laugh at about 3 to 4 months of age, indicating an early response to humorous behaviors or events (Reddy, 2008). Infants repeat actions that elicit adults' laughter (Reddy, 2001), such as making funny faces, playing peek-a-boo, and making noises and movements (such as kicking their legs) designed to elicit a response. In the first year of life, the response to humor generally involves non-verbal stimuli (e.g., adults use of a squeaky voice), tactile stimuli (e.g., bouncing a baby on the adult's knee or lap), and other actions frequently performed by adults to elicit children's laughter (Hoicka, 2014). At about 12 months of age, children enjoy silly actions, such as watching someone misuse an item (e.g., putting a bowl on his head to represent a hat). Falsehoods consist of using an object to represent another object (e.g., using a shoe to be a hat on a head). As early as 15 months of age, children can understand that falsehoods are meant to be jokes. Preschoolers develop more sophisticated understanding and use of humor.

SCHEMAS

A **schema** is an organized representation of knowledge. In children's early cognitive development, a schema allows them to process information and organize knowledge about the world (Piaget, 1954). Schemas also provide children with the ability to construct a representation of the entities and events that appear around them (Witt, 1998). Schemas develop when children first encounter a thing or event, as in the following example.

> Children first encounter a bird in the park, such as a pigeon. They form a schema that represents this entity based on the perception of the entity's structural attributes: two legs, feathers, movable parts (legs and wings), and the ability to fly.

These schemas are psychological structures that allow a child to organize knowledge about objects, entities (e.g., humans, animals, and insects), concepts (e.g., ideas, beliefs, and thoughts), and actions. Sche-

mas are formed when children first are exposed to an entity. This initial exposure allows them to identify the characteristics of this entity, store these characteristics, and associate a name or label with the entity.

> A schema is a cognitive system for understanding knowledge about concepts. Concepts represent things and living entities, along with the relationship these concepts have with other things, actions, and events.

There are instances when children encounter something that does not fit into an existing schema, such as when children are told that a *penguin* is a bird. Most children do not believe that a penguin is a bird, as they do not see it fly. To accept the penguin as a *bird*, the schema for *bird* must change. **Adaptation** is the process of changing a schema in response to a new entity. **Assimilation** is a cognitive process that involves fitting this new entity into an existing schema, and **accommodation** involves changing an existing schema to make the new entity fit. **Equilibrium** (cognitive balance) is the goal that is achieved through assimilation or accommodation.

Piaget's (1973) stages were part of an influential theory that contributed to our current understanding of children's development. In this theory, the sensorimotor stage is the first stage of cognitive development, occurring between birth and 2 years of age. In this stage, infants discover the environment and learn through sensory perception and motor activity. Infants learn through their sensory abilities (taste, smell, sight, hearing, and touch) and their motor abilities (e.g., movements used to explore the environment or their own bodies). The preoperational stage follows, at ages 2 to 7 years, with children forming ideas based on their perceptions. The concrete operational stage follows, at ages 7 to 12 years, with reasoning skills emerging along with more logical thinking patterns. The formal operations stage follows through adulthood, with children now able to reason and employ abstract thought. Abstract thought involves the ability to reason, consider all aspects of a situation, and think about things in a logical manner. Young children begin to develop abstract thinking skills through their pretend play when they use an object to represent something else (e.g., a block to represent a phone).

> Stimuli are things or events that excite or stimulate infants' sight, sound, touch, taste, or smell. Stimuli cause a response, as these are things or events that interest or excite the infant. For example, infants are stimulated by things (look longer at them) that are dynamic or moving as opposed to attempts at stimulation that are static or unmoving (Shaddy & Columbo, 2004).

At 8 to 12 months, infants can anticipate events. They are also able to establish goals and a method to obtain their goals (**means-end behavior**). They understand that an object remains the same even when it is viewed from a different perspective, such as upside-down (**object constancy**). Infants understand that actions have a cause (**causality**) and remember that an object exists when it is absent from their sight (**object permanence**). Intentional or goal-directed behaviors also appear, such as pulling a string to acquire a toy. The

movement to meaningful or intentional goal-directed behaviors reflects **practical intelligence**.

> Practical intelligence has been defined as the knowledge needed to achieve or accomplish a goal. This is knowledge that was not explicitly taught or talked about to the infant (Sternberg et al., 2001). Instead, it is knowledge that is possessed by the infant. The skills involved with practical intelligence can be thought of as applied to practical skills (e.g., what an infant must do to obtain a goal or solve a problem).

Deferred imitation appears between 12 and 18 months of age. This occurs when children observe an activity, establish this action in their memory, and imitate the action at a later time. **Symbolic functions** appear with the production of first words, when words are used to represent an entity (e.g., *dog* to represent the thing that is furry, has four legs, and barks) or activity (e.g., *drink* to represent drinking from a cup). Children produce their first words when the entity is present in the environment (**referent present**). However, they achieve symbolic knowledge when using the word to label an entity absent from the environment (**referent absent**), showing that children have established an internal representation of this entity.

At 18 to 24 months, **representational thought** appears when children understand the world through mental operations rather than actions. Now they can solve problems through thought rather than physical means. For example, a child now considers how to solve a problem in her mind, before using physical means to solve the problem. Prior to the appearance of representational thought, a child will attempt physical means before mentally considering solutions. We next examine children's play, along with the connection between play and children's language development.

THE DEVELOPMENT OF PLAY

There is a close relationship between pretend play and the development of language (Patterson & Westby, 1998), given that symbolic or pretend play and language are dependent on representational skills (Orr & Geva, 2015). Representational skills appear when a child uses items to represent real objects (e.g., toy blocks to represent a phone) and when a child uses *words* to represent things in the world (e.g., the word *block* to represent a toy block). Pretend (symbolic) play demonstrates the ability to decontextualize (to separate an object from its immediate context). This occurs when a child uses a block to represent a train or telephone and uses *words* to represent a thing, even when the thing (*block*) is not the thing itself (e.g., *train* or *telephone*).

Pretend play appears at around 12 months of age, when children pretend to sleep or to drink from a cup. Play with dolls or adventure figures develops after age 2, with a child able to use different voices in pretend play at about 4 years of age (Galotti, 2017). The correlation between play and early language development involves four factors (Weisberg, Zosh, Hirsh-Pasek, & Golinkoff, 2013), shown in Table 4–5.

Children first engage in pretend play by using their own daily activities (e.g., preschool or familiar experienced activities). Next, they engage in pretend play that involves others' activities, using dolls and stuffed animals to create play schemes that involve playing house, taking care of a baby, going to work, or events that take place at school. Creating roles for other children in a play scheme reflects **decentration**, defined as the ability to consider multiple aspects of a situation (e.g., other children's roles in the play scheme and the actions involved in the play scheme). When children use symbols (e.g., a block to stand for a car, telephone, or loaf of bread), this represents a **semiotic function**. This occurs when a sign (a word, image, sound, or gesture) is used to create meaning.

Table 4–5. *The Correlation between Play and Early Language Development*

Symbolic thought	The use of props for real objects (e.g., a block for bread or for a telephone)
Social interaction	Collaboration among children to create a play scheme (e.g., going shopping) that also involves creating roles (e.g., shopper and vendor)
Language input	Peer and adult interaction in play involving language use
Engagement	Children's interaction within the play scheme

Semiotics explores how signs (words) create *meaning*. For example, when children create an imaginary world in pretend play, they use objects (e.g., a block) to stand for or represent items in this play scheme (e.g., cars, tea, a market, a train).

Early pretend play depends on real objects as props to support the play scheme. Late in the second year of life, children are less dependent on props. This reflects increased cognitive skills as children can mentally construct a play scheme (imaginative play without props) and are able to use language to construct the play scheme (language used to create the play scheme and events involved in this scheme). For example, a child can now symbolically create a play scheme using one object to represent another (e.g., *cardboard box* for *stove*) and use words to create the pretend play scheme (e.g., . . . *now you are the daddy and you just came home from work* . . .).

The opportunity for pretend play differs depending on the external environment. Some contemporary playgrounds consist of anchored structures, natural elements, and paths for riding bikes. These types of playground may have mazes, slides built into stonework, climbing devices, climbing walls, and tunnels. In contrast, traditional playgrounds consist of swings and slides. The richer environment of the contemporary playground was found to enhance the complexity of children's pretend play, allowing for richer social interaction (Li, Hestenes, & Wang, 2016).

There are stages that characterize children's play development (Westby, 1980), with early play schemes drawn from events that children have observed in their own environments (Table 4–6). Note that language skills advance throughout the stages of play development, as more complex play requires the use of more complex language (e.g., If I could . . . If you would . . . We might . . .). Children use their language skills to develop more complex play schemes and to explain these schemes to other children to engage their participation.

There are two factors that play a role in children's pretend play: **causal cognition** and **counterfactual reasoning** (Gopnik & Walker, 2013). Causal cognition allows children to understand the relationship between cause and effect, such as what object causes another object to move, make noise, or light up. These skills also play a role in children's understanding of how another individual's desires, emotions, and beliefs are the *cause* of their actions (Gopnik, Sobel, Schulz, & Glymour, 2001). For example, children can understand why another child might be upset when something he or she treasures is broken, such as a favorite toy. Causal cognitive skills also allow children to make predictions about the future, based on cause and effect (e.g., *if I spill my drink on the sofa, I am going to get into trouble*) and to provide causal explanations (e.g., *I think he is crying because someone took his ball*).

Multicultural Differences and Play

The language and themes in pretend play differ across cultures (Hwa-Froelich, 2004). The type of play in a culture is dependent on parents' cultural beliefs and goals regarding a child's development (Vandermaas-Peeler, 2002). In some

Table 4–6. *Children's Play Development*

Stage I (9 to 12 months)	Means-end skills allow children to use methods to achieve goals, such as pulling a string to play with a toy. Object permanence allows children to find a hidden object.
Stage II (13 to 17 months)	Children explore and discover the mode of operation of a toy (e.g., levers or other movable parts).
Stage III (17 to 19 months)	Children begin to engage in pretend play (e.g., pretending to sleep or other daily activities).
Stage IV (19 to 22 months)	Symbolic play continues to emerge, defined by the child using one thing to represent something else (e.g., a block as a telephone or a box used to represent a car). Play schemes can also include feeding a doll, putting the doll to bed, and general care of the doll, which represents a live baby.
Stage V (24 months)	Children engage in play schemes that represent daily activities that they have observed (e.g., shopping or playing house).
Stage VI (2½ years)	More varied experiences appear in play (e.g., trips to the doctor).
Stage VII (3 years)	Play schemas continue to use props (realistic objects), while play consists of sequenced events (e.g., getting breakfast, going shopping, putting baby in bed to nap, and other activities that represent the sequence of these events).
Stage VIII (3 to 3½ years)	Realistic props, previously used in play, are replaced by the use of imagination to create a play scheme. Children may use blocks to create an enclosure (e.g., a house, school, barn) or a row of chairs to represent a bus.
Stage IX (4 years)	Hypothetical events (not yet experienced) are used to create play schemes and projects (e.g., building a city, a farm, an airport or some other scheme that requires materials). Children begin to take account of future events (e.g., what would happen if . . .), resulting in behaviors that require planning to create the play scheme (e.g., a barn yard that will keep the animals from running away).
Stage X (5 years)	Collaborative play appears as interaction involves imaginative play schemes (e.g., a super hero, home making, a classroom play scheme). Children are now able to coordinate multiple activities within a play event by creating roles for other children in the play scheme (e.g., the teacher, the bus driver, and the children).

Source: Reproduced with permission from the American Speech-Language-Hearing Association, from C. E. Westby (1980). Assessment of cognitive and language abilities through play. *Language, Speech, and Hearing Services in Schools, 11,* 154–168.

cultures, parents engage in play with their children, while older siblings engage in play in other cultures. Across cultures, parents provide varying degrees of support and guidance. For example, Italian mothers were found to consider play a child's activity not requiring the need for adult intervention, while American mothers take a more active role in their children's play (Chessa et al., 2012).

A study of the beliefs and attitudes of Greek and Cypriot parents found play was valued for their children's development (Shiakou & Belsky, 2013). However, education was also highly valued, with children reported to spend greater time with academic lessons than play at home. An investigation of New York City immigrant Indo-Caribbean parents' attitudes toward play found that 67% of mothers and 48% of fathers believed that play contributed to cognitive abilities, social skills, and emotional development (Roopnarine & Jin, 2012).

In summary, it is important to consider that cultural differences are an important factor when assessing children's play, given the variability in the attitudes toward and styles of play across cultures. It is also important to respect parents' goals and cultural beliefs when planning interventions for children from multilinguistic and multicultural backgrounds.

MORPHOLOGICAL DEVELOPMENT

Morphology is concerned with the structure or organization of words, and **morphemes** are the minimal (smallest) meaningful units of words. For example, the lexical morpheme *hat* /hæt/ cannot be broken down into smaller parts (e.g., *ha* or *at*), as this would lead to the loss of the meaning of the word *hat*. Children's morphological development is presented in Table 4–7.

> Children's sentence length is also expanded by the inclusion of articles (e.g., *a, an, the*), prepositions (*in, on, under*), pronouns (*I, me, he*), and auxiliary verbs (*am, is, are*).

Morphosyntactic Development

Morphosyntactic development describes the relationship between morphemes and sentences, given that children's sentences expand when they begin to attach morphemes to words. For example, the addition of the inflectional morphemes *-ed* and *-ing* to the word *walk* adds meaning by indicating that an action has occurred in the past (past tense *-ed*) or that an action is now occurring and ongoing in the present (present progressive *-ing*).

Walk + ed (regular past tense inflectional morpheme): walk**ed**

Walk + ing (present progressive inflectional morpheme): walk**ing**

Children's morphosyntactic development goes through the stages (Bernstein, 2011; Bernstein & Levey, 2009) shown in Table 4–8.

Mean Length of Utterance

Mean length of utterance (MLU) is the average number of morphemes in children's utterances (Lund & Duchan, 1993).

Table 4–7. The Order of Development of Children's Grammatical Morphemes*

Grammatical Morpheme	Example	Age of Mastery (months)
Present progressive verb ending –ing	Going, playing	19–28
Preposition in	Put in cup	27–30
Preposition on	Put on shoes	27–30
Regular plural -s	Want blocks	24–33
Past irregular verbs came, fell, went, broke	He broke it	25–46
Possessive 's	Mommy's shoe	26–40
Uncontractible copula (be as main verb) am, is, are, was, were, be, been	He was nice	27–39
Articles a, an, the	The boy ran home	28–46
Past regular -ed	He walked home	26–48
Third person singular regular -s	He walks	26–46
Third person singular irregular has, does	He does walk	28–50
Uncontractible auxiliary (be verbs preceding another verb)	The boy is walking	29–48
Contractible copula	I'm happy	29–49
Contractible auxiliary	I'm jumping	30–50

*Used correctly 90% of the time in obligatory or required contexts.

Source: Reproduced with permission from *A First Language: The Early Stages*, by Roger Brown. Cambridge, MA: Harvard University Press, Copyright 1973 by the President and Fellows of Harvard College.

Table 4–8. Children's Morphosyntactic Development

I. The production of single-word utterances (e.g., *cookie, milk,* and *juice*) expands to include two-word utterances (*more cookie, drink milk,* and *gimme juice*).

II. The appearance of grammatical morphemes (e.g., -*ing,* plural -*s*), and prepositions (*in* and *on*). Utterances such as *I eating, put shoe on,* and *see cats* are characteristic of this stage. Children begin to produce additional grammatical morphemes (e.g., present progressive -*ing,* plural -*s,* possessive '*s,* and regular past-tense -*ed*).

III. Children's utterance length continues to grow as they produce simple declarative sentences (*That's my ball*), imperatives (*Don't take my ball*), Wh- questions (*Where's my toy?*), and simple negative sentences (*No wanna go*).

IV. Children's language expands to contain complex constructions. In this stage, children produce **compound** sentences (*Daddy is working **and** Mommy is reading*) and **complex sentences** (*That boy, **who is in my school**, is my friend*), with embedded clauses (e.g., *The man, **who drives the bus**, is nice*).

For example, the word *walk* is a single morpheme, whereas *walked* (*walk* + *ed*) and *walking* (*walk* + *ing*) are each composed of two morphemes when an inflectional morpheme is added (i.e., *-ed* and *-ing*). We calculate MLU by counting the number of morphemes in each utterance produced, usually assessing at least 50 separate utterances. After counting all morphemes, we divide the number of morphemes by the number of utterances. For example, if a child produces 150 morphemes in 50 utterances, the MLU would be 3.0 (e.g., 150 morphemes divided by 50 utterances).

> The method for calculating the number of morphemes in children's utterances involves counting some two- and three-word phrases as only a single word, as children do not perceive these two- and three-word utterances to consist of multiple words. For example, they do not view *big bird* as a bird that is big. Instead, they view some multiple word names as a single word, such as *Big Bird*, *Cookie Monster*, and *New York City*.

Morphological Differences

It is important to understand that languages and dialects differ in morphemes, so it is only appropriate to use these examples of MLU to assess English-speaking children. Using Mainstream American English (MAE) as a model for calculating the MLU of the speakers of different dialects or languages may incorrectly signal a disorder. For example, one of the rules found in several languages and dialects is to omit elements that repeat informa-

tion. African American English (AAE) is an example of a language that omits redundant (unnecessary) elements, such as omitting the plural when the adjective (*three*) already signals plurality (e.g., *three boy*). When we omit the redundant elements, note the differences in MLU between the first and second examples below that illustrate the difference between MAE and AAE.

MAE: I saw three boys = 5 morphemes (*I*, *saw*, *three*, *boy*, *-s*)

AAE: I saw three boy = 4 morphemes (*I*, *saw*, *three*, *boy*)

Given that this may be a rule in certain languages, it is important not to use MAE as the measure of typical or atypical development when working with children who speak other languages or dialects. It would be an error to consider morphological differences across dialects or languages as signs of a disorder. Instead, these are *differences* that contribute to the interesting variability across languages and dialects.

The morphological and syntactic differences between MAE and AAE speakers shown in Table 4–9 derive from the many contributions to AAE from West African languages (e.g., Bambara, Ewe, Fanta, Twi, Mende, Wolof, and Yoruba), along with contributions from Native American languages, French, and English. Again, it is important to understand that the differences found in language dialects and English-learning children signal *differences* and not *disorders*.

There are also differences between the morphological patterns found in native Spanish-speaking children learning English and native English-speaking children (Table 4–10).

Table 4–9. *Characteristics of African American English Morphology and Syntax*

AAE Feature/ Characteristic	Mainstream American English	Sample AAE Utterance
Omission of noun possessive	That's the woman's car. It's John's pencil	That **the woman** car. It **John** pencil.
Omission of noun plural	He has 2 boxes of apples. She gives me 5 cents.	He got 2 **box** of **apple**. She give me 5 **cent**.
Omission of third person singular present tense marker	She walks to school. The man works in his yard.	She **walk** to school. The man **work** in his yard.
Omission of "to be" forms, such as "is, are"	She is a nice lady. They are going to a movie.	**She a** nice lady. **They going** to a movie.
Present tense "is" may be used regardless of person/ number	They are having fun. You are a smart man.	**They is** having fun. **You is** a smart man.
Utterances with "to be" may not show person number agreement with past and present forms	You are playing ball. They are having a picnic.	You **is** playing ball. They **is** having a picnic.
Present tense forms of auxiliary "have" are omitted	I have been here for 2 hours. He has done it again.	I been here for 2 hours. He done it again.
Past tense endings may be omitted	He lived in California. She cracked the nut.	He **live** in California. She **crack** the nut.
Past "was" may be used regardless of number and person	They were shopping. You were helping me.	They **was** shopping. You **was** helping me.
Multiple negatives (each additional negative form adds emphasis to the negative meaning)	We don't have any more. I don't want any cake. I don't like broccoli.	We **don't** have **no** more. I **don't never** want **no** cake. I **don't never** like broccoli.
"None" may be substituted for "any"	She doesn't want any.	She don't want **none**.

Table 4–9. continued

AAE Feature/ Characteristic	Mainstream American English	Sample AAE Utterance
Perfective construction; "been" may be used to indicate that an action took place in the distant past	I had the mumps last year. I have known her for years.	I **been had** the mumps last year. I **been known** her.
"Done" may be combined with a past tense form to indicate that an action was started and completed	He fixed the stove. She tried to paint it.	He **done fixed** the stove. She **done tried** to paint it.
The form "be" may be used as the main verb	Today she is working. We are singing.	Today **she be** working. **We be** singing.
Distributive "be" may be used to indicate actions and events over time	He is often cheerful. She's kind sometimes.	**He be** cheerful. **She be** kind.
A pronoun may be used to restate the subject	My brother surprised me. My dog has fleas.	My brother, **he** surprise me. My dog, **he** got fleas.
"Them" may be substituted for "those"	Those cars are antiques. Where'd you get those books?	**Them cars**, they be antique. Where you got **them books**?
Future tense "is, are" may be replaced by "gonna"	She is going to help us. They are going to be there.	She **gonna** help us. They **gonna** be there.
"At" is used at the end of "where" questions	Where is the house? Where is the store?	Where is the house **at**? Where is the store **at**?
Additional auxiliaries are often used	I might have done it.	I **might could have** done it.
"Does" replaced by "do"	She does funny things. It does make sense.	**She do** funny things. **It do** make sense.

Source: Reproduced with permission from Roseberry-McKibbin, C. (2014). Examples of Acceptable Utterances by Speakers of African American English (Table 4.1 on pages 77–78). Oceanside, CA: Academic Communication Associates.

Table 4–10. *Morphological Differences Between Native English Speakers and Spanish-English Speakers*

	Native English Speakers	Spanish-English Speakers
Past tense (-ed) (regular)	Yesterday, I paint**ed**.	Yesterday I paint.
Plurals (-s)	The flower**s** are pretty.	The flower are pretty.
Possessive ('s)	My friend**'s** coat.	My friend coat.
Negative	She does **not** walk.	She no walk.
Interrogative (question inversion)	**Is** Juan coming?	Juan is coming?

Source: Reproduced with permission from Bernstein, D. K. (2011). Morphological Differences: MAE and Spanish-English Speakers (Table 8.9 on p. 157). San Diego, CA: Sage Publications.

MORPHOPHONOLOGY

Morphophonology describes the connection between morphemes and phonology. Morphophonological rules apply to changes in phonemes due to their sound environment (the sounds that surround another sound by coming before or following that sound). For example, note that the production of the final plural sound *-s* varies, depending on the sound that it follows.

Cat + s = cats /kæts/

Dog + s = dogs /dɔgz/

As described in Chapter 1, the plural *-s* remains intact as the unvoiced fricative /s/ when following the unvoiced stop-plosive /t/ in the word *cat*. However, the sound /s/ changes to the voiced fricative /z/ when it follows the voiced stop-plosive /g/ in the word *dog*. This is an example of the interaction between morphemes and phonology described as morphophonology.

We next review children's syntactic development, beginning with the production of two-word utterances to form simple sentences (e.g., *Want cookie*). By the end of the stages described in this chapter, children begin to produce longer utterances with a wider set of meanings.

SYNTACTIC DEVELOPMENT

Syntax describes rules for producing sentences through the combination of words (e.g., The + apple + is + on + the + table). As described in Chapter 1, syntax emerges when children begin to produce two-word utterances at about 18 months of age. At this stage of syntactic development, children produce utterances that indicate requests and observations of the world (e.g., *pick up, see doggy, push ball, all gone doggy, wanna snack, sock off, daddy go*).

In early sentence production, children omit the subject in the noun phrase, producing sentences such as *Want cookie*. Dropping the subject pronoun (pro-drop) occurs less frequently at around age 2½, when children's utterances increase to around three-word lengths (MacWhinney & Snow, 1985; Valian, Hoeffner, & Aubry, 1996). Note that there are languages that generally allow for omitting the subject pronoun, as shown in the following examples of pro-drop languages (Italian and Spanish) and non-pro-drop languages (English and French). Thus, the differences shown in Table 4–11 must be considered when working with multilingual speakers.

Children's early sentence productions are composed of nouns (*dogs, boys, snow*) and verbs (*bark, run, falls*). Nouns label entities (e.g., people, animals, and things) and verbs label actions (e.g., *run, eat, sleep*). There is also a class of verbs termed **mental state verbs** (e.g., *frighten, like, disappoint*) that refer to a person's mental state. Children's production of mental state verbs is an indicator of their ability to understand others' mental or internal states. The term *internal* or *mental state* refers to what an individual knows, thinks, feels, believes, and other types of mental activities. The internal mental state refers to the speaker's mind, while the external state refers to that which is physical or what you can see. Internal states are characterized by emotions (e.g., likes, dislikes, or fears), visceral states by bodily status (e.g., hunger, fatigue, thirst), and cognitive states by how the world is being processed, thought about, or understood (e.g., knowing, believing, thinking, understanding, recognizing, and remembering) (Oosterwijk et al., 2015).

PRONOUN ACQUISITION

Pronouns first appear at 31 to 34 months of age. There is an association between children's **perspective-taking** and correct pronoun use (Ricard, Girouard, & Decarie, 1999). Perspective-taking involves understanding that the points of view of others differ from the child's own. Thus, the correct use of the pronouns *you* and *I* requires understanding that perspective (viewpoint) changes, depending on who is speaking at that time. Younger children frequently confuse pronouns, producing sentence such as *Pick you up* (meaning to say, *Pick me up*).

Table 4–11. Pro-Drop Differences Across Languages

Italian	Vado al cinema stasera. (I) go to the cinema tonight.
Spanish	Salieron a las ocho. (They) left at eight.
English	I go to the cinema tonight.
French	Nous sommes partis à huit heures. We left at eight o'clock.

The speech-language pathologist (SLP) sat across from Tania, planning to work on the pronouns *you* and *I*. When the SLP used the pronoun *I*, little Tania was confused, given that she was also expected to use the pronoun *I* to refer to herself. The SLP realized the problem and moved to sit next to Tania to solve the confusion between these pronouns.

An example of a pronoun error is found in Micah's production of the utterance *I want me* to pick *you* up, when requesting to be picked up at age 2½. Children must be able to shift roles and see another's perspective or point of view to acquire the difference between these pronouns (Perner, 1991).

The pronouns that refer to *self* (*I, mine, my,* and *me*) emerge early, whereas those that refer to others (*he, she,* and *they*) emerge later. Children acquire objective pronouns (*him, her,* and *them*) before they acquire possessive pronouns (*mine, yours, his, hers, ours,* and *theirs*). The **reflexive pronouns** (*himself, herself, ourselves,* and *themselves*) are generally not mastered until 5 years of age. Table 4–12 presents the general order of pronoun acquisition (Moorehead & Ingram, 1973).

Objective pronouns are those that are the object or recipient of the action (*Give the book to him*). Possessive pronouns indicate possession (*That book is **hers***). Reflexive pronouns refer to someone's *self* (*I did it myself, she/he did it her/himself, they did it themselves*).

The Development of Nouns and Verbs

Nouns

Nouns comprise the largest category of words in a child's early vocabulary. Nouns label a person, place, or thing. When children acquire words, almost half are nouns, one-quarter are verbs and adjectives, and one-quarter are function words (e.g., prepositions, pronouns, determiners, conjunctions, and auxiliary verbs) (Bates et al., 1994). A description of these elements is presented in Table 4–13.

The definite article *the* refers to a specific entity that has already been referred to in conversation, while the indefinite article *a* refers to a nonspecific entity. Children may have difficulty distinguishing between these two article types until age 4 or later.

Children's earliest words are shown in the examples below (Gleason & Bernstein

Table 4–12. *Pronouns*

Stage	Pronoun
Level I	*I*
Level II	*my, it, me, mine*
Level III	*you, your, she, them*
Level IV	*we, he, they, us, you, him, his, theirs*
Level V	*her, its, our, herself, himself, ourselves, yourselves, themselves*

Source: Reproduced with permission from the American Speech-Language-Hearing Association, from D. Moorehead & D. Ingram (1973). The development of base syntax in normal and linguistically deviant children. *Journal of Speech and Hearing Research, 16,* 330–352.

Table 4–13. *Elements that Compose Sentence Formation*

Prepositions	Provide information about where (*in, on, under*), when (*after*), or descriptive information (*with*)
Pronouns	Take the place of nouns (e.g., *I, he, she, we, they*)
Determiners	Express the definiteness and specificity of a noun (a book vs. the book)
Conjunctions	Connect words and sentences (toys and games; apples or oranges)
Auxiliary verbs	Used with a main verb to show the verb's tense or to form a negative or question (e.g., *am, is, are, were, was*)

Ratner, 2017, p. 85). Note that these early words reflect children's experiences and that the environment plays a role in their learning.

Food and drink: *Apple, banana, cookie, cheese, juice, milk*

Body parts and clothing: *Diaper, ear, eye, foot, hair, hand, hat, mouth, nose, shoe*

Household/outdoor objects: *Blanket, chair, cup, door, flower, keys, spoon, tree, TV*

People: *Baby, daddy, grandma, grandpa, mommy*

Toys and vehicles: *Ball, balloon, bike, boat, book, bubbles, toy*

Families that have immigrated from regions that differ in foods, animals, and the environment will not share the same vocabulary expected by those unaware of these differences. For example, a child who has lived in a desert region may not have seen some of the animals experienced by a child who has lived in a city. Thus, we should not expect that the vocabulary items produced by children from different language backgrounds will be the same.

A student clinician in the U.S. was administering a vocabulary test to a child from one of the African countries. The child was presented with a picture of a baseball and labeled it as *soccer ball*. The student clinician was confused by the child's response. The clinical supervisor explained that soccer was played in most parts of the world, while baseball was not.

Children's early acquisition of nouns is associated with two factors: their semantic properties (the description of an entity or thing) and concrete object reference (the physical characteristics that can be perceived). Consequently, children learn nouns based on the characteristics of a thing, such as the shape and color of a piece of fruit (e.g., apples). Nouns are mapped onto perceptual qualities (e.g., *shape* and *use*). These perceptual skills allow children to label things such as *chair, door, tree,* and *dog*.

Verbs are more complex than nouns because they convey the meaning associated with actions or events and lack the characteristics associated with nouns. For example, it is easier for a child to learn the noun *cup* before understanding *run*. Learning verbs requires exposure to actions and events, along with understanding of these activities (e.g., *Dogs bark*). Consider the difficulty of distinguishing among the verbs *walk, jog,* and *run*. It may be difficult for children to distinguish between these actions, whereas *apple* is relatively easy to identify and remember.

> The semantic properties of a word play a role in learning. Nouns appear early, as they refer to the concrete aspects of things that we can perceive, such as people, animals, and objects in the environment. Concrete object reference refers to the characteristics of things that we can perceive, such as an *apple* that is usually *red* and *round.*

Word Learning and the Mutual Exclusivity Bias

Children's word-learning has been explained by various factors. One of the explanations of learning new words is the **mutual exclusivity bias**. When children are presented with a new word and a new object (e.g., *bunny*), they gaze at the only object in the room that is new to them and the object for which they have no name.

> When children hear a new word, they apply the new label to an unfamiliar object that has not been previously named.

For example, picture a scene that contains several objects that the child is familiar with: *car, ball, teddy bear,* and *doll.* When an adult places a new object within this array of toys (a *bunny*) and asks the child to "Look at the bunny," the child will look at the novel object, the bunny. Children use this strategy until about 17 to 22 months of age (Hansen & Markman, 2009), holding to the principle that each referent or thing can only have one name.

VERBS

The first verbs produced by young children describe simple actions (Bloom, Lightbown, & Hood, 1978), such as *eat, read, do,* and *fix.* These verbs are followed by *put, go,* and *sit.* Later acquired verbs include the mental verbs *want, have,* and *know.* When children first learn verbs, they use them in the context in which they were initially acquired (Tomasello, 1992, 2003). For example, if children learn *cut* when watching someone cut paper, they use the verb only for cutting paper. Children extend the meaning of this verb beyond the learning context to apply to another type of cutting, such as fingernails or bread, when they are exposed to more examples of the use of this word.

There is a connection between verb learning and children's awareness of syntactic structure (Gleitman & Gleitman, 1992). For example, certain verbs, such as *hit*, are transitive verbs that require a direct object noun to complete their meaning. In contrast, the verb *cry* is an intransitive verb that does not require a direct object noun to complete its meaning. Transitive verbs express a relationship between two things (e.g., *Daddy hit the ball*). In contrast, *cry* does not express a relationship between two things, as we cannot *cry* something in the way we can *hit* something. The following examples demonstrate these differences between intransitive and transitive clauses:

Transitive: Subject + verb + object: *She wanted* **an apple.**

Intransitive: Subject + verb: *She cried.*

> There is more complexity involved in constructing a sentence that requires a direct object (*He hit the ball*) versus a sentence that does not require a direct object (*She sneezed*). Consequently, intransitive forms first appear in children's productions (e.g., *cry, smile, frown*), followed later by transitive forms (e.g., *want, kick, like*). Note that the transitive forms require a direct object (*I want a cookie, I kick the ball, I like cookies*).

The regular past tense of a verb is formed by adding *-ed* (e.g., *walked, talked, voted*). Children often **overgeneralize** the regular verb form (add *-ed*) to produce an irregular verb, as shown in the following examples of the irregular verb form targets *ate, threw,* and *went.*

I eated it

I throwed the ball

I goed there

Auxiliary verbs (e.g., *am, is, are, was, were, be,* and *been*) are also termed *helping verbs* because they are used in conjunction with main verbs to express time or tense.

*He **is** walking*

*We **are** eating*

*They **were** here yesterday*

> The verb *walk* is not marked for tense or time. When we add the auxiliary verb *is*, we can mark it as expressing the present tense of an ongoing action (i.e., *He **is** walking*).

The auxiliary modal verbs *will, shall, may, might, can, could, must, ought to, should, would, used to,* and *need to* are used to express certain attitudes, such as disapproval (*You might have asked before taking a cookie*), possibility (*I may give you a cookie tomorrow*), or ability (*I can throw a ball far*). Children begin to use modal auxiliaries around age 2 to 3, with the earlier production and understanding of the modal verb *can* (Leonard, Deevy, Wong, Stokes, & Fletcher, 2007; Richards, 1990). The acquisition of auxiliary verbs for the majority of children follows this pattern of development (Wells, 1979).

Early acquisition: *do, can, will, going to*

Preschool-age acquisition: *have to, shall, could*

There are certain verb contrasts that present children with difficulty, such as *ask* versus *tell* (Macaulay, 2006). The verbs *ask* and *tell* may present difficulty until children reach school age. At age 3½, Micah said that he was going to *ask* his mother that he had hurt his arm.

The Phonological Features of Irregular Verb Forms

Children's difficulty with the correct production of irregular verb forms is associated with the phonological changes required by certain verbs (Shipley, Maddox, & Driver, 1991, p. 118). For example, note that some irregular past tense verbs do not change in the present tense form to the past tense form (e.g., I am going to *cut* the bread/Yesterday, I *cut* the bread). In contrast, other verbs undergo greater change between present and past tense forms (e.g., *catch/caught*). In this case, the change consists of the consonant "ch" to the consonant "t," along with the change of the vowel "ae" to the vowel "au." The interaction between phonology and irregular verb form production is shown in the examples in Table 4–14. Children have no difficulty with the production of the *no change* category (e.g., *cut/cut* and *hit/hit*), given that these verbs do not change from present to past tense form.

> *Watch me **cut** the paper*
> *Yesterday, I **cut** the paper*

Greater difficulty appears in the verbs that require more complex sound changes from the present to past form changes (e.g., *caught, ate, went*).

> *Watch me **catch** the ball*
> *Yesterday, I **caught** the ball*
>
> *Watch me **eat** the cookie*
> *Yesterday, I **ate** the cookie*

Table 4–14. *The Relationship Between Phonology and Verb Changes*

No change in vowels or consonants	*cut/cut*
Internal vowel change of /ʌ/ to /e/	*come/came*
Internal vowel change with final change from /p/ to /t/	*sweep/swept*
Final consonant change from /d/ to /t/	*build/built*

> *Watch me **go** down the hill*
> *Yesterday, I **went** down the hill*

Overgeneralization occurs most often with irregular past tense verbs with internal vowel change (e.g., *take/took*) and final change from /d/ to /t/ (e.g., *build/built*). In this case, children produce the past tense forms as *taked* and *builded*. The minimal difference in voicing between these sounds (e.g., /d/ voiced and /t/ unvoiced) may present children with perceptual difficulties in noting this change. The irregular past tense verbs *go/went* may be produced correctly at 3½ to 4 years of age, *see/saw* at 4 to 4½, and *eat/ate* by 4½ to 5. Children may not master the change from /d/ to /t/ until 9 years of age.

In summary, children's accuracy is greater for *no change* verbs (e.g., *hit/hit*). The greatest difficulty appears with change from /d/ to /t/ (e.g., *bend/bent*, *build/built*, and *send/sent*). These difficulties are found in phonological changes in some verbs to past tense. Regular verbs present less difficulty, as the child merely adds *-ed* to the root forms *walk, talk*, and *bake* (*walked, talked, baked*).

THE DEVELOPMENT OF NEGATIVE, INTERROGATIVE, AND IMPERATIVE SENTENCE FORMS

Negative Sentence Forms

Children at the one- and two-word utterance stage express three types of negation.

Nonexistence to indicate disappearance: *All gone juice*

Rejection to indicate not wanting something: *No milk*

Denial to indicate an untruth: *Not book*

Three phases of negative construction development have been described (Bellugi, 1967; Bloom, 1991; Klima & Bellugi, 1966). Table 4–15 presents the development of negative sentence forms.

Indefinite negative words such as *nobody*, *no one*, and *nothing* present young language learners with difficulty. Younger children often say, *I want anything*, when they mean, *I want nothing* (Seymour & Roeper, 1999). Older school-age children might say, *I don't got no books*, and even adults might say, *I don't see nobody*.

We may also find that children who are learning English as a new language or English dialect speakers may produce sentences that include negative concord (double negatives). Negative concord consists of the use of more than one negative element in a sentence. Negative concord is often considered ungrammatical if the listener is unaware that negative concord is considered grammatically correct across many languages and dialects (Peccei, 1999; Zanuttini, 2014). Negative concord is a standard feature in Portuguese, English, Persian, Russian, Spanish, Neapolitan, and Italian. Examples of the use of negative concord in English dialects have been found in American English speakers of Alabama White English (Feagin, 1979), African American English (Labov, 1972; Green, 2002; White-Sustaita, 2010), Appa-lachian English (Wolfram & Christian, 1976), and West Texas English (Foreman, 1999). Despite the double negative, we interpret the sentence as being negated only once. It is important for practitioners to understand that double negation does not reflect a language disorder, as it is an accepted rule across many languages and dialects. An example of negative concord is shown below.

Nobody don't like me

> Examples of negative concord include *Nobody **ain't** doin' **nothing** wrong*, found in West Texas English (Foreman, 1999) and ***I don't never** have **no** problems*, found in African American English (Green, 2002).

Interrogative Sentence Forms

Yes/no questions (*Do you want a cookie?*) require that the listener simply answer the question with either a *yes* or a *no* word. To form yes/no questions, children must learn to invert (reverse) the subject (the boy) and the auxiliary verb (is), as shown in the following example.

Declarative sentence: *The boy **is** eating.*

Inversion: ***Is** the boy eating?*

Table 4–15. *Negative Sentence Development*

First stage	Children produce the negative element outside the sentence (*No bed*).
Second stage	Children embed the negative element *no* (*I no want milk*) while also producing the negative form *not* (*That not cookie*).
Third stage	The negative contractible forms *can't* and *don't* emerge (*I don't have a cookie*) when MLU reaches 4.0.

Wh-questions (beginning with *who, what, when, where, why,* or *how*) require more information than a *yes/no* response. Answering *why, how,* and *when* questions require greater knowledge than is present in the immediate context (e.g., *Why was the doggie bad?*). Children must look for this information from another context or previous **discourse** or discussion (e.g., *why, how,* and *when did something happen*). Discourse is a continuous stretch of speech, such as conversation. In conversation, discourse is constructed between participants, with each taking a turn and responding to what the other has said (Leahy, 2004, p. 71). The complexity and order of acquisition of *Wh*-questions are presented in Table 4–16.

> The learning of *Wh*-words occurs when children can engage in conversations with adults or more advanced language users about past and future events, which will help children to think about themselves at different points in time (Hudson, 2006).

It is necessary to perform two operations to produce a *Wh*-question. The more complex process of forming *Wh*-questions explains children's ability to perform this operation only at a later stage of language development. The operations in producing a *Wh*-question are the following:

1. Transpose (reverse the order of) the subject (*The boy*) and the auxiliary verb (*is*).
2. Add the *Wh*-form to the beginning of the sentence.

The following sequence demonstrates these operations.

> Declarative sentence: *The boy **is** eating.*

> Inversion: **Is** *the boy eating?*

> Add the *Wh*-form: *What **is** the boy eating?*

Four phases of development characterize question development (Bloom, 1991; Klima & Bellugi, 1966), as shown in Table 4–17.

Table 4–16. *Wh-Question Complexity*

- *What* questions require knowledge of an object (e.g., *What is that?*).
- *What doing* questions require knowledge of an action or event (e.g., *What did he do?*).
- *Where* questions require knowledge of location (e.g., *Where is my ball?*).
- *Who* questions require knowledge of identity (e.g., *Who took my book?*).
- *When* questions require knowledge of temporal (time) information (e.g., *When do you eat breakfast?*).
- *Why* questions require knowledge of causation (e.g., *Why is she crying?*).
- *How* questions require knowledge of the way something works (*How does this work?*), the way something happened (*How did he get that bruise?*), the quality of an experience (*How was your vacation?*), or the extent or degree of something (*How far, how long, how many, how much,* and *how old?*).

Table 4–17. *Four Phases of Question Sentence Development*

Phase 1	Rising intonation and some *Wh*-forms occur between 27 and 30 months of age.	*Cookie now?* *Go car?*
	Younger children simply attach a *Wh*-word to an assertion.	*Where daddy?* *What dat?*
	Where and *what* questions are the more prominent *Wh*-questions produced, with difficulty understanding *why* questions (treating them as *what* questions).	Question asked: **Why** *do you eat breakfast?* Child's response: *Cereal*
Phase 2	Between 27 and about 34 months, children understand and respond to *what, who,* and *where* questions, while auxiliary verbs may be absent.	*Where my car?* *What you doing?*
Phase 3	Between 31 and 40 months, there is limited use of inversion in *Wh*-questions until children reach 3.5 MLU (O'Grady, 1997).	*Where you?* *Where you are?* *Where are you?*
	At this stage, children are able to invert the subject and verb to produce yes/no questions.	*We are going?* Inversion absent *Are we going?* Inversion present
Phase 4	Inversion in positive *Wh*-questions appears at about 35 months (MLU 3.5+). Children now invert the subject and the auxiliary verb when asking positive *Wh*-questions.	*What is the man doing?*
	Difficulty appears with inversion when producing negative *Wh*-questions.	*Why I can't have cookie?*

Imperative Sentence Forms

Imperative sentences consist of requests, demands, and commands for a listener to perform an action to satisfy a speaker's intent (goals and meaning). Imperatives have the following syntactic structure: uninflected verbs (no morphemes attached) and the subject *you* omitted (e.g., *Come here!*). At the prelinguistic level, children express imperatives by pointing and gesturing. Later in develop-

ment, children's production of two-word imperative utterances takes the following forms.

Eat cookie!

No bed!

More complex imperative sentence forms appear as children approach age 3.

Throw the ball to me.

SEMANTIC DEVELOPMENT

Semantics describes how meaning is conveyed through words, sentences, and discourse. Vocabulary development begins at about 12 months, when children produce words that label familiar entities, actions, and objects in the environment. This demonstrates the connection between children's vocabulary development and their environmental experiences.

Vocabulary Development

Children have an expressive vocabulary of one or more words at 12 months and a 200- to 300-word vocabulary at 24 months. By age 6, a child's vocabulary consists of 10,000 words (Anglin, 1993). Children's receptive vocabulary generally exceeds their expressive vocabulary, and they can understand at least 50 words when their expressive vocabulary consists of approximately 10 words. Some children's vocabulary shows a *vocabulary burst, vocabulary spurt,* or *naming explosion* when they acquire a 50-word vocabulary during the second year of life. However, not all children show this pattern of rapid vocabulary growth (Ganger & Brent, 2004). Consequently, the variation in children's development must be considered in assessment.

There is also variation in vocabulary development for children learning a second language. This requires that all languages spoken be considered when assessing vocabulary skills. In this case, a child's true vocabulary knowledge is scored, rather than the language that is being learned. This approach to assessment is termed *conceptual scoring* (Gross, Buac, & Kaushanskaya, 2014). An example of this type of scoring follows when a Spanish/English-speaking child's vocabulary skills are assessed for describing a picture of a *ball*. This child is in the process of learning English as a second language.

"Striped" . . . "round" . . . "grande" . . . "rossa"

If this child were scored for only English, the score would be "2." If credited for the child's native language (Spanish) and second language (English), the score would be "4." If only one language is considered, the child's true vocabulary knowledge would not be considered.

Young children frequently use the perceptual characteristics of entities to extend the meaning beyond that entity (**overextension**), such as labeling all four-legged animals *doggie*. Overextensions derive from the perceptual or functional characteristics of the target word (Peccei, 1999), such as the number of legs on the animal. Functional characteristics form the basis for a child using the word *hat* to label a hat, scarf, ribbon, or hairbrush, given the similar function of putting something on or near your head.

Frequently, children also produce overextensions when lacking the appropriate word. In this case, they produce a word such as *doggy* for another four-legged animal, as a way of asking *what's that?* Children also sometimes make up words when they lack a word to describe things, such as the phrase, *I'm crackering my soup* (Clark, 1981) to describe putting crackers in their soup. Overextension occurs until about 3 years of age, when children's vocabulary skills increase (Bernstein & Levey, 2009).

Underextension can also appear in children's word productions when they have a restricted definition of a word. For example, Daniel was horrified when told that the picture of his dog's grandfather was on the cover of a dog manual, asking *Is Shanti's grandfather a dog?* Children may also deny that their mother's high heels are *shoes*, pointing to their own and saying *No, dis shoe.*

Relational Terms

Semantic development includes the acquisition of **relational terms**. Relational terms mark the relationship of things. Examples consist of existence (*all gone*) or recurrence (*more*). Relational terms also describe temporal relations (time), physical relations (descriptions), locative relations (location), and kinship terms (family relations) (Table 4–18).

An investigation of early relational words produced by children from 12 to 20 months showed the production of *that* used to indicate an object of interest, along with the relational use of *gone* to indicate disappearance (Gopnik, 1988). When children are aware that something is absent, they will code the meaning of **recurrence,** produced when children have finished all the juice in their cups and ask for *more.* Learning relational terms is fundamen-

tal to language development (Göksun, Hirsh-Pasek, & Golinkoff, 2009), given that these terms allow children to express greater meaning.

Exposure to spatial relational terms also acts to facilitate children's encoding and mapping of spatial relations in the world (Loewenstein & Gentner, 2005). For example, understanding locative relations allows children to describe the spatial relation between objects, such as *the cup is on the table.* Children who have acquired relational terms are also better at noticing, using, and maintaining memories of similar relationships in the environment (Loewenstein & Gentner, 2001), such as the use of *all gone* to refer to entities that have disappeared (e.g., *Cookies all gone!*).

The locational relation terms that children learn by 3 years of age are *in, on,* and *under* (Johnston, 1988). Children learn relational terms that are less complex to conceptualize, such as *big/little, tall/short,* and *high/low,* before *thick/thin, wide/narrow,* and *deep/shallow* (Owens, 2016). In addition, the relational terms *in, on, under,* and *next to* are learned in that order, followed by the more complex spatial concepts *in back/in front of, above,* and *below.*

Table 4–18. *Relational Terms*

Temporal relations	*before, after, first, next, last*
Dimensional relations	*big/little, tall/short, long/short, large/small, high/low, thick/thin, wide/narrow, deep/shallow*
Quantitative relations	*more, less*
Object relations	*all gone, more*
Physical relations	*hot/cold*
Locative relations	*in, on, under, next to, behind*
Spatial relations	*close/far, up, down, open, in front of/behind, beside*
Kinship relations	*mother, brother, cousin*

Concepts are mental representations of things and living entities (objects, ideas, people, animals, times) that children perceive and experience (Galotti, 2017). There are five classes of concepts: spatial (location), temporal (time), quantity (number), quality (description), and social-emotional (feelings).

The temporal concepts that refer to a sequence of events (*before* and *after*) are learned late. Younger children rely on the *order of mention* for understanding the terms *before* and *after* (Bever, 1970). This means that children interpret the first thing mentioned in a sentence as the first object of action. Consequently, they misinterpret the following direction that asks the child to **first** put the toy in the box.

> *Before you put the **ball** in the box, put the* ***toy*** *in the box.*

Given that *ball* was mentioned first, children interpret this sentence to mean *put the ball in the box* first and *put the toy in the box* second. Children begin to better understand syntactic structure in the later preschool stages, with less reliance on the order of mention (Owens, 2012).

There are two classes of temporal relations: temporal order (*after* and *before*) and temporal duration (*since* and *until*). Examples of these relational terms follow.

Temporal order
He came into the class after John.
She went into the room before John.

Temporal duration
He has been here since the room opened.
She will stay until it gets dark outside.

Children understand the temporal-order sentence structures *before* and *after* earlier than the duration terms *since* and *until* (Feagans, 1980). Duration terms are not fully understood before 7 years of age. Younger children also have difficulty understanding the relational terms *more, less, long*, and *short*. Understanding the relational terms *in front of, behind*, and *beside* depends on an object that has a clearly defined front, back, or side. It is important to understand that children first understand spatial concepts by using their own bodies as reference (e.g., *in front of* and *in back of* the child's body). Consequently, this aspect of learning spatial terms should be considered when addressing learning these concepts.

Cultural Differences and Relational Terms

Cultural differences also play a role in understanding certain relational terms. Children from different language backgrounds may use varied methods or schemas to create concepts of space and objects in that space. For example, some cultures schematize a table in the following manner: Table top plus legs. In other words, a table is conceptualized to resemble a solid object with top and sides. This schema was found for Atsugewi speakers (a native American tribal language of Northern California), who view the table with top and four sides (Talmy, 1983). In contrast, other cultures may schematize a table as having only a table top, with nothing else under or on the sides of the table. In this case, the table has only a single dimension (the top) and the legs are disregarded when conceptualizing a table. Consequently, children's description of the path of a ball thrown under a table may result in two different answers: through the table (given the concept of a table with legs) or under the table (given the concept of a table with only a top). Consequently, it is important to consider that there may be linguistic differences in the schematization of space across cultures.

Kinship Relationship Terms

Another category of relationship terms refers to *kinship* or a child's relationship to family members. Piaget's early study (1928) was replicated 34 years later (Elkind, 1962), with similar results for children's understanding of kinship relations. The order of the acquisition of kinship terms follows (Owens, 2016):

Mother, father, brother, sister

Daughter, son, grandmother, grandfather

Uncle, aunt, cousin

Children's early understanding of kinship reveals difficulty understanding reciprocity. In other words, children have difficulty understand that the kinship term *brother* applies to both the child and to the child's brother. Later, children understand that *to have a brother* means that *you might be a brother too.* Most kinship terms are established by age 10.

Semantic Roles and Semantic Relations

Another area of development is children's production of **semantic roles** (Bernstein & Levey, 2009). These semantic roles include *agent, action, object/affected, location, possession, rejection, disappearance, nonexistence,* and *denial.* At 12 to 18 months, semantic roles are expressed in children's one-word speech productions, as presented in Table 4–19.

At about 18 months, children begin to produce two-word utterances. When they

Table 4–19. *Semantic Roles: Produced at the One-word Stage of Language Development*

Semantic Role	Definition	Example
Agent	Doer of an action	*daddy* (pointing to daddy kicking a ball)
Action	Event	*kick* (pointing to daddy kicking a ball)
Affected	Entity acted upon	*ball* (pointing to ball that was kicked)
Location	Place	*bed* (indicating that the dog is *in* his bed)
Possessor	Owner	*mommy's* (while pointing to her shoe)
Possession	Entity owned	*shoe* (while bringing mommy's shoe to her)
Attribute	Characteristic	*hot* (while pointing to stove)
Recurrence	Repetition	*more* (while pointing to cookie plate)
Negation	Rejection	*no* (going to bed rejected)

Source: Reproduced with permission from Levey, S. (2011). Semantic roles (Table 7.1, p. 127). Los Angeles, CA: Sage Publications.

acquire at least 20 words, they combine semantic roles (e.g., *mommy* and *go*) to create **semantic relations**: agent (*mommy*) + action (*go*). Examples of these semantic relations are presented in Table 4–20 (Levey, 2011).

Semantic relations describe the relationship between things, such as *mommy go* or *doggy barking*. These examples describe the relationship between the agents (*mommy* and *doggy*) and the actions (*going* and *barking*). Semantic relations mark children's productions of new meanings and expanded ways to express meaning.

PRAGMATIC DEVELOPMENT

Pragmatics involves the use of language in interaction, adapting the language used for different listeners and situations, and following certain rules to achieve successful

Table 4–20. *Semantic Relations*

Semantic Relations	Examples
Agent + action	*Mommy kiss*
Action + affected	*Kick ball*
Action + location	*Sleep bed*
Entity + location	*Baby bed*
Possessor + possession	*Mommy shoe*
Entity + attribute	*Doggy big*
Nomination	*That car*
Recurrence	*More juice*
Negation	*No bed*

Source: Reproduced with permission from Levey, S. (2011). Semantic Relations (Table 3.5, p. 46). Los Angeles, CA: Sage Publications.

communication. Examples of these three pragmatic factors follow in Table 4–21.

Early Pragmatic Development

Infants are capable of producing **intentional** communication to indicate their wants and needs. Infants communicate intentionality with gesture and/or vocalization coupled with eye contact (James, 1990). Infants begin communication through the use of gesture, with reaching for a desired object used as a signal for a *request* and pointing as a signal to indicate some interest in an item in the environment (Owens, 2016). Infants frequently combine a gesture (e.g., pointing) with verbalization (e.g., *doggy*). Capone (2007) points out that gesture and language originate in the same neural regions of the brain, suggesting that gestures are an indication of a child's future language development.

Children at the one-word stage use language to regulate others' behaviors, establish joint attention, and engage in social interaction (James, 1990). A child's early attempt to communicate an **intention** (meaning or request) consists of the following functions (Bernstein & Levey, 2009; Halliday, 1975).

Instrumental function, used to obtain a goal and to have wants and needs met (the child holds out a cup and says *more*)

Regulatory function, used to control others' behaviors (the child gives a ball to an adult to request play and says *ball*)

Interaction function, used to obtain joint attention (the child calls *mama*)

Table 4–21. *Pragmatic Factors in Language Interaction*

Language use	Greetings: *Hello, goodbye, how are you?*
	Informing: *I'm going home now.*
	Demanding: *I want to play with your new doll.*
	Promising: *I promise to share my new toy with you.*
	Requesting: *Can I play with your new doll?*
Adapting and accommodating to different listeners	Talking differently to a baby than to an adult and to a teacher than to a friend
	Giving enough information so that the listener understands what you are talking about, how or why something happened, or how to play a game
Following rules in conversation	Taking turns in conversation as speaker and listener
	Introducing topics of conversation that are relevant to the topic at hand
	Staying on topic
	Making conversational repairs when communication breakdowns occur
	Learning to interpret signals (e.g., when someone is bored with the conversation or anxious to add something to the conversation)
	Appropriate distance between speaker and listener
	Eye contact

Personal function, used to express feelings or attitudes (the child says *yum* while eating a cookie)

Children's pragmatic requests develop over time, as shown in the following examples of children requesting a cookie:

1 year	*Waa* (and reaching)
1½ years	*Cookie*
2 years	*Wannacookie*
3 years	*Cookie please*
7 years	*That cookie sure looks yummy*

Conversational abilities appear at about 2 years of age, with the child able to engage in a short number of turns as speaker and listener. Verbal responses increase at 2 years of age, with an increase in verbal interaction at 3 years of age (Owens, 2016).

Speech Acts

A speaker's intent or meaning can be categorized as a **speech act** (Cameron-Faulkner, 2014; Searle, 1983). The term *speech act* refers to a speaker's goal or intention (meaning) when producing a word, sentence, or longer utterance. Speech acts are called *acts* for two reasons: first, because speech is considered an action or act and second, because speech acts can have some sort of action or effect on a listener. Examples of speech acts are statements (*I'm hungry*), requests (*Give me a hug*), warnings (*Watch out for the crack in the sidewalk*), advice (*Take your umbrella because it looks like rain*), commands (*Put on your shoes*), and promises (*I promise to clean my room*). To understand a speech act, the listener must understand the speaker's intention (meaning or goal). There are five speech act categories that label a speaker's intent (meaning or goal) when producing a sentence (Cameron-Faulkner, 2014, p. 39). These speech act categories are shown in Table 4–22.

Speech acts can be direct (e.g., *Pass the salt*) or indirect (e.g., *Can you pass the salt?*). Note that the indirect speech act has the syntactic form of a question (i.e., *Can you . . . ?*) but has the intention or meaning that an action be performed by the listener (i.e., *pass the salt*). Indirect speech acts convey a request in a manner that is more appropriate or polite, given that the request for action is conveyed in a subtle manner through the use of modal auxiliaries (e.g., *can, could, would, should, couldn't*). Children begin to understand indirect speech acts at about 3 years of age (Bucciarelli, Colle, & Bara, 2003). The production of indirect speech acts appears at about 30 months, when children acquire the modal auxiliary *can,* with later production of the modal auxiliaries *will, shall,* and *could* (Wells, 1979).

NARRATIVE DEVELOPMENT

Narrative plays a role in social interaction, effective communication, and the development of literacy skills and is a good predictor of subsequent literacy achievement. The sequence of children's narrative development follows the following stages (Bliss & McCabe, 2011), shown in Table 4–23.

> A narrative can consist of telling a story, recounting something that happened in a story, or giving a description of something that has happened.

Vocabulary skills play an essential role in narrative development, giving children a wide variety of words to describe events. Narrative also becomes more organized as children learn connectives, such as *and then, therefore, however,* and *nevertheless.*

Table 4–22. *Five Speech Act Categories*

Representatives: assertion or statements	*This is a pretty flower.*
Directives: commands or requests	*Please put all of your toys away.*
Commissives: promises or threats	*I promise to mail the letter today.*
Expressives: thanks, compliments, accusations	*Thank you for your gift.*
Declaratives: official acts	*I declare you husband and wife.*

Table 4–23. The Stages of Narrative Development

A one-event narrative has only one specific past tense action.	*I played.* (when asked what he did in school that day)
A two-event narrative is characterized by two actions.	*I dropped my cookie. Mommy gave me new cookie.*
A leap-frog narrative includes events that are not sequenced appropriately and/or omits major events so that the listener must infer a logical causal sequence and any missing events.	*I went to the zoo. My brother got popcorn. I went on the subway.*
A chronological narrative contains a chronological sequence or listing of events without much coherence and/or evaluation; so it sounds like a travel itinerary.	*We went to the ball game. I ate a hot dog. It was raining. We went inside. I didn't get wet.*
A classic narrative is complete with information on characters involved, what happened, where the event happened, when it happened, and the elements of cause and effect.	*I went to the lake house and played Wii. We went bowling and I won three games but we had to leave 'cause Grampa got tired of playing. We went to Tanzy's for lunch and had curly fries. I spilled my drink but nobody got mad. We came back to the lake house and watched a movie.*

Source: Reproduced with permission from Bliss, L. S., & McCabe, A. (2011). *Language Development: Understanding Diversity in the Classroom* (p. 213). Los Angeles, CA: Sage Publications.

The man climbed up the ladder. **And then** he started to paint the star.

He wanted to stay and play. **However,** he had to go home to eat dinner.

She was full from eating all the popcorn. **Nevertheless,** she managed to eat some candy.

The narrative story or grammar model describes the rules for recounting the events in a story: setting (where the story took place), event or events (what happened), sequence (the order of events), and conclusions (what were the results).

The Narrative Grammar Model

The narrative grammar model describes the structure of stories in children's books (Stein & Glenn, 1979).

It is essential that children develop an understanding of this structure because this knowledge helps them better understand and remember elements of the stories read to them at home or at school. Exposure to narratives in storybooks allows children to internalize this structure. Once in preschool, this internalized structure helps them achieve better understanding of stories. Children are not able to produce a complete episode, including all elements of the narrative structure, until age 7 or 8. Internal responses (words that describe the characters' feelings) are largely absent in younger children (Apel & Masterson, 1998). An example of narrative structure is shown in Table 4–24. The description of a logical sequence of events appears in children's narratives by 3 to 5 years of age (Owens, 2016).

Multicultural Differences and Narratives

There are cultural differences across languages in children's narrative production. Speech-language pathologists must be aware of these differences to provide evidence-based assessment and intervention. Chinese children's narratives were found to focus on social engagement, morals, and authority themes (Wang & Leichtman, 2000). Narratives included characters helping one another and positive relationships among characters. American English-speaking children were found to focus on characters' personal likes and dislikes, along with avoidances.

Some children may produce topic-associating narratives (Bliss & McCabe, 2011). These narratives are characterized by relatively lengthy descriptions of several situations in one narrative, with situations linked semantically (through meaning) rather than chronologically (through a sequence of events). Some characteristics found in Spanish-speaking children's narratives are broad topic maintenance, conversationally focused narrative, infor-

Table 4–24. *Narrative Structure*

Setting	Introduction of characters, time, and place	*Winnie the Pooh looked into his honey pot.*
Initiating event	Problem	*His honey pot was empty.*
Internal response	Character's feelings about the initiating event	*He felt sad—and hungry.*
Internal plan	Statement about fixing the problem	*"I should fill my pot again."*
Attempt	Action to solve problem	*He went out to search for more honey to fill his pot.*
Consequence	Event or events following the attempt	*He found a bee's nest and the friendly bees said, "We'll share our honey with you."*
Resolution or reaction	The final state of affairs following the attempt	*Winnie the Pooh said, "Thank you" and went home with a full pot of honey.*
Ending	A statement ending the story	*Winnie the Pooh was happy and he also had made new friends.*

mation presented by descriptive statements, and redundant subjects of utterances (Bliss & McCabe, 2011). An example of a narrative style, produced by Chinese- and Korean-speaking children, shows the omission of a redundant element, i.e., the repeated use of the subject pronoun *I* (Minami & McCabe, 1991):

I went to school . . . found a dollar . . . gave it to my mother . . .

In summary, it is essential to consider cultural differences in narratives when assessing children from different language backgrounds. Rules differ and the richness of these differences are positive across languages.

- ◆ The role of innate cognitive skills in children's language development
- ◆ Children's phonological, morphological, syntactic, semantic, and pragmatic development
- ◆ Multilinguistic differences found in diverse dialects and languages

The highlights of children's hearing, understanding, and talking can be found in Appendix 4–A. Chapter 5 traces the development of language as children develop their language skills beyond age 3, during the preschool stage of language development.

SUMMARY

We have traced the development of children's language, beginning at birth and continuing to age 3. In this period of development, children produce their first words, establish a theory of mind, understand many types of *Wh*-questions, begin to produce narratives, express requests in a more appropriate and polite manner, and engage in more complex play schemes. In this chapter, we have learned:

- ◆ What infant perception tells us about the human mind
- ◆ The role of the theory of mind in language development
- ◆ The development of infants' productions, beginning with the babbling stage
- ◆ The important role of joint attention and joint action in language development

KEY WORDS

Accommodation

Adaptation

Assimilation

Auditory perception

Causal cognition

Causality

Cognition

Counterfactual reasoning

Decentration

Deferred imitation

Denial

Discourse

Equilibrium

Incidental learning

Innate

Instrumental function

Intention

Intentional

Interaction function

Jargon

Joint action

Joint attention

Means-end behavior

Mean length utterance (MLU)

Mental state verbs

Mirror neurons

Morphemes

Morphology

Morphophonology

Morphosyntactic development

Mutual exclusivity bias

Narrative

Nonexistence

Object constancy

Object permanence

Overextension

Overgeneralization

Overgeneralize

Perception

Perceptual

Personal function

Perspective-taking

Phonemic representations

Phonetically consistent forms

Phonological awareness

Practical intelligence

Pragmatics

Processing

Recurrence

Reduplicated babbling

Referent absent

Referent present

Reflexive pronouns

Regulatory function

Rejection

Relational terms

Representational thought

Schemas

Semantic relations

Semantic roles

Semiotic function

Speech act

Symbolic functions

Syntax

Theory of mind (TOM)

Underextension

Variegated babbling

Working memory

STUDY QUESTIONS

1. Discuss the importance of the theory of mind in children's language development.

2. Explain why joint attention and joint interaction play a role in children's language development.

3. Explain why children may have difficulty with understanding the pronouns *you* and *I*.

4. Describe the connection between play and language in children's development.

5. Explain the production of the irregular past tense verbs as *comed* and *standed*.

REFERENCES

Acharya, S., & Shukla, S. (2012). Mirror neurons: Enigma of the metaphysical modular brain. *Journal of Natural Science, Biology and Medicine, 3*(2), 118–124.

Akhtar, N., Jipson, J., & Callanan, M. A. (2001). Learning words through overhearing. *Child Development, 72,* 416–430.

American Speech-Language-Hearing Association. (2009). *How does your child hear and talk?* Retrieved from http://www.asha.org/public/speech/development/chart.htm

Anglin, J. M. (1993). Vocabulary development: A morphological analysis. *Monographs of the Society for Research in Child Development, 58*(10, Serial No. 238), 1–165.

Apel, K., & Masterson, J. (1998). *Assessment and treatment of narrative skills: What's the story?* Rockville, MD: American Speech-Language-Hearing Association.

Baddeley, A. (2003). Working memory and language: An overview. *Journal of Communication Disorders, 36,* 189–208.

Baddeley, A. D., & Larson, J. D. (2007). The phonological loop unmasked? A comment on the evidence for a "perceptual-gestural" alternative. *Quarterly Journal of Experimental Psychology, 60*(4), 497–504.

Barna, J., & Legerstee, M. (2005). Nine- and twelve-month-old infants relate emotions to people's actions. *Cognition and Emotion, 19*(1), 53–67.

Bartsch, K., & Wellman, H. M. (1995). *Children's talk about the mind.* New York, NY: Psychological Corporation.

Bates, E., & Elman, J. (1996). Learning rediscovered: A perspective on Saffran, Aslin, & Newport. *Science, 274,* 1849–1850.

Bates, E., Marchman, V., Thal, D., Fenson, L., Dale, P., Reznick, . . . Hartung, J. (1994). Developmental and stylistic variation in the composition of early vocabulary. *Journal of Child Language, 21*(1), 85–124.

Beier, J. S., & Spelke, E. S. (2012). Infants' developing understanding of social gaze. *Child Development, 83*(2), 486–496.

Bellugi, U. (1967). *The acquisition of negation* (Doctoral dissertation). Cambridge, MA: Harvard University Press.

Bernstein, D. K. (2011). Language development from ages 3 to 5. In S. Levey & S. Polirstok (Eds.), *Language development: Understanding language diversity in the classroom* (pp. 139–160). Los Angeles, CA: Sage.

Bernstein, D. K., & Levey, S. (2009). Language development: A review. In D. K. Bernstein & E. Tiegerman-Farber (Eds.), *Language and communication disorders in children* (pp. 28–100). Boston, MA: Pearson.

Berwick, R. C., & Chomsky, N. (2016). *Why only us: Language and evolution.* Cambridge, MA: MIT Press.

Bever, T. G. (1970). The cognitive basis for linguistic structure. In J. R. Hayes (Ed.), *Cognition and the development of language.* New York, NY: John Wiley.

Bliss, L. S., & McCabe, A. (2011). Educational implications of narrative discourse. In S. Levey & S. Polirstok (Eds.), *Language development: Understanding language diversity in the classroom* (pp. 209–226). Los Angeles, CA: Sage.

Bloom, L. (1991). *Language development from two to three.* Cambridge, UK: Cambridge University Press.

Bloom, L., Lightbown, P., & Hood, L. (1978). Pronominal-nominal variation in child language. In L. Bloom (Ed.), *Readings in language development* (pp. 231–253). New York, NY: John Wiley & Sons.

Bucciarelli, M., Colle, L., & Bara, B. G. (2003). How children comprehend speech acts and communicative gestures. *Journal of Pragmatics, 35,* 207–241.

Bushnell, I. W. R. (2001). Mother's face recognition in newborn infants: Learning and memory. *Infant and Child Development, 10,* 67–74.

Bushnell, I. W. R., Sai F., & Mullen J. T. (1989). Neonatal recognition of mother's face. *British Journal of Developmental Psychology, 7*(1), 3–15.

Cameron-Faulkner, T. (2014). The development of speech acts. In D. Matthews (Ed.), *Pragmatic development in first language acquisition* (pp. 37–52). Amsterdam and Philadelphia: John Benjamin.

Capone, N. C. (2007). Tapping toddlers' evolving semantic representation via gesture. *Journal of Speech-Language-Hearing Research, 50*(3), 732–745.

Carter, A. S., Davis, N. O., Klin, A., & Volkmar, F. R. (2005). Social development in autism. In F. R. Volkmar, R. Paul, A. Klin, & D. Cohen (Eds.), *Handbook of autism and pervasive developmental disorders: Diagnosis, development, neurobiology, and behavior* (Vol. 1). Hoboken, NJ: John Wiley & Sons.

Chessa, D., Lis, A., Di Riso, D., Delvecchio, E., Mazzeschi, C., Russ, S. W., & Dillon, J. (2012). A cross-cultural comparison of pretend play in U.S. and Italian children. *Journal of Cross-Cultural Psychology, 44*(4), 640–656.

Chomsky, N. (1957). *Syntactic structures*. The Hague, Netherlands: Mouton.

Chomsky, N. (1965). *Aspects of the theory of syntax*. Cambridge, MA: MIT Press.

Clark, E. V. (1981). Lexical innovations: How children learn to create new words. In W. Deutsch (Ed.), *The child's construction of language* (pp. 299–328). London, UK: Academic Press.

Columbo, J., Kapa, L., & Curtindale, L. (2011). Varieties of attention in infancy. In L. M. Oakes, C. H. Cashon, M. Casasola, & D. H. Rakison (Eds.), *Infant perception and cognition: Recent advances, emerging theories, and future directions* (pp. 3–26). New York, NY: Oxford University Press.

Elkind, D. (1962). Children's conceptions of brother and sister: Piaget replication study V. *Journal of Child Language, 6*, 313–327.

Feagans, L. (1980). Children's understanding of some temporal terms denoting order, duration, and simultaneity. *Journal of Psycholinguistic Research, 9*(1), 41–57.

Feagin, C. (1979). *Variation and change in Alabama English: A sociolinguistic study of the white community*. Washington, DC: Georgetown University Press.

Foreman, J. (1999). Syntax of negative inversion in non-standard English. In K. Shahin, S. Blake, & E. Sook Kim (Eds.), *The Proceedings of the 17th West Coast Conference on Formal Linguistics*, 205–219. Stanford, CA: Center for the Study of Language and Information.

Galotti, K. M. (2017). *Cognitive development: Infancy through adolescence* (2nd ed.). Los Angeles, CA: Sage.

Ganger, J., & Brent, M. R. (2004). Reexamining the vocabulary spurt. *Developmental Psychology, 40*(4), 621–632.

Gleason, J. B., & Bernstein Ratner, N. B. (2017). *The development of language* (9th ed.). Boston, MA: Pearson.

Gleitman, L. R., & Gleitman, H. (1992). A picture is worth a thousand words, but that's the problem: The role of syntax in vocabulary acquisition. *Current Directions in Psychological Sciences, 1*, 31–35.

Göksun, T., Hirsh-Pasek, K., & Golinkoff, R. M. (2009). Trading spaces: Carving up events for learning language. *Perspectives on Psychological Science, 5*, 33–42.

Gopnik, A. (1988). Three types of early word: The emergence of social words, names and cognitive-relational words in the one-word stage and their relation to cognitive development. *First Language, 8*, 49–69.

Gopnik, A., Meltzoff, A. N., & Kuhl, P. K. (1999). *The scientist in the crib: What early learning tells us about the mind*. New York, NY: Harper.

Gopnik, A., Sobel, D. M., Schulz, L. E., & Glymour, C. (2001). Causal learning mechanisms in very young children: Two-, three-, and four-year-olds infer causal relations from patterns of variation and covariation. *Developmental Psychology, 37*, 620–629.

Gopnik, A., & Walker, C. A. (2013). Considering counterfactuals: The relations between causal learning and pretend play. *American Journal of Play, 6*(1), 15–28.

Green, L. (2002). *African American English: A linguistic introduction.* New York, NY: Cambridge University Press.

Gross, M., Buac, M., & Kaushanskaya, M. (2014). Conceptual scoring of receptive and expressive vocabulary measures in simultaneous and sequential bilingual children. *American Journal of Speech-Language Pathology, 23,* 574–586.

Gruber, D. R. (2016). The extent of engagement, the means of invention: Measuring debate about mirror neurons in the humanities and social sciences. *Journal of Science Communication, 15*(2), 2–17.

Halliday, M. A. K. (1975). *Learning how to mean: Explorations in the development of language.* New York, NY: Elsevier.

Hansen, M. B., & Markman, E. M. (2009). Children's use of mutual exclusivity to learn labels for parts of objects. *Developmental Psychology, 45*(2), 592–596.

Harris, P. L., de Rosnay, M., & Pons, F. (2005). Language and children's understanding of mental states. *Current Directions in Psychological Sciences, 14*(2), 69–73.

Hillenbrand, J. (1983). Perceptual organization of speech sounds by infants. *Journal of Speech and Hearing Research, 26,* 268–282.

Hoicka, E. (2014). Pragmatic development of humor. In D. Matthews (Ed.), *Pragmatic development in first language acquisition* (pp. 219–238). Amsterdam, Netherlands: John Benjamin.

Hudson, J. A. (2006). The development of future time concepts through mother-child conversation. *Merrill-Palmer Quarterly, 52*(1), 70–95.

Hurtado, N., Marchman, V. A., & Fernald, A. (2008). Does input influence uptake? Links between maternal talk, processing speed and vocabulary size in Spanish-learning children. *Developmental Science, 11*(6), 31–39.

Hwa-Froelich, D. A. (2004). Play assessment for children from culturally and linguistically diverse backgrounds. *Perspectives on Language, Learning and Education and on Communication Disorders and Sciences in Culturally and Linguistically Diverse Populations, 11*(2), 6–10.

James, S. L. (1990). *Normal language acquisition.* Boston, MA: Allyn & Bacon.

Johnston, J. R. (1988). Children's verbal representation of spatial location. In J. Stiles-Davis, M. Kritchevsky, & U. Bellugi (Eds.), *Spatial cognition: Brain bases and development* (pp. 195–206). Hillsdale: NJ: Erlbaum.

Jusczyk, P. W. (1992). Developing phonological categories from the speech signal. In C. A. Ferguson, L. Menn, & C. Stoel-Gammon (Eds.), *Phonological development: Models, research, implications* (pp. 17–64). Timonium, MD: York Press.

Keysers, C., Kaas, J. H., & Gazzola, V. (2010). Somatosensation in social perception. *Nature Reviews Neuroscience, 11*(6), 417–428.

Klima, E., & Bellugi, U. (1966). Syntactic regularities in the speech of children. In J. Lyons & R. Wales (Eds.), *Psycholinguistic papers* (pp. 183–208). Edinburgh, UK: Edinburgh University Press.

Labov, W. (1972). Negative attraction and negative concord in English grammar. *Language, 48,* 773–818.

Lamm, C.,& Majdandžić, J. (2015). The role of shared neural activations, mirror neurons, and morality in empathy—a critical comment. *Neuroscience Research, 90,* 15–24.

Leahy, M. M. (2004). Therapy talk: analyzing therapeutic discourse. *Language, Speech, and Hearing Services in Schools, 35,* 70–81.

Lee, E. C., & Rescorla, L. (2008). The use of psychological state words by late talkers at ages 3, 4, and 5 years. *Applied Psycholinguistics, 29*(1), 21–39.

Legerstee, M. (2000). Domain specificity and the epistemic triangle: The development of the concept of animacy in infancy. In F. Lacerda, C. von Hofsten, & M. Heinemann (Eds.), *Emerging cognitive abilities in early infancy* (pp. 193–212). Mahwah, NJ: Lawrence Erlbaum Associates.

Legerstee, M., Anderson, D., & Schaffer, A. (1998). Five- and eight-month-old infants recognize their faces and voices as familiar and social stimuli. *Child Development, 69,* 37–50.

Leonard, L. B., Deevy, P., Wong, A. M.-Y., Stokes, S. F., & Fletcher, P. (2007). Modal verbs with and without tense: A study of English- and Cantonese-speaking children with specific language impairment. *International Journal of Language and Communication Disorders, 42*(2): 209–228.

Levey, S. (2011).Typical and atypical language development. In S. Levey & S. Polirstok (Eds.), *Language development: Understanding language diversity in the classroom* (pp. 37–58). Los Angeles, CA: Sage.

Levey, S., & Schwartz, R. G. (2002). Syllable omission by two-year-old children. *Communication Disorders Quarterly, 23*(4), 169–177.

Li, J., Hestenes, L. L., & Wang, Y. C. (2016). Links between preschool children's social skills and observed pretend play in outdoor child environments. *Early Education Journal, 44*(1), 61–68.

Loewenstein, G., & Gentner, D. (2001). Spatial mapping in preschoolers: Close comparisons facilitate far mappings. *Journal of Cognition and Development, 2,* 189–219.

Loewenstein, G., & Gentner, D. (2005). Relational language and the development of relational mapping. *Cognitive Psychology, 50,* 315–353.

Lund, N., & Duchan, J. (1993). *Assessing children's language in naturalistic contexts* (3rd ed.). Englewood Cliffs, NJ: Prentice Hall.

Macaulay, R. (2006). *Language and its uses* (2nd ed.). New York, NY: Oxford Press.

MacWhinney, B., & Snow, C. (1985). The child language data exchange system. *Journal of Child Language, 12,* 271–295.

Maekawa, J., & Storkel, H. L. (2006). Individual differences in the influence of phonological characteristics on expressive vocabulary development by young children. *Journal of Child Language, 33,* 439–459.

Mandel, D. R., Jusczyk, P. W., & Pisoni, D. B. (1995). Infants' recognition of the sound patterns of their own names. *Psychological Sciences, 6,* 315–318.

Mazzone, M. (2009). Pragmatics and cognition: Intentions and pattern recognition in context. *International Review of Pragmatics, 1,* 321–347.

Minami, M., & McCabe, A. *Haiku* as a discourse regulation device: A stanza analysis of Japanese children's personal narratives. *Language in Society, 20*(4), 577–599.

Moorehead, D., & Ingram, D. (1973). The development of base syntax in normal and linguistically deviant children. *Journal of Speech and Hearing Research, 16,* 330–352.

Moses, L. J., Baldwin, D. A., Rosicky, J. G., & Tidball, G. (2002). Evidence for referential understanding in the emotions domain at twelve and eighteen months. *Child Development, 3,* 718–735.

Newbury, J., Klee, T., Stokes, S. F., & Moran, C. (2016). Interrelationships between working memory, processing speech, and language development in the age range 2 to 4 years. *Journal of Speech, Language, and Hearing Research, 59*(5), 1146–1158.

Oakes, L. M., Kannass, K. N., & Shaddy, D. J. (2002). Developmental changes in endogenous control of attention: The role of target familiarity on infants' distraction latency. *Child Development, 73*(6), 1644–1655.

Oller, D. K. (1980).The emergence of the sounds of speech in infancy. In G. Yeni-Komshian, J. F. Kavanagh, & C. A. Ferguson (Eds.), *Child phonology: Production* (Vol. 1, pp. 93–112). New York, NY: Academic Press.

Oosterwijk, S., Mackey, S., Wilson-Mendenhall, C., Winkielman, P., & Paulus, M. P. (2015). Concepts in context: Processing mental state concepts with internal or external focus involves different neural systems. *Social Neuroscience Journal, 10*(3), 294–307.

Orr, E., & Geva, R. (2015), Symbolic play and language development. *Infant Behavior and Development, 38,* 147–161.

Osman, H., & Sullivan, J. R. (2014). Children's auditory working memory performance in degraded listening conditions. *Journal of Speech, Language, and Hearing Research, 57,* 1503–1511.

Owens, R. E. (2012). *Language development: An introduction* (8th ed.). Boston, MA: Pearson.

Owens, R. E. (2016). *Language development: An introduction* (9th ed.). Boston, MA: Pearson.

Pan, B. A., Rowe, M. L., Singer, J. D., & Snow, C. E. (2005). Maternal correlates of growth in toddler vocabulary production in low-income families. *Child Development, 76*(4), 763–782.

Patten, E., Belardi, K., Baranek, G. T., Watson, L. R., Labban, J. D., & Kimbrough Oller, D. (2014). Vocal patterns in infants with autism spectrum disorder: Canonical babbling status and vocalization frequency. *Journal of Autism and Developmental Disorders.* Retrieved from http://libres.uncg.edu/ir/uncg/f/J_Labban_Vocal_2014.pdf

Patterson, J. L., & Westby, C. E. (1998). The development of play. In W. O. Haynes & B. B. Shulman (Eds.), *Communication development: Foundations, processes, and clinical applications* (pp. 135–163). Baltimore, MD: Williams and Wilkins.

Peccei, J. S. (1999). *Child language* (2nd ed.). London, UK: Routledge.

Perner, J. (1991). *Understanding the representational mind.* Cambridge, MA: Bradford Books/MIT Press.

Phillips, A. T., Wellman. H. M., & Spelke, E. S. (2002). Infants' ability to connect gaze and emotional expression to intentional action. *Cognition, 85,* 53–78.

Piaget, J. (1928). *Judgment and reasoning in the child.* London, UK: Routledge and Kegan Paul.

Piaget, J. (1954). *The construction of reality in the child.* New York, NY: Basic Books.

Piaget, J. (1973). *The child and reality: Problems of genetic psychology.* New York, NY: Grossman.

Poll, G. H. (2011). Increasing the odds: Applying emergentist theory in language acquisition. *Language, Speech, and Hearing Services in Schools, 42,* 680–591.

Reddy, V. (2001). Infant clowns: The interpersonal creation of humour in infancy. *Enfance, 53*(3), 247–256.

Reddy, V. (2008). *How infants know minds.* Cambridge, MA: Harvard University Press.

Rescorla, L., Alley, A., & Christine, J. B. (2001). Word frequencies in toddlers' lexicons. *Journal of Speech, Language, and Hearing Research, 44,* 598–609.

Ricard, M., Girouard, P. C., & Decarie, T. G. (1999). Personal pronouns and perspective taking in toddlers. *Journal of Child Language, 26*(3), 687–697.

Richards, B. (1990). *Language development and language differences: A study of auxiliary verb learning.* Cambridge, UK: Cambridge University Press.

Roopnarine, J. L., & Jin, B. (2012). Indo Caribbean immigrant beliefs about play and its impact on early academic performance. *American Journal of Play, 4*(4), 441–463.

Roseberry-McKibbin, C. (2014). *Multicultural students with special language needs: Practical strategies for assessment and intervention.* Oceanside, CA: Academic Communication Associates.

Ruston, H. P., & Schwanenflugel, P. J. (2010). Effects of a conversation on the expressive vocabulary development of prekindergarten children. *Language, Speech, and Hearing Services in Schools, 41,* 303–313.

Sai, F. Z. (2005). The role of the mother's voice in developing mother's face preference: Evidence for intermodal perception at birth. *Infant and Child Development, 14,* 29–50.

Seidenberg, M. S., & Elman, J. (1999). Do infants learn grammar with algebra or statistics? *Science, 284,* 5413.

Searle, J. (1983). *Intentionality: An essay in the philosophy of mind* (Vol. 9). Cambridge, UK: Cambridge University Press.

Seymour, H. N., & Roeper, T. (1999). Grammatical acquisition of African American English. In L. B. Leonard & O. L. Taylor (Eds.), *Language acquisition across North America: Cross-cultural and cross-linguistic perspectives* (pp. 109–152). San Diego, CA: Singular.

Shaddy, D. J., & Colombo, J. (2004). Developmental changes in infant attention to dynamic and static stimuli. *Infancy, 3,* 355–365.

Shatz, M., Wellman, H. M., & Silber, S. (1983). The acquisition of mental verbs: A systematic investigation of the first reference to mental state. *Cognition, 14,* 301–321.

Shiakou, M., & Belsky, J. (2013). Exploring parent attitudes toward children's play and learning in Cyprus. *Journal of Research in Childhood Education, 25,* 17–30.

Shipley, K. G., Maddox, M. A., & Driver, J. E. (1991) Children's development of irregular past tense forms. *Language, Speech and Hearing Services in Schools, 22,* 115–122.

Shneidman, L. A., Arroyo, M. E., Levine, S. C., & Goldin-Meadow, S. (2012). What counts as effective input for word learning? *Journal of Child Language, 10,* 1–15.

Simion, F., & Di Giorgio, E. (2015). Face perception and processing in early infancy: Inborn predispositions and development changes. *Frontiers in Psychology, 6* (969), 1–11.

Sosa, A. V., & Stoel-Gammon, C. (2006). Patterns of intraword phonological variability during the second year of life. *Journal of Child Language, 33,* 31–50.

Stein, N., & Glenn, C. (1979). An analysis of story comprehension in elementary school children. In R. D. Freedle (Ed.), *Advances in discourse processes: New directions in discourse processing* (Vol. 2, pp. 53–119). Norwood, NJ: Ablex.

Sternberg, R. J., Nokes, C., Wenzel Geissler, P., Prince, R., Okatcha, F., Bundy, D. A., & Grigorenko, E. L. (2001). The relationship between academic and practical intelligence: A case study in Kenya. *Intelligence, 29,* 401–418.

Talmy, L. (1983). How language structures space. In H. L. Pick & L. P. Acredolo (Eds.), *Spatial orientation; Theory, research, and application* (pp. 225–282). New York: Plenum Press.

Tomasello, M. (1992). *First verbs: A case study of early grammatical development.* Cambridge, UK: Cambridge University Press.

Tomasello, M. (1998). Reference: Intending that others jointly attend. *Pragmatics and Cognition, 6,* 219–243.

Tomasello, M. (2003). *Constructing a language.* Cambridge, MA: Harvard University Press.

Tomasello, M., Carpenter, M., & Liszkowski, U. (2007). A new look at infant pointing. *Child Development, 78*(3), 705–722.

Tomasello, M., & Todd, J. (1983). Joint attention and lexical acquisition style. *First Language, 4,* 197–212.

Valian, V., Hoeffner, J., & Aubry, S. (1996). Young children's imitation of sentence subjects: Evidence of processing limitations. *Developmental Psychology, 32*(1), 153–164.

Vandermaas-Peeler, M. (2002). Cultural variations in parental support of children's play. *Online Readings in Psychology and Culture, 6*(1). http://dx.doi.org/10.9707/2307-0919.1054

Wang, Q., & Leichtman, M. D. (2000). Same beginnings, different stories: A comparison of American and Chinese children's narratives. *Child Development, 71,* 1329–1346.

Weisberg, D., Zosh, J., Hirsh-Pasek, K., & Golinkoff, R. M. (2013). Talking it up: Play, language development and the role of adult support. *American Journal of Play, 6,* 39–54.

Wells, C. (1979). Learning and using the auxiliary verb in English. In V. Lee (Ed.), *Language development.* Beckenham, UK: Croom Helm.

Westby, C. E. (1980). Assessment of cognitive and language abilities through play. *Language, Speech, and Hearing Services in Schools, 11,* 154–168.

White-Sustaita, J. (2010). Reconsidering the syntax of non-canonical negative inversion. *English Language and Linguistics, 14,* 429–455.

Wilkinson, N., Paikan, A., Gredebäck, G., Rea, F., & Metta, G. (2014). Staring us in the face? An embodied theory of innate face preference. *Developmental Science, 17*(6), 808–825.

Witt, B. (1998). Cognition and the cognitive-language relationship. In W. O. Haynes & B. B. Shulman (Eds.), *Communication development: Foundations, processes, and clinical applications* (pp. 101–133). Baltimore, MD: Williams and Wilkins.

Wolfram, W., & Christian, D. (1976). *Appalachian Speech.* Arlington, VA: Center for Applied Linguistics.

Zanuttini, R. (2014). *Our language prejudices don't make no sense.* Retrieved from https://psmag.com/our-language-prejudices-don-t-make-no-sense-85f224844bca#.1ve3w4pig

APPENDIX 4–A

Highlights of Children's Language Development

Birth to One Year

Hearing and Understanding	Talking
Birth–3 Months ◆ Startles to loud sounds ◆ Quiets or smiles when spoken to ◆ Seems to recognize your voice and quiets if crying ◆ Increases or decreases sucking behavior in response to sound	**Birth–3 Months** ◆ Makes pleasure sounds (cooing, gooing) ◆ Cries differently for different needs ◆ Smiles when sees you
4–6 Months ◆ Moves eyes in direction of sounds ◆ Responds to changes in tone of your voice ◆ Notices toys that make sounds ◆ Pays attention to music	**4–6 Months** ◆ Babbling sounds more speech-like, with many different sounds, including *p, b,* and *m* ◆ Chuckles and laughs ◆ Vocalizes excitement and displeasure ◆ Makes gurgling sounds when left alone and when playing with you
7 Months–1 Year ◆ Enjoys games like peek-a-boo and pat-a-cake ◆ Turns and looks in direction of sounds ◆ Listens when spoken to ◆ Recognizes words for common items like "cup," "shoe," "book," and "juice" ◆ Begins to respond to requests (e.g., "Come here" or "Want more?")	**7 Months–1 Year** ◆ Babbling has both long and short groups of sounds, such as "tataupupbibibibi" ◆ Uses speech or noncrying sounds to get and keep attention ◆ Uses gestures to communicate (waving, holding arms to be picked up) ◆ Imitates different speech sounds ◆ Has one or two words (hi, dog, dada, mama) around first birthday, although sounds may not be clear

continues

APPENDIX 4–A. *continued*

One to Two Years

Hearing and Understanding	Talking
◆ Points to a few body parts when asked ◆ Follows simple commands and understands simple questions ("Roll the ball," "Kiss the baby," "Where's your shoe?") ◆ Listens to simple stories, songs, and rhymes ◆ Points to pictures in a book when named	◆ Says more words every month ◆ Uses some one- or two-word questions ("Where kitty?" "Go bye-bye?" "What's that?") ◆ Puts two words together ("more cookie," "no juice," "mommy book") ◆ Uses many different consonant sounds at the beginning of words

Two to Three Years

Talking	Hearing and Understanding
◆ Has a word for almost everything ◆ Uses two or three words to talk about and ask for things ◆ Uses *k, g, f, t, d,* and *n* sounds ◆ Speech understood by familiar listeners most of the time ◆ Often asks for or directs attention to objects by naming them	◆ Understands differences in meaning ("go-stop," "in-on," "big-little," "up-down") ◆ Follows two requests ("Get the book and put it on the table") ◆ Listens to and enjoys hearing stories for longer periods of time

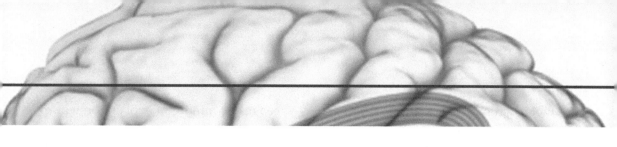

5

Preschool Language Development

Diana Almodovar and Sandra Levey

Case Study

José is 3 years of age and enrolled in a preschool class. He produces lengthy sentences and is able to understand and remember lengthy directions (e.g., go into the garage, get the broom, and give it to grandpa). He also engages in appropriate *play with peers, such as asking if he can share a toy rather than crying or grabbing. After reading this chapter, you will understand the changes that occur when children enter the preschool stage of language development.*

CHAPTER OBJECTIVES

This chapter describes preschoolers' language development. Children's developmental milestones during this stage can be found in Appendix 5–A. After reading this chapter, you will understand:

◆ Language development during the preschool stage (3 to 5 years of age)
◆ The major changes in vocabulary, syntax, morphology, semantics, and pragmatics that occur during this period of development

◆ The major changes in children's cognitive skills that play a role in language development

AN OVERVIEW OF PRESCHOOL LANGUAGE DEVELOPMENT

From age 3, children demonstrate a tremendous amount of linguistic and cognitive growth. By age 5, typically developing children have acquired roughly 90% of their syntax, their connected speech is intelligible, and they can maintain conversations for longer periods of time. Their play becomes more complex, with more elaborate imaginative and dramatic play evident. Their overall social, language, and play skills reflect their advanced stages of cognitive development. During this stage, children begin to develop the requisite skills for academic success, such as reading and writing. We begin with a review of preschoolers' cognitive development.

COGNITIVE DEVELOPMENT

One of the most important cognitive developments in the preschool years is the emergence of symbolic thought. Symbolic thought is the ability to mentally represent objects, actions, and events. Children's symbolic thought is applied in play. For example, children may use a wooden block to represent many other objects (e.g., a baby bottle, a telephone, or a loaf of bread). Children express symbolic thought when they engage in pretend play and model the actions of adults when creating a play scheme. In this play scheme, they may take on the role of these adults, while imitating the actions that they have observed in their environment (e.g., caring for a baby, shopping).

Conceptual Development

Conceptual development consists of mental representations of things in the world. Concepts consist of properties (e.g., *happiness, color, hunger*) or abstract ideas (e.g., *truth* or, *fairness*). Concepts are sets of

ideas in the mind that explain the world (Goswami, 2009). Concepts allow children to represent information in an efficient manner by grouping information under general categories (e.g., *cat, tail, legs, fur*). Concepts are organized in the following hierarchy:

Subordinate level: German Shepherd

Basic level: dog

Superordinate level: mammal

The subordinate level is the most specific, however, preschoolers tend to learn basic level terms before superordinate or subordinate (Galotti, 2017). Children who develop an interest in a particular area, such as dinosaurs, are more likely to learn the higher-level terms that refer to this interest (e.g., *Brachiosaurus, Tyrannosaurus,* and *Diplodocus*).

Theory of Mind

One of the most important components of cognitive development is the acquisition of a **theory of mind (TOM),** introduced in Chapter 1. TOM describes a child's ability to understand someone else's mental state (Rhodes & Brandone, 2014). When children acquire a TOM, they have a better understanding of others' thoughts, beliefs, and feelings (Baron-Cohen, 1993, 1996; Wellman, 2014). A TOM provides the ability to predict how someone will act and to explain why a person acted in a certain manner. Children also are able to describe the motivation that supports people's actions using **mental state verbs** (e.g., *think, know, feel,* and *believe*). Growth in the use of mental state verbs occurs between the ages of 3 and 5.

Children with a TOM are able to express their own feelings and thoughts while also able to interpret those of others. This leads to improved interaction and conversation with peers and others because children are better able to understand others' intentions or meaning during these events. TOM is also essential for understanding stories because children are able to then understand a character's actions (e.g., *why* the wolf dressed as Little Red Riding Hood's grandmother). Narrative knowledge helps children develop a TOM because stories often contain information about a character's feelings, beliefs, and thoughts, along with the language associated with these concepts (e.g., Little Red Riding Hood was *afraid* because she didn't *know* . . . the bears were *upset* because they *thought* . . .).

Conversation also plays a role in developing a TOM, given that adults frequently converse about others' beliefs and mental states, along with possible explanations for others' actions. Children also develop an understanding of false beliefs when exposed to conversations about others' mental states (Gola, 2012). A false belief is a misconception about something that results from poor reasoning. An example of a false belief task that has been used to assess the presence of a TOM is presented below.

A child, Sally, leaves a marble in her basket and goes outside to play. While she is playing outside, another child, Anne, moves the marble from the basket to a box. Anne is asked, when Sally comes back, where will she look for her marble?

If children report that Sally will look for her marble in her basket, this indicates the presence of a TOM. Children can solve this type of false belief task by age 5 (Rhodes & Brandone, 2014). The absence of a TOM is shown if a child reports that Sally will look for her marble in the box.

Executive Functions

Executive functions are another cognitive factor that plays a role in children's development. Executive functions are mental processes that include planning, generating goal-directed behavior, organizing, maintaining attention, using **working memory**, managing time and space, and problem solving. Without executive functions, strategic problem-solving skills are absent (Baddeley, 1997, 2003; Baddeley & Larson, 2007). Strategic problem-solving skills consist of identifying a problem, planning a solution, executing a plan, and evaluating the results. At the preschool stage of cognitive development, children may not consider all aspects of a problem when planning a solution (Galotti, 2017).

Working Memory

Working memory, described in earlier chapters, allows children to retain information for processing and facilitates the temporary maintenance and manipulation of information. Working memory allows children to store information in their minds to make this information available for processing in long-term memory. Consequently, children with intact working memory are able to retain lengthier directions and remember past events. The ability to consider stored information allows children to anticipate what might happen in the future, especially when there are similarities between current and prior experiences. *Anticipation* denotes the ability to predict the occurrence of an event, because it is preceded by a particular cause. An example is that a juice cup may spill if placed too close to the end of the table. Subsequently, children are now able to predict *what might happen next* in current or future situations.

Divergent Thought

Cognitive development also includes **divergent thinking**. Divergent thought is essential for creative thought and problem solving, allowing children to generate a number of solutions to a particular dilemma. For example, when one child wants to take another child's toy (a frequent occurrence in children's experiences), this ability allows children to think of an appropriate response, rather than a physical tug-of-war over the toy. Divergent thinking is essential for children's imaginative thought (Addis, Pan, Musicaro, & Schacter, 2016). This allows children to develop pretend play schemes that rely on their imagination.

Magical Thinking

During the preschool stage of development, we see that children engage in **magical thinking** (Subbotsky, 2010). Magical thinking occurs when a child assigns animacy to certain inanimate objects (e.g., the belief that a child's favorite TV character actually lives in the television set). Learning to distinguish between fantasy and reality is an element of cognitive development. Magical thinking appears when children believe that a certain action will influence the world around them (e.g.,

food will taste good if eaten with a pink spoon) (Ryan, 2017). At age 3, children still practice magical thinking and may take adult comments literally, such as an adult saying, *Your nose is running.* A child may interpret this in a concrete manner and say the following: *My nose can't run because it doesn't have any legs.* Children begin to understand the difference between fantasy and reality as they move through the preschool period, but some fantasy continues to age 7 or 8, such as the belief in the existence of mythical figures (e.g., Superman).

Expanded Symbolic Play Skills

Children's growing cognitive skills also appear in expanded symbolic play. Symbolic play emerges when children use objects to represent other things (e.g., a box to represent a train) and use language to describe the activities associated with the play scheme (e.g., *Let's all get on the train*). Play skills expand at about 30 months, when children's cognitive skills play a role in terms of insight, flexibility, and divergent thinking (Wallace & Russ, 2015). These skills are essential to create pretend play schemes and to take on various roles in these schemes (e.g., mother, father, baby, doctor).

Multischeme play sequences appear at about 3 years of age, when children expand single scheme play (e.g., making a cake for a doll) to create a series of events (e.g., getting the ingredients to make a cake for the doll's birthday party, making the cake, serving the cake, cleaning up, and putting the doll to bed for the night). Another change occurs at around 3 to 3½, when children create a dialogue between themselves and their dolls or stuffed toys and talk for the toys. Younger children rely on more familiar roles for pretend play (e.g., playing house), while older preschoolers create more elaborate play schemes that may involve superheroes (Galotti, 2017). Preschoolers' imagination develops when they take on different roles in play. At this stage, they take on the roles of firefighter and other familiar figures.

Play is an important factor in the development of language. Children must achieve the language skills to create and explain the play scheme to other children. For example, play involves the use of narrative structures to develop a play scheme. Preschoolers must use their language skills to explain the goals, events, plans, and outcomes of the play scheme. Preschoolers who engage with peers in play demonstrate higher receptive vocabulary skills than children who predominantly engage in parallel play (Holmes, Romero, Ciraola, & Grushko, 2015). In addition, more complex play skills predict better narrative skills during the school-age years (Stagnitti & Lewis, 2015). By 3 to 5 years of age, children use their language skills to create and maintain play schemes, relying less on the use of props.

At age 5, when symbolic and pretend play skills involve coordinated sequences of events (e.g., shopping, cooking, and putting baby to bed), time relations appear, such as *first*, *next*, *before*, and *after*. Children acquire the distinction between the temporal relations *before* and *after* in later stages of preschool development.

> Children's cognitive and play skills develop during this stage. They have now achieved the language and cognitive skills that allow for the type of imaginative play that includes interaction with peers.

Next, we explore children's linguistic development as they enter the preschool age.

LINGUISTIC DEVELOPMENT

As reviewed in previous chapters, language consists of five areas: phonology, morphology, syntax, semantics, and pragmatics. Bloom and Lahey (1978) identified three major components comprising language: form, content, and use.

Language form includes phonology, morphology, and syntax. These language areas are similar in that they define the structure and rules of language.

Language content refers to the area of semantics, or the meaning of words and the relationship of these words to one another.

Language use describes the pragmatic and social components of language.

While these five areas are each distinct, they also interact dynamically with one another. For example, as a preschooler's vocabulary increases, she or he is able to produce lengthier sentences. This reflects the interaction between semantic, morphological, and syntactic skills.

Phonology

Phonology is the part of language that contains rules that govern the structure, distribution, and sequencing of speech sounds to create words. Initially, children make production errors that are termed *phonological processes* (Table 5–1).

Table 5–1. *Phonological Processes*

Phonological Process	Adult Target	Child's Production
Unstressed syllable deletion	banana	"nanuh"
Reduplication	daddy	"dada"
Consonant cluster reduction	stop	"top"
Final consonant deletion	bus	"bu"
Initial consonant deletion	cup	"up"
Syllable repetition	daddy	"dada"
Fronting (back sound produced as a front sound)	cup	"tup"
Backing (front sound produced as a back sound)	top	"cop"
Assimilation	dog	"gog"
	cat	"cac" or "tat"
Vocalization	car	"cah"
Prevocalic voicing	top	"dop"
Depalatization	chew	"too"
Gliding	run	"wun"
	lip	"wip"
Epenthesis	cup	"cupuh"

Studies on phonemic and phonological development in children have demonstrated a wide range of ages in which children demonstrate the mastery of specific speech sounds (Bauman-Waengler & Davis, 2016).

Phonological processes are typically described in three broad categories: **syllable structure processes, substitution processes**, and **assimilation processes**. Children demonstrate selectivity to words containing specific speech sounds in their early word productions, and children's production errors have been attributed to their weak representations or knowledge of phonemes (Stoel-Gammon, 2011).

Syllable structure refers to the composition and sequencing of consonants and syllables within a word. An example of syllable structure process is a child's deletion of a syllable from a word that consists of two or more syllables, such as *puter* produced in place of the word *computer*. This phonological process is also referred to as syllable deletion or reduction. Syllable reduction is the deletion of a syllable from a word containing two or more syllables.

> The simplest syllable for children to produce is an **open syllable** structure. An open syllable is one in which the final sound in the syllable is a vowel (V), e.g., *bee*. A **closed syllable** is one that ends in a consonant (C), e.g., *beet*.

Whole word processes include reduplication, final consonant deletion, cluster reduction, and unstressed syllable omission.

Reduplication: Daddy /dædi/ produced as *dada* /dædæ/

Final consonant deletion: Bus /bʌs/ produced as *buh* /bʌ/

Cluster reduction: Stop /stɑp/ produced as *top* /tɑp/

Unstressed syllable omission: Banana /bənænə/ produced as *nana* /nænə/

> An example of the difference between a stressed and unstressed syllable is in the difference in the meaning of the following words: PREsent and preSENT. In the first example, the meaning of the word is a gift (e.g., I gave her a birthday present). In the second example, the meaning of this word is to give something to someone (e.g., presenting an award).

Substitution processes consist of the substitution of one phonemic class (e.g.,

stops) for another (e.g., fricatives). Examples include the following.

Stopping   *ton* /tʌn/ for *sun* /sʌn/

Fronting   *tea* /ti/ for *key* /ki/

Gliding   *wabbit* /wæbɪt/ for *rabbit* /ræbɪt/

Assimilation processes consist of the production of a speech sound that is similar to another sound in the same word, as shown in the example below. Progressive assimilation consists of a speech sound taking on the characteristics of a preceding sound within the word (i.e., initial phoneme /k/ produced in place of the final phoneme /t/).

kak /kæk/ for *cat* /kæt/

Regressive assimilation consists of a speech sound that takes on the characteristics of a succeeding sound (i.e., the final phoneme /t/ produced in place of the initial phoneme /k/).

tat /tæt/ for *cat* /kæt/

Some children have difficulty discriminating the difference between two similar phonemes, which typically will result in substitution processes (e.g., f/v, s/z, and p/b). As children achieve the ability to judge the correct production of a sound, their productions achieve adult forms of the target words. While there is variability in children's accurate word production, most phonological processes disappear by age 4. The **intelligibility** of a child's speech is how clear and easily understood the speaker's speech is to a listener. By age 4, a child's speech is typically judged to be 100% intelligible to strangers, with intelligibility at 50% at age 2 and at 75% at age 3 (Flipsen, 2006).

Morphology

Morphemes are the smallest units of meaning in a language. Note that the word *cat* cannot be reduced to one or two phonemes (e.g., /k/ or /t/) without the loss of the meaning of the word *cat*. At approximately age 3, a child's grammatical morphology begins to emerge. Grammatical morphemes can be free or bound. A **free morpheme** is a whole-word morpheme that can stand alone as a word, while bound morphemes must be attached to other morphemes. Free morphemes include **content words** and **function words**.

Content words: nouns, verbs, adjectives, and adverbs

Function words: modify or link content words together within a sentence

Function words include determiners (*a, an, the, that*), conjunctions (*and, or, but*), prepositions (*in, on, under*), pronouns (*she, he, we, they*), auxiliary verbs (*am, is, are, was, were, be, been*), modals (*can, could, shall, should, may, might*), and quantifiers (*some, an, much, many, few*).

> Function words, such as determiners (e.g., *the, a, an*), do not have content meanings, such as nouns and verbs. Instead, their definition is based on their use or function.

A **bound morpheme** serves a grammatical purpose and can be attached to a free morpheme. Bound morphemes can be either **inflectional** or **derivational**. Inflectional morphemes maintain the word's grammatical category (e.g., noun, or verb.) and add a grammatical feature to that word, such as indicating possession or tense. Children's grammatical morpheme development is shown in Table 5–2.

Table 5–2. *Grammatical Morpheme Development Ages 3–5*

Age	Morpheme	Example
3	Regular plural -*s*	The boy<u>s</u> are playing.
3	Possessive *'s*	That is the girl<u>'s</u> hat.
3	Uncontractible copula	She is. (in response to "who is pretty?)
3	Articles	I have <u>a</u> ball. Mommy pulled <u>the</u> wagon.
4–5	Regular past tense	He kick<u>ed</u> me.
4–5	Contractible auxiliary	Daddy<u>'s</u> eating.

Source: Reproduced with permission from *Language Development: Understanding Language Diversity in the Classroom* (p. 144), by S. Levey & S. Polirstok (Eds.), 2011, Los Angeles, CA: Sage.

Possession	*mommy's hat*
Tense	*I walk**ed** home*

There are differences in the use of inflectional morphemes, shown in the irregular adjective forms that are exceptions to the rule of adding the inflectional regular suffixes *-er* and *-est*. Examples are shown for the words *good* and *bad*.

Comparative Form	*better, worse*
Superlative Form	*best, worst*

Derivational morphology emerges in the later preschool and early school-age stages. Derivational morphemes change the grammatical category of the word, as shown in the example of the verb *teach* becoming the noun *teacher* (i.e., *teach + er*).

SYNTACTIC DEVELOPMENT

Syntax describes how words, phrases, clauses, and sentences are combined within a language to form sentences (Angell, 2009). The early precursors to syntactic development can be found in children's word combinations (Singleton & Shulman, 2013). Developmental growth occurs rather rapidly in this domain, with early syntactic connections mastered at approximately 30 months of age and adult-like syntax evident by age 4 (Owens, 2016). Table 5–3 provides examples of typical utterances produced by preschoolers.

One theory of syntactic development is that children rely on a strategy called **bootstrapping**. In this theory, children utilize syntactic or semantic cues in language in order to "pull" themselves up to more advanced linguistic skills (Gleitman, 1990; Hacquard, 2014; Jin & Fisher, 2014). Syntactic bootstrapping is a child's ability to utilize grammatical cues in an adult's language productions in order to facilitate comprehension and development of grammatical categories. For example, the use of an article (e.g., *the*) would indicate to a child that the following word is a noun. Semantic bootstrapping refers to conceptual approaches to learning. For example, children create grammatical categories with objects and living entities placed in the category noun, while actions are placed in the category of verb. Children utilize this semantic information (the meaning of a word and its relationship to other objects or entities) to infer meaning and its place within a sentence. These categories are expanded with other language factors, such as morphemes.

Sentence Types

A sentence is a syntactic structure that presents a complete thought (Justice & Ezell, 2016). Once children begin to combine two words to produce sentences, they demonstrate the emergence of syntax. The earliest sentence structures to emerge are **declarative sentences**, which follow a subject + verb + object (SVO) structure, e.g., *The dog ate the cookies*. Examples of preschoolers' syntactic development are shown in Table 5–4.

Interrogative sentences, consisting of questions, appear at approximately age 3. An interrogative sentence requires subject inversion and auxiliary verbs (e.g., *am, is, are, was, were*), as shown in the development of interrogative sentence productions shown below.

Sleep?

Mommy sleeping?

Is Mommy sleeping?

Table 5–3. *Typical Utterances Produced by Preschoolers*

Communicative Function	Example
Requesting information (using a variety of questions)	What's that? Can I go now? Is he eating candy? Where are you going? Why can't I have it?
Responding to requests (answering a question or supplying information)	It's in my closet. I don't want it. I didn't do it. He did it.
Describing events, objects, or properties	It's a red truck. He's building it slowly. That's a tractor. There's a crane.
Stating facts, feelings, attitudes, and beliefs	I feel sick. Ghosts are not real. I don't like it.
Encoding from a picture book	The boy and the girl got into the van and the van took them to the train.
Describing a plan	First, I'll build the tracks, then I'll make the train.
Describing a past experience	She pushed me so hard I fell down and hurt myself.
Complaining	You always give the big one to him.
Criticizing	Your picture is yucky.
Annoying	I'll do it again and again and again and again.
Threatening	Give it back or I will tell Mommy.

Source: Reproduced with permission from *Language Development: Understanding Language Diversity in the Classroom* (p. 149), by S. Levey & S. Polirstok (Eds.), 2011, Los Angeles CA: Sage.

Table 5–4. *Syntactic Development Ages 3–5*

Age	Morphosyntactic Characteristics	Examples
3	Simple sentences and difference sentence types are in the child's repertoire	
	a. Declaratives	a. I'm eating
	b. Interrogatives	b. What are you eating?
	c. Imperatives	c. Push the truck.
	d. Negatives	d. No more chicken.
	e. Use of quantities	e. I have two trucks.
	f. Use of adjectives	f. He has a red ball.
	g. Use of adverbs	g. She runs fast.
3½–4	Embedded phrases in sentences.	The man <u>in the hat</u> is driving.
	Subordinate clauses in sentences.	<u>Before you go</u>, put on your coat.
4–5	Conjoined sentences using conjunctions "and," "because," and "but"	I play the drums and she plays the piano.
		I cried because he hit me.
		I like cookies but not fish.

Source: Reproduced with permission from *Language Development: Understanding Language Diversity in the Classroom* (p. 144), by S. Levey & S. Polirstok (Eds.), 2011, Los Angeles, CA: Sage.

At 35 to 40 months of age, children begin to produce indirect and embedded *Wh*-questions.

Direct question: Danny asked, "Can I come to play?"

Indirect question: Danny asked me if I can come to play.

Embedded *Wh*-questions: I don't know **what** happened; I don't know **when** it happened.

At 31 to 34 months of age, interrogative reversals are produced, with an increased use of *Wh*-questions emerging (e.g., *Why I can't go?*). Negative interrogatives do not emerge until approximately age 5, when children acquire negative modal auxiliary verbs (e.g., *can't* and *don't*).

Can't I have a cookie with my juice?

Negative sentences are productions in which the child demonstrates a rejection or protest, shown in the following development of negative sentences.

No juice

I don't want juice

I don't want juice with my cake

Imperative sentences include a demand or request. Children transition from labeling an item as a command to producing full sentences.

Ball

Give me the ball

Throw the ball to me

Sentence Elements

Noun Phrases

Noun phrases contain the main subject of the sentence, including words that modify the noun, such as:

Articles: *a, an, the*

Quantifiers: *some, many, all*

Possessive pronouns: *mine, your*

Demonstratives: *this, that*

Numerical terms: *one, two, three*

Adjectives: *happy, black, large*

Ordinals: *first, second, third*

Children typically go through four stages of noun phrase development, which correspond to Brown's (1973) stages of development. During stage I (ages 18 to 25 months), children produce predominantly single words. During this stage, syntax has not begun to fully emerge, as two-word utterances provide the structure required for syntactic development.

At stage II (27 to 30 months), sentence production is expanded, as shown in the following example.

Mommy makes cookies.

During stage III (31–34 months), the sentences are expanded with modifiers and articles.

*My mommy makes **yummy** cookies.*

At stage IV (34 months +), children's utterances expand to include a wider variety of modifiers and an increased usage of pronouns.

*That boy kicked the **red** ball to **his** friend.*

Verb Phrases

During stage I of development, a child produces single verbs, as syntactic structures have yet to develop (e.g., *drink, play, go*). By stage II (27–30 months), children produce verbs with early acquired grammatical morphemes, such as the present progressive *-ing* (e.g., *playing*). Early infinitives begin to emerge (e.g., *I want **to play***).

> Infinitives refer to the use of the word *to* before a verb, e.g., *She wanted to swim, to drive, to run, to eat.*

At stage III, auxiliaries are acquired (e.g., *am, is, are, don't, can't*) and the past tense *-ed* is observed in regular verbs (e.g., *walked*). The past tense *-ed* is also produced in the overregularization of irregular verbs (*goed* instead of *went*). Prepositional phrases are attached to verb phrases to mark the location of the object in the sentence (i.e., *on the bed*) (Figure 5–1).

By stages IV and V, **modal auxiliaries** appear in children's productions (e.g., *can, could, would, should*). Modal auxiliaries are verbs that are combined with other verbs to express obligation (*You **should** eat your*

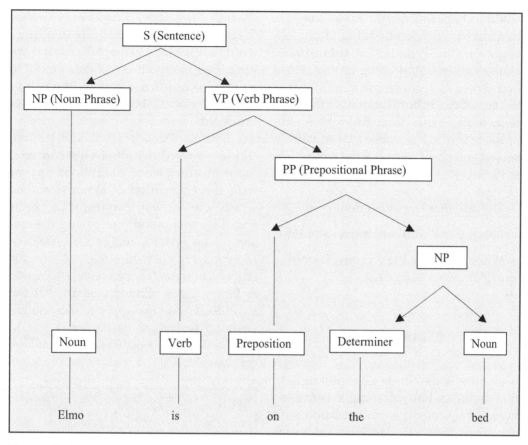

Figure 5–1. *The structure of a sentence to demonstrate a prepositional phrase.*

dinner), uncertainty (*I **could** go to the movies if my mother says okay*), ability (*I **can** lift this stone*), permission (*You **can** use my bike*), or future possibilities (*I **will** go to the party*). Modal auxiliaries are acquired in the following order of development: *can, could, shall, should, will, would, may, might,* and *must* (Wells, 1985).

By stage V, most children have fully acquired regular and irregular past tense verbs (Owens, 2016). Examples consist of the regular past tense verbs *walked* and *talked* and the irregular past tense verbs *caught* and *threw*. Conjunctions (e.g., *and, but, if, because*) are also produced, which allow the creation of more complex sen-

tences (e.g., *I would like to come, but I have to finish my homework*).

Embedding and Conjoining

Between 36 and 48 months of age, children advance from simple sentences to longer and more complex sentences. The emergence of complex sentences begins with **conjoined** or coordinated sentences, referred to as **compound sentences**. These sentences comprise two main clauses that are conjoined by the conjunction *and, or, but,* or *because*. The conjunction *and* is the first conjunction produced by preschoolers. Between 48 and 60 months of age, children begin to demonstrate complex sentences in their **embedding** of phrases and subordinate clauses. A **subordinate clause** cannot stand alone in a sentence and serves as a grammatical unit within the sentence. **Subordination** contributes to increased syntactic complexity. A subordinate clause is a clause that contains a subject and predicate but is not a complete sentence.

The dog **that lives next door** is nice.

I played ball **until my mom called me**.

Whoever broke the window should explain what happened.

SEMANTICS

Semantics is the component of language that describes how meaning is conveyed by words, sentences, conversation, and narratives. Semantic development begins with children's vocabulary development. Vocabulary increases rapidly, starting at age 2 (Golinkoff, Mervis, & Hirsh-Pasek, 1994) with 900 to 1,000 words at 3 years of age, 1,500 words at 4 years of age, and over 2,000 words acquired by age 5 (Owens, Farinella, & Metz, 2014). Over time, children expand and extend the meaning of words to apply to related objects or entities. For example, many animal names are first learned from books read to young children (e.g., *cat*). The meaning of the word *cat* is extended to other entities when a child visits a zoo. When this occurs, children learn that the word *cat* can refer to *kitty cat, tiger*, and *lion*.

New words are learned quickly following initial representations in both didactic (direct teaching) and informal contexts (Apel, Kahmi, & Dollaghan,

1985; Oetting, Rice, & Swank, 1995; Rice & Hoffman, 2015). The ability to acquire words is attributed to the skill of **fast mapping**. Fast mapping is a child's ability to internalize or learn a symbol (the word/vocabulary item) after minimal exposures to a word.

During the late preschool period, children's word definitions are **concrete**. More abstract word definitions appear with the acquisition of synonymy (i.e., words with similar features, such as *sick* and *ill*), explanation (i.e., giving the reason for an action), and specifications of categorical relationships (e.g., placing *dog* and *bird* in the category *animal*) (Bernstein & Levey, 2009). Children learn that the word *block* can now apply to their neighborhood (*going around the block*) and to obstructions (*He blocked me and I couldn't get through*).

> Abstract lexical terms do not label objects or observable actions. Abstract terms label concepts, such as time, while concrete terms label observable things and actions that can be pointed at in the environment.

Abstract lexical terms, such as words for time (*before, later, soon*), present difficulties for younger children because their meaning is not apparent or visible. For example, utterances that indicate time (e.g., *in a minute*) are always difficult for a child to understand when asking *When can I get a cookie?* During the preschool stage, children have an incomplete understanding of more abstract terms that refer to the actual duration of time (Shatz, Tare, Nguyen, & Young, 2010). For example, children were asked questions including, *How long does it take to see a movie? How long does it take to eat breakfast?* and *How long does it take for puppies to grow up to be dogs?* They were given the option of answering *days, hours,* or *years.* Preschoolers' knowledge of these terms was found to be incomplete, with better understanding of these terms at age 6.

The Mental Lexicon

The **mental lexicon** is a mental dictionary that holds all the words that an individual has acquired. Children's mental lexicon is organized according to phonological similarity, with words that differ by one phoneme, referred to as phonological neighbors. Words that are phonologically similar to many other words are said to "reside" in phonologically dense neighborhoods. A word's neighborhood size, also referred to as its neighborhood density, has been defined as the number of words similar to one another (e.g., *mat* and *rat* as neighbors of the word *cat*). Children learn new words faster if the words are of low phonological density, while the organization of these words is restructured as children are introduced to new vocabulary (Hoover, Storkel, & Hogan, 2010).

There are some aspects of language that present younger preschoolers with difficulty, such as certain determiners and quantifiers. The determiner *the* refers to a specific thing (*the book*) and *a* refers to a general set of things (*a book*). Children frequently make mistakes in article use until age 4 (Zdorenko & Paradis, 2011). The quantifiers *some* and *any* also present younger preschoolers with difficulty (Hurewitz, Papafragou, Gleitman, & Gelman, 2006). Some 3-year-olds interpret *some* to mean *at least some* and possibly *all.* The difference between the quantifiers *some* and *any* is acquired by 4 years of age.

Children learn new concepts and how to code these concepts linguistically by forming sentences to convey their ideas and knowledge. The main concepts acquired between 2 and 5 years of age consist of spatial concepts (location), temporal concepts (time), quantity concepts (number), quality concepts (description), and social emotional concepts (feelings), as shown in the following examples:

Spatial concepts: *in, on, over, between, across, along*

Temporal concepts: *before, after, later*

Quantity concepts: *more, less, empty, full*

Quality concepts: *rough, smooth, hard, soft*

Social emotional concepts: *happy, sad*

The terms *more/less* and *same/different* present difficulty for preschoolers. They may choose the size of an object to interpret both *more* and *less* (Owens, 2016). For example, younger preschoolers may choose a larger object, rather than a larger number of objects, to represent *more.*

Semantic Relations

Single words express meaning, such as the words *daddy* and *go.* When these words are combined to form a sentence, a **semantic relation** exists. Examples of semantic relations expressed by preschoolers can be found in Table 5–5. Semantic relations

Table 5–5. *Semantic Relations Produced by Preschoolers*

Agent + action	*He is throwing the ball.*
Action + object	*I am eating the pear.*
Demonstrative	*That's a ball.*
Entity + attribute	*The stove is hot.*
Entity + location	*The doggie is in the bed.*
Possessor + possession	*This is my doll.*
Recurrence	*Can I have more juice?*
Disappearance	*The juice is all gone.*
Negation	*I don't want to go to bed.*

describe the relationship among words in the sentence. For example, the words *big* and *bug* each have a meaning. When a younger child combines thee words to form the phrase *Big bug,* a semantic relationship is created (i.e., attribute + entity).

Relational Terms

During the preschool years, children acquire relational terms that apply to temporal (time), spatial (location), and physical (place) concepts. Children also begin to acquire relational terms that apply to kinship relations. Examples of these relational terms include:

Temporal relational terms: *before/after*

Locational relational terms: *in/on*

Physical relational terms: *high/low*

Kinship terms: *mother/father*

Examples of the development of locational, physical, and kinship relational terms can be found in Table 5–6.

Temporal Relations

Temporal relations include the terms *before, after, when, since,* and *while.* Children first acquire terms that refer to sequencing (*then, before, after*), followed by the acquisition of terms that refer to simultaneity (*while, at the same time*). Terms that refer to sequence and duration (*since, until*) are acquired at the school-age stage (Winskel, 2003).

Preschool-age children must achieve knowledge of syntactic structure to understand the terms *before* and *after.* Instead of relying on the syntactic structure of sentences that contain these terms, younger children rely on the *order of mention.* The order of mention refers to the order of events that are reported in a spoken utterance. The following example presents the chronological order of events (first, put on his shoes; second, ate a cookie) that are consistent with the order of mention (first, put on his shoes; second, ate a cookie).

He put on his shoes before he ate a cookie.

Table 5–6. The Acquisition of Locational, Physical, Temporal, and Kinship Terms

Age	Locational Relationship	Physical	Kinship Term
3–4	Under	Big/little	Mommy/Daddy
		Heavy/light	
4–4.6	Next to	Tall/short	Mother/father
	Behind	Long/short	Sister/brother
	In back of	Hard/soft	
	In front of		
School age	Right/left	Deep/shallow	Uncle/cousin

Source: Reproduced with permission from *Language Development: Understanding Language Diversity in the Classroom* (p. 147), by S. Levey & S. Polirstok (Eds.), 2011, Los Angeles, CA: Sage.

In the following example, the order of mention does not follow the chronological order of events. In this example, the order of mention (first, ate a cookie; second, put on his shoes) is not consistent with the chronological order of events (first, put on his shoes; second, ate his cookie).

Before he ate his cookie, he put on his shoes.

Children rely on the order of mention until 4 to 6 years of age, with better understanding of syntax and the terms *before* and *after* at age 7 (Blything, Davies, & Cain, 2015; Owens, 2016).

Temporal relations, such as *yesterday* and *tomorrow,* are better understood with exposure to adults' use of these terms (Hudson, 2006). By age 4, children are better able to conceptualize the timeframe for events occurring in the past or future, which contributes to their understanding of the terms *yesterday* and *tomorrow.* Exposure to the use of these terms allows children to better understand the connection between events and time.

Children are able to recall and discuss past events at 2 to 3 years of age, but reference to the actual time of past events may not occur until 35 to 40 months of age (Peterson, 1990). Children frequently use *yesterday* as a term for any period in the past.

Physical Relations

Children acquire the physical relations *big/little* as young as 2 years of age (Sandhofer & Smith, 2001), while other physical relations are learned later.

Big/little

Tall/short and long/short

High/low

Thick/thin

Deep/shallow

Wide/narrow

Locational Terms

Children must establish a good grasp of the environment before they learn the words associated with spatial concepts. Spatial terms begin with simple configurations, such as *in/on*. Children begin by describing one target object (e.g., *a book*) in relation to a single landmark (e.g., *on a table*). Children understand support relations (*in/on*) before proximity relations (*by* and *next to*). Configurations learned later are *between, across,* and *along* (Weist, 2002). Consequently, children will have a better understanding of *the toy is **in** the bag* than *the toy is **next to** the bag* or *the book is **between** the bag and the box*. Before age 4, children use *in, on,* and *over* to label object location, whereas *up, down,* and *off* are used as locational prepositions (e.g., *stand up, sit down*) (Owens, 2016).

> Prepositions expressing spatial relations can address location or direction. Prepositions of location appear with verbs describing a state or condition of an object or entity (e.g., *in the box*). Prepositions of direction appear with verbs of motion (e.g., *stand up*).

We now explore the development of children's narrative skills. Learning this aspect of semantics begins when young children are exposed to the structure of narratives in stories that are read to them.

Narrative Development

Narrative is a form of discourse that differs from conversation because narratives do not require a listener's response. In contrast to conversational interaction, narratives consist of an extended monologue that incorporates the use of intonation, gesture, and prosody, along with the description of an event. Narrative involves a story structure that includes the setting (who are the characters, when did the event take place, and where did the event take place), the action being discussed, feelings associated with the action or event, and some sort of outcome. The elements of a narrative must be connected and expressed according to the actual sequence of events (i.e., what happened first, next, last).

There may also be differences in the structure of narratives produced by speakers of different languages. However, all narrative styles include sharing and recounting of personal events and experiences, self-generated stories, telling and retelling of familiar tales, and the retelling of stories from movies, books, and television shows. Initially, children's narrative development lacks a cohesive or complete order of events, as shown in Table 5–7 (Bernstein, 2011). The full order of narrative elements emerges at age 5.

At 3 years of age, children produce *additive chains,* a set of events that relate to a central topic, with no particular temporal order. This level of narrative consists of sequences of events that can be arranged in any order with no effect on the meaning of the narrative. Apel and Masterson (1998, p. 5) provide an example of this level of narrative produced by a child aged 4 years and 5 months.

My mom went to outer space. And she saw a monster. And she ate moon cake. And she saw everything but nothing else. That was it.

Temporal chains are produced between 3 and 5 years of age, when narrative is

Table 5–7. *Narratives Produced by Preschoolers*

Age	Narrative Type	Example
3	Primitive	Has a concrete core with minimal detail
4	Unfocused chains	Presents a story, at times drifts off
5	Focused chains	Has a main character and a series of events
5+	True narratives	Thematic bonds and complex syntax which hold narratives together. Stories contain setting information, a series of events, as well as consequences and motivations.

Source: Reproduced with permission from *Language Development: Understanding Language Diversity in the Classroom* (p. 151), by S. Levey & S. Polirstok (Eds.), 2011, Los Angeles, CA: Sage.

structured to include sequential information, expressed by temporal or timed sequences of events.

One day, I went to the park. A big boy pushed a little boy and he fell down. He cried. The end.

At around 5 years of age, children produce simple causal chains that present an *episode* (a set of smaller scenes strung together to make a longer story). This level of narrative structure consists of *initiating event, attempt,* and *consequence.* The elements that are absent include *setting, internal response, internal plan, resolution,* and *ending.* In the causal chain, events are related by causal dependency because events cause other events. By 7 to 8 years of age, children produce a complete episode, summarized next.

Setting: Introduction of characters, time, and place

Initiating event: Problem (e.g., a broken toy)

Internal response: Characters' feelings about the initiating event

Internal plan: Statement about fixing the problem

Attempt: Action to solve a problem

Consequence: Event or events following the attempt

Resolution/reaction: The final state following the attempt

Ending: A statement ending the story

With all elements present, the *Winnie the Pooh* story would include the following elements (bolded) to provide a full narrative episode.

One day, Winnie the Pooh lost his honey pot. **He was sad. He decided to go out and find more honey.** *He met some bees. The bees told him to take some honey from the tree.* **He was happy because he got more honey. He lived happily ever after.**

Two types of narratives are produced by older preschool-age children: **personal narratives**, a description of "what happened," and **fictional narratives**, drawn from a child's imagination. Children use personal narratives to describe their own experiences. Personal narratives can consist of **decontextualized narratives** that are descriptions of people, objects, and events absent from the immediate environment. Personal narrative can also consist of **contextualized narratives** that consist of every day conversation. **Cohesive devices** are used to provide a well-organized narrative by creating a connection between elements of the story. These are linguistic devices that refer to a previously stated person or object (Gabig, 2014) and are used to connect parts of a conversation or narrative. Examples consist of *and, then, when, because, so, then, if, but,* and *that.* These are terms that are learned beginning with *and.* Cohesive devices consist of additive, temporal, and causal conjunctions.

Additives	Conjunctions that link clauses through addition (e.g., *and*)
Temporal	Conjunctions that link clauses temporally (e.g., *then, next*)
Causal	Conjunctions that link clauses causally (e.g., *because, so*)

METALINGUISTIC AWARENESS

Metalinguistic awareness appears during the preschool years, providing children with the ability to consciously reflect on the nature and properties of language. This ability allows children to reflect on the form and structure of language, such as rules for forming sentences and phonological features that form and distinguish words and the meaning of words (Berko Gleason & Bernstein Ratner, 2017). Metalinguistic awareness allows children to recognize syntactic, semantic, and phonological components that may contain errors, as shown in the following examples (Kahmi & Koenig, 1985, p. 209):

Syntactic awareness: Where "he go?" versus Where *is he going?*

Semantic awareness: Jill "eats" cards versus Jill *plays* cards

Phonological awareness: He "locks" to school versus He *walks* to school

Typically developing children can identify and revise errors by age 4, but metalinguistic skills do not fully develop until age 7 or 8. Metalinguistic skills require the development of intact language skills and differentiate typical from atypical language development. Metalinguistic awareness is also a factor in developing intact literacy skills for reading and writing abilities. For example, metalinguistic awareness plays a role in phonological skills, providing children with the ability to recognize rhymes (e.g., *cat, hat,* and *bat*) and to identify sounds in words (e.g., the word *cat* contains the three sounds "c," "a," and "t"). In summary, metalinguistic awareness is present when children develop the ability to think about language itself (Yopp & Yopp, 2010).

PRAGMATICS

Pragmatics involves the appropriate use of language based on three major communication skills:

◆ The use of language to greet, inform, and request (e.g., saying hello, giving information, asking for something in an appropriate manner)

◆ The ability to change and adapt language to different persons and situations to maximize their understanding (e.g., providing background information so the listener will understand the topic and simplifying language so younger listeners can understand)

◆ The ability to follow rules in conversation (e.g., turn-taking, maintaining a topic, staying on topic).

Children first understand how to produce polite requests to achieve a better outcome when asking for something. By age 3, children begin to use the word *please*. Later, children produce **indirect speech acts** (e.g., *Can I go to the playground?*) at about 3½ to 4 years of age (Bates, 1976; Leech, 2016). Preschoolers are also better able to elaborate on topics and discuss activities (Berko Gleason & Bernstein Ratner, 2017).

Pragmatics also describes the rules for communicative interaction. Examples include adapting to a listener's needs, initiating a conversation, turn taking in a conversation, and forming polite requests (Westby, 1980). From 36 to 48 months, conversations are maintained through extended turn-taking. Children make conversational repairs and correct others. Humor is inserted into social exchanges and language begins to become more abstract and figurative. Preschoolers are able to advocate for themselves and provide justifications in their reasoning. As they get older, children begin to ask more questions for clarification, to gain information and word meanings. During the preschool years, joint play with peers begins to emerge. By the end of age 3, children rely on verbal language, rather than physicality, to communicate.

Indirect Requests

In the preschool period, children begin to understand and use indirect requests (Bates, 1976; Wells, 1985). When children acquire modal auxiliaries (e.g., *can, could, would,* and *might*), they begin to understand that an indirect request is a more appropriate form to convey the underlying intention (e.g., *to get a cookie* or *to go to the playground*). Between 3 and 4 years of age, children produce indirect requests through the use of modal auxiliaries (e.g., *Can I have a cookie?*). Modals first appear with the production of *can* at about 30 months of age.

can and *will*: 2 years and 6 months

should and *could*: 2 years 9 months to 3 years

may, might, and *must*: 3 years

The negative forms of the earlier learned modal auxiliaries may appear as early as 30 months (*can't, won't,* and *don't*) (Owens, 2016). Inversion appears around age 3 for earlier acquired modal auxiliaries.

Why can't you come?

There are indirect speech acts that require a child to infer a meaning that goes beyond the words that are being used. For example, when a speaker says, "This is a *salad* fork," the child must draw the inference that this fork is only to be used for eating salad, along with the understanding that the other forks in the kitchen are to be used for other foods. This inference is made through understanding the meaning that is being communicated by the indirect speech act. The ability to understand the inference of a speaker's utterance begins to appear in preschool-aged children (Horowitz & Frank, 2016).

Conversational Development

Conversation is a communicative event that requires a speaker and a listener. Conversation involves a setting, a topic, rules for taking turns as speaker and listener, and common knowledge shared between the speaker and listener to ensure a successful interaction. Children's early conversation lacks these conventions that govern successful communication. Frequently, their conversation begins with the assumption of shared information. For example, a 2-year-old held up a toy to a telephone receiver and said, *Mommy, look at my new toy*, based on the assumption that his mother shared his perspective. These early conversational attempts lack a TOM because children lack an understanding of what a listener sees or knows (which differs from the child's own perspective of the situation or context).

Children achieve the principles that govern conversation once they develop the language skills and rules for conversational interaction (Brinton & Fujiki, 1989), as shown in the following conversational rules that are acquired when children develop more advanced language and pragmatic skills:

Introduce topics with appropriate referents (background information)

Do not interrupt other speakers

Contribute to a topic

Understand the main point of the conversation

Make sure the topic is understood by others in the interaction

Preschool-age children learn to take turns in a conversation, to maintain the conversational topic, and to contribute new and relevant information. Children are able to maintain a topic established by a speaker by age 3½. There is considerable growth in the length, variety, and complexity of children's conversational narratives from 3 to 5 years of age. By age 4, children may produce three to nine sentences in narrative conversation, whereas 3-year-olds produce four. By age 5, the major change is providing greater information for the listener in terms of temporal orientation (*when something has occurred*).

The conversational topics of 4-year-olds consist of enacting scenarios, describing, and problem solving (Schober-Peterson & Johnson, 1989). At ages 3 to 5, children will attempt to repair a breakdown by repeating the previous word or utterance, rather than providing a clarification.

A communication breakdown occurs when a listener has difficulty understanding what has been communicated. Conversational breakdowns can result from articulation difficulties, incomplete information, or lack of attention to the topic (Roth & Spekman, 1984).

At age 2½, children are inconsistent in their understanding of the need to repair a breakdown when communication fails (Shatz & O'Reilly, 1990). At age 2, clarification requests consist of confused facial expressions. Young preschool-age children request clarification by asking

Huh? or *What?* (Ninio & Snow, 1996). It is not until the early school-age years that children are able to request specific clarification for better understanding of a speaker's message.

By age 4, children can adopt different roles in conversation by adjusting pitch and loudness. For example, they use a deeper and louder voice when taking on a male role in play. By age 4, children are able to use **motherese** (child-directed speech) when interacting with younger children. This consists of a higher pitch and quieter voice. **Register** refers to the language style used for a specific purpose or to adapt to a specific social context. For example, when speaking before a class, a speaker will be careful to use a more formal style of speech. Register also includes the politeness forms developed when preschoolers learn that vocabulary and grammar play a role in communication, such as the use of indirect requests (e.g., *Can I have a cookie?*). By age 5, they purposefully use polite forms. Topic maintenance ensures **cohesion** (connection between elements) in a conversation. At age 2, only half of contributions to a conversation are on topic.

By age 3½, children can sustain a topic of conversation about 75% of the time but are better able to sustain a topic when they are interested or actively engaged in the topic at hand. Turn-taking is also a factor in conversation. This refers to taking turns as speaker and listener. Children have difficulty sustaining that topic beyond one or two turns at ages 2½ to 3, but 5-year-olds can sustain a conversation for about 12 turns, based on more advanced vocabulary and language skills (Hoyte, Degotardi, & Torr, 2015). Conversation frequently requires referring to entities or events that are absent from the context, defined as **decontextualized language**. During the preschool years, children learn to talk about objects absent from the immediate environment, events in the past and future, and personal experiences.

HUMOR

Conversational skills frequently involve the use of humor. By age 2, children invent their own jokes (Hoicka & Akhtar, 2011). Examples consist of handing an adult the incorrect object (giving a spoon when asked for a cup) or making up names for things (calling a cup a silly or another name). At age 3, children are more likely to laugh when mislabeling items in this manner. Examples of children's development of humor include the use of incongruity (e.g., a bowl for a hat at 18 to 24 months), appreciation of jokes (2 to 7 years of age), and enjoyment of puns, satire, and ambiguous meanings as children develop greater vocabulary skills at later ages (e.g., she has *bear* feet versus *bare* feet; McGhee, 1980). Humor also plays a role in children's socialization, with most research showing a relationship between play and humor.

Understanding humor depends on a child's ability to recognize incongruity (an absurd or strange situation or action). Incongruity involves an event or story resulting in an illogical conclusion or action (e.g., a shoe used as a hat). The understanding of the incongruity of an unexpected outcome is humor, with the response of laughter. Understanding that there was an unexpected, incongruous result reflects a child's ability to understand humor (Southam, 2005).

Children begin to enjoy riddles at ages 3 to 4 (*What do you call a rabbit who tells jokes? A funny bunny*) (Southam, 2005). Humor in riddles and jokes requires understanding that words may sound the same but are spelled differently and have different meanings (*bear/bare*) (Bernstein & Levey, 2009). For older children, humor often involves linguistic ambiguity, such as the example of phonological ambiguity shown below (i.e., *sick-tick*).

Why did the clock go to the doctor?

Because he was tick.

In summary, infants show an appreciation of humor, while preschoolers truly appreciate the use of humor when interacting with peers.

SUMMARY

Children's language skills develop during the preschool period. By 4 years of age, children achieve adult-like speech and language skills with respect to their production of more complex and lengthy sentence structures, interactive communication, the correct production of sounds, vocabulary development, and phonological awareness.

◆ Cognitive development is reflected in children's interest in learning how things work, better planning, and problem solving.

◆ Cognitive development is also reflected in children's awareness of the concepts of time (e.g., when and how long), space (e.g., where), and quantity (e.g., how many and how much).

◆ Theory of mind develops and children can engage in more successful conversation and interaction because children can put themselves into the listener's shoes and understand others' feelings, beliefs, and intended meanings.

◆ Syntactic development is characterized by the production of a greater range of sentence types and expanded sentence length.

◆ Syntactic skills reflect greater sentence complexity at around age 3 with the production of sentences that include a main clause (e.g., *I think*) and a subordinate clause (e.g., *that*) to produce sentences such as *I think that I like that.*

◆ Children now produce auxiliary verbs (e.g., *is, are*) and morphological inflections (inflectional and derivational morphemes).

◆ Pragmatic development reflects the use of more polite forms of request, such as the use of *please* by younger children, and indirect speech acts (e.g., *Can I*) at about age 3 or 4.

◆ Children's word productions are closer to those of adults as their phonological skills develop.

◆ Phonological awareness develops when children become more aware of sounds in words and the connection between spoken sounds and written letters.

◆ Semantic skills increase when children develop a better understanding of language and acquire more abstract word meanings (e.g., *toy block, don't block the doorway, around the block*).

◆ Semantic skills also develop as children produce stories with a central topic and temporal order (e.g., *This is a story about and first . . . then . . . next*).

◆ Children begin to gain knowledge about print, which further develops their literacy skills in later grades.

◆ Humor appears in preschoolers' conversations with peers. This shows an understanding of more abstract language.

Chapter 6 traces the development of language during the school-age stage of language development.

KEY WORDS

Assimilation processes

Bootstrapping

Bound morpheme

Closed syllable

Cohesion

Cohesive devices

Complex sentence

Compound sentence

Concrete

Conjoined sentences

Content words

Contextualized narrative

Declarative sentence

Decontextualized language

Decontextualized narrative

Derivational morpheme

Divergent thinking

Embedding

Fast mapping

Fictional narrative

Free morpheme

Function word

Imperative sentences

Indirect speech acts

Inflectional morpheme

Intelligibility

Interrogative sentences

Language content

Language form

Language use

Magical thinking

Mental lexicon

Mental state verbs

Metalinguistic awareness

Modal auxiliaries

Negative sentences

Open syllable

Personal narratives

Register

Semantic relations

Subordinate clause

Subordination

Substitution processes

Syllable structure processes

Theory of mind (TOM)

Working memory

STUDY QUESTIONS

1. Describe the role of morphemes in children's syntactic development.

2. Provide an example from this chapter that demonstrates the relationship between two language areas.

3. Explain the role of modal auxiliaries in children's interaction with others.

4. Explain the importance of meta-linguistic awareness in language development.

5. Explain the role of narrative in children's language learning.

REFERENCES

Addis, D. R, Pan, L., Musicaro, R., & Schacter, D. L. (2016). Divergent thinking and constructing episodic simulations. *Memory, 24*(1), 89–97.

Angell, C. (2009). *Language development and disorders: A case study approach.* Boston, MA: Jones & Bartlett.

Apel, K., Kahmi, A., & Dollaghan, C. (1985, November). *Fast mapping skills in young children: Name that word.* Paper presented at the American Speech-Language-Hearing Association Convention, Washington, DC.

Apel, K., & Masterson, J. (1998). *Assessment and treatment of narrative skills: What's the story?* Rockville, MD: American Speech-Language-Hearing Association.

Baddeley, A. (1997). *Human memory: Theory and practice.* Hove, East Sussex, UK: Psychology Press.

Baddeley, A. (2003). Working memory and language: An overview. *Journal of Communication Disorders, 36,* 189–208.

Baddeley, A. D., & Larson, J. D. (2007). The phonological loop unmasked? A comment on the evidence for a "perceptual-gestural" alternative. *Quarterly Journal of Experimental Psychology, 60*(4), 497–504.

Baron-Cohen, S. (1993). From attention-goal psychology to belief-desire psychology: The development of a theory of mind, and its dysfunction. In S. Baron-Cohen, H. Tager-Flusberg, & D. J. Cohen (Eds.), *Understanding other minds: Perspectives from autism* (pp. 59–82). New York, NY: Oxford University Press.

Baron-Cohen, S. (1996). *Mind blindness: An essay on autism and theory of mind.* Cambridge, MA: MIT Press.

Bates, E. (1976). *Language and context: The acquisition of pragmatics.* San Diego, CA: Academic Press.

Bauman-Waengler, J., & Davis, A. (2016). *Articulation and phonology in speech sound disorders: A clinical focus* (5th ed.). Boston, MA: Pearson Education.

Berko Gleason, J., & Bernstein Ratner, N. (2017). *The development of language.* Boston, MA: Pearson.

Bernstein, D. K. (2011). Language development from ages 3 to 5. In S. Levey & S. Polirstok (Eds.), *Language development: Understanding language diversity in the classroom* (pp. 139–160). Los Angeles, CA: Sage.

Bernstein, D. K., & Levey, S. (2009). Language development: A review. In D. K. Bernstein & E. Tiegerman-Farber (Eds.), *Language and communication disorders in children* (6th ed., pp. 28–100). Boston, MA: Allyn & Bacon.

Bloom, L., & Lahey, M. (1978). *Language development and language disorders.* New York, NY: John Wiley & Sons.

Blything, L. P., Davies, R., & Cain, K. (2015). Young children's comprehension of temporal relations in complex sentences: The influence of memory on performance. *Child Development, 86*(6), 1922–1934.

Bowerman, M. (1982). Reorganizational processes in lexical and syntactic development. In E. Wanner & L. Gleitman (Eds.), *Language acquisition: The state of the art* (pp. 319–346). New York, NY: Academic Press.

Brinton, B., & Fujiki, M. (1989). *Conversational management with language-impaired children: Pragmatic assessment and intervention.* Rockville, MD: Aspen.

Brown, R. (1973). *A first language: The early stages.* Boston, MA: Harvard University Press.

Flipsen, P., Jr. (2006). Measuring the intelligibility of conversational speech in children. *Clinical Linguistics and Phonetics, 20*(4), 202–312.

Gabig, C. S. (2014). Language development in middle and late childhood and adolescence. In S. Levey (Ed.), *Introduction to language development* (pp. 211–246). Los Angeles, CA: Sage.

Galotti, K. M. (2017). *Cognitive development: Infancy through adolescence* (2nd ed.). Los Angeles, CA: Sage.

Gola, A. A. H. (2012). Mental verb input for promoting children's theory of mind: A training study. *Cognitive Development, 27*(1), 64–76.

Gleitman, L. (1990). The structural sources of verb meanings. *Language Acquisition, 1*(1), 3–55.

Golinkoff, R. M., Mervis, C. B., & Hirsh-Pasek, K. (1994). Early object labels: The case for a developmental lexical principles framework. *Journal of Child Language, 21*(01), 125–155.

Goswami, U. (2009). *Cognitive development: The learning brain.* East Sussex, UK: Psychology Press.

Hacquard, V. (2014). Bootstrapping attitudes. *Proceedings of SALT, 24,* 330–352. Retrieved from http://ling.umd.edu/assets/publications/Hacquard-14-SALT24-Bootstrapping Attitudes.pdf

Hoicka, E., & Akhtar, N. (2011). Preschoolers joke with jokers, but correct foreigners. *Developmental Science 14,* 848–858.

Holmes, R. M., Romeo, L., Ciraola, S., & Grushko, M. (2015). The relationship between creativity, social play, and children's language abilities. *Early Child Development and Care, 185*(7), 1180–1197.

Hoover, J. R., Storkel, H. L., & Hogan, T. P. (2010). A cross-sectional comparison of the effects of phonotactic probability and neighborhood density on word learning by preschool children. *Journal of Memory and Language, 63*(1), 100–116.

Horowitz, A. C., & Frank, M. C. (2016). Children's pragmatic inferences as a route for learning about the world. *Child Development, 87*(3), 807–819.

Hoyte, F., Degotardi, S., & Torr, J. (2015). What is it all about: Topic choices in young children's play. *International Journal of Play, 4*(2), 136–148. http://dx.doi.org/10.1080/21594 937.2015.1060566

Hudson, J. A. (2006). The development of future time concepts through mother-child conversation. *Merrill–Palmer Quarterly, 52*(1), 70–95.

Hurewitz, F., Papafragou, A., Gleitman, L., & Gelman, R. (2006). Asymmetries in the acquisition of numbers and quantifiers. *Language Learning and Development, 2*(2), 77–96.

Jin, K. S., & Fisher, C. (2014). Early evidence for syntactic bootstrapping: 15-month-olds use sentence structure in verb learning. *Boston University Conference on Language Development.* Retrieved from http://www.bu.edu/bucld/files/201404/jin.pdf

Justice, L. M., & Ezell, H. K. (2016). *The syntax handbook* (2nd ed.). Austin, TX: Pro-Ed.

Kahmi, A. G., & Koenig, L. A. (1985). Metalinguistic awareness in normal and language-disordered children. *Language, Speech, and Hearing Services in Schools, 16,* 199–210.

Leech, G. N. (2016). *Principles of pragmatics.* London, UK: Routledge.

McGhee, P. (1980). *Humor: Its origin and development.* New York, NY: W.H. Freeman & Co.

Ninio, A., & Snow, C. E. (1996). *Pragmatic development.* Boulder, CO: Westview Press.

Oetting, J. B., Rice, M. L., & Swank, L. K. (1995). Quick incidental learning (QUIL) of words by school-age children with and without SLI. *Journal of Speech, Language, and Hearing Research, 38*(2), 434–445.

Owens, R. E. (2016). *Language development: An introduction* (9th ed.). Boston, MA: Pearson Education.

Owens, R. E., Farinella, K. A., & Metz, D. E. (2014). *Introduction to communication disorders: A lifespan evidence-based perspective.* Boston, MA: Pearson Education.

Peterson, C. (1990). The who, when and where of early narratives. *Journal of Child Language, 17*(02), 433–455.

Rhodes, M., & Brandone, A. C. (2014). Three-year-olds theories of mind in actions and words. *Frontiers in Psychology.* Retrieved from https://static1.squarespace.com/static/56d88d0c0442624b79f94337/t/56e 1cb2ba3360c4beb0694e1/1457638188496/ Rhodes+Brandone+2014.pdf

Rice, M. L., & Hoffman, L. (2015). Predicting vocabulary growth in children with and without specific language impairment: A longitudinal study from 2;6 to 21 years of age. *Journal of Speech, Language, and Hearing Research, 58*(2), 345–359.

Roth, F. P., & Spekman, N. J. (1984). Assessing the pragmatic abilities of children part 1: Organizational framework and assessment parameters. *Journal of Speech and Hearing Disorders, 49*(1), 2–11.

Ryan, M. (2017). *Signs of magical thinking in small children.* Retrieved from https://www.verywell.com/the-signs-of-magical-thinking-in-children-290168

Sandhofer, C. M., & Smith, L. B. (2001). Why children learn color and size words so differently: Evidence from adults' learning of artificial terms. *Journal of Experimental Psychology, 130*(4), 600.

Schober-Peterson, D., & Johnson, C. J. (1989). Conversational topics of 4-year-olds. *Journal of Speech, Language, and Hearing Research, 32*(4), 857–870.

Shatz, M., & O'Reilly, A. W. (1990). Conversational or communicative skill? A reassessment of two-year-olds' behaviour in miscommunication episodes. *Journal of Child Language, 17*(01), 131–146.

Shatz, M., Tare, M., Nguyen, S. P., & Young, T. (2010). Acquiring non-object terms: The case for time words. *Journal of Cognition and Development, 11*(1), 16–36.

Singleton, N. C., & Shulman, B. B. (2013). *Language development: Foundations, processes, and clinical applications.* Burlington, MA: Jones & Bartlett.

Southam, M. (2005). Humor development: An important cognitive and social skill in the growing child. *Physical and Developmental Therapy in Pediatrics, 25*(1/2), 105–117.

Stagnitti, K., & Lewis, F. M. (2015). Qual-ity of pre-school children's pretend play and subsequent development of semantic organization and narrative re-telling skills. *International Journal of Speech-Language Pathology, 17*(2), 148–158.

Subbotsky, E. (2010). *Magic and the mind: Mechanisms, functions, and development of magical thinking and behavior.* New York, NY: Oxford University Press.

Wallace, C. E., & Russ, S. W. (2015). Pretend play, divergent thinking, and math achievement in girls: A longitudinal study. *Psychology of aesthetics, creativity, and the arts. American Psychological Association, 9*(3), 296–305.

Weist, R. M. (2002). Temporal and spatial concepts in child language: Conventional and configurational. *Journal of Psycholinguistic Research, 31*(3), 195–210.

Wellman, H. (2014). *Making minds: How theory of mind develops.* New York, NY: Oxford University Press.

Wells, G. (1985). *Language development in the preschool years.* New York, NY: Cambridge University Press.

Westby, C. E. (1980). Assessment of cognitive and language abilities through play. *Language, Speech, and Hearing Services in Schools, 11*(3), 154–168.

Winskel, H. (2003). The acquisition of temporal event sequencing: A cross-linguistic study using an elicited imitation task. *First Language, 23*(1), 65–95.

Yopp, H. K., & Yopp, R. H. (2010). *Purposeful play for early childhood phonological awareness.* Huntington Beach, CA: Shell Education.

Zdorenko, T., & Paradis, J. (2012). Articles in child L2 English: When L1 and L2 acquisition meet at the interface. *First Language, 32*(1–2), 38–62.

APPENDIX 5–A
Developmental Milestones, Ages 3 to 5

Three to Four Years of Age

Hearing and Understanding	Talking
◆ Hears you when you call from another room. ◆ Hears television or radio at the same loudness level as other family members. ◆ Answers simple who?, what?, where?, and why? questions.	◆ Talks about activities at school or at friends' homes. ◆ People outside of the family usually understand child's speech. ◆ Uses a lot of sentences that have four or more words. ◆ Usually talks easily without repeating syllables or words.

Four to Five Years of Age

Hearing and Understanding	Talking
◆ Pays attention to a short story and answers simple questions about it. ◆ Hears and understands most of what is said at home and in school.	◆ Uses sentences that give lots of details ("the biggest peach is mine"). ◆ Tells stories that stick to topic. ◆ Communicates easily with other children and adults. ◆ Says most sounds correctly except a few like l, s, r, v, z, ch, sh, th. ◆ Says rhyming words. ◆ Names some letters and numbers. ◆ Uses the same grammar as the rest of the family.

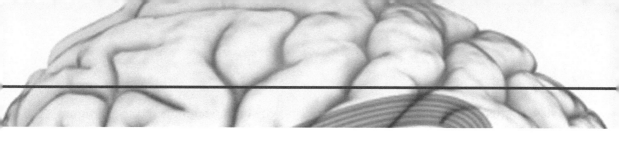

6

Language Development in Middle and Late Childhood and Adolescence

María R. Brea-Spahn and Sandra Levey

Case Study

Ginger is an 8-year-old in the third grade. She has a diverse vocabulary. She is a good student and enjoys reading books and writing in her journal. After reading this *chapter, you will be able to understand the language factors that contribute to a child's ability to achieve successful academic skills during the school-age years.*

CHAPTER OBJECTIVES

This chapter presents language development in early childhood (6 to 8 years), late childhood (9 to 12), and adolescence (13 to 19). School-age children and adolescents add sophistication to their language content, form, and use as a result of exposure to the academic context through textbooks and the language spoken by teachers.

Their language also develops through participation in after-school programs and peer relationships (Nippold, 2000). We begin this chapter with a discussion of the factors that support language development during the school-age period. Next, we provide a description of advances in the semantic, syntactic, and discourse levels of language. Finally, we discuss literacy development during the school-age stages. After reading this chapter, you will be able to understand:

- The factors that contribute to success in developing school-age and adolescent academic skills
- The language development of school-age children and adolescents
- The impact of reading and writing on the language skills of early and late elementary school-age children and adolescents

LANGUAGE IN MIDDLE AND LATE CHILDHOOD AND ADOLESCENCE: SOURCES OF DEVELOPMENT

In comparison with the rapid language learning of infants, toddlers, and kindergarteners, there is a gradual and subtle process of language development in school-age children and adolescents. Language skills continue to develop into middle childhood (6–8 years), late childhood (9–12), and adolescence (13–19) (Nippold, 2007). By age 5, children participate in conversations and negotiate demands, such as providing reasons for parents to purchase a desired game or toy (Nippold, 1998). As children progress through school, opportunities for learning different subjects and participating in extracurricular activities promote their language development. There is advancement in semantic knowledge, syntactic complexity, and discourse comprehension and use. School-age children's development includes the following language, cognitive, and social skills (Gabig, 2014, p. 211).

Advanced metalinguistic skills

More abstract vocabulary skills

The understanding and use of figurative language

More complex linguistic forms

The use of derivational morphemes

Advanced social and pragmatic skills

Examples of the linguistic attainments of typically developing children at age 10 and adolescents at age 15 can be found in Table 6–1 (Nippold, 2007).

METALINGUISTIC AWARENESS

Metalinguistic awareness involves the ability to reflect on and consciously think about language and how it is used. Metalinguistic awareness is necessary for the development of reading skills. This is essential when school-age children are presented with riddles or jokes, as shown in the following example (Nippold, 2007, p. 234).

Why did the hungry man go to the *lamp* store? Because he wanted a *light* snack.

Growth in metalinguistic awareness depends on a maturing cognitive system. Cognitive development and metalinguistic awareness develop within social contexts, in which school-age children and adolescents thrive. This, in turn, supports the emergence of abstract thought. Abstract thought involves the ability to conceptualize (to form a concept or idea about an occurrence or an event) and to solve a problem or develop a plan by thinking of the solution or a path of action, rather than the use of an actual action to solve the problem. An example of a child

Table 6–1. Linguistic Attainments of Typical Development: Age 10 and Age 15

Linguistic Skills	Age 10	Age 15
Lexical Development		
Understands word meaning	20,000 words	30,000 words
Understands psychological meaning	*sweet, hard, cold, bright*	*bright, sharp, dull*
Uses morphological cues for word identification	Identifies unknown words	Identifies unknown words
Word definition	Defines concrete nouns	Defines abstract nouns
Verbal Reasoning		
Analogies	Can solve second-order analogies	Can solve third-order analogies
Syllogisms	Can understand logical syllogisms	Can understand illogical syllogisms
Figurative Language		
Metaphors understood	Common, transparent metaphors	Difficult opaque metaphors
Enjoys jokes and riddles	Linguistic ambiguity understood	Linguistic ambiguity explained
Proverbs understood	Common, concrete proverbs	Some abstract proverbs
Syntax		
Length in conversational discourse	7+ words	8+ words
Length in expository discourse	9+ words	10+ words
Persuasive writing mean length of utterance	11+ words	12+ words
Subordinate conjunctions	*because, before,*	*even though, so that,*
Adverbial conjuncts	*also, then, so, besides*	*furthermore, nevertheless*
Discourse and Pragmatics		
Stories and narratives	Uses all grammar story elements	Complete episodes and elaboration
Discourse	Uses conjunctions as cohesive elements	
	Explains rules of a game accurately	Detailed explanations of games
Conflicts	Negotiates with peers	Mutual collaboration with peers

Source: Adapted with permission from *Later Language Development: School-Age Children, Adolescents, and Young Adults—Third Edition* (pp. 361–366), by M. A. Nippold, 2007, Austin, TX: Pro-Ed. Copyright 2007 by Pro-Ed, Inc.

using abstract thought to plan a path of action is shown below.

> Jay was thinking about how he might ask his parents for a new bike. He thought about the things he would say, along with how he might explain the problems with his old bike.

> Abstract thought develops early, when children engage in pretend play (e.g., using an object to represent other things, such as a box to represent a car, rocket ship, or stove). Abstract thought allows children to create a mental image of an object that represents something else. In addition, abstract thought allows younger school-aged children to recognize that alphabet letters represent sounds and meaning, as well as understand that numbers represent physical quantities. Abstract thought allows older children to plan ahead by anticipating or imagining what might occur in the future.

Four Types of Metalinguistic Knowledge

There are four types of metalinguistic knowledge that characterize the school-age child's language development (Berko Gleason & Ratner, 2017): **phonological awareness**, semantic awareness, syntactic awareness, and **pragmatic** awareness (Table 6–2).

Phonological awareness grows during the early school-age period, when children can use strategies to identify a word by its sound patterns. Semantic awareness expands around age 10, when children

Table 6–2. *Metalinguistic Skills*

Phonological awareness	Knowledge that words are composed of syllables and phonemes
Semantic awareness	The ability to provide word definitions and understand figurative language forms (simile, metaphor, and idiom)
Syntactic awareness	Understanding of syntactic (sentence structure) rules and the ability to correct syntactic errors
Pragmatic awareness	Awareness of the connection between language and its use in social interaction

can define words, with greater vocabulary development through exposure to reading. Syntactic awareness appears in adolescence, when complex sentences are understood and produced (Justice & Ezell, 2016). Pragmatic awareness appears during later childhood and adolescence, when children can successfully participate in appropriate communication with others through a better understanding of their mental states and needs.

Metalinguistic competence is another factor that appears during the school-age stage of development. Competence involves the awareness that language is composed of syntactic, semantic, morphological, phonological, and pragmatic domains that can be synthesized, analyzed, and reorganized.

◆ Synthesis refers to the consideration of prior learning or ideas when developing new ideas, plans, or tasks.

- Analytical skills involve the ability to interpret, observe, detect patterns, and process information, such as understanding frequent occurrences or frequent behavioral patterns in others.
- Organization involves the use of a systematic approach to problem solving by creating order and gathering the necessary materials to complete a goal, such as the study materials needed to prepare for a test.

Metalinguistic skills are dependent on the development of cognitive abilities. Younger school-age children (age 7–11 years) are in the **concrete operations stage** of cognitive development (Piaget & Inhelder, 1969). In this stage, children use logical thought to process or understand events and to solve problems. They possess the ability to draw on prior experience to understand and to explain others' behaviors and actions. In addition, their attention span increases, allowing children to maintain a task for about 15 minutes at 6 years of age and for an hour at age 9. Piaget (1954) placed adolescents in the **formal operations** stage. At this stage, their cognitive skills allow them to understand more abstract concepts (Dijkstra, Eerland, Zijlmans, & Post, 2014).

> Concrete concepts refer to objects in the physical world, such as a tree in a forest, along with physical actions (e.g., running, drinking). Abstract concepts refer to entities that have no direct representation in the physical world, including emotions, figurative language (e.g., metaphors), and abstract action (thoughts and emotions).

Verbal Reasoning

Verbal reasoning is a cognitive skill that involves the ability to draw conclusions, solve problems, and make decisions. Children who possess verbal reasoning can answer questions such as, *What would happen if . . . ?* and *Why do you think . . . ?* Two examples of verbal reasoning are found in the ability to process **analogies** and **syllogisms**. Both analogy and syllogism tasks are associated with reasoning methods that are used in daily problem solving.

- An analogy presents the relations between the features of sets of things, relying on a correspondence or partial similarity.
- A syllogism involves a deductive process: a formal argument consisting of a major and minor premise and a conclusion.

An example of analogy follows.

Eyes are to *see* as *ears* are to _____.

The goal is to analyze the relationship between the first and second terms (*eyes: see*) and apply this relationship to the third and fourth terms (*ears: hear*). As shown in Table 6–1, older children understand more complex analogies as their verbal reasoning and vocabulary skills have progressed. More advanced vocabulary skills are essential to understand complex analogies, such as the example below (Nippold, 2007, p. 121). In this example, the child must know the words *apex*, *base*, and *anterior*. In addition, the word *posterior* must be present in the child's **lexicon**.

Apex is to base as anterior is to (posterior).

Analogical processes can be found in daily activities, such as explaining something to a younger child. For example, *email* can be explained by describing the similarity between receiving a message on the computer and receiving a message by mail. This explanation employs analogical reasoning to draw this comparison.

Email is to the *computer* as *letter* is to the *mailbox*.

A syllogism is a formal argument that consists of a major and minor premise and a conclusion, used to convince others or to inform others of facts. Syllogisms play a role in academic and other general skills, given the need to formulate and understand logical arguments. In the classroom, logical arguments appear in academic texts, with children asked to draw conclusions from what they have read. Children must also understand if an argument is logical and not presenting a false conclusion.

Syllogisms also play a role in conversation, as shown in the following example (Tessler & Goodman, 2017). In this example, someone is telling a friend that officemates are out with the flu.

Major premise: All officemates are out with the flu.

Minor premise: Some officemates with the flu are out for weeks.

What would be a logical conclusion?

Conclusion 1: Therefore, some officemates are out for weeks.

Conclusion 2: Therefore, all officemates are out for weeks.

In conversation, a listener would draw the logical conclusion that only *some* office-mates are out for weeks. It would not be logical to assume that *all officemates* are out for weeks. An example of an illogical syllogism is shown in the following example (Markovits, Schleifer, & Fortier, 1989, p. 793). In this case, the second premise (*All red things have a nose*) does not share any terms with the first premise (*Every Zobole is yellow*).

Major premise: Every *Zobole is yellow.*

Minor premise: All *red things* have a nose.

Conclusion: Therefore, Zoboles have a nose.

As shown in Table 6–1, illogical syllogisms are not detected until children reach age 15, given that advanced cognitive skills play a role in children's ability to process more abstract cognitive tasks (Galotti, 2017). At this age, a child might say, "That makes no sense because we only know that a Zobole is yellow."

Note the difference between the illogical syllogism and the logical syllogism. In the logical syllogism, there is a connection between the premises and the conclusion. The illogical syllogism shown in the example shows no connection between the first and second premise.

Critical-thinking skills are an essential factor for school-age children when presented with illogical beliefs or ideas. Critical thinking involves the analysis of the content of a spoken or written text for accuracy and logic (Nippold et al., 2014). This analysis allows the child to judge the logic of the ideas being expressed.

We next discuss the language development that occurs in early, middle, and later grades. These changes appear in semantics (vocabulary, **narrative**, conversation, expository discourse, and figurative language), syntax and morphology, pragmatics, and literacy.

> We can say **Many** *houses are being built* or *They spilled* **much** *of the salt onto the floor*, but we cannot say **Much** *houses* or **Many** *sands.* The correct use of the terms *many* and *much* are acquired by the late elementary school years.

SEMANTICS

Vocabulary

At 6 years of age, children have acquired approximately 18,000 words, with an increase in vocabulary when children begin to read. By the time children reach adulthood, they will have acquired 60,000 words (Nippold, 2006). Many words are learned through **incidental learning** (Akhtar, Jipson, & Callanan, 2001), when children are not directly taught these words. In this case, words are learned in conversations and other contexts. In contrast, other words are learned when they are explicitly taught through direct instruction (Beck, McKeown, & Kucan, 2013). During the period of learning new words, certain vocabulary terms are learned as children are exposed to the correct use of these words:

◆ Irregular past tense verbs (e.g., *eat/ate, catch/caught, throw/threw*). Children produce irregular verbs (e.g., *ate, caught, threw*) correctly after 8 years of age.
◆ Reflexive pronouns (e.g., *myself, yourself, themselves*), produced by about 9 years of age.
◆ Mass and count nouns (e.g., *water* vs. *house*). Mass nouns label nonindividual substances, such as *water, salt,* and *sand*, and count nouns label individual objects, such as *house* and *car.*

Within the classroom, teachers focus on children learning three types of vocabulary words that target three tiers of word knowledge (Beck et al., 2013). Tier 1 consists of basic and concrete vocabulary items that children learn even before entering school. Examples include *book, girl, boy, dog, big, small, house,* and *table.* Tier 2 consists of high-frequency words that are more abstract and occur in written text and adult conversation. These vocabulary items are important for reading comprehension. Examples include *consistent, expectation, justify,* and *predict.* Tier 3 words appear in academic texts and specific domains (e.g., geography). **Domain-specific** vocabulary items are specialized to an area or field of study. Examples include terms such as *isotope, peninsula,* and *evolution,* learned in the domains associated with physics, geography, and biology, respectively.

> There are differences in vocabulary across languages and cultures. For example, a child who lives in a desert region will have vocabulary differences from a child who lives in a busy city. Despite these differences, most children are familiar with zoo animals (Nelson & Nelson, 1990).

Mental state verbs are another category of vocabulary terms that depend on cognitive abilities. The use and understanding of these terms is based on the ability to understand the thoughts, feelings, and ideas of others. These terms consist of metalinguistic verbs (which refer to spoken language) and metacognitive verbs (which refer to thoughts). These vocabulary items are often used in classroom discussions of history and philosophy (Nippold, 2007, p. 42).

Metalinguistic verbs refer to spoken language: *assert, imply, predict*

Metacognitive verbs refer to thoughts: *remember, conclude, assume*

Older children and adolescents acquire **metalinguistic strategies** that support vocabulary skills (Nippold, 2006), described in Table 6–3. An example of a metalinguistic strategy involves using surrounding words in a written text to understand the meaning of a new word. The following example shows how **context clues** can be used to identify the meaning of the word *extinct*.

Dinosaurs disappeared approximately 65 million years ago, with many different explanations for what caused the dinosaurs to become *extinct*.

Over time, vocabulary skills continue to develop, given direct instruction or through the metalinguistic strategies shown in Table 6–3: semantic mapping, semantic feature analysis, and context clues (Ram, Marinellie, Benigno, & McCarthy, 2013). Vocabulary skills expand when children are exposed to books, comics, magazines, and media events (e.g., movies and television shows). Reading skills have considerable influence on the vocabulary development of children beyond grade 4 (Gabig, 2014), when children transition from learning to read to reading to learn. Adolescents are exposed to abstract vocabulary that is found in figurative expressions (e.g., **idioms, metaphors, similes**, and **proverbs**). Specialized vocabulary is also found in **expository discourse**, when children enter the later grades.

Table 6–3. *Metalinguistic Strategies*

- Semantic mapping (graphic organizers) involves creating maps or webs of words to visually display the meaning-based connections between a word and related words or concepts. For example, if there is a lesson about *bugs*, the children will organize a map that shows differences and similarities across different bugs (e.g., wings/no wings, number of legs, color, and size). In this way, prior knowledge is used and vocabulary learning occurs.

- Semantic feature analysis involves comparing how word meanings differ or are similar. For example, children may have a lesson about animals and their characteristics (e.g., general appearance). Next, the children will use a plus or minus sign to indicate whether each animal does or does not have that feature. In this way, children are required to analyze semantic features that identify these differences. In addition to vocabulary development, semantic processing is developed.

- Context clues involve using other words in a sentence or a paragraph to understand an unknown word. In this way, vocabulary is expanded, and a reading strategy is provided to develop literacy skills.

Expository discourse refers to academic language found in textbooks and classroom lectures. Examples include comparison (compare/contrast), causation (cause/effect), procedural (temporal sequence), problem/solution, and collection/description (Ward-Lonergan & Duthie, 2014, p. 44).

Figurative Language

Figurative language consists of idioms, similes, metaphors, and proverbs. Riddles and puns are also included in this language category. Figurative language is found in books, television shows, movies, and magazines. Idioms are expressions that cannot be understood from the meanings of their separate words, as shown in the following example:

They are walking on eggshells.

Clearly, the speaker does not truly mean that these individuals are actually walking on eggshells. Instead, this idiom means that they are being very careful when presented with a delicate or sensitive topic. Similes are expressions in which two unlike things are explicitly compared by using the words *like* or *as* (e.g., *Busy as a bee*). We know that bees are frequently seen flying about while looking for pollen or nectar. This figure of speech makes a comparison between the activities of a bee and a person's workload. A metaphor is a figure of speech that makes a comparison between two things that are unrelated but share some common characteristics (*He was boiling mad*). We know that water boils when the temperature is high enough. This comment makes a comparison between boiling water and the person's anger. Proverbs are expressions that express a thought or truth (e.g., *Practice makes perfect*). This figure of speech expresses a truth that additional practice may be a factor in greater success. The understanding of figurative expressions emerges during the school-age years.

Understanding figurative language requires abstract language processing, as a child must understand the meaning of these expressions by going beyond the basic meaning of the words used. For example, the idiom *Going by the book* does not mean moving or walking past a book. Instead, this expression means *following rules*. The following example demonstrates the use of this figurative expression (Nippold and Duthie, 2003, p. 792).

Ben and his mother were driving to the ski resort for the weekend. Ben wanted to get there quickly, so he asked his mom to drive faster. She said she wouldn't go any faster. Ben said to himself, "Mom goes by the book."

Idiom

Idiom comprehension is affected by a variety of factors. One factor is familiarity, or how often a child has previously heard the idiom used. Another factor is transparency (how close the figurative meaning of the idiom is to its literal meaning). A transparent idiom is: *I don't think you can trust her—she will **stab you in the back**.* In this case, the transparency is found in the knowledge that a stab in the back is an attack. The actual meaning of this idiom is that someone may betray your trust.

The opposite of a transparent idiom is an opaque idiom, whose figurative and literal language is not easily discernible, such as *Barking up the wrong tree*. This idiom is based on the idea that a dog is barking at the wrong tree (i.e., the squirrel being sought is hiding in another tree). The actual meaning of this idiom is that a person is on the wrong track, looking in the wrong place, or considering an incorrect idea. School-age children find transparent idioms easier to comprehend than opaque expressions (Nippold & Duthie, 2003). Preadolescent children may understand certain idioms if they have previously heard these terms used, know the meanings of the words embedded in the idiom, and can *read between the lines* for the intended, yet unexpressed, meaning (Nippold & Rudzinski, 1993).

Simile

Similes make comparisons between two different subjects by using the words *like* or *as* (e.g., *As stubborn as a mule* or *As light as a feather*). Frequently, figurative language is found in children's literature. Examples consist of the following examples, taken from children's books:

> *He is as stubborn as a mule.* (Mules are resistant to being told or urged to move.)
>
> *My best friend is as sharp as a pencil.* (The term *sharp* is associated with intelligence.)
>
> *I woke up as fresh as a daisy.* (You woke up feeling good.)

Over time, children learn that many words have various meanings, such as *sharp, dull, deep,* and *shallow*. Although the meaning of these words applies to physical meanings (e.g., sharp or dull objects, and deep or shallow water), the more abstract meanings apply to intelligence and personal traits.

Metaphor

A metaphor makes a comparison between two entities that are not related but share some common characteristics.

> *The exam was a breeze.*

In this example, the metaphor means that the exam was easy, with comparison to a gentle breeze. By age 6, children understand simple metaphors (Nippold, Leonard, & Kail, 1984), with more complex metaphors understood by adolescence. Examples of metaphors found in children's books consist of *You are toast* (someone is being told he or she is in trouble) and *My school is a zoo* (the school is full of kids acting out or behaving like wild animals).

Proverbs

Proverbs express a practical or basic truth, as shown in the following examples.

- ◆ Two wrongs don't make a right. (When someone has done something wrong, do not do something wrong in return.)
- ◆ The pen is mightier than the sword. (Using words is often more effective than forcing people to do what you want.)

Children have difficulty understanding proverbs before age 12. Additionally, proverbs may pose a significant difficulty for children from diverse cultural or linguistic backgrounds (Roseberry-McKibbin, 2007), given that proverbs are specific to different languages and cultures. An example is the Indonesian proverb *Like an owl yearning for the moon.* The meaning of this proverb is to wish for something that is impossible to attain.

Riddles and Puns

A riddle is a question or statement that requires an answer, as shown in the following example (Nippold, 2007, p. 242).

Question: *Why can't the bicycle stand up by itself?*

Answer: *Because it is two-tired.*

A pun is a joke that makes use of the different possible meanings of a word, as shown in these two examples.

What do you call an alligator in a vest? An investigator!

Why can't you feed a teddy bear? Because they are always stuffed!

Both types of humor are understood by older school-age children and play a role in children's interaction with others.

Narrative, Conversation, and Expository Discourse

Discourse forms include conversation, narrative, expository, and persuasion (Nippold, 2014). Conversation involves the use of language in social interaction. Narrative discourse involves the use of language to express a series of connected events or a story, often involving personal, fictional, or nonfictional events. Expository discourse is found in textbooks, classroom lectures, technical papers, and documen-

taries (Ward-Lonergan, 2010). This form of discourse also involves the explanation of games. Persuasive discourse involves a speaker expressing logical reasons to persuade or motivate others to engage in an activity or to accept an idea or an opinion.

There are differences between conversation, narrative, and expository discourse. Conversation discourse takes place in more informal social contexts, as when a student engages in conversation about a favorite movie or a vacation trip with a group of friends. Narratives are meant to convey stories and events. The plot of a narrative may follow a chronological order of events (e.g., first, then, next). Expository discourse consists of the use of language to convey information (Bliss, 2002).

Narrative

School-age children learn to produce or write narratives that involve fictional events or past experiences. These narratives may also involve stories from events, television shows, or movies. Narratives contain an underlying structure that consists of the following elements (Stein & Glenn, 1979).

Setting: Characters, place, and time

Initiating event: A problem or an event, such as a surprise party

Internal response: Reaction of the character(s) to the initiating event

Plan: The method to solve a problem or to respond to an event

There is also an outcome that summarizes the narrative elements (e.g., *and they lived happily ever after when the wolf ran away).* The ability to understand the structure of a story is established by 9 to 10 years of age (Berman & Slobin, 1994). Older school-age children, around 12 to 13 years of age, produce narratives with a greater proportion of complete episodes than younger children, as described in Chapter 5. An example of a school-age narrative follows (Nippold, 2007, p. 295), with the speaker expressing an event that occurred. This narrative continues beyond this example, with a friend asking more about the spider and what happened next.

> I going to tell you what happened to me this morning. I was playin' on the monkey bars. A boy came along with a big, huge, giant spider in his hand.

Conversation

Conversation involves cognitive and perceptual abilities (Avivi-Reich, Jakubczyk, Daneman, & Schneider, 2015). Cognitive abilities involve focused attention to the conversation while avoiding distractions, switching attention from one speaker to another, keeping track of the topics, extracting the meaning of the information being discussed, and keeping information in memory for the future. Perceptual abilities involve listening and comprehension of the topic being discussed. This allows for successful participation in the conversation. Conversational growth during the school-age years appears as children achieve the following abilities (Nippold, 2007, p. 286).

- Improved and longer topic maintenance
- Appropriate turn-taking
- A greater number of relevant comments

- Consideration of participants' thoughts and feelings
- Repairs used to clarify understanding if others are confused

Expository Discourse

Expository discourse consists of language that is typically found in textbooks, classroom lectures, and technical papers. This type of discourse is based on factual information with a focus on the following factors (Ward-Lonergan, 2010):

Comparison: Compare and contrast ideas

Causation: Explain a cause and the resulting effect

Problem: Provide a solution

Collection/description: Provide a description of the elements

Enumeration: Provide a definition and example

Expository discourse may be used to inform, to express facts, or to argue a point of view. This type of discourse requires different cognitive skills than those required by narrative discourse, and is more linguistically complex (Nippold, Hesketh, Duthie, & Mansfield, 2005; Sun & Nippold, 2012). This complexity is based on the use of a greater number of words and more advanced syntax. An example from a high school text can be found in Table 6–4, showing the elements that characterize expository discourse (Lundine & McCauley, 2016, p. 308).

When children reach grade 4, they begin to use linguistic skills that distinguish narrative from expository discourse (Berman, 2004). However, children do

Table 6–4. Expository Discourse

Descriptive	A definition of global warming (*for instance, such as*)
Procedural	Procedures to slow global warming (*first, next, until, during*)
Enumerative	Physical changes to the earth because of global warming (*another, also*)
Cause/effect	Reasons for global warming (*because, effect of, so, consequently*)
Compare/ contrast	Climate changes over time (*however, as opposed to, in comparison*)
Problem/ solution	Solutions for global warming (*problem, concern, issue, possible solution*)

not incorporate the elements of sentence structure and vocabulary that distinguish narrative and expository writing until adolescence (Berman, 2004; Berman & Nir-Sagiv, 2007).

Another form of discourse involves persuasion. Persuasion requires the knowledge to convince others to agree with an idea or an action. Consequently, it is essential to possess the skills to persuade others in an appropriate manner to achieve success.

Persuasion

Persuasion is the discourse genre that involves convincing others to accept a point of view or argument, with progress in persuasion occurring after grade 3. Adolescents achieve the ability to produce a persuasive argument that appeals to others' values and beliefs (Nippold, 1998). At this stage of development, they are able to see another person's point of view when engaged in a persuasive argu-

ment. Persuasion discourse abilities progress during school age and adolescence, as shown in the following examples (Nippold, 2007, p. 306).

Adjustment to listeners' characteristics (e.g., age, needs, beliefs)

Provision of advantages to persuade the listener to agreement

Anticipation and response to counterarguments

Provision of a variety of different arguments

In summary, conversation, narrative, and expository discourse skills continue to develop with age and experience. Children also develop an understanding of figurative language. In this case, meaning must be found by going beyond the basic meaning of the words that are used (e.g., *He goes by the book*).

There are narrative differences across languages. For example, children from Spanish-speaking backgrounds may produce narratives as conversational and descriptive statements. Chinese and Korean children may express multiple experiences in a brief narrative style. Redundant elements are often omitted, such as the use of "I" in subsequent sentences.

SYNTACTIC AND MORPHOLOGICAL DEVELOPMENT

Syntactic Development

School-age children's syntactic development is reflected in the increased length and complexity of their utterances. A 6-year-old may produce sentences composed of six words, while adults produce utterances that contain at least ten words (Nippold, 2006). The mean length of response or mean number of words used per sentence may be related to the complexity and length required for certain language events. For example, expository discourse requires greater syntactic complexity than conversation (Nippold, Hesketh, Duthie, & Mansfield, 2005), given that more complex tasks must be explained and understood by the listener (e.g., the explanation of rules for a game).

Syntactic Elaboration

Syntactic elaboration involves the increased length and complexity of sentences. The main characteristic of a complex sentence is that it contains two or more main verbs

(Steffani, 2007), as shown in the following example:

> I **went** to school, and then I **came** home and **watched** TV.

Subordination is one of the factors that contributes to increased syntactic complexity. A **subordinate clause** contains a subject and predicate (e.g., *Mary drove*) but does not express an independent or complete sentence. An independent clause is a complete sentence with a subject (S), verb (V), and object noun (O) (e.g., *Mary drove to the store*). By grade 8, the use of a greater number of subordinate and embedded clauses appear (Nippold & Sun, 2010).

A subordinate clause is sometimes termed a dependent clause. This is a clause that cannot stand alone as a complete sentence, since a complete thought is not expressed. An embedded clause (words that include a subject and verb) is within another clause and typically marked by commas. The following examples illustrate the use of subordinate clauses (in boldface):

> She lives in the city, **which is convenient.**

> Always lock the door, **because it keeps you safe.**

The following example is an embedded clause:

> The dog **who lives next door** is friendly.

A subordinate clause is introduced by a subordinating conjunction or a relative pronoun. Examples of **subordinating conjunctions** are *after, although, as, if, as if, because, before, even if, even though, since, though, unless, until, whatever, when, whenever, whether,* and *while.* Examples of relative pronouns are *which, that, who, whom,* and *whose.*

> Independent clause (SVO): *The **dog ate** the **cookies.***

> Subordinating conjunction: ***Because** the dog ate the cookies . . .*

> Relative pronoun: *The dog, **who** lives next door, ate the cookies.*

The terms *if* and *although* may not be used consistently until age 15 (Bernstein & Levey, 2009).

> *I will come, **if** I finish my homework in time.*

> *I went to school, **although** I had to come home because I was sick.*

Syntactic elaboration also consists of **noun phrase** or **verb phrase** elaboration. Both processes emerge during middle and late childhood.

> Noun phrase elaboration: *The dog; The **big** dog*

> Verb phrase elaboration: *The dog barks; The dog barks **loudly***

Verb phrase elaboration can also be accomplished with the use of modal auxiliary verbs (e.g., *can, could, shall, should, will, would, may, might*).

> *I **could** climb the mountain if I wanted to.*

Verb phrase elaboration also occurs when **conjunctions** (e.g., *although, and, because, but, either*) are used.

> *She likes snow **because** she likes to ski.*

Another example of complex sentence structure that emerges during the school-age period is passive sentence structure. In the following sentence, the *dog* is the subject (S), the word *chased* is the verb (V), and *the cat* is the direct object noun (O).

> SVO: *The dog chased the cat.*

To form a passive structure, the sentence structure SVO is transformed to the passive structure OVS, as shown in the following example.

> OVS: *The cat was chased by the dog.*

Younger children may understand passive sentence forms, but they are not produced until age 7 or 8 (Snyder & Hyams, 2015).

> There are two types of passive forms: reversible and irreversible. Some passive forms are irreversible (*The window was broken by the boy*) because the reverse form (*The boy was broken by the window*) is not possible. However, a reversible passive sentence (*The boy was kissed by the girl*) can be logically reversed (*The girl was kissed by the boy*).

The complex sentences produced at age 10 to 11 contain mental state verbs and adverbial conjuncts (Bernstein & Levey, 2009). Mental state verbs describe someone's thoughts, beliefs, feelings, or intentions and consist of terms such as *believe, think, know, understand, perceive, feel, guess, recognize, notice, want,* and *imagine*. Examples of adverbial conjunct terms consist of *also, consequently, finally, instead, meanwhile, nevertheless, now, thus,* and *therefore.*

> Mental state verb: *I **think** he likes me.*

> Adverbial conjunct: ***Finally**, the girl found her bicycle.*

The Analysis of Syntactic Complexity

One approach to the analysis of syntactic complexity takes account of sentences that contain an independent clause (IC), adverbial clause (ADV), or nominal (NOM) clause (Table 6–5). Examples of these syntactic components are presented in Table 6–6 (Nippold, 2009, p. 870). These examples, based on conversations between an adult and a child age 12, include a discussion about chess and a general conversation about pets. Note that the child employed more complex language in the explanation of the chess game than in the general conversation about her pets. For example, the conversation about chess included independent, adverbial, and nominal clauses, while the conversation about pets consisted of independent clauses alone. These samples illustrate the difference between expository discourse (game explanation) and conversation (information report). As noted earlier, expository discourse requires greater syntactic complexity than conversation, given that more complex tasks must be explained more carefully to be understood by the listener (Nippold et al., 2005).

Syntactic complexity is measured in T-units and clausal density. A T-unit consists of a main clause plus all subordinate clauses and nonclausal structures that are attached to or embedded within. An example of this analysis is shown in Table 6–7 (Scott & Nelson, 2007). In this sample, there are 14 clauses and 8 T-units, resulting in a clause density of 1.75 (14 clauses/8 T-units).

Morphological Development

English includes free morphemes, which can stand on their own and have meaning, as well as bound morphemes—word parts that only have meaning when attached to other words. Inflectional morphemes add specificity to verbs. School-age children use inflectional morphemes to indicate grammatical meaning with the use of the plural (*cat* + *s*), past-tense forms (*walk* + *ed*), and morphemes that indicate present and ongoing action (*go* + *ing*). In this way, semantic content and sentence length are increased.

Derivational morphemes act to modify the meaning or grammatical function of the words to which they are attached.

Table 6–5. *Syntactic Complexity: T-Unit Elements*

An independent clause can stand alone and expresses a main idea (e.g., *The dog ate a cookie*)—while a phrase does not contain both a subject and a verb (e.g., *a red book*, *running away*, and *in the box*).

An adverbial clause is used as an adverb that indicates time, place, or condition (e.g., clauses beginning with *after, although, unless, until, when*).

A nominal clause is a dependent clause that acts as the subject or object of a sentence, naming a person, place, or thing (e.g., clauses beginning with *who, what, which, where*).

A relative clause is a dependent clause that modifies an independent clause and is introduced by a relative pronoun (e.g., *who, which, that, whose, whom*).

Table 6–6. *A Conversation About Chess and a Conversation About Pets*

A Conversation about Chess	A Conversation about Pets
Examiner: Now tell me why you enjoy chess. Child: I enjoy [IC] it for the social part of it because I get [ADV] to talk to a lot of people and also because it can help [ADV] me in school. It's helped [IC] a lot in math. And also I get [IC] to go different places for the Nationals. This year I'll be going [IC] to Texas. Examiner: Tell me how it helps you with math. Child: With math, it's [IC] different things like understanding. So I'll have [IC] to understand how different things work [NOM] in chess. And then I'll also have [IC] to understand things like algorithms and things like that in math too. Examiner: Do you have any other reasons why you enjoy chess? Child: I just enjoy [IC] it because it's [ADV] something fun to do, and I can kind of enjoy [ADV] my time there, and it's [ADV] better than sitting at home watching TV or something.	Examiner: Do you have any pets at home? Child: Two cats. Examiner: What are their names? Child: R and S. Examiner: How old are they? Child: They'll be [IC] three in May. Examiner: Can you tell me more about them? What colors are they? Child: They're [IC] gray and white tabbies. We got [IC] them from the cat adoption. So they were [IC] named after perfumes. So we couldn't really think [IC] of any names for them. Examiner: Do you have any other pets? Child: No.

Source: Reproduced with permission from Nippold (2009). School-age children talk about chess: Does knowledge drive complexity? 2009, *Journal of Speech and Hearing Research, 52,* p. 870. Republished with permission from the American Speech-Language-Hearing Association.

Table 6–7. *Sentence Complexity Analysis*

1. Yanis' father was a farmer (1)
2. And he wanted him to be a farmer (2)
3. And then Yanis let the little goats out to go up the mountain and stuff (2)
4. And one went off (1)
5. And he was going to go after it (2)
6. And he got to the top of the mountain and saw the sea (2)
7. And he had a dream that night (1)
8. And he told his dad that he could be a fisherman and be back in a couple of days (3)

Source: Reproduced with permission from the American Speech-Language-Hearing Association, from C. M. Scott and N. W. Nelson (2007, November). *Common measures of naturalistic language: What they do and don't tell us.* Paper presented at the Meeting of the American Speech-Language-Hearing Association, Boston, MA.

Derivational morphemes consist of prefixes (e.g., *un-, im-, re-,* and *ex-*) and suffixes (e.g., *-ish, -ous, -er, -ate,* and *-able*). Examples of free, derivational, grammatical, and inflectional morphemes are shown in Table 6–8.

Derivational morphemes form new words. For example, *-er* is a derivational suffix that changes a verb into a noun (*paint* to *painter*) or a noun to a verb (*painter* to *paint*). Derivational morphemes are acquired at the late preschool and early school-age levels. The derivational morphemes that are acquired during the later school-age years are *-ful, -less, -ly, -ness, -al,* and *-ance*.

Delight	Delightful
Happy	Happiness
Slow	Slowly
Origin	Original
Distant	Distance

While morphemes add to the complexity of children's sentence production and writing, children may also use a morphological approach to decipher a word's meaning. By interpretation of a root word that is known, the meaning of a word can be understood. The examples below are taken from a fourth-grade morphology test (Kieffer & Lesaux, 2007), with root words followed by derived words based on morphological additions. Which of the following derived words may be the easiest for children when using a morphological approach to decoding or analyzing the meaning of a word?

Grow	Growth
Decide	Decision
Five	Fifth
Admit	Admission

Note that the words *decision, fifth,* and *admit* involve sound and spelling changes between the root and derived form. If you chose the word *growth*, you would be correct, as the word *growth* does not contain these changes. Examples of the use of grammatical morphemes in forming words and sentences are shown in Table 6–9.

There are differences found in morphology across languages. Given that many children within classrooms are learning English as a new language, these differences should not be viewed as a disorder.

Table 6–8. *Morphemes*

Free lexical morphemes	Nouns, verbs, adverbs, and adjectives
Derivational morphemes	The prefixes *un-, -re, -im* and suffixes *-ish, -ous,* and *-able* (e.g., *un + likely* and *understand + able*)
Grammatical morphemes	Articles, prepositions, conjunctions, and pronouns (e.g., *in, and, they*)
Inflectional morphemes	Plural *-s*, possessive *'s*, third person present singular *-s* (e.g., *two cats, daddy's hat,* and *she eats only vegetables*)

Table 6–9. *Grammatical Morphemes*

Present progressive	They are go**ing**.
Plural	She has one cat and he has two cat**s**.
Irregular plural forms	elf/elves; man/men; child/children
Past irregular	eat/ate; catch/caught; drive/drove
Possessive inflection	Mary**'s** hat is lost.
Uncontractible copula/auxiliary	She **is**. (response to who is crying)
Past regular *-ed*	They walk**ed** to school.
Third person regular *-s*	He walk**s** to school.
Third person irregular	She **has** a book.
Contractible copula	He**'s** big.

Differences may appear in production between Spanish and English speakers (Roseberry-McKibbin, 2014, p. 107): the omission of the possessive morpheme *-'s* (*The girl book is* brown) and the past tense form *-ed* (*They walk to the store yesterday*). Differences may also appear between Asian and English speakers (Roseberry-McKibbin, 2014, p. 134): the omission of the plural morpheme *-s* (*Here are two piece of toast*) and the possessive morpheme *-'s* (*Mom food is cold*). Differences may also appear between mainstream American English (MAE) and African American English (AAE) speakers: omission of the plural morpheme *-s* (*He got three box of crayons*), the possessive morpheme *-'s* (*That my brother bike*), and the past tense morpheme *-ed* (*She live in New York*). These differences emerge from the influence of West African languages, Native American languages, French, and English on AAE.

In summary, growth in the domain of syntax for children in the middle to late school-age years and adolescence is characterized by an increase in word length and sentence complexity, including the use of morphology, modal auxiliary verbs, passive sentence forms, and subordination. The progress in syntactic complexity is related to academic language exposure. As children are introduced to the language spoken by teachers and the language used in textbooks, their language is transformed. A description of children's sentence development during the school-age period is presented in Table 6–10.

PRAGMATIC DEVELOPMENT

Pragmatics involves the use of language in social interaction. Early social interaction largely involves family. As children enter later grades, there is greater interaction

Table 6–10. Sentence Development

Description	Example
Full propositional complement: contains a cognitive verb such as *think, guess, wish, know, hope, wonder, show, remember, pretend, mean, forget, say, tell,* may or may not contain *that*	I *hope* (that) we go to lunch soon.
Gerund: contains an *-ing* form that functions as a noun	*Swimming* is fun.
Participle: contains an *-ing* form that functions as an adjective (modifies a noun or a pronoun)	I see the man *driving* down the street. I hear the dog *barking* loudly.
Simple infinitive: contains *to* followed by a verb	I need *to go.*
Infinitive clause (to + verb) with different subject: Contains an infinitive; the subject of the infinitive clause is different from the main clause	I want *the baby* to eat.
Unmarked infinitive: contains *make, help, watch,* or *let* without a *to* marker	Watch me run.
Simple *Wh*-clause: contains *who, what, where, when, why, how*; does not contain an infinitive *to* marker	See how fast I am.
Wh-infinitive: contains a *Wh*-word and an infinitive	I don't know *what* to wear.
Relative clause: contains an embedded phrase that functions as an adjective; modifies an object or subject noun phrase; may be marked by *who, which, that*	That is the one that I like.
Simple conjoining: contains two clauses that are joined by a conjunction; can be coordination (*and, but, or,* etc.) or subordination (*because, after,* etc.)	I ate fast so I could leave. I like cake and I like ice cream.
Embedded and conjoined: contains both an embedded and conjoined clause; may include a catenative (a verb often followed by a function word such as *to* or *on*); will have three or more verbs	I want *to stay* here, *but* my mommy says no.
Multiple embedding: contains more than one embedded clause; one verb may be a catenative; will have three or more verbs	I *know* that we have *to eat* soon.

Source: Reproduced with permission from the American Speech-Language-Hearing Association, from S. A. Stefani (2007). Identifying embedded and conjoined complex sentences: Making it simple. *Contemporary Issues in Communication Sciences and Disorders, 34,* p. 46.

with peers. The social context becomes the backdrop for changes in social language interaction. The pragmatic changes that occur during adolescence consist of progress in topic maintenance, relevance to the topic of conversation, appropriate turn-taking during conversation, the contribution of new information, the expression of empathy and understanding, and the ability to focus on a conversational topic (Nippold, 1998).

There is increased insight into others' thoughts and feelings during this period of development. This is reflected in school-age children becoming more adept at taking the perspective of others and accomplishing social perspective-taking (Nippold, 2007). Perspective-taking involves considering another person's perspective or point of view, such as the opinions, beliefs, feelings, and needs of others. The social skills that ensure successful peer acceptance for school-age children are relevant comments, novel ideas, and amusing comments during social interaction (Nippold, 1998, 2000).

Children's interaction also becomes more appropriate when making requests with the use of modal auxiliary terms (e.g., *Can you . . . , could you . . . , would you . . . ?*) used to produce indirect requests (*Can I use your bike today?*). Indirect requests are a more appropriate type of a request, in comparison to a direct request (*Give me your bike today*). At age 10, children begin to use indirect requests more frequently within interaction.

In addition to the linguistic aspects of pragmatics, there are pragmatic rules that govern interaction. These are rules that apply to greetings, providing information, and adapting language to different listeners (age and status). Pragmatic rules also apply to turn-taking in conversation, clarification if not understood, eye contact during interaction, and distance or proximity to other speakers in an interaction. The pragmatic skills required for successful communication are reflected in conversation, narrative, and persuasive discourse (Nippold, 2006, p. 371). It is important to understand that pragmatic rules differ across languages and cultures, while many of these rules apply to most contexts of interaction. Grice (1975) provided pragmatic rules that specify appropriate conversation: Be brief and to the point, be honest, and avoid misunderstandings (Table 6–11).

In summary, language development in school-age children is associated with growth in metalinguistic, cognitive, and social skills. These are the factors that develop when children are exposed to

Table 6–11. Pragmatic Rules that Govern Appropriate Conversation

The maxim of quantity	Be as informative as possible, giving as much information as is needed and no more.
The maxim of quality	Be truthful and do not give information that is false or lacks evidence.
The maxim of relation	Be relevant to the topic being discussed.
The maxim of manner	Be clear, brief, and orderly in what you are saying to avoid any chance of obscurity or ambiguity.

varied experiences, along with the experiences provided through reading, the language spoken by teachers, and social interaction with peers. We now review the language skills that support literacy skills during the school-age period.

LITERACY SKILLS IN EARLY, MIDDLE, AND LATER GRADES

For most school-age children and adolescents, written language plays a pivotal role in the development of more complex oral language skills. Before children become proficient at understanding the symbolic nature of language necessary for reading comprehension, they must become phonologically aware. Phonological awareness includes consciousness about lexical units (words) and sublexical units (phonemes, syllables, and onset/rime).

> Onset refers to the initial sound or sounds in a word (e.g., *stop*), while the rime refers to the vowel and any following consonants in the word (e.g., *stop*).

Phonological awareness develops over the course of the early elementary school-age period, with awareness that words are composed of smaller units of language (syllables, onset-rime, and phonemes). Phonological awareness that appears during the school-age years includes the following examples:

◆ Alliteration skills signal awareness of shared phonemes across words (e.g., *big bad bears*).
◆ Phoneme awareness reveals the ability to sequentially isolate a sound

from a word, such as the sounds that compose the word *cat* (e.g., *c – a – t*) and to blend spoken sounds that compose words (e.g., to blend or combine the spoken sounds "c," "a," "t" to form the word *cat*)
◆ Elision consists of the ability to delete a sound in a word to form a new word (e.g., *stop → top*)

Gillon (2004) presents the following tasks that characterize phonological awareness skills (Table 6–12).

Once phonological awareness skills are acquired in the early elementary years, the focus is on reading fluency (accuracy and rate of reading). Following their mastery of single-word decoding, children are taught to read from connected text found in stories and books. Writing follows a similar path, with children in the first grade introduced to spelling common words with regular phonetic patterns (*dog, ran, cat*). In the second grade, children read and write at a basic level and have an understanding of riddles and puns, described in the explanation of figurative language development.

In the third grade, children can provide a summary of what they have read. In the fourth grade, the focus is on reading complex, domain-specific texts that contain more technical vocabulary items that are related to the domain (e.g., history or science). In the fifth grade, learners understand a story plot, the characters' behaviors and thoughts, as well as the function of quotation marks to denote dialogues within story episodes. Their writing skills have also developed and they are able to write more complex narratives about events or experiences. In the sixth grade, children can organize, revise, and edit their written work.

Table 6–12. *Phonological Awareness Skills*

Age 4	Rhyme
Age 5	Recognition of phonemic changes in words (*Hickory Dickory "clock"* versus *Hickory Dickory Dock*)
	Syllable awareness (awareness that the word *banana* has three syllables)
	Blending onset and rime (th-umb)
	Producing a rhyme (What rhymes with *cat*?)
	Matching initial sounds; isolating an initial sound (Say the first sound in the word *ride*)
	Compound word deletion (Say *cowboy*. Say it again but don't say *cow*)
Age 6	Blending of two and three phonemes (*z-oo; sh-o-p; h-ou-se*)
	Phoneme segmentation (Say the word as you move a chip for each sound: sh-e; m-a-n; l-e-g)
	Phoneme substitution to build new words (Change the /a/ in *cane* to /o/)
Age 7	Sound deletion (Say the word *stop* without the /s/)
Age 8	Sound deletion that includes blends (Say *prank*; now say it without the /p/)
Age 9	Sound deletion that includes medial and final blends (Say *snail*. Say it again, without the /n/; say *fork*. Say it again without the /k/)

By grade 7, children can understand and compare written texts (e.g., poems, stories, other written texts). In grade 8, children are expected to analyze texts for their ideas and to write arguments with correct capitalization, punctuation, and spelling. By grade 12, children are able to identify the main idea and purpose in a written text, make simple connections between ideas within a text, and provide general evaluations of the meaning or purpose of the text. At this stage, they must possess the cognitive skills to integrate text ideas, explain **causal relationships**, and evaluate complex information.

In a causal relationship, there is an evident relationship between two things. This relationship makes something happen. For example, if an alarm clock caused you to wake up this morning, there is a causal relationship between the alarm and this event. In school, children must understand cause and effect.

An overview of children's language development, based on literacy and communication from kindergarten through grade 5, can be found in Table 6–13.

Table 6–13. *An Overview of Language Development. Literacy and Communication: Expectations from Kindergarten Through Third Grade*

Kindergarten
1. Follows one- to two-step directions in sequence
2. Listens to and understands stories read to the class
3. Answers simple yes/no and *Wh*-questions (e.g., "What did you . . . ?")
4. Produces clear speech
5. Asks for information
6. Participates in and initiates conversation
7. Understands reading from top to bottom and left to right
8. Understands words that rhyme
9. Can match words based on their sounds
10. Matches some sounds with letters
11. Has sight word recognition for some words
12. Prints names
13. Draws a picture to tell a story

First Grade
14. Understands and can recall information
15. Follows two- to three-step directions in sequence
16. Answers more complex questions
17. Can tell and retell stories with logical order of events
18. Produces a variety of sentence types and supplies directions
19. Stays on topic during a conversation
20. Asks and answers *Wh*-questions (i.e., *who, what, where, why,* and *when*)
21. Can match spoken with written words and can identify sounds in shorter words
22. May sound out unfamiliar words when reading
23. Prints words and spells frequently used words correctly
24. Can write short stories

Table 6–13. *continued*

Second Grade

25. Follows three- to four-step directions

26. Understands concepts that involve location and time

27. Can answer questions about a story

28. Produces more complex sentences

29. Can explain words and ideas

30. Uses language in more complex ways (e.g., to inform, persuade, entertain)

31. Maintains topic and turn-taking in conversation

32. Displays intact phonological awareness for the correspondence between sounds, syllables, words, and longer spoken utterances with written forms

33. Has expanded sight word recognition

34. Monitors reading accuracy by rereading

35. Can explain the main ideas of a story

36. Writes clearly and uses a range of sentence types

37. Moves from inventive to accurate spelling

Third Grade

38. Shows good listening skills and continued progress in conversation skills

39. Can summarize, predict, and explain when working with reading tasks

40. Displays prediction and mastery of phonics in reading skills

41. Uses learned information to learn new topics

42. Uses topic-specific vocabulary in conversation and classroom discussion

43. Can explain material that has been learned in the classroom

44. Can ask and answer questions related to material learned in the classroom

45. Makes continued progress in monitoring reading accuracy

46. Composes stories and spells simple words correctly while using details in writing

47. Asks and answers questions about reading materials

48. Rereads and corrects errors

49. Spells most words correctly

Source: Reproduced and adapted with permission from D. Wellman Owre and M. Kennedy Brennan (2002). An overview of language development. *Literacy and communication: Expectations from kindergarten through fifth grade.*

SUMMARY

Children's language continues to develop during the school-age years. Progress appears in academic skills and social interaction.

◆ Vocabulary development with the acquisition of 3,000 words per academic year
◆ Advances in syntax characterized by noun and verb phrase elaboration, along with the production of longer and more complex sentence forms
◆ The development of narrative discourse in earlier grades, with the emergence of expository discourse in later grades
◆ The development of reading and writing skills, based on phonological awareness and vocabulary development

KEY WORDS

Analogies

Causal relationships

Concrete operations stage

Conjunctions

Context clues

Critical thinking

Derivational morpheme

Discourse

Domain-specific

Expository discourse

Formal operations

Idioms

Incidental learning

Lexicon

Mental state verbs

Metalinguistic awareness

Metalinguistic competence

Metalinguistic strategies

Metaphors

Narrative

Noun phrase

Phonological awareness

Pragmatics

Proverbs

Similes

Subordinate clause

Subordinating conjunctions

Subordination

Syllogisms

Verb phrase

Verbal reasoning

STUDY QUESTIONS

1. Explain the role of pragmatics in successful peer interaction.

2. Describe the importance of verbal reasoning in children's academic skills.

3. Explain the role of morphology in expanding sentence length.

4. Explain the differences between narrative and expository discourse.

REFERENCES

Akhtar, N., Jipson, J., & Callanan, M. A. (2001). Learning words through overhearing. *Child Development, 72,* 416–430.

Avivi-Reich, M, Jakubczyk, A., Daneman, M., & Schneider, B. A. (2015). How age, linguistic status, and the nature of the auditory scene alter the manner in which listening comprehension is achieved in multitalker conversations. *Journal of Speech, Language, and Hearing Research, 58,* 1570–1591.

Beck, I. L., McKeown, M. G., & Kucan, L. (2013). *Bringing words to life: Robust vocabulary instruction* (2nd ed.). New York, NY: Guilford Press.

Berko Gleason, J., & Bernstein Ratner, N. (2017). *The development of language.* Boston, MA: Pearson.

Berman, R. A. (2004). Between emergence and mastery: The long developmental route of language acquisition. In R. A. Berman (Ed.), *Language development across childhood and adolescence* (pp. 9–34). Amsterdam, Netherlands: Benjamin.

Berman, R. A., & Nir-Sagiv, B. (2007). Comparing narrative and expository text construction across adolescence: A developmental paradox. *Discourse Processes: A Multidisciplinary Journal, 43*(2), 79–120.

Berman, R. A., & Slobin, D. I. (1994). *Relating events in narrative: A crosslinguistic developmental study.* Hillsdale, NJ: Lawrence Erlbaum Associates.

Bernstein, D. K., & Levey, S. (2009). Language development: A review. In D. K. Bernstein & E. Tiegerman-Farber (Eds.), *Language and communication disorders in children* (5th ed., pp. 27–94). Boston, MA: Allyn & Bacon.

Bliss, L. S. (2002). *Discourse impairments: Assessment and intervention applications.* Boston, MA: Allyn & Bacon.

Dijkstra, K., Eerland, A., Zijlmans, J., & Post, L. S. (2014). Embodied cognition, abstract concepts, and the benefits of new technology for implicit body manipulation. *Frontiers in Psychology, 5,* 1–8. https://doi.org/10.3389/fpsyg.2014.00757

Gabig, C. S. (2014). Language development in middle and late childhood and adolescence. In S. Levey (Ed.), *Introduction to language development* (pp. 211–246). Los Angeles, CA: Sage.

Galotti, K. M. (2017). *Cognitive development: Infancy through adolescence.* Los Angeles, CA: Sage.

Gillon, G. T. (2004). *Phonological awareness: From research to practice.* New York, NY: Guilford Press.

Grice, H. P. (1975). Logic and conversation. In P. Cole & J. Morgan (Eds.), *Studies in syntax and semantics III: Speech acts* (pp. 183–198). New York, NY: Academic Press.

Justice, L. M., & Ezell, H. K. (2016). *The syntax handbook* (2nd ed.). Austin: TX. Pro-Ed.

Kieffer, M. J., & Lesaux, N. K. (2007). Breaking down words to build meaning: Morphology, vocabulary, and reading comprehension in the urban classroom. *The Reading Teacher, 61*(2), 134–144.

Lundine, J. P., & McCauley, R. J. (2016). A tutorial on expository discourse: Structure, development, and disorders in children and adolescents. *American Journal of Speech-Language Pathology, 25,* 306–320.

Markovits, H., Schleifer, M., & Fortier, L. (1989). Development of elementary deductive reasoning in young children. *Developmental Psychology, 25*(5), 787–793.

Nelson, K., & Nelson, A. P. (1990). Category production in response to script and category cues by kindergarten and second-grade children. *Journal of Applied Developmental Psychology, 11,* 431–446.

Nippold, M. A. (1998). *Later language development: The school-age and adolescent years* (2nd ed.) Austin, TX: Pro-Ed.

Nippold, M. A. (2000). Language development during the adolescent years: Aspects of pragmatics, syntax, and semantics. *Topics in Language Disorders, 20*(2), 15–28.

Nippold, M. A. (2006). Language development in school-age children, adolescents, and adults. In K. Brown (Ed.), *Encyclopedia of language and linguistics* (2nd ed., pp. 368–373). Philadelphia, PA: Elsevier

Nippold, M. A. (2007). *Later language development: School-age children, adolescents, and young adults.* Austin, TX: Pro-Ed.

Nippold, M. A. (2009). School-age children talk about chess: Does knowledge drive syntactic complexity? *Journal of Speech, Language, and Hearing Research, 52,* 856–871.

Nippold, M. A., & Duthie, J. K. (2003). Mental imagery and idiom comprehension: A comparison of school-age children and adults. *Journal of Language and Hearing Research, 46*(4), 788–799.

Nippold, M. A., Frantz-Kaspar, M. W., Cramond, P., Kirk, C., Hayward-Mayhew, C., & MacKinnon, M. (2014). Conversational and narrative speaking in adolescents: Examining the use of complex syntax. *Journal of Speech, Language, and Hearing Research, 57,* 876–886.

Nippold, M. A., Hesketh, L. J., Duthie, J. K., & Mansfield, T. C. (2005). Conversational versus expository discourse: A study of syntactic development in children, adolescents, and adults. *Journal of Speech, Language, and Hearing Research, 48,* 1048–1064.

Nippold, M. A., Leonard, L. B., & Kail, R. (1984). Syntactic and conceptual factors in children's understanding of metaphors. *Journal of Speech and Hearing Research, 27,* 197–205.

Nippold, M. A., & Rudzinski, M. (1993). Familiarity and transparency in idiom explanation: A developmental study of children and adolescents. *Journal of Speech and Hearing Research, 36,* 728–737.

Nippold, M. A., & Sun, L. (2010). Expository writing in children and adolescents: A classroom assessment tool. *Perspectives on Language Learning and Education: Adolescent Language, 17,* 100–107. Published by Division 1, American Speech-Language-Hearing Association.

Owre, D., & Kennedy Brennan, M. (2002). *An overview of language development: Literacy and communication: Expectations from kindergarten through fifth grade.* Retrieved from http://www.asha.org/uploadedFiles/Build-Your-Childs-Skills-Third-to-Fifth-Grade.pdf

Piaget, J. (1954). *The construction of reality in the child.* New York, NY: Basic Books.

Piaget, J., & Inhelder, B. (1969). *The psychology of the child.* New York, NY: Basic Books.

Ram, G., Marinellie, S. A., Benigno, J., & McCarthy, J. (2013). Morphological analysis in context versus isolation: Use of a dynamic assessment task with school-age children. *Language, Speech, and Hearing Services in Schools, 24,* 32–47.

Roseberry-McKibbin, C. (2007). *Language disorders in children: A multicultural and case perspective.* Boston, MA: Allyn & Bacon.

Roseberry-McKibbin, C. (2014). *Multicultural children with special language needs: Practical strategies for assessment and intervention* (4th ed.). Oceanside, CA: Academic Communication Associates.

Snyder, W., & Hyams, N. (2015). Minimality effects in children's passives. In E. di Domenico, C. Hamann, & S. Matteini (Eds.), *Structures, strategies and beyond: Studies in honour of Andrea Belletti* (pp. 343–368). Amsterdam, Netherlands: John Benjamin.

Steffani, S. A. (2007). Identifying embedded and conjoined complex sentences: Making it simple. *Contemporary Issues in Communication Sciences and Disorders, 34,* 44–54.

Stein, N., & Glenn, C. (1979). An analysis of story comprehension in elementary school children. In R. Freedle (Ed.), *New directions in discourse processing* (Vol. 2). Norwood, NJ: Ablex.

Sun, L., & Nippold, M. A. (2012). Narrative writing in children and adolescents: Examining the literate lexicon. *Language, Speech, and Hearing Services in Schools, 43,* 2–13.

Tessler, M., & Goodman, N. D. (2017). *Some arguments are probably valid: Syllogistic reasoning as communication.* Retrieved from https://web.stanford.edu/~ngoodman/papers/cogsci14-syllogisms_tessler.pdf

Ward-Lonergan, J. M. (2010). Expository discourse abilities in school-age children and adolescents with language disorders: Nature of the problem. In M. A. Nippold & C. M. Scott (Eds.), *Expository discourse in children, adolescents, and adults: Development and disorders* (pp. 155–189). New York, NY: Psychology Press/Taylor and Francis.

Ward-Lonergan, J. M., & Duthie, J. K. (2014). *Expository discourse intervention for adolescents with language disorders.* Retrieved from https://coe.uoregon.edu/cds/files/2011/09/Expository-Discourse-Intervention.pdf

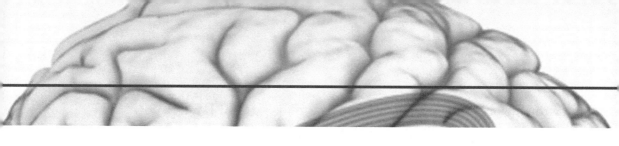

1

The Development of Literacy Skills

Sylvia F. Diehl

Case Study

Pat is 4 years old. He loves to point out his favorite stores to his Mother when riding in the car. He frequently points out signs, especially McDonald's and Toys R Us. Pat loves to read books with his big sister and will often use his toys to act out the stories they read. He is beginning to learn what sound /p/ makes and that it is in his name (i.e., the sound and symbol relationship). He can identify his own name and enjoys finding the special letters in his name on signs and in books. After reading this chapter, you will understand why these abilities are important in providing the foundation for literacy development.

Literacy encompasses the ability to read, write, speak, listen, and think effectively (Meltzer, Smith, & Clark, 2001). The purpose of reading is to gather meaning from the printed page (Dickenson, Golinkoff, & Hirsch-Paseki, 2010). The development of literacy is indivisibly linked with the development of language (Goodrich, Mudrich, & Robinson, 2015; Nelson, 2010). One usually thinks of the development of language as starting in infancy, with literacy skills beginning during formal school instruction. It is true that the process of identifying letters and words is best when systematically taught, and this instruction typically occurs at school. Think for a moment about Pat's identification of the fast food sign. This shows print awareness that Pat developed before formal teaching. Moreover, comprehension of the written word is a very complex skill that includes language and cognitive abilities whose building blocks are achieved before formal teaching (Kamhi, 2009). The process of acquiring literacy cannot be viewed as beginning with school instruction. Instead, the acquisition of literacy begins in infancy (Newman, Ratner, Juszcyk, & Juszcyk, 2006). Language and literacy skills foster one another and help each other to flourish. Oral language nourishes reading and writing development, while reading and writing development promotes growth in oral language. In short, literacy skills are a means for a child to learn and think about the world in increasingly complex ways (Morrow, 2015; Teale & Sulzby, 1986).

CHAPTER OBJECTIVES

The purpose of this chapter is to explore normal literacy development from infancy through adolescence. After reading this chapter, you should understand:

◆ The interdependence of language and literacy
◆ The importance of metalinguistics
◆ The developmental stages of literacy in the preschool through adolescent years
◆ Methods to support literacy development across all ages

This chapter begins with an examination of the relationship between language and literacy, followed by a review of the development of literacy for preschoolers, elementary school-age children, and adolescents. A brief discussion concerning methods to support literacy development follows each section.

THE DEVELOPMENT OF LITERACY

In infancy, when children are beginning to learn speech and language, abilities are acquired that form the framework for later literacy learning. For instance, when a child's mother says, "Here comes your Daddy," the child learns to comprehend the word *Daddy* separately from the whole stream of words. This segmentation skill provides the foundation for formal segmentation tasks, such as, "What is the first sound in *nap*?" Children also become aware of print well before school-age when exposed to books, magazines, grocery lists, advertisements, television shows, and educational toys.

Children learn that pictures or symbols stand for ideas. For example, young children easily identify the trademark symbol of their favorite fast food restaurant or identify the black and white outline in the book as a "cow." These are just a few examples of the early foundational learning experiences that provide the underpinnings for conscious formal learning (Dickinson, Golinkoff, & Hirsch-Pasek, 2010).

EMERGENT LITERACY

Emergent literacy is typically associated with the preschool years (Storch & Whitehurst, 2001; Whitehurst & Lonigan, 1998). From 3 to 5 years of age, children gather information about print and sounds. They make sense out of reading and writing in very elementary ways related to symbols or codes (i.e., awareness of print; appreciation of rhyming in songs; early draw-ing and writing) and language-related skills (i.e., vocabulary, syntax, story struc-ture) before they experience formal lit-eracy instruction (Justice & Ezell, 2004; Westerveld, Trembath, Shellshear, & Paynter, 2016). This foundation supports the development of abilities for accu-rate fluent reading with comprehension (National Institute of Child Health and Human Development [NICHD], 2008). During this time, the child starts to learn to think about language in a more mind-ful way. This represents a transition from using language automatically for com-munication to conscious thought about the use of language. This ability is called **metalinguistic knowledge**, which means "thinking about language."

Metalinguistic skills are essential for learning to read and write (Laurent & Mar-tinot, 2009; van Kleeck, 1994). In addition, learning another language acts to promote metalinguistic awareness (Naqvi, Thorne, Pfitscher, Nordstokke, & McKeough, 2013). As the child progresses through school, each area of language becomes the focus of metalinguistic examination (Justice, 2006). Early metalinguistic skills typically involve **print awareness** and **phonological awareness** (Justice, 2006; Justice & Ezell, 2004). Developing print and phonologi-cal awareness is a gradual developmental process (Suortti & Lipponen, 2016). Young children exhibit print awareness by real-izing that the print underneath a picture gives additional information.

DEVELOPMENT OF CODE-RELATED LITERACY

Phonological awareness begins in the early preschool years and continues throughout the early elementary school years (Troia, Stone, Silliman, Ehren, & Wallach, 2014). Phonological awareness refers to an individual's awareness of the phonological structure, or sound struc-ture, of words. It starts with an interest in the sounds in words and with enjoyment of rhymes, songs, and chants. At 2 years of age, many children can detect rhyme and alliteration (van Kleeck & Schuele, 1987). Later this matures into more conscious metalinguistic awareness of **onset**, **rimes**, and individual phonemes. This kind of gradual progression proceeds through the aspects of phonological awareness, including a child's ability to understand how the sounds of language relate to one another to form the meaning of words. Phonological awareness involves iden-tifying and manipulating whole words, syllables, initial consonants, and word chunks at the end of words (rime). Exam-ples of children's phonological awareness follow:

Awareness of the sound structure of words

Understanding that the word *dog* has one syllable and *banana* has three syllables

Understanding that the word *cat* consists of three alphabet letters

Having the ability to identify rhyming words and, later, to generate rhyme

Identifying the ending sound of the word *hat*

By 4 years of age, children become aware that print has certain conventions. For example, they learn that print is orga-nized from left to right and that a grocery list is organized differently than a storybook. Children learn that print can represent distinct names, depending on the varied order of letters in words (Justice & Ezell, 2004). At this stage of development, children's phonological awareness becomes much more visible, graduating to the ability to segment sound units in words. Development goes from larger segments, such as parsing sentences into words, to smaller segments, such as dividing multisyllabic words into syllables (e.g., *ba-na-na* and *mon-key*) (Moats, 2009). They also begin to recognize when words rhyme (e.g., *hat-cat*).

As children grow, phonological awareness increases and more complex phonological awareness tasks are mastered. Earlier tasks typically involve matching letters (i.e., Can you find another "G"?), blending (i.e., What word does /b/-/i/-/n/ make?), and adding sounds to form new words (i.e., add /s/ to the beginning of the word *top*). Later developing phonological tasks involve analysis, such as counting the number of segments in words (i.e., How many sounds are in the word *cough*?), segmenting (i.e., Say each sound in the word *sun*), and deleting sounds (i.e., Say *spot* without the /s/) (Yopp & Yopp, 2009).

LITERACY DEVELOPMENTAL MILESTONES (MEANING RELATED)

The preschool years are an eventful time for building the foundation for literacy development (Chall, 1996; Justice, 2006; Moats, 2009; Shipley & McAfee, 2009; Tompkins, 2003; van Kleeck, 2006; Wolfersberger, Reutzel, Sudweeks, & Fawson, 2004; Wood, 2007; Yopp & Yopp, 2009) (Table 7–1). By age 3, children are starting to think and communicate about their

world in more complex ways. They are learning to communicate about people, objects, and events that are not actually present. This involves **decontextualized language**, or language used to refer to things not present in the immediate environment. Experience with decontextualized language is crucial to later reading development and text comprehension (Olaussen, 2016). In fact, comprehension of complex language is the best predictor of reading comprehension. During the preschool years, children also develop an understanding of simple **narratives** or stories. Vocabulary develops as children learn new words from books. This, in turn, feeds the growth of a larger and more varied vocabulary along with the ability to retell events.

> Very early print awareness begins to appear when children develop an interest in print and realize that print carries meaning (Justice & Ezell, 2004). They first begin with an understanding of the letters in their own names and, in this way, learn that alphabet letters are "special" (Wood, 2007).

By age 4, children's vocabulary and sentences continue to develop into more and more complex forms. Children are now able to tell stories that remain mostly on topic but do not have a typical story structure (Stadler & Ward, 2005). A description of children's narrative development is provided in Chapter 6, showing that children begin with simple recounts of events. This early knowledge of stories matures into an awareness of narrative **text structure** (Hedberg & Westby, 1993). Text structure refers to the organization of written text. Examples of the features and

Table 7–1. Preschool Literacy Development and Literacy Activities

Print Concepts	Phonological Awareness	Spelling	Vocabulary	Narrative Development	Writing	Supporting Preschool Literacy Development
• Interest in print	• Enjoys playing with the sounds in words and songs	• Scribbling common	• Ever-expanding vocabulary for words in their environment	• Retells stories that stay mostly on topic	• Starts out scribbling, which turns into writing that looks like letters and words	• A literacy-rich environment
• Groups of letters have meaning	• Can separate sentences into words and words into syllables	• May use letter symbols but no sound symbol correspondence	• Able to use subordinating and coordinating words to form more complex sentences	• Relates stories to personal experience	• Will interpret his or her writing and drawing for others to form a whole meaning	• Book sharing or dialogic reading
• Turns pages one at a time	• Knows words are made of sounds	• May be able to spell name		• By age 4, answers *wh*-questions about read-aloud stories		• Pointing out details about print
• Looks from left to right and top to bottom	• Produces words that rhyme	• Direction of writing on page				• Songs
		• Some letter sound matches by age 4				• Fingerplay that promotes sound play and manipulation of the sounds in words
						• Dramatic play
						• Varied writing experiences

183

organization of text structure for narrative (story) elements of fiction follow:

Characters: People involved in the story

Setting: Places where the action occurs

Problem: Challenges that the characters face

Solution: How the challenge is resolved

Plot: Events that make up a story

As stories are read to preschoolers, the narrative elements become expected and start to be included in their retelling. Other types of text structure related to nonfiction are incorporated in the same way. With exposure, these formats become familiar and the framework for their structure is incorporated into the preschoolers' repertoire. Here are some examples of the features and organization of the text structure for nonfiction:

Cause and effect: A discussion of how one action can cause another action to occur

Sequence of events: The chronological order of actions or events

Description: A topic that is explained in terms of characteristics, features, and examples

Comparison and contrast: An explanation of how two or more events are alike and/or different

Knowledge of text structure supports children's comprehension of both fiction and nonfiction texts by providing them with the format for the ideas presented in various types of texts, along with the relationship among these ideas. With knowledge of the framework of text structure, children can comprehend how words and sentences are arranged within varied types of texts, from a simple grocery list to the popular *Harry Potter* series. For example, children must organize their thinking to match the thought of the author of the text and arrive at an understanding of the sequence of events and the motivations of the characters in narratives (i.e., the reasons for their actions). Children without exposure to text structure may approach reading without a basic framework or plan which makes comprehension of the story more difficult.

Metalinguistic abilities are an integral part of language and literacy learning, because children must be aware of how to determine word meaning. In terms of word meaning (semantics), readers often consciously wonder about the meaning of an unfamiliar word. They may try to decipher the word in context (i.e., by determining the meaning via other words that surround it) or look it up in a dictionary.

SUPPORTING LITERACY DEVELOPMENT IN THE PRESCHOOL YEARS

Support for literacy skills in the preschool years is intended to ensure that a child has a variety of literacy experiences. During this stage of development, children are exposed to varying text structures and are given the opportunity to engage in prewriting activities (e.g., scribbling and drawing). Four strategies are recommended to support literacy development in the preschool years: providing: (1) a print-rich environment and prewriting activities; (2) book sharing; (3) phonological awareness activities; and (4) symbolic play (see Table 7–1).

Print-Rich Environment

Scribbling and drawing is an important part of children's literacy development. It provides the beginning motor practice for formal writing and provides additional information about the sound symbol connection. Additionally, children have interesting narratives and imaginative play entwined with their scribbling and early drawing. Listening to children as they draw reveals their inner fantasies. Children often use drawing to test out their knowledge (Coates & Coates, 2016). Therefore, it is important to provide a print-rich environment at home as an important ingredient in this experiential effort to support children's literacy development (Guo, Justice, Kaderavek, & McGinty, 2012; Roskos & Neuman, 2001; Wolfersberger et al., 2004).

There are a variety of reading materials that support different genres such as stories, poetry, directions, grocery lists, and recipes. An assortment of materials set the stage for purposeful encounters, including writing paper, construction paper, whiteboards, easels, chalk, crayons, markers, and glue and stickers. Modeling writing and drawing with young children encourages their prewriting experience. Adults should listen to children's narrations of their drawings (Coates & Coates, 2016). Early drawing and writing attempts should be celebrated and

proudly displayed in the classroom and on the refrigerator at home.

> Children's early writing begins with a mix of drawing efforts with attempts to "write." Very young children begin their attempts to write with scribbling and move to drawing. There is a connection between these early writing attempts and children's oral language skills (Coates & Coates, 2016; Dyson, 2000), as the combination of writing, drawing, and language is integrated to form meaning.

Book Sharing

Book sharing has been shown to provide an important experience for preschoolers (Pentimonti et al., 2012; Towson, Gallagher, & Bingham, 2016; van Kleeck, 2006; Zevenbergen & Whitehurst, 2003), allowing the novice reader to have a dialogue with a peer or an adult who is a more experienced reader (van Kleeck, 2006). Effective book sharing is interactive and involves more than just reading books with a child. This kind of book sharing is called **dialogic reading**. It encourages a gradual shift in the conversational roles of the adult and child during shared interactive reading (van Druten-Frietman, Strating, Denessen, & Verhoeven, 2016). The final outcome in dialogic reading is for the child to become the storyteller and the adult an active listener (Towson, Gallagher, & Bingham, 2016; Zevenbergen & Whitehurst, 2003). Here are some factors to consider before, during, and after shared interactive reading (Colmar, 2011, 2014; Lonigan & Whitehurst, 1998; Justice, Kaderavek, Bowles, & Grimm, 2005;

Koppenhaver, Erickson, & Skotko, 2001; van Kleeck, Vander Woude, & Hammett, 2006; Whitehurst et al., 1994; Zevenbergen, Whitehurst, & Zevenbergen, 2003; Ziolkowski & Goldstein, 2008):

♦ Before reading, consider the choice of book being read. The content and length of the book and the complexity of the language should be a good match with the child's interest, attention span, and comprehension abilities. A child should be encouraged to make predictions about the book's content from its cover.

♦ During reading, it is important that the adult make the experience a positive one by reading with expression and interest. With unfamiliar books, the adult should do more of the talking. As the child becomes more familiar with the book, the balance should shift to the child (Whitehurst et al., 1994). Adults should periodically pause to encourage commenting by the child. When the child volunteers a comment, the comment could be expanded. Fill-in-the-blanks (e.g., *I think he is going to ___*), *wh*-questions (e.g., *who, what, where,*and *why*), or prediction questions (e.g., *What do you think will happen next?*) are useful to encourage the child to repeat the expanded comment or fill in new information. Point out features of print that would be special to the child, such as the letters in their name. This kind of active interaction should be periodic so it does not interrupt the meaning of the book.

♦ After reading, it is important to talk about the story that has been read. Elements of text structure should be included when appropriate (e.g., characters, settings, problems, solutions,

and the plot). The child and adult could also discuss how the content relates to their lives and discuss the new words that they have encountered, along with what they would like to read the next time.

> Shared interactive reading should be done frequently and routinely to help the child learn about the organization of books and the text structure found in them. New vocabulary words should be discussed as they appear in the text, along with periodic questions and comments about the story (Huebner, 2000; van Kleeck, 2008). Indicating aspects of print during reading, such as pointing to words while reading, has been shown to have a positive effect on reading acquisition (Pentimonti et al., 2012).

Phonological Awareness Activities

Playing with sounds helps build the phonological abilities needed when formal reading instruction begins (Phillips, Clancy-Menchetti, & Lonigan, 2008). Songs, poems, alliterative games, and rhyming books help provide early experiences with manipulating sound. For young children, these phonological awareness activities should not be seen as schoolwork but as an extension of play (Yopp & Yopp, 2009).

Sociodramatic Play Experiences

Sociodramatic play experiences are also foundational for successful literacy development (Vygotsky, 1967). In sociodramatic play, children use an object to represent something other than what it is (e.g., a box for a car or a block for a telephone). The ability to substitute or represent one thing for another is a rung on the ladder to realizing that letters grouped together can represent the spoken word. In other words, children realize that alphabet letters are symbols that represent spoken sounds and that these letters can be connected to represent words. Symbolic play also encourages the language growth needed in literacy attainment (Wilford, 2000). Sociodramatic play has six ingredients, according to Smilansky (1968). These ingredients are: (1) make-believing using objects, (2) assuming a make-believe role, (3) make-believing about a situation or action, (4) persisting or being able to continue the play in face of challenges, (5) using language to communicate the context of play, and (6) interacting socially while playing. For example, children were observed in a preschool classroom acting out a book called *Mrs. Wishy Washy* that they had previously read as a class. This is a story about a farmwoman who washes her animals but they keep getting dirty. The teacher had the objects of the farm animals, a play bathtub, and a brown towel out in the reading center. The children pretended to be the animals and the farm woman. They would get the animals "dirty" by throwing them on the brown towel and repeating repetitive lines in the book like, "Oh, lovely mud!" One child even suggested getting the animals dirty by coloring them with water-based markers. When they couldn't find any markers, they agree to pretend. They worked together enacting the story many times and changing roles. This play context helped cement the important language and literacy factors discussed, such as symbol development, character perspective, and expressive vocabulary. Sociodramatic play has been found to benefit literacy development in both monolingual and bilingual children (Banerjee, Alsalman, & Alqafari, 2016; Eisenchlas, Schalley, & Moyes, 2016).

Technology and Literacy

Despite mixed feelings by many on the subject, the impact of technology on literacy must be recognized. Children are now exposed to digital media from a young age (Kozminsky & Asher-Sadon, 2013). Young children are frequently using Internet applications, such as Starfall.com and PBS.kids, which read stories to them or present phonological awareness and phonic games. In the classroom, technology is being used as teaching aids. Whiteboards and computers are being used to motivate, provide greater visual supports for the concepts being taught, and monitor progress. Research on this practice produces varied results. For instance, Dennis, Whalon, Kraut, and Herron (2016) studied the effects of using iPads in teaching vocabulary. They found that both digital and nondigital approaches were effective. Korat and Segal-Drori (2016) compared e-book versus printed book reading and found that the e-book showed more positive effects.

LITERACY DEVELOPMENT IN THE ELEMENTARY SCHOOL YEARS

The elementary school years mark a time of enormous growth in literacy development (Blachman, 1997; Chall, 1996; Kaderavek & Justice, 2004; Shipley & McAfee, 2009; Tompkins, 2003; Wood, 2007) (Tables 7–2 and 7–3). Children go from identifying sound and letter pairings in kindergarten to

Table 7–2. *Literacy Development from Kindergarten Through Grade 2*

Grade	Phonological Awareness	Spelling	Vocabulary	Fluency	Comprehension	Writing
K	• Segments onset and rime (*m* followed by *-an*) • Finds words that start with the same phoneme • Blend sounds together	• Knows the letters and their sounds • Identifies all upper- and lowercase letters • Can identify words in the same word family	• Can talk about things that are not physically present • Knows about 2,000 to 3,000 words	• Expands vocabulary using more words not in immediate environment	• Sight reads high-frequency words and some CVC words	• Predicts what is next in stories • Answers questions about read-aloud stories • Draws and writes
1	• Changes phonemes by adding, deleting, or substituting phonemes • Has more advanced abilities to blend sounds together	• Understands that words have a distinct spelling • Spells by sounding out • Spells CVC and sight words	• Knows about 2,000 to 3,000 words • Understands the word relations of antonyms and synonyms	• Creates meaning while reading • Rereads to get words right	• Answers questions about text • Follows simple written instructions	• Begins with capital letters • Ends with period • Spacing irregular
2	• Reads longer words by sounding out using phonic abilities • Reads words with one and two syllables	• Traditional spelling increases • Consonant blends and digraphs are acquired • Some morphological structures are used	• Uses context of reading to help decode words • Begins to use root words, prefixes, and suffixes to decode words	• Reading speed increases	• Sequences events of story • Uses context clues to help comprehension	• Writes narrative and expository text with model • Variety of sentence forms • Writing has beginning, middle, and end • Legible writing • Regular spacing

Table 7–3. *Literacy Development from Grades 3 Through 10*

Grade	Spelling	Vocabulary	Fluency	Comprehension	Writing
3	• Mostly adultlike spelling • Long vowel and control vowel spelling patterns • Complex consonant patterns	• Vocabulary continues to be enriched through reading • Knows between 4,000 and 6,000 words	• Reads at 114 words per minute • Word analysis skills when reading	• Monitors comprehension while reading • Clarifies when does not comprehend • Knows fact/opinion • Knows cause/effect	• Narratives, letters, simple expositories • Uses more cohesive devices
4–6	• Identifies misspellings by using orthographic knowledge • Applies inflectional endings • Uses syllabication	• Uses vocabulary effectively in writing • Knows between 5,000 and 8,000 words	• Fluent reading • Understands an increasing number of text structures	• Makes inferences from text • Can summarize and paraphrase	• Organizes writing into beginning, middle, and end • Main idea is evident • Develops characters and plots • Reviews and revises
7–10	• Uses phonological, orthographic, and morphologic knowledge to spell • Latin and Greek affixes and root words • Etymologies	• Attains vocabulary needed in content areas	• Reads fluently for learning and for entertainment	• Reads independently for new knowledge and research projects	• Complex sentences in writing • Coherent and cohesive writing • A variety of text structures are explored

reading a variety of text genres (e.g., types of text) fluently by the fifth grade. Literacy development occurs across the critical literacy areas below:

◆ Phonological awareness
◆ Vocabulary
◆ Reading comprehension
◆ Spelling
◆ Reading fluency
◆ Writing

Phonological Awareness and Literacy Learning

Formal reading instruction begins in earnest when a child enters kindergarten. Phonological awareness is now a large part of formal literacy learning. Phonological awareness is a broad term that incorporates the size of a sound unit and how that sound unit is used in different contexts (Yopp & Yopp, 2009). There are levels of complexity for the sound units being learned:

Larger sound units—beginning with sentences, then moving to words

Smaller sound units—beginning with syllables (e.g., ba–na–na), then moving to individual phonemes in words (e.g., /b/)

Children gradually develop awareness of the size of units, proceeding from the larger units of sentences and syllables in the preschool years to individual phonemes or sounds in the kindergarten years. The way in which sound units are manipulated (i.e., matching, blending, segmenting, substituting, and deleting) develops from kindergarten through grade 2 (see Table 7–2).

In kindergarten, a child can identify the first sound of a spoken word and separate it from its rime. For example, the word *pin* begins with /p/, which is the onset, and the rime is "in."

Monosyllabic words can be split into two parts—the onset and the rime. The onset is the initial consonant sound (*b-* in *bag* and *sw-* in *swim*) and the *rime* is the vowel and the rest of the syllable that follows (*-ag* in *bag* and *-im* in *swim*).

In grade 1, children continue to manipulate the sounds of words through compound word construction (e.g., *railroad*) and syllable deletion (e.g., omitting a syllable from a word). Examples consist of saying the word *railroad* without *road* and saying the word *fishing* without the *-ing*. By the end of the first grade and into second grade, children begin to work with even smaller sound segments. They can now count the number of phonemes or sound units in a word (e.g., *nut* has three sounds). They may be asked to delete the initial or final phoneme of a word (e.g., Say *stop* without the /s/). In addition to deleting sounds, the first grader is able to blend sounds together to form words (Moats, 2009), such as blending "c-a-t" to form the word *cat*.

Some words are recognized by sight at this stage of development, but many words are sounded out phoneme by phoneme. Additionally, during the second grade, word patterns are learned (i.e., the pattern of letters that form certain frequently encountered words, such as *the, is, are, these,* and other examples that occur frequently in written text). Word pattern recognition acts to speed up reading skills.

Vocabulary Development and Reading Comprehension

Vocabulary knowledge is a powerful predictor of reading development. However, there is variance in the vocabulary knowledge that children possess when entering school (Cervetti, Wright, & Hwang, 2016). Differences are likely related to the experience base of the children and the frequency of words the children are exposed to at home. In fact, vocabulary size in first grade is a predictor of reading comprehension in the eleventh grade (Cunningham & Stanovich, 1997). Another factor in reading comprehension and vocabulary development is the amount of reading experience. For example, exposure to new words enhances children's memory for the pronunciation, spelling, and meaning of that word (Rosenthal & Ehri, 2008). Because of the differences related to their literary experience, the developmental ranges presented here are only an estimate of typically developing children.

In kindergarten, the child's ability to read and discuss decontextualized ideas expands. Typically, topics discussed in the classroom are not physically present. For example, a preschool-age child may talk about a policeman when he sees a policeman on the street. In the kindergarten classroom, a discussion might be held about community helpers, such as policemen and firemen, but they need not be present for this discussion to occur. Ideas are discussed using oral language, pictures, and books. The kindergartner also expands his or her ability to tell stories or narratives that follow a sequential order of events (Stadler & Ward, 2005).

It is estimated that a first grader acquires 2,000 to 3,000 words and will learn about 3,000 words a year in the following years (Carlisle & Katz, 2005). By the third grade, vocabulary continues to develop and children are beginning to understand complex word relationships. Children enjoy nonliteral language, such as humor, idioms, and early **figurative language** (e.g., groups of words that change or exaggerate meaning because they are grouped together). The first grader uses this vocabulary to gather comprehension clues about pictures, titles, and headings within a book. He or she can make accurate predictions using this information.

In the second grade, language skills continue to expand and children are able to identify root words (*stand*), prefixes (*mis-*), and suffixes (*-ing*). This is an important step in helping the child move away from sound-by-sound reading into more fluent comprehension of text and words (e.g., *misunderstanding*). Second graders also have more fully developed narratives (Stadler & Ward, 2005). They can create a full episode including setting, plot, character, and resolution. Second graders start to comprehend written text without the aid of an adult (Wood, 2007). They become more independent in their reading and new word learning. They may use dictionaries and other resources to support comprehension. As they mature through elementary school, children are able to comprehend lengthier texts, such as books with chapters.

By the fourth grade, independent reading is well developed (Wood, 2007). By the fifth grade, children's vocabulary continues to develop and they become more interested in exploring nonfiction reading and enjoy biographies.

Spelling

Learning about spelling supports reading development by increasing children's knowledge of phonemic awareness, increasing their knowledge of the alphabetic principle, and making sight words easier to remember. Recent studies have shown the importance of formal spelling instruction (Graham & Santangelo, 2014). The development of spelling involves a blend of three types of linguistic knowledge (Bourassa & Treiman, 2001). It is the integration of these three types of linguistic knowledge that leads to spelling expertise:

> The first type of linguistic knowledge is phonological knowledge, helping a child to form a link between sounds and letters.

> The second type of linguistic knowledge is orthographic knowledge, allowing a child to understand that a sound can be represented in print in different ways (e.g., the "*oo*" sound in the word sh*oo*t can also be spelled as "*oe*" in the word sh*oe*).

> The third type of linguistic knowledge is morphological knowledge, providing the knowledge of inflections such as *-er* and *-ing* (e.g., *bigger* and *running*).

Kindergartners and first graders primarily depend on their phonological knowledge (Ehri, 2000), using their understanding of the sound-symbol relationship to spell words. For example, children may spell the word *you* as "u" or the word *night* as "nit."

Next, children begin to spell words with short vowels in consonant-vowel-consonant (CVC) form (e.g., *cat, rip, men*). They are able to spell words with two consonants together, such as the blends *sm* and *st*. At this stage of development, children are also able to spell words with **digraphs**, or words that have two consonants that make one sound (i.e., *th, sh, ch*, used to spell *thumb, shoe*, and *chin*). Note that the phonetic representation of these sounds is a single phoneme: *th* /θ/, *sh* /ʃ/, and *ch* /tʃ/, as described in Chapters 1 and 3.

By the second grade, children begin to learn that words that "sound the same" may have different meanings and spellings (e.g., *two, too,* and *to*), and they are challenged by the different spellings of these words. When a child must choose between alternative spellings (i.e., *for* versus *four*), words that the children have frequently seen in print provide orthographic guidance (Wright & Ehri, 2007). More exposure to reading provides children with the ability to recognize the meaning of these words, along with the ability to spell them.

In the second grade, children are now reading more frequently and independently and are exposed to more words in print. By the end of second grade, the use of inflections begins to appear with the use of past tense and plurals evident in children's productions (Carlisle, 1988; Walker & Hauerwas, 2006). Examples consist of the use of the past tense verb form *-ed* (e.g., *walked*) and the plural form *-s* (e.g., *cats*).

By the third grade, the use of morphological knowledge in spelling becomes commonplace and affixes are consistently used correctly (Tompkins, 2003). An affix is a word element, such as a prefix or suffix, that can only occur attached to a base, stem, or root, as demonstrated in the following examples:

Prefixes that occur before a root/stem:

un + kind	unkind
mis + lay	mislay
mis + understand	misunderstand

Suffixes that occur at the end of a root/stem:

care + ful	careful

danger + ous   dangerous

happy + ness   happiness

Third graders are able to use meaningful chunks or segments of words in their spelling. More advanced inflectional endings are present, such as *-ness* or *-ship* (e.g., *happiness* and *ownership*). As children learn how to spell words, errors in adding prefixes, suffixes, inflectional endings, along with doubling errors, are common (e.g., "hamer" for *hammer*). Children who can integrate the three types of linguistic knowledge in their spelling—phonological, morphological, and orthographic—are on their way to being good spellers.

Reading Fluency

When children are first learning to read, their reading rate is quite slow because they are putting significant mental effort into the phonological process of sounding out the words sound by sound. In order to increase their rate, children must integrate their other linguistic abilities with spelling skills. These other linguistic abilities consist of orthographic skills (which allow children to quickly identify sight words) and morphologic skills (which allow children to identify prefixes and suffixes). They must also connect their orthographic skills with word meaning or semantic knowledge. When these abilities work in an integrative and automatic fashion, the child is said to read fluently and his or her reading rate typically increases. It is thought that if children spend less cognitive resources decoding a text, they have more resources available to devote to understanding the meaning of the passage (Lingo, 2014).

The National Reading Panel (National Institute of Child Health and Human Development [NICHD], 2008) defines **fluency** as the ability to read a text quickly and accurately and with proper expression. Fluent reading is connected with good reading comprehension, with the added requirement of good decoding skills. The correlation between the rate of oral reading and reading comprehension is strong during the elementary school years (Pinnell et al., 1995), but rapid reading skills do not always mean that the reader comprehends the text. Most readers, but not all, who can read text quickly are also good comprehenders. However, some children have the ability to read words quickly but do not understand what they are reading. The ability to read fluently is a complex skill that develops over time.

Reading fluency requires a cognitive process of analysis, in which children apply their knowledge of a wide number of unrelated facts about the world, along with an understanding of the relationship among various concepts (ideas about things) (Bialystok, 2001). Beginning and more advanced fluent reading (and writing) are based on different levels of cognitive processing and require different levels of language skills.

Consider the cognitive demands of conversation (low cognitive demands) versus giving a book report in class (high cognitive demands). In a similar manner, fluent reading depends on more advanced cognitive processes and language skills. Fluent reading also requires that the reader apply higher cognitive processes to comprehension, rather than the lower level processes assigned to recognizing individual words (Stanovich, Cunningham, & Freeman, 2009). The fluent reader holds sequences of words in short-term memory, the site of operation of comprehension processes on the words that have been read. This process leads to meaningful phrasing while reading and to the integration of words into a meaningful conceptual structure that can be stored in long-term memory. In short, the more fluent the reader, the less chance for misinterpretation of the text (Rubin, 2016).

Writing

As discussed earlier, children's earliest writings are combined with drawing. Their first written word is often their own name (Bloodgood, 1999). Children expand from that name knowledge and begin to pepper their drawings with letters (Harste, Woodward, & Burke, 1984). In kindergarten, children's early writing reflects their burgeoning phonological development and maturing motor skills.

> Most kindergartners can stay within the lines on big writing paper, and their writing flows from left to right and top to bottom (Wood, 2007). There is inconsistency in their spacing but there are also attempts to group words separately.

In the beginning stages of writing, children typically prefer uppercase letters. Invented spelling is common (Moats, 2009)—for example, *mommy* written as "MBXBC." By the first grade, writing is legible but still larger than typical writing. It is not unusual to see a mix of upper- and lowercase letters. Although there is variability, basic writing conventions are followed, such as using capital letters when appropriate and ending with a period.

By the second grade, children still rely on lines to guide their placement of letters but writing has become more automatic. The diminished motor demands help children focus more on the content in their written efforts. By this stage of development, connected writing expands and children's written essays have a beginning, middle, and end (Wood, 2007). They develop more interest in writing **expository** text structure or informational assignments.

> The primary goal of expository text is to deliver information about a subject, a common issue, a way to do something, or an idea. This represents the beginning of a journey into a variety of expository text structures, each of which has a different function (i.e., descriptive, sequence, comparison-contrast, cause-effect, and problem-solution) (Westby, 1999).

By the third grade, children are typically motorically fluent writers. They are ready to begin the draft and revision process for their writing efforts. Their plots include character development but may sometimes be fanciful and hard to believe. Fourth graders are ready to write at more length using information resources to develop the topic. Their budding ability to understand idioms and early figurative language appears in their attempts to include humor in their writing. They write in multiple genres, including narratives and expositories, from letters to basic research papers.

Fifth graders continue to perfect the draft and revision process. Their plots become more complex and may include more than one episode (e.g., a story within another story). They continue to expand their enjoyment of different written genres through poetry writing, cartooning, and journaling (Wood, 2007). Their writing shows more awareness of who will read what they have written.

Because oral language and written language are so closely connected, children's oral language feeds the complexity of their written language. Their increasing language skills are especially important in the development of **cohesion** and **coherence** in their writing. Cohesion is how the ideas relate to each other. A paper with good cohesion is comprehensible and consistent. One thought naturally leads to another. Coherence can be conceived as the grammatical and lexical links from one part of a text to another. This includes use of synonyms (words with the same meaning), lexical sets (a set of words with the same topic, function, or form), pronouns (words that replace nouns), verb tenses (verb forms that express the time an action took place), time references (words that indicate when an event occurs, occurred, or will occur), and grammatical forms (proper nouns, adjectives, prepositional phrases, and relative clauses), as shown in the following examples:

Synonyms: **Myths** often narrate historical beliefs. These **narratives** tell a story about what some people believe.

Lexical sets: We were looking for the lost **cat**. This **feline** was our pet.

Pronouns: **Peter** was lost and **he** didn't know where **he** was.

Verb tenses: He **went** *yesterday* and decided to **go** again tomorrow.

Time references: **First**, he ate; **next**, he took a nap; **and then** he watched TV.

Grammatical forms: The **little** girl ran **quickly around** the track.

Adept use of cohesive ties helps writing grow in coherence and increases the clarity of the writing as the complexity increases (Dyson & Freedman, 2003). Both abilities grow throughout children's lives and well into adulthood.

SUPPORTING LITERACY DEVELOPMENT IN THE ELEMENTARY SCHOOL YEARS

A child's literacy program in the elementary school years should include five areas recommended by the National Reading Panel (NICHD, 2000): (1) phonemic awareness, (2) phonics, (3) fluency, (4) vocabulary, and (5) text comprehension. The child's reading program should be balanced, integrating all areas that play a role in literacy development, rather than a focused concentration on one or the other.

Phonemic Awareness

Phonemic awareness is an aspect of phonological awareness that deals with the phoneme. As stated in Chapters 1 and 3, a phoneme is the smallest sound unit of language. Whereas younger children deal with larger units like words and syllables, school-age children deal with phonemes. Phonemic awareness helps children realize that sounds can be put together to form words. Meaningful activities given to beginning readers provide practice with segmenting and blending individual sounds (Torgesen et al., 2001). Once children become aware of the individual sounds in words, they are able to understand *blending* and *segmenting* sounds in words. Segmenting involves breaking words into syllables (e.g., *ba-na-na*) or individual sounds (e.g., *cat = c-a-t*), whereas blending involves combining individual sounds to produce a word (e.g., *c-a-t = cat*).

Phonics

Whereas phonemic awareness deals with spoken language sounds, **phonics** describes the relationship between phonemes (sounds) and graphemes (written language). In other words, phonics teaches the child the connection between the sound that the phoneme makes and the letter representation. When presenting phonemic awareness activities, the connections to the grapheme(s) or the written letter or letters that correspond with sounds should be made obvious to the child (NICHD, 2000; Torgesen et al., 2001). Phonics should be explicitly and systematically taught and children should be encouraged to use their phonic skills when reading or writing (NICHD, 2000).

Reading Fluency

Gaining fluency skills depends both on exposure to models of fluent reading and on experience with reading aloud. There are numerous ways of providing repeated experiences, such as student–adult reading, partner reading, choral reading, tape-assisted reading, and readers' theater. Repeated readings have been shown to be effective in typically developing children, children with learning disabilities, and children learning a second language (Rubin, 2016). In student–adult reading and partner reading, the readers take turns reading aloud, whereas in choral reading, the whole class reads together at the same time. Tape-assisted reading allows the student to read along while an experienced reader reads the book on an audiotape. As the child becomes more fluent, he or she could read in concert with the audiobook and then independently. Readers' theater allows students to rehearse a play that comes from their reading. The script is then performed for classmates with a minimum of preparation or props. Because it is in play form, it is a natural vehicle to increase fluent reading presentation.

Vocabulary

Vocabulary is learned both incidentally (implicitly) and by direct teaching (explicitly) (Nagy & Herman, 1985). Some word meanings are taught explicitly. Explicit word learning strategies include pre-teaching vocabulary words, repeated exposure to vocabulary words, the key word method, word maps, the Cloze procedure, and root analysis. Even with the use of these strategies, it is impossible for teachers to directly teach all the word meanings needed. Therefore, students must be able to learn new words incidentally from oral language or by inferring meaning from context when reading. Teachers can support incidental word learning, however, by inspiring interest and inquisitiveness about learning new words. Modeling word-learning strategies and interest in word learning can help capitalize on incidental word learning while students are reading independently (NICHD, 2000).

Strategies That Support Reading Comprehension

Vocabulary knowledge is not all there is to reading comprehension. Understanding what is read takes more than just knowing the individual word meanings. Good readers think about meaning as they are reading, integrating the written text with what they already know.

There are many strategies that aid reading comprehension. These strategies include using graphic organizers, answering and asking questions about what was read, discussing text structure, and summarizing texts (NICHD, 2000). One method incorporates four of these strategies (Palincsar & Brown, 1986). This method is called Reciprocal Teaching. In this method, the more experienced reader models and encourages asking questions about what is being read, clarifying unknown words, predicting what might happen next, and summarizing or using self-review. Another strategy, Question Answer Relationship, has been found to support reading comprehension and the ability to answer questions (Green, 2016). In this strategy, four types of comprehension questions are taught (*right there*, *think and search*, *the author and you*, and *on your own*). Knowing the expectation of the question helps readers determine the correct source for the answer.

Technology and School-Age Children

Technology is being increasingly used to address literacy instruction in our schools (International Reading Association, 2001). Text formats are increasingly presented via multimedia or hyperlinks and are impacting the way students integrate information (Warschauer, 2006). Sources for information are timely and searches for information have innovative formats. Social opportunities are also available in the use of email, texts, and chats. Writing is increasingly expressed using digital means and has changed the way that texts are planned, produced, and shared

(Kervin & Mantei, 2016). The right balance between these technologies is a constant issue for teachers and is impacted by the technology available and by their attitudes and beliefs about new technologies (Hew & Brush, 2007).

LITERACY DEVELOPMENT IN ADOLESCENCE

This review highlights several common instructional elements—such as explicit instruction in comprehension, writing, and cooperative learning—that could be explored in future research. Common instructional elements can help inform increasingly effective practices. Systematic combinations of these elements and organizational components (such as extended instruction or professional development) could continue to be investigated to determine which elements are necessary and how many are sufficient to demonstrate positive effects (Biancarosa & Snow, 2006.) By adolescence, children are fluent readers, but this does not mean that their literacy development is complete (see Table 7–3). To meet the expectations in the content areas in the upper grades, it is imperative that their vocabulary, comprehension, fluency, and writing abilities continue to grow and expand. In this section, growth in these areas is highlighted along with methods to support adolescents' continued literacy growth.

Genre, Vocabulary, and Reading Comprehension

Throughout adolescence, children learn to enjoy, use, and comprehend a variety of genres or types of text, both fiction and nonfiction (Wood, 2007). In middle school, they begin reading newspapers, magazines, and biographies. These continue in high school along with song lyrics, poetry, drama, short stories, and novels. As noted earlier, familiarity with different types of text structure supports the comprehension of a text. This is especially helpful if the content of the text is unfamiliar to the reader (Wallach & Butler, 1994).

> Knowing different kinds of text structure also helps support vocabulary development. When a student reads about the same subject in a variety of types of print, there is more frequent exposure to related vocabulary. This helps the adolescent to learn a variety of high-frequency (more common) and low-frequency (less common) words related to the subject (Adams, 2011).

Along with varying text structure, comprehension in content areas depends on being able to master the oral and written language requirements presented in the varied subject areas found in different texts (Beck & Jeffrey, 2009). For example, each academic subject area has its own academic language register. An academic register is a specialized way of speaking or writing in accord with disciplinary requirements (Wilkinson & Silliman, 2008). Reading and understanding social studies is quite different from reading and understanding science.

As adolescents travel through middle school and high school, a significant percentage of their new vocabulary development is related to their subject study. Content area texts contain vocabulary that is challenging because it is often more scholarly and includes the specialized vocabulary of the discipline being studied (Silliman & Scott, 2009). For instance, let us consider this sample question taken from a high school science state examination (NYSED, 2011):

> *When the bacterium,* Serratia marcescens, *is grown on a sterile culture medium in a petri dish at 30°C, the bacterial colonies are cream colored. When this same bacterium is cultured under identical conditions, except at a temperature of 25°C, the colonies are brick red. This difference in color is most likely due to the effect of temperature on the expression of the gene for color.*

The preceding passage contains advanced vocabulary, such as *sterile, medium,* and *expression,* along with specialized scientific vocabulary, such as *bacterium, culture,* and *gene.* This text also presents the adolescent reader with increased syntactic complexity: The second sentence contains a dependent clause and a phrase, in addition to the independent clause. These elements increase the length of the sentence and the density of ideas being communicated. Thus, the adolescent reader must possess good language skills when faced with this level of complexity.

Social literacy demands are also increasing during this period, given the variety of technologies that are available and widely used, such as texting, instant messaging, and other social networking media. There is greater motivation to fit in with peers. Consequently, the adolescent learns to meet the language demands found in humor and sarcasm. The closely related skills involved in the comprehension of figurative language (e.g., simile, metaphor, personification, hyperbole) are also increasing (Wood, 2007).

Reading Fluency

Adolescents vary significantly in reading fluency, as fluency is affected by the four following factors (Barth, Catts, & Anthony, 2009).

The **first factor** in reading fluency is word accuracy. Word accuracy is the ability to read or decode words using the phonological, orthographic, and morphological abilities described earlier in the chapter. The integration of phonological, orthographic, and morphological knowledge leads to more rapid recognition of a word.

The **second factor** in reading fluency is the ability to name the word quickly. It is thought that this quick naming retrieval plays a bigger part in fluency in younger than in older readers (Barth, Catts, & Anthony, 2009).

The **third factor** in reading fluency is working memory. This means that the reader can remember and manipulate information at the same time.

The **fourth factor** in reading fluency is language comprehension, which plays a large part in reading fluency for adolescents (Barth, Catts, & Anthony, 2009). This is the ability to create meaning from the text. This can be influenced by the students' familiarity with the text structure and content. Unfamiliar structure and content may need to be read more slowly than familiar structure and content.

Greater experience with reading helps make these four factors work in concert more quickly. The beginning reader may have to focus almost entirely on the decoding process, reading one word at a time. Reading becomes more automatic to the more experienced adolescent readers, and fluency continues to develop throughout the reader's lifetime.

Writing

Writing development in adolescence centers on improving the ability to revise written work, the ability to write in a variety of genres, and the ability to use multiple perspectives in writing. Writing in most classrooms consists of cycles of planning, writing, and reviewing (Graham & Sandmel, 2011). Beginning in early adolescence, the responsibility for the reviewing process shifts more formally from the teacher to the student. Students use dictionaries and thesaurus references independently while paying more attention to proper writing mechanics. Students are able to evaluate their own work with guidance from a checklist or a rubric and make successive revisions. They may also participate in critiquing their peers' work. As their ability to comprehend different text structures increases, so does their ability to write in different genres.

Adolescents begin to take notes effectively and enjoy writing autobiographies, song lyrics, and poetry (Wood, 2007). They may enjoy formal collaborative writing in the form of the school newspaper or wikis. Throughout adolescence, the ability to look at a problem or life situation from different points of view continues to grow. Consequently, the ability to write persuasively matures.

SUPPORTING ADOLESCENT LITERACY DEVELOPMENT

Supporting adolescent literacy development successfully requires the use of many of the direct methods for comprehension support discussed for the elementary school-age child. These supports consist of explicit vocabulary instruction, awareness of text structure, self-monitoring, summarization, and activating schemas or prior knowledge (Biancarosa & Snow, 2004). For adolescents, there is an increased expectation of being able to interpret texts with more depth, rather than just obtaining basic information. For this reason, opportunities for extended discussion of the meaning and interpretation of text should be provided (Kamil et al., 2008). A recent meta-analysis investigated current adolescent programs for their efficacy. They found that explicit instruction in comprehension writing and the use of cooperative learning showed positive effects on the reading abilities of adolescents (Herrera, Truckenmiller, & Foorman, 2016). Various organizational components (such as extended instruction and professional development) could continue to be investigated to determine which elements are necessary and how many are sufficient to demonstrate positive effects (Biancarosa & Snow, 2004).

With adolescents, motivation and engagement become especially important. Adolescents face self-esteem and identity challenges that can significantly influence their academic achievement (Wood, 2007). If an adolescent has had previous literacy experiences that were unsuccessful, this can translate into reduced motivation and effort (Ehren, Lenz, & Deshler, 2004). Therefore, it is important to provide a positive learning environment that provides relevant connections to the students' lives (Kamil et al., 2008).

SUMMARY

This chapter discussed the relationship of language and literacy and the development of literacy from preschool through adolescence. It also briefly reviewed supportive practices for teaching in literacy-related areas.

◆ Language and literacy development are interwoven and benefit each other. Good oral language makes learning to read easier, and reading increases oral language abilities.
◆ Many underlying skills needed for literacy development are seen before formal literacy learning begins.
◆ Evidence-based practices for supporting literacy in preschool include providing a print-rich environment, shared book reading, phonological awareness play, and symbolic play.
◆ Literacy development in kindergarten is primarily focused on learning the sound-symbol relationship. In first and second grades, development targets use phonological awareness and phonics skills to blend and segment when reading and writing. Older elementary school students integrate phonological, orthographic, morphological, and semantic linguistic elements to become fluent in reading and writing.
◆ The National Reading Panel (NICHD, 2000) has designed a balanced reading program that includes phonemic

awareness, phonics, fluency, vocabulary, and reading comprehension.

◆ Adolescent literacy development involves an expansion of fluency and knowledge of text structure along with an expansion of vocabulary needed for content area knowledge.

◆ Supports for reading comprehension should include knowledge of text structure, activating prior knowledge, questioning, self-monitoring, and summarization.

◆ Adolescent literacy instruction accounts for self-esteem and motivational issues along with the need to discuss texts on a more integrative level.

KEY WORDS

Coherence

Cohesion

Decontextualized language

Dialogic reading

Digraphs

Emergent literacy

Expository

Figurative language

Fluency

Metalinguistic knowledge

Myths

Narratives

Onset

Phonemic awareness

Phonics

Phonological awareness

Print awareness

Rime

Text structure

STUDY QUESTIONS

1. Discuss the connection between language and literacy development.

2. What is involved in the development of emergent literacy?

3. How do you support literacy in the preschool years?

4. After third grade, children become increasingly fluent readers. Discuss what abilities aid this process.

5. Consider the five areas of the reading program recommended by the National Reading Panel (NICHD,2000) and illustrate how they should overlap to produce a balanced reading program.

6. What is the role of text structure in reading comprehension?

7. Identify and discuss five strategies that support adolescent literacy development.

REFERENCES

Adams, M. (2011). Advancing our students' language and literacy: The challenge of complex texts. *American Educator, Winter*, *34*(53), 3–11.

Banerjee, R., Alsalman, A., & Alqafari, S. (2016). Supporting sociodramatic play in preschools to promote language and literacy skills of English language learners. *Early Childhood Education Journal, 44*(4), 299–305.

Barth, A., Catts, H., & Anthony, J. (2009). The component skills underlying reading fluency in adolescent readers: A latent variable analysis. *Reading and Writing, 22,* 567–590.

Beck, S. W., & Jeffery, J. V. (2009). Genre and thinking in academic writing tasks. *Journal of Literacy Research, 41*(2), 228–272.

Bialystok, E. (2001). *Bilingual development: Language, literacy, and cognition.* Cambridge, UK: Cambridge University Press.

Biancarosa, G., & Snow, C. E. (2004). *Reading next: A vision for action and research in middle and high school literacy: A report to the Carnegie Corporation of New York.* Washington, DC: Alliance for Excellent Education.

Blachman, B. A. (1997). Early intervention and phonological awareness: A cautionary tale. In B. A. Blachman (Ed.), *Foundations of reading acquisition and dyslexia* (pp. 409–430). Mahwah, NJ: Erlbaum.

Bloodgood, J. (1999). What's in a name? Children's name writing and literacy acquisition. *Reading Research Quarterly, 34,* 342–367.

Bourassa, D. C., & Treiman, R. (2001). Spelling development and disability: The importance of linguistic factors. *Language, Speech, and Hearing Services in Schools, 32,* 172–181.

Carlisle, J. F. (1988). Knowledge of derivational morphology and spelling ability in fourth, sixth, and eighth graders. *Applied Psycholinguistics, 9,* 247–266.

Carlisle, J. F., & Katz, L. A. (2005). Word learning and vocabulary instruction. In J. Birsch (Ed.), *Multisensory teaching of basic language skills* (2nd ed.). Baltimore, MD: Paul H. Brookes.

Cervetti, G. N., Wright, T. S., & Hwang, H. (2016). Conceptual coherence, comprehension, and vocabulary acquisition: A knowledge effect? *Reading and Writing, 29*(4), 761–779.

Chall, J. S. (1996). *Stages of reading development.* New York, NY: McGraw-Hill.

Coates, E., & Coates, A. (2016). The essential role of scribbling in the imaginative and cognitive development of young children. *Journal of Early Childhood Literacy, 16*(1), 60–83.

Colmar, S. (2011). A book reading intervention with mothers of children with language difficulties. *Australasian Journal of Early Childhood, 36*(2), 104–112.

Colmar, S. (2014). A parent-based book-reading intervention for disadvantaged children with language difficulties. *Child Language Teaching and Therapy, 30*(1), 79–90.

Cunningham, A. E., & Stanovich, K. E. (1997). Early reading acquisition and its relation to reading experience and ability 10 years later. *Developmental Psychology, 33*(6), 934–945.

Dennis, L. R., Whalon, K., Kraut, L., & Herron, D. (2016). Effects of a teacher versus iPad-facilitated intervention on the vocabulary of at-risk preschool children. *Journal of Early Intervention, 38*(3), 170–186.

Dickinson, D., Golinkoff, R., & Hirsch-Pasek, K. (2010). Speaking out for language: Why language is central to reading development. *Educational Researcher, 39,* 305–310.

Dyson, A. (2000). Writing and the sea of voices: Oral language in, around, and about writing. In R. Indrisano & J. Squire (Eds.), *Perspectives on writing* (pp. 45–65). Newark, DE: International Reading Association.

Dyson, A. H., & Freedman, S. W. (2003). Writing. In J. Flood, D. Lapp, J. R. Squire, & J. M. Jensen (Eds.), *Handbook of research on teaching the English language arts* (2nd ed., pp. 967–992). Mahwah, NJ: Erlbaum.

Ehren, B., Lenz, B., & Deshler, D. (2004). Enhancing literacy proficiency with adolescents and young adults. In C. A. Stone & E. R. Silliman (Eds.), *Handbook of language and literacy* (pp. 681–702). New York, NY: Guilford Press.

Ehri, L. (2000). Learning to read and learning to spell: Two sides of a coin. *Topics in Language Disorders, 20*(3), 19–49.

Eisenchlas, S. A., Schalley, A. C., & Moyes, G. (2016). Play to learn: Self-directed home language literacy acquisition through online games. *International Journal of Bilingual Education and Bilingualism, 19*(2), 136–152.

Goodrich, S., Mudrick, H., & Robinson, J. (2015). The transition from early child care to preschool: Emerging toddler skills and readiness for group-based learning. *Early Education and Development, 26*(7), 1035–1056.

Graham, S., & Sandmel, K. (2011). The process writing approach: A meta-analysis. *Journal of Educational Research, 104*, 396–407.

Graham, S., & Santangelo, T. (2014). Does spelling instruction make students better spellers, readers, and writers? A meta-analytic review. *Reading and Writing: An Interdisciplinary Journal, 27*(9), 1703–1743.

Green, S. (2016). *Two for one: Using QAR to increase reading comprehension and improve test scores.* Retrieved from http://online library.wiley.com/doi/10.1002/trtr.1466/abstract

Guo, Y., Justice, L., Kaderavek, J., & McGinty, A. (2012). The literacy environment of preschool classrooms: Contributions to children's emergent literacy growth. *Journal of Research in Reading, 35*, 308–327.

Harste, J. C., Woodward, V. A., & Burke, C. L. (1984). *Language stories and literacy lessons.* Portsmouth, NH: Heinemann Educational Books.

Hedberg, N. L., & Westby, C. E. (1993). *Analyzing storytelling skills: Theory to practice.* Tucson, AZ: Communication Skill Builders.

Herrera, S., Truckenmiller, A. J., & Foorman, B. R. (2016). *Summary of 20 years of research on the effectiveness of adolescent literacy programs and practices.* Retrieved from https://ies.ed.gov/ncee/edlabs/regions/southeast/pdf/REL_2016178.pdf

Hew, K. F., & Brush, T. (2007). Integrating technology into K–12 teaching and learning: Current knowledge gaps and recommendations for future research. *Education Technology and Research Development, 55*, 223–252.

Huebner, C. E. (2000). Promoting toddlers' language development through community-based intervention. *Journal of Applied Developmental Psychology, 21*(5), 513–535.

International Reading Association. (2001). *Integrating literacy and technology in the cur-riculum: A position statement.* Retrieved from www.reading.org/downloads/positions/ps1048_technol ogy.pdf

Justice, L. (2006). *Communication sciences and disorders: An introduction.* Upper Saddle River, NJ: Pearson Education.

Justice, L., & Ezell, H. (2004). Print-referencing: An emergent literacy enhancement technique and its clinical applications. *Language, Speech, and Hearing Services in Schools, 35*, 185–193.

Justice, L. M., Kaderavek, J., Bowles, R., & Grimm, K. (2005). Language impairment, parent-child shared reading, and phonological awareness: A feasibility study. *Topics in Early Childhood Special Education, 25* (3) 143–156.

Kaderavek, J., & Justice, L. (2004). Embedded-explicit emergent literacy: II. Goal selection and implementations in the early childhood classroom. *Language, Speech, and Hearing Services in Schools, 35*, 212–228.

Kamhi, A. (2009). Prologue: The case for the narrow view of reading. *Language, Speech, and Hearing Services in Schools, 40*(2), 174–177.

Kamil, M. L., Borman, G. D., Dole, J., Kral, C. C., Salinger, T., & Torgesen, J. (2008). *Improving adolescent literacy: Effective classroom and intervention practices: A practice guide* (NCEE #2008-4027). Washington, DC: National Center for Education Evaluation and Regional Assistance, Institute of Education Sciences, U.S. Department of Education. Retrieved from http://ies.ed.gov/ncee/wwc

Kervin, L., & Mantei, J. (2016). Digital writing practices: A close look at one grade-three author. *Literacy, 50*(3), 133–140.

Koppenhaver, D. A., Erickson, K. A., & Skotko, B. G. (2001). Supporting communication of girls with Rett syndrome and their mothers in storybook readings. *International Journal of Disability, Development, and Education, 48*(4), 395–410.

Korat, O., & Segal-Drori, O. (2016). E-book and printed book reading in different contexts as emergent literacy facilitator. *Early Education and Development, 27*(4), 532–550.

Kozminsky, E., & Asher-Sadon, R. (2013). Media type influences preschooler's literacy development: E-book versus printed book reading. *Interdisciplinary Journal of E-Learning and Learning Objects, 9,* 233–247.

Laurent, A., & Martinot, C. (2009) Bilingualism and phonological segmentation of speech: The case of English-French pre-schoolers. *Journal of Early Childhood Literacy, 9,* 29–49.

Lingo, A. S. (2014). Tutoring middle school students with disabilities by high school students: Effects on oral reading fluency. *Education and Treatment of Children, 37*(1), 53–75.

Lonigan, C. J., & Whitehurst, G. J. (1998). Examination of the relative efficacy of parent and teacher involvement in a shared-reading intervention for preschool children from low-income backgrounds. *Early Childhood Research Quarterly, 17,* 265–292.

Meltzer, J., Smith, N. C., & Clark, H. (2001). *Adolescent literacy resources: Linking research and practice.* Providence, RI: Brown University, Northeast and Islands Regional Educational Laboratory.

Moats, L. C. (2009). Knowledge foundations for teaching reading and spelling. *Reading and Writing: An Interdisciplinary Journal, 22,* 379–399.

Morrow, L. (2015). *Literacy development in the early years: Helping children read and write.* Upper Saddle River, NJ: Pearson Education.

Nagy, W. E., & Herman, P. A. (1985). Incidental vs. instructional approaches to increasing reading vocabulary. *Educational Perspectives, 23*(1), 16–21.

Naqvi, R., Thorne, K. J., Pfitscher, C. M., Nordstokke, D. W., & McKeough, A. (2013). Reading dual language books: Improving early literacy skills in linguistically diverse classrooms. *Journal of Early Childhood Research, 11*(1), 3–15.

National Institute of Child Health and Human Development (NICHD). (2008). *Report of the National Reading Panel. Teaching children to read: An evidence-based assessment of the scientific research literature on reading and its implications for reading instruction.* Retrieved from https://www.nichd.nih.gov/publications/pubs/nrp/Documents/report.pdf#search=report and reading panel

Nelson, N. W. (2010). *Language and literacy disorders: Infancy through adolescence.* Boston, MA: Allyn & Bacon.

Newman, R., Ratner, N., Juszcyk, A., & Juszcyk, P. (2006). Infants' early ability to segment the conversational speech signal predicts later language development: A retrospective analysis. *Developmental Psychology, 42,* 643–655.

New York State Education Department. (NYSED). (2011). *Living Environment Regents Examination Sampler.* Retrieved from http://www.p12.nysed.gov/ciai/mst/pub/livenvirsam1.pdf

Olaussen, B. S. (2016). Classroom discourse: The role of teachers' instructional practice for promoting student dialogues in the Early Years Literacy Program (EYLP). *Universal Journal of Educational Research, 4*(11), 2595–2605.

Palincsar, A. S., & Brown, A. L. (1986). Interactive teaching to promote independent learning from text. *The Reading Teacher, 39,* 771–777.

Pentimonti, J., Zucker, T., Justice, L., Petscher, Y., Piasta, S., & Kaderavek, J. (2012). A standardized tool for assessing the quality of classroom-based reading: Systematic assessment of book reading. *Early Childhood Research Quarterly, 27,* 512–528.

Phillips, B. M., Clancy-Menchetti, J., & Lonigan, C. J. (2008). Successful phonological awareness instruction with preschool children: Lessons from the classroom. *Topics in Early Childhood Special Education, 28*(1), 3–17.

Pinnell, G., Pikulski, J., Wixson, K., Campbell, J., Gough, P., & Beatty, A. (1995). *Listening to children read aloud.* Washington, DC: Office of Educational Research and Improvement, United States Department of Education.

Rosenthal, J., & Ehri, L. C. (2008). The mnemonic value of orthography for vocabulary learning. *Journal of Educational Psychology, 100,* 175–191.

Roskos, K. A., & Neuman, S. B. (2001). Environment and its influences for early literacy teaching and learning. In S. B. Neuman & D. K. Dickinson (Eds.), *Handbook of early literacy research* (pp. 281–294). New York, NY: Guilford Press.

Rubin, D. I. (2016). Growth in oral reading fluency of Spanish ELL students with learning disabilities. *Intervention in School and Clinic, 52*(1), 34–38.

Shipley, K. G., & McAfee, J. G. (2009). *Assessment in speech-language pathology: A resource manual.* Florence, KY: Cengage.

Silliman, E. R., & Scott, C. M. (2009). Research-based oral language intervention routes to the academic language of literacy: Finding the right road. In S. Rosenfield & V. W. Berninger (Eds.), *Implementing evidence-based academic interventions in school settings* (pp. 107–145). New York, NY: Oxford University Press.

Smilansky, S. (1968). *The effects of sociodramatic play on disadvantaged preschool children.* London, UK: Wiley.

Stadler, M. A., & Ward, G. C. (2005). Supporting the narrative development of young children. *Early Childhood Education Journal, 33*(2), 73–80.

Stanovich, K. E., Cunningham, A. E., & Freeman, D. J. (2009). Intelligence, cognitive skills, and early reading progress. *International Reading Association, 19*(3), 278–303.

Storch, S. A., & Whitehurst, G. J. (2001). The role of family and home in the literacy development of children from low-income backgrounds. *New Directions for Child and Adolescent Development, 92*, 53–71.

Suortti, O., & Lipponen, L. (2016). Phonological awareness and emerging reading skills of two- to five-year-old children. *Early Child Development and Care, 186*(11), 1703–1721.

Teale, W., & Sulzby, E. (1986). *Emergent literacy: Writing and reading.* Norwood, NJ: Ablex.

Tompkins, G. (2003). *Literacy for the 21st century.* Upper Saddle River, NJ: Pearson Education.

Torgesen, J., Alexander, A., Wagner, R., Rashotte, C., Voeller, K., & Conway, T. (2001). Intensive remedial instruction for children with severe reading disabilities: Immediate and long-term outcomes from two instructional approaches. *Journal of Learning Disabilities, 34*, 33–58.

Towson, J. A., Gallagher, P. A., & Bingham, G. E. (2016). Dialogic reading: Language and preliteracy outcomes for young children with disabilities. *Journal of Early Intervention, 38*(4), 230–246.

Troia, G., Stone, C., Silliman, E., Ehren, B., & Wallach, G. (2014). *Handbook of language and literacy: Development and disorders.* New York, NY: Guilford Press.

van Druten-Frietman, L., Strating, H., Denessen, E., & Verhoeven, L. (2016). Interactive storybook-based intervention effects on kindergartners' language development. *Journal of Early Intervention, 38*(4), 212–229.

van Kleeck, A. (1994). Metalinguistic development. In G. Wallach & K. Butler (Eds.), *Language learning disabilities in school-age children and adolescents.* New York, NY: Merrill.

van Kleeck, A. (2006). Fostering inferential language during book sharing with prereaders: A foundation for later text comprehension strategies. In A. van Kleeck (Ed.), *Sharing books and stories to promote language and literacy* (pp. 269–317). San Diego, CA: Plural.

van Kleeck, A. (2008). Providing preschool foundations for later reading comprehension: The importance of and ideas for targeting inferencing in storybook-sharing interventions. *Psychology in the Schools, 45*(7), 627–643.

van Kleeck, A., & Schuele, M. (1987). Precursors to literacy: Normal development. *Topics in Language Disorders, 7*(2), 13–31.

van Kleeck, A., Vander Woude, J., & Hammett, L. (2006). Fostering literal and inferential language skills in Head Start preschoolers with language impairment using scripted book-sharing discussions. *American Journal of Speech-Language Pathology, 15*(1), 85–95.

Vygotsky, L. S. (1967). Play and its role in the mental development of the child. *Soviet Psychology, 5*, 6–18.

Walker, J., & Hauerwas, L. B. (2006). Development of phonological, morphological, and orthographic knowledge in young spellers: The case of inflected verbs. *Reading and Writing, 19*, 819–843.

Wallach, G., & Butler, K. (1994). *Language learning disabilities in school-age children and adolescents.* New York, NY: Merrill.

Warschauer, M. (2006). *Laptops and literacy: Learning in the wireless classroom.* New York, NY: Teachers College Press.

Westby, C. (1999). Assessing and facilitating text comprehension problem. In H. W. Catts & A. G. Kamhi (Eds.), *Language and reading disabilities* (pp. 154–221). Boston, MA: Allyn & Bacon.

Westerveld, M. (2016). A systematic review of the literature on emergent literacy skills of preschool children with autism spectrum disorder. *Journal of Special Education, 50*(1), 1–37.

Westerveld, M. F., Trembath, D., Shellshear, L., & Paynter, J. (2016). A systematic review of the literature on emergent literacy skills of preschool children with autism spectrum. *Journal of Special Education, 50*, 37–48.

Whitehurst, G. J., Epstein, J. N., Angell, A. L., Payne, A. C., Crone, D. A., & Fischel, J. E. (1994). Outcomes of an emergent literacy intervention in Head Start. *Journal of Educational Psychology, 86*(4), 542–555.

Whitehurst, G. J., & Lonigan, C. J. (1998). Child development and emergent literacy. *Child Development, 69*(3), 848–872.

Wilford, S. (2000). *From play to literacy: Implications for the classroom* (Occasional paper No. 2). Bronxville, NY: Child Development Institute, Sarah Lawrence College.

Wilkinson, L. C., & Silliman, E. R. (2008). Academic language proficiency and literacy instruction in urban settings. In L. Wilkinson, L. Morrow, & V. Chou (Eds.), *Improving literacy achievement in urban schools: Critical elements in teacher preparation* (pp. 121–142). Newark, DE: International Reading Association.

Wolfersberger, M. E., Reutzel, D. R., Sudweeks, R., & Fawson, P. C. (2004). Developing and validating the Classroom Literacy Environmental Profile (CLEP): A tool for examining the "print richness" of early childhood and elementary classrooms. *Journal of Literacy Research, 36*(2), 211–272.

Wood, C. (2007). *Yardsticks: Children in the classroom ages 4–14.* Turner Falls, MA: Northeast Foundation for Children.

Wright, D., & Ehri, L. C. (2007). Beginners remember orthography when they learn to read words: The case of doubled letters. *Applied Psycholinguistics, 28*, 115–133.

Yopp, H. K., & Yopp, H. (2009). Phonological awareness is child's play! *Young Children, 64*(1), 12–18.

Zevenbergen, A. A., & Whitehurst, C. J. (2003). Dialogic reading: A shared picture book reading intervention for preschoolers. In A. van Kleeck, S. A. Stahl, & E. B. Bauer (Eds.), *On reading books to children: Parents and teachers.* Mahwah, NJ: Erlbaum.

Zevenbergen, A. A., Whitehurst, G. J., & Zevenbergen, J. A. (2003). Effects of a shared-reading intervention on the inclusion of evaluative devices in narratives of children from low-income families. *Journal of Applied Developmental Psychology, 24*(1), 1–15.

Ziolkowski, R. A., & Goldstein, H. (2008). Effects of an embedded phonological awareness intervention during repeated book reading on preschool children with language delays. *Journal of Early Intervention, 31*, 67–90.

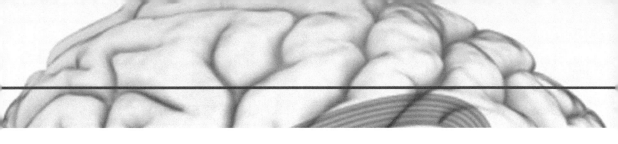

8

Bilingual Children's Language Development: Assessment and Intervention

Brian A. Goldstein

Case Study

Yaitza is a 5-year-old native Spanish-English-speaking bilingual child who began to acquire English in preschool at age 4. After reading this chapter, you will understand how her language skills will develop. You will also learn basic information about how to assess her languages and treat her language problem should she be diagnosed with a language disorder. The following questions should be considered: Should Yaitza be assessed in English, Spanish, or both languages? How will you differentiate a possible language disorder from a language difference? What home and school factors might influence Yaitza's language development? Should an interpreter be used in the assessment and treatment of Yaitza's language disorder? If warranted, should intervention take place in English, Spanish, or both languages?

There are almost 5 million children in the schools in the United States who are learning English as a second language. Thus, it is essential that students majoring in speech-language pathology programs acquire knowledge of bilingual populations to provide them with evidence-based assessment and intervention when these services are required. The purpose of this chapter is to provide information on language development and disorders in bilingual children. Prior to reading this chapter, review the following statements and think about and/or discuss whether you think they are myths or facts.

MYTH OR FACT?

- Bilingualism is defined as the ability to speak two languages fluently.
- We should try to determine in which language the bilingual child is dominant.
- Bilinguals who are typically developing acquire their languages more slowly than monolinguals.
- Language development for bilinguals proceeds at a steady pace over time.
- Bilingual children show the same language skills in each language.
- All bilingual children undergo a silent period.
- Children learn second languages quickly and easily, especially when learning a language at a young age.
- Being raised bilingually will confuse children. Therefore, each language should be spoken by different people.
- The frequency of transfer is high in bilingual children.
- Transfer is greatest if both parents "mix" languages.
- Language proficiency is control over grammar and speech sounds.

By the end of this chapter, you should know whether these statements are myths or facts. Your knowledge of these statements will provide insight and knowledge about how bilingual children acquire their languages and the characteristics of speech and language disorders in such children.

CHAPTER OBJECTIVES

After reading this chapter, you should understand and be able to:

- Describe sociocultural factors related to bilingual language acquisition
- Summarize bilingual language development
- Apply best practice principles for assessment
- Describe cross-linguistic and bilingual approaches to intervention

The reader will learn and understand definitions of bilingualism and related terms, including:

- Dialect
- Code switching
- The stages of second-language learning
- Typical speech and language development in bilingual children
- Deceleration
- Acceleration
- Language proficiency
- Characteristics of bilingual children with speech and language disorders
- Appropriate assessment and intervention approaches
- Use of interpreters and translators

WHAT'S IN A NAME?

There are numerous terms for children who are acquiring more than one language. You will hear them commonly referred to as:

- Limited English proficient
- Non-English proficient

- ◆ Culturally and linguistically diverse
- ◆ English-language learners
- ◆ **Dual language learners**
- ◆ Bilingual
- ◆ **Multilingual**

Although these terms differ in meaning, they are often used interchangeably. Throughout this chapter, the term **bilingual** is used to refer to the children under discussion. This approach is taken to emphasize the fact that in bilingual speech and language development, *both* languages have an impact on acquisition. terms like **limited English proficient**, **non-English proficient**, and **English-language learners** (ELL) tend to emphasize only one of the child's languages, and a term such as **culturally and linguistically diverse** denotes not only those who are acquiring more than one language but also those who might be using more than one **dialect** (i.e., a rule-governed variant of a language, such as African American English).

Bilinguals then are those individuals who are acquiring more than one language, or as one of my students once said, "Bilinguals are those who are not monolingual" (DiMarzio, personal communication). Her definition was quite perceptive because we know that the speech and language development of bilinguals is not identical to that of monolingual children in either language. We will return to this issue later in the chapter.

As Baker (2006) has said, however, "[d]efining who is or is not bilingual is essentially elusive and ultimately impossible. Some categorization is often necessary and helpful to make sense of the world." (p. 13) It is in that spirit that the main types of bilinguals are presented. Bilinguals are often categorized as one of

two main types: **simultaneous bilinguals** and **sequential bilinguals**.

Simultaneous bilinguals are those who acquire both languages before the age of about 5 years. Simultaneous bilinguals who acquire both languages from birth are known to be undergoing **bilingual first-language acquisition** (de Houwer, 2009). That is, they are acquiring *two* first languages from birth. Sequential bilinguals are those who acquire a second language after a foundation in their first language.

The distinction between simultaneous bilinguals and sequential bilinguals is usually based on the age at which the second language is introduced.

If the two languages are introduced before about age 5 (and often age 3), then the child is typically considered a simultaneous bilingual (McLaughlin, 1984; Meisel, 2004). If, however, the second language is introduced after age 5 (and often after age 3), then the child is typically considered a sequential bilingual (Paradis, Genesee, & Crago, 2011).

COMPLEXITY IN DEFINING *BILINGUAL*

Although the categories just described are the main labels used to group bilinguals, they are only one method used to classify bilinguals. Those two categories are based on one criterion—the age at which the second language was introduced.

Bilingualism, however, is somewhat more complex than that because bilingualism is not an absolute condition but rather a relative one in that bilingual individuals can be [either] slightly bilingual or very bilingual (Valdés & Figueroa, 1994). What Valdés and Figueroa mean is that bilingual skills reside on a continuum. Being bilingual does *not* mean that one is equally skilled in both languages. That is, the speech and language skills that bilinguals have in one language are not simply mirrored in the other language. One can have superior skills in Language A over Language B. For example, a child acquiring Vietnamese and English might have superior speech and language skills in Vietnamese compared with skills in English. Over time, however, that balance might change (Paradis, 2016). As the child becomes more embedded in the U.S. educational system, for example, her English skills might become stronger than her skills in Vietnamese.

Bilingual development is further complicated by the fact that a bilingual child's skills can vary by language domain (i.e., syntax, semantics, lexicon, phonology, and pragmatics). For example, a bilingual child theoretically could have greater skills in syntax in Language A but superior skills in phonology in Language B. Additionally, a bilingual child's speech and language skills are not equally distributed. Thus, the child might have knowledge in one language that he or she does not have in the other (Paradis et al., 2011). For example, a bilingual child might be able to label an object in one language but not in the other (Peña, Bedore, & Rappazzo, 2003).

When bilinguals are said to have skills in one language but not in the other, they are often referred to as having (language) *dominance* in one linguistic system over the other. **Language dominance**, however, is a term that is difficult to define and validly assess. Moreover, the term should be used with great caution because it is often misunderstood and misused (e.g., MacSwan & Rolstad, 2006). Language dominance most often connotes greater skill in one language over the other. As alluded to previously, bilingualism exists on a continuum, likely influenced by language domain. Thus, a bilingual child will have some skills that are superior in Language A and other skills that are superior in Language B. For example, Peña and colleagues (2003) found such an effect in Spanish-English bilingual children. In their study, the children found receptive functions (e.g., *show me what you do with a hammer*) to be easier when asked in Spanish than when those same children were prompted about receptive functions in English. These results question the validity of language dominance, as it is traditionally defined. Moreover, results from other studies are equivocal on the usefulness of such a construct.

In a group of Welsh-English bilingual children ages 2;6 to 5;0, Ball, Müller, and Munro (2001) found that Welsh-dominant children acquired the trill earlier than their peers who were English dominant.

In a group of 2-year-old French-English bilingual children, Paradis (2001) found that English-dominant bilinguals preserved a higher frequency of second syllables in words (e.g., gi-RAFFE, *giraffe*) than did French-dominant bilinguals. However, French-dominant bilinguals preserved a higher frequency of third syllables (e.g., e-le-PHANT, *elephant*) than did English-dominant bilinguals.

In a group of Cantonese- and Putonghua-speaking bilingual children ages 2;6 to 4;11, Law and So (2006) found that both Cantonese-dominant and Putonghua-dominant children acquired Cantonese phonology first. That is, regardless of which language was considered the dominant one, the children learned Cantonese before Putonghua.

These equivocal results related to language dominance question its validity. What is necessary from a practical point of view is to determine the bilingual child's relative strengths and weaknesses in each of their languages across all domains of language. Attempting to determine dominance as an omnibus measure appears not to be warranted, especially as it relates to speech and language development.

BILINGUAL SPEECH AND LANGUAGE ACQUISITION

In discussing speech and language acquisition, it is helpful to embed it within a theoretical context. One such theory is the **Interactional Dual Systems Model** of bilingual language acquisition (Paradis, 2001). This model assumes that bilingual children develop distinct linguistic systems for each language. Those two systems, however, interact and thus, are, interdependent. Interdependence could serve to speed up (i.e., **acceleration**) and/or slow down (i.e., **deceleration**) speech and language development relative to that of monolinguals (Fabiano-Smith & Goldstein, 2010; Paradis et al., 2011). There is evidence that both acceleration and deceleration occur in bilingual speech

and language acquisition when the skills of bilingual children are compared with monolinguals. For example, Bialystok (2001) noted a cognitive advantage in terms of executive control functions, such as activation, selection, attention, inhibition, and organization of information (problem solving, planning) in bilinguals compared with monolinguals. By the way, this advantage in bilinguals increased commensurate with the amount of language the children heard in their environment and their levels of proficiency (i.e., how well they use each of their languages). Thus, the more of each language that second-language learners hear and the more skilled they are in speaking each one, the greater the cognitive advantage. These results seem to show support for acceleration of the language skills in bilinguals compared with monolinguals.

Although bilingual children might exhibit acceleration in their language skills in comparison to monolinguals, they might show deceleration as well. Deceleration indicates that development occurs more slowly in bilingual children than in monolingual children. Such a result has been shown for syntax, morphology, and phonology (Gildersleeve-Neumann, Kester, Davis, & Peña, 2008; Swain, 1972; Vihman, 1982). For example, in a group of Spanish-English bilingual 3-year-olds, Gildersleeve et al. (2008) found that overall consonant accuracy (i.e., how well children produce speech sounds) was lower in bilinguals than in monolinguals.

The speech and language skills of bilinguals relative to monolinguals might be accelerated or decelerated, but what is important to realize, however, is that "[d]espite the acquisition of two languages, bilingual children do *not* appear to be 'remarkably delayed nor remarkably advanced' relative to that of . . . monolingual children" (Nicoladis & Genesee, 1996, p. 264, emphasis added). That is, the speech and language skills of bilinguals are similar, although not identical, to those of monolinguals in each constituent language (Goldstein, 2012). This result has been found across various domains of language such as syntax (Paradis & Genesee, 1996) and phonology (e.g., Goldstein, Fabiano, & Washington, 2005).

It is important to point out, however, that bilingual children do not proceed through the same linguistic stages at the same time in each language. Merino (1992) found that the order of acquisition of grammatical forms was different for monolinguals and bilinguals. For example, monolinguals first acquired the active tense (e.g., *ella come pan* [she eats bread]) followed by gender (*gato rojo* [cat red]), plural (*gatos* [cats]), regular past tense (*ella comió pan* [she ate bread]), and finally irregular past (*ellos fueron a la casa* [they went home]). In contrast, bilingual children first acquired the active tense followed by gender, present progressive (*ella está comiendo* [she is eating]), plural, and finally regular past. Findings such as these indicate that even though bilingual children might show overall commensurate language skills with monolinguals, there will be differences in those skills across each constituent language. It is likely that bilinguals will have skills that are greater in one language over the other. For example, bilinguals might exhibit more advanced syntactic skills in Language A vs. Language B (Paradis et al., 2011).

The speech and language trajectory of children who acquire a second language after some facility with a first language (i.e., sequential bilinguals) is somewhat different from that of monolingual children in either language. For example, Paradis (2007) found that after 21 months

of exposure to English, 40% of the sequential bilinguals exhibited morphological skills within the normal range of monolinguals, 65% for receptive vocabulary, and 90% for story grammar. Additionally, after an average of 8 months of exposure to English, overall consonant accuracy for sequential bilinguals (ages 4;6 to 6;9) averaged 90% (Gilhool, Goldstein, Burrows, & Paradis, 2009). More specifically, consonant accuracy was less than 90% (average of 83%) for only 2 of 10 children. These data show that even children who acquire speech and language skills after experience in their first language approach monolingual norms after a relatively short time period.

LANGUAGE DEVELOPMENT IN SECOND-LANGUAGE ACQUISITION

Children undergoing second-language acquisition go through five primary stages of speech and language development (Hearne, 2000). It should be noted that these stages are meant to be general in nature, given the known individual variation of speech and language development of second-language learners (and all children, in general).

Stage I: Preproduction. In this stage, children often undergo a silent period. That is, they focus more on **receptive language** (i.e., language comprehension) than on **expressive language** (i.e., language production). The silent period is relatively short—usually not more than 6 months (Tabors, 1997). It should be noted, however, that often during this phase, children use some expressive language (in the second language) with each other but less so with adults in the environment (Tabors, 1997). Also during this stage, children respond to simple commands and have a receptive vocabulary of about 500 words.

Stage II: Early Production. In this stage (approximately 3 to 6 months after introduction of the second language), the children are still focused more on receptive language than on expressive language. Specifically, they are comprehending yes/no and who/what/where questions. They typically use one- to three-word phrases and formulaic expressions (*gimme five*). Their receptive and expressive vocabulary consists of approximately 1,000 words.

Stage III: Speech Emergence. In this stage (approximately 6 months to 2 years after introduction of the second language), the children show increased comprehension and increased grammatical complexity, but exhibit grammatical errors; use simple sentences by expanding vocabulary; and have a receptive and expressive vocabulary of around 3,000 words.

Stage IV: Intermediate Fluency. In this stage (approximately 3 years after introduction of the second language), the children show improved comprehension, a receptive and expressive vocabulary of around 6,000 words, adequate face-to-face conversational skills, and more complex statements in which they express thoughts and opinions with few grammatical errors.

Stage V: Advanced Language Proficiency. In this stage (approximately

5 to 7 years after introduction of the second language), the children use specialized vocabulary related to content areas, use English grammar and vocabulary comparable to a native speaker, and are able to actively participate in grade level classroom activities.

TRANSFER AND CODE-MIXING

Bilingual children exhibit both acceleration and deceleration relative to monolingual development. They also show patterns of transfer. **Transfer** is defined as language-specific features found in productions of the other language (Paradis, 2001). This term is often used synonymously with **cross-linguistic effects**. Cross-linguistic effects usually connote that the features are bidirectional; that is, from Language A to Language B and vice versa.

Transfer is a hallmark of bilingual speech and language development. An example might be when a native Spanish speaker produces *red house* as *house red* because, in Spanish, nouns precede the adjectives that modify them. It should be noted that features of transfer are variable (Schnitzer & Krasinski, 1994, 1996), occur in both languages (Gildersleeve-Neumann et al., 2008), and are *not* equally represented in both languages (Goldstein, 2008). From a practical point of view, features of transfer are not true errors and thus would not be treated if the bilingual child had a speech or language disorder and required intervention.

Code-mixing is the "use of phonological, lexical, morphosyntactic, or pragmatic patterns from two languages in the same utterance or stretch of conversation" (Paradis et al., 2011, p. 89). According to

Paradis et al. (2011), there are a number of types of code-mixing:

- Intra-utterance:. *Alguien se murió en ese cuarto* [someone died in that room] *that he sleeps in.*
- Inter-utterance:. *Pa ¿me vas a comprarun jugo?* [are you going to buy me juice] *It cos' 25 cents.*
- Mixing words:. *Estamos como marido y* [we are like man and] *woman.*
- Mixing clauses:. *You know how to swim but no te tapa* [it won't be over your head]

As is the case with transfer, code-mixing is a typical linguistic phenomenon in bilinguals. Code-mixing does *not* mean that the bilingual speaker lacks control or proficiency over the two languages. It is a natural occurrence in acquiring a second language. However, the more the bilingual child's parents code-mix, the more likely it is that he or she will code-mix (Lanza, 1992).

LANGUAGE LOSS/ LANGUAGE DISORDER

Another phenomenon typical in bilingual speakers is **language loss** (also termed *language attrition*) (Anderson, 2012). Language loss occurs when the speech and language features of the first language are no longer utilized by the speaker because he or she hears and uses less of the first language over time. Examples of language loss include the following:

- Deletion of grammatical markers (e.g., plural)
- Decreased number of different words (i.e., speakers will tend to use the same core group of words over and over rather than using a robust number of different words)
- Increased number of false starts, pauses, hesitation, and decreased organizational skills.

Unfortunately, these characteristics often are similar to those features that signal a true language disorder (i.e., not related to learning a second language). It is possible, however, to stave off language attrition with programs that support the first language (Gutiérrez-Clellen, Simón Cereijido, Restrepo, 2013; Restrepo & Gray, 2012).

Features of language attrition should *not* be confused with a true language disorder. That said, there is no doubt that bilingual speakers (be they simultaneous or sequential bilinguals) can exhibit a language disorder. What is interesting about language disorders in these children is that they show commensurate language skills to monolinguals with language impairments (Paradis, 2005), and they exhibit the same type and frequency of grammatical errors as monolinguals with language impairments (Paradis, Crago, Genesee, & Rice, 2003). Moreover, bilingual children with Down syndrome (DS) showed commensurate language skills to monolingual children with DS (Kay-Raining Bird et al., 2005), and bilingual children with language impairments exhibited (protracted) periods of plateaus or regressions in grammatical development, just as did monolinguals with language impairments (Kohnert, 2008).

Some speech-language pathologists (SLPs) and other practitioners are often wary of providing intervention to bilingual children in their non-English language. Their rationale is that bilingual children with language disorders will be even more "confused" by receiving services in the non-English language. The evidence presented previously seems to obviate that concern. Both languages of the bilingual benefit from input in the two languages. As Kohnert (2008, pp. 143–144) says, "[a] disorder in bilinguals is not caused by bilingualism or cured by monolingualism."

ASSESSMENT OF SPEECH AND LANGUAGE DISORDERS IN BILINGUAL CHILDREN

Identification of bilingual children for being at risk for language disorders (specifically semantics and syntax) is *not* predicted by being bilingual (Peña, 2016; Peña, Gillam, Bedore, & Bohman, 2011). Thus, although being bilingual does not "cause" or exacerbate a speech or language disorder, it does complicate diagnosing them differentially.

In assessing all children, it is necessary for the SLP to complete a case history in which he or she begins to determine the presenting problem and the possible medical, psychosocial, and environmental factors related to the speech or language disorder. When a child is acquiring more than one language (i.e., is not monolingual), the SLP must gather the following additional information, specific to bilingual children:

♦ The sociocultural characteristics of the community: It is important to understand the culture of the family and the community (e.g., Lynch & Hanson, 2011). The SLP might need a **cultural broker** to aid in understanding the community's culture. A cultural broker is an individual, usually from the family's cultural background, who can provide an "insider's" information on that culture and aid in the interpretation of the family's linguistic and nonlinguistic characteristics.

♦ The structure of the non-English language: vocabulary, grammar, word meaning, speech sounds, and pragmatics.

♦ Age of acquisition: Is the child a simultaneous or sequential bilingual? Also, at what age did the child begin to hear and use each language?

♦ **Language use**: how often and with whom each language is used.

♦ **Language proficiency**: how well each language is used.

Once the case history is completed, the SLP conducts testing to discern whether the child has a speech or language disorder and what the child's strengths and weaknesses are in each of the two languages. Testing can be either formal or informal in nature. In speech-language pathology, formal tests are often standardized. A standardized test is used to measure a client's performance in one or more domains. That performance is then compared with that of a similar group on a measure that is not influenced by the person administering or interpreting the test (Tomblin, 2000). This standardized procedure allows us to assume that differences in performance are based on ability rather than on the testing procedure. The difficulty in utilizing such tests with bilingual children is that they rarely include bilingual children in the normative data. In fact, they usually are specifically excluded. Even for non-English tests, bilingual children are rarely included. Finally, standardized tests that include bilingual children do not test the full range of bilingual skills (i.e., from "a little" bilingual to "a lot" bilingual). Thus, there are few standardized tests available to use with bilingual children. In the consideration of using standardized tests with bilingual children, it is important to determine if:

◆ The normative data include bilingual children.
◆ The bilingual children in the normative group are similar to the group with whom you will use the test.
◆ **Confidence intervals** (i.e., the score a child would receive if he or she theoretically took the test multiple times) are provided.
◆ The test manual reports data on:
  ◆ **Sensitivity** (i.e., percentage of individuals correctly identified with a disorder)
  ◆ **Specificity** (i.e., percentage of individuals correctly identified as typically developing)

Informal Assessment Procedures

Because there are so few standardized tests available to use with bilingual children, informal means of assessment are implemented with them (e.g., Arias & Friberg, 2016). SLPs often use standardized tests in an informal way. That is, they use the stimulus items from the tests but do not report the scores. Some examples of such informal procedures include:

◆ Giving more detailed explanations of tasks because not all children will have experience taking such tests
◆ Adding practice items, again because of the lack of experience taking tests
◆ Repeating stimuli and/or rewording the test

◆ Testing beyond the test's ceiling (i.e., above the point where administration of the test would stop if it were being scored according to the instructions in the test manual)
◆ Asking children to explain their answers in order to determine if they have understood the question
◆ Utilizing informal checklists (Roseberry-McKibbin, 2002) and parent questionnaires (Restrepo, 1998)
◆ Comparing data from the child being evaluated with published data on similar children
◆ Focusing more on process-based measures (rate and quality of "learning") rather than on static measures (Hwa-Froelich & Matsuo, 2005; Peña & Quinn, 1997)
◆ Analyzing narratives/conversational samples by measuring aspects, such as number of different words, number of clauses per utterance, and cohesion (Gutiérrez-Clellen, 2012)

Dynamic Assessment

One commonly used alternative assessment approach is **dynamic assessment**, based on the work of Vygotsky (1978) and his concept of the zone of proximal development; that is, the "distance between the level of performance a child can reach unaided and the level of participation that can be accomplished when guided by a more knowledgeable participant" (Campione & Brown, 1987, p. 83). This zone can be interpreted as "potential." The goals of dynamic assessment are to profile learners' abilities; to observe learners' modifiability; to induce an active, self-regulated learning; and to inform intervention.

What dynamic assessment allows the assessor to do is to tap future skills, or the child's **modifiability** (i.e., change through mediation) (Peña, 1996). Modifiability involves three factors: child responsiveness (how the child responds to and uses new information); examiner effort (quantity and quality of effort needed to make a change); and transfer (generalization of new skills). All three factors are critical in determining if a child fails on a task because of experience or ability.

The format for dynamic assessment is test-teach-retest. In the test phase, the examiner determines the child's areas of weakness and the base level of functioning, without any aid or assistance. In the teach phase, the assessor models the target behaviors and strategies in meaningful contexts, makes the child aware of how the strategies are to be applied, allows the child to lead some of the time, and increases demands as the skills are mastered. In order to determine how the child has progressed after the teach phase, she is retested, measuring examiner effort (i.e., how much aid is needed by individuals to maximize their performance), child responsiveness (i.e., how rapidly the child changes in response to teaching), and transfer (i.e., the generalization of the task to other tasks and other domains). Dynamic assessment has been used successfully to differentiate children's lack of experience from their lack of ability (Peña, Iglesias, & Lidz, 2001).

Do's and Don'ts

The process outlined previously indicates the type of assessment that should be completed with bilingual children. Equally important is the kind of testing that should be avoided; that is, testing "don'ts." These include:

◆ Don't use norm-referenced tests only.
◆ Don't use only a language sample or multiple assessments to qualify someone for services.
◆ Don't use tests administered in English only.
◆ Don't assume that features of a second language are characteristics of a disorder (overdiagnosis).
◆ Don't assume that errors related to a true disorder are features of a second language (underdiagnosis).
◆ Translated tests should not be used for the following reasons:
  ◆ There are differences in structure and content of each language.
  ◆ Using translated tests implies (mistakenly) that all children receive similar socialization, language input, and academic instruction in both languages.
  ◆ Differences in the frequency of target words vary from language to language.
  ◆ Grammatical forms may not be equivalent.
  ◆ Such tests do not tap into a child's ability to acquire language.

Interpreters and Translators

In some sense, all SLPs are monolingual. That is, no SLP can possibly speak every language that her clients speak. It is estimated that only 6% of certified SLPs meet the definition of a bilingual service provider (ASHA, 2016). Thus, it is highly likely that monolingual SLPs will be providing services to bilinguals. The American Speech-Language-Hearing Association

(ASHA) (1985) has outlined a number of tasks that monolingual SLPs can perform with bilinguals, including:

◆ Testing in English
◆ Performing an oral-peripheral exam
◆ Conducting hearing screenings
◆ Completing nonverbal assessments
◆ Conducting a family interview (with an interpreter or translator)
◆ Being an advocate for the client and family

It is likely, however, that at some point an SLP will need to utilize the services of an **interpreter** (conveys information from one language to another when the message is oral) or a **translator** (conveys information from one language to another when the message is written) to assess a bilingual child. Here we focus on interpreters, that is, the individual who serves as the bridge between the SLP and the family/child (Langdon & Cheng, 2002). The use of an interpreter does not negate the role of the SLP. It is the SLP's job to construct the assessment session (and the intervention) and to train the interpreter in how to work effectively. The training of an interpreter should include not only verbal interaction but also nonverbal cues, cultural effects, and contextual knowledge (i.e., how the environment of the assessment has shaped the interaction). Interpreters should be professionals who regularly serve in this role. It is not appropriate to have friends, neighbors, siblings, or relatives serve in this role because they do not have the objectivity needed to provide such services.

Langdon and Cheng (2002) outline a three-step process for the session. The first phase is termed *briefing*. In this phase, the SLP plans the session, trains the interpreter, and reviews the critical questions and/or issues. The second phase is *interaction*. During this phase, the SLP and the interpreter interact with the client and her or his family. The role of the SLP during this phase is to make observations on the body language of the child and note if the interpreter uses too many words when instructing the child. The interpreter should record all responses and ask for clarification when questions arise. In the *debriefing* phase, the SLP and the interpreter review the outcomes. The SLP reviews the interpreter's impressions and the SLP and interpreter discuss any difficulties related to the process. All reports should state that an assessment was performed with the assistance of an interpreter. In the end, the SLP makes the final recommendations.

In summary, assessment for bilinguals is complex and multidimensional. It is far more important to describe in detail the child's skills in all domains in both languages rather than trying to determine, for example, in which language the child is "dominant." Moreover, rather than focusing on the *type* of bilingualism, *etiology* of the disorder, or *scores* on a standardized assessment, focus should be on behaviors, symptoms, and characteristics.

INTERVENTION

Although there have been several research studies that focus on the assessment of bilingual children, there are far fewer related to intervention for bilingual children with speech and language disorders (e.g., Thordardottir, Cloutier, Ménard, Pelland-Blais, & Rvachew, 2016). This relative lack of studies has made it difficult to apply principles of **evidence-based practice** (EBP) to such children. EBP is an approach to clinical decision making in which valid, reliable evidence is given more validity than intuition, anecdote, and expert authority (Dollaghan, 2007; Justice & Fey, 2004). EBP includes not only the best available evidence but also clinical expertise and client values (Dollaghan, 2007). Thus, EBP requires the application of evidence in combination with the clinician's experience, or clinical craft, and understanding of the child's and family's unique demographic characteristics and sociocultural perspectives (Justice & Fey, 2004). As Kamhi (2011) has noted, however, "the scientific method, with its emphasis on theoretical coherence, replicability, unbiased measurements, and logic, is diametrically opposed to flexible, dynamic, spontaneous, reactive, and creative clinical practice" (p. 61). It is such practice that must be provided to bilingual children with speech and language disorders given the paucity of research studies related to intervention.

Six-Step Process for Intervention

For bilingual children, the purpose of intervention is to systematically improve their communication skills *in both languages*, through intervention carried out by a culturally and linguistically competent professional. To do so, a six-step process for intervention is proposed here (see Appendix 8–A for a complete description of these steps).

Step 1: Choose goals

Step 2: Choose targets

Step 3: Choose the goal attack strategy

Step 4: Choose the intervention approach

Step 5: Choose the language of intervention

Step 6: Monitor progress

MYTH OR FACT? REVISITED

Now that you have read this chapter, you should be able to answer myth or fact to the following statements. As before, read the statements and think about and/or discuss whether you think they are myths or facts and indicate what evidence underlies your decision. As you read and discuss these statements, be aware that the answers are not likely to be straightforward. Just like bilinguals themselves, the answers are complex.

- Bilingualism is defined as the ability to speak two languages fluently.
- We should try and determine in which language the bilingual child is dominant.
- Bilinguals who are typically developing acquire their languages more slowly than monolinguals. Thus, language development for bilinguals is slower than that of monolinguals.
- Language development for bilinguals proceeds at a steady pace over time.
- Bilingual children show the same language skills in each language.
- All bilingual children undergo a silent period.
- Children, especially the young ones, learn second languages quickly and easily.
- Being raised bilingually will confuse children. Therefore, each language should be spoken by different people.
- The frequency of transfer is high in bilingual children.

- Transfer is greatest if both parents "mix" languages.
- Language proficiency is control over grammar and speech sounds.

SUMMARY

Acquiring more than one language is a complex, multilayered task that is neither quick nor easy. That said, bilingual language acquisition is similar, although not identical, to monolingual language acquisition. This holds true for bilingual children with speech and language disorders as well. That is, even children who have speech and language disorders are able to acquire two languages. Finally, there is significant interchild variation in the skills of bilingual children.

KEY WORDS

Acceleration

Bilingual

Bilingual first-language acquisition

Code-mixing

Confidence intervals

Cross-linguistic effects

Cultural broker

Culturally and linguistically diverse

Deceleration

Dialect

Dual language learners

Dynamic assessment

English-language learners

Evidence-based practice

Expressive language

Interactional Dual Systems Model

Interpreter

Language dominance

Language loss

Language proficiency

Language use

Limited English proficient

Modifiability

Multilingual

Non-English proficient

Receptive language

Sensitivity

Sequential bilinguals

Simultaneous bilinguals

Specificity

Transfer

Translator

STUDY QUESTIONS

1. List three alternative methods to assess bilingual children with speech and language disorders. Furthermore, indicate how these three ways are less biased than using standardized tests to assess these children.

2. In planning intervention for bilingual children, explain why the language of intervention is not the first decision to be made in this process.

3. How would you explain to a class-room teacher that using more than one language by bilingual children will not necessarily slow down their overall language development?

4. Explain why characteristics of code-mixing are not features of a language problem in bilinguals.

REFERENCES

American Speech-Language-Hearing Association. (1985). *Clinical management of communicatively handicapped minority language populations* [Position statement]. Retrieved from http://www.asha.org/policy

American Speech-Language-Hearing Association. (2016). *Demographic profile of ASHA members providing bilingual services*. Retrieved from http://www.asha.org/uploadedFiles/Demographic-profile-Bilingual-Spanish-Service-Members.pdf

Anderson, R. (2012). First language loss in Spanish-speaking children. In B. Goldstein (Ed.), *Bilingual language development and disorders in Spanish-English speakers* (2nd ed., pp. 193–212). Baltimore, MD: Brookes.

Arias G., & Friberg, J. (2016). Bilingual language assessment: Contemporary versus recommended practice in American schools. *Language, Speech, and Hearing Services in Schools, 48*, 1–15.

Baker, C. (2006). *Foundations of bilingual education and bilingualism*. Clevedon, UK: Multilingual Matters.

Ball, M. J., Müller, N., & Munro, S. (2001). The acquisition of the rhotic consonants by Welsh-English bilingual children. *International Journal of Bilingualism, 5*, 71–86.

Bialystok, E. (2001). *Bilingualism in development: Language, literacy, and cognition*. New York, NY: Cambridge University Press.

Campione, J., & Brown, A. (1987). Linking dynamic assessment with school achievement. In C. Lidz (Ed.), *Dynamic assessment:*

An interactional approach to evaluating learning potential (pp. 82–115). New York, NY: Guilford Press.

de Houwer, A. (2009). *Bilingual first language acquisition*. Clevedon, UK: Multilingual Matters.

Dollaghan, C. (2007). *The handbook of evidence-based practice in communication disorders*. Baltimore, MD: Brookes.

Fabiano-Smith, L., & Goldstein, B. (2010). Early-, middle-, and late-developing sounds in monolingual and bilingual children: An exploratory investigation. *American Journal of Speech-Language Pathology, 19*, 66–77.

Fey, M. (1986). *Language intervention with young children*. San Diego, CA: College-Hill Press.

Gildersleeve-Neumann, C., Kester, E., Davis, B., & Peña, E. (2008). English speech sound development in preschool-aged children from bilingual English-Spanish environments. *Language, Speech, and Hearing Services in Schools, 39*, 314–328.

Gilhool, A., Goldstein, B., Burrows, L., & Paradis, J. (2009, November). *English phonological skills of English language learners*. Seminar presented at the convention of the American Speech-Language-Hearing Association, New Orleans, LA.

Goldstein, B. (2008). Integration of evidence-based practice into the university clinic. *Topics in Language Disorders, 28*, 200–211.

Goldstein, B. (Ed.). (2012). *Bilingual language development and disorders in Spanish-English speakers* (2nd ed.). Baltimore, MD: Brookes.

Goldstein, B., Fabiano, L., & Washington, P. S. (2005). Phonological skills in predominantly English-speaking, predominantly Spanish-speaking, and Spanish-English bilingual children. *Language, Speech, and Hearing Services in Schools, 36*, 201–218.

Gutiérrez-Clellen, V. F. (1999). Language choice in intervention with bilingual children. *American Journal of Speech-Language Pathology, 8*, 291–302.

Gutierréz-Clellen, V. (2012). Narrative development and disorders in bilingual children. In B. Goldstein (Ed.), *Bilingual language development and disorders in Spanish-English speakers* (2nd ed., pp. 233–249). Baltimore, MD: Brookes.

Gutiérrez-Clellen, V., Simón Cereijido, G., & Restrepo, M. A. (2013). *Improving the vocabulary and oral language of bilingual Latino preschoolers: An intervention for speech-language pathologists.* San Diego, CA: Plural.

Hearne, D. (2000). *Teaching 2nd language learners with learning disabilities.* Oceanside, CA: Academic Communication Associates.

Hwa-Froelich, D. A., & Matsuo, H. (2005). Vietnamese children and language-based processing tasks. *Language, Speech, and Hearing Services in Schools, 36,* 230–243.

Justice, L. M., & Fey, M. E. (2004, September 21). Evidence-based practice in schools: Integrating craft and theory with science and data. *The ASHA Leader, 4–5,* 30–32.

Kamhi, A. G. (2011). Balancing certainty and uncertainty in clinical practice. *Language, Speech, and Hearing Services in Schools, 42,* 59–64.

Kay-Raining Bird, E., Cleave, P., Trureau, N., Thordardottir, E., Sutton, A., & Thorpe, A. (2005). The language abilities of bilingual children with Down syndrome. *American Journal of Speech-Language Pathology, 14,* 187–199.

Kohnert, K. (2008). *Language disorders in bilingual children and adults.* San Diego, CA: Plural.

Kohnert, K., & Derr, A. (2012). Language intervention with bilingual children. In B. Goldstein (Ed.), *Bilingual language development and disorders in Spanish-English speakers* (2nd ed., pp. 337–356). Baltimore, MD: Brookes.

Langdon, H. W., & Cheng, L. L. (2002). *Collaborating with interpreters and translators in the communication disorders field.* Eau Claire, WI: Thinking Publications.

Lanza, E. (1992). Can bilingual two-year-olds code-switch? *Journal of Child Language, 19,* 633–658.

Law, N. C. W., & So, L. K. H. (2006). The relationship of phonological development and language dominance in bilingual Cantonese-Putonghua children. *International Journal of Bilingualism, 10,* 405–428.

Lopez, L., & Greenfield, D. (2004). The cross-linguistic transfer of phonological skills of Hispanic Head Start children. *Bilingual Research Journal, 28,* 1–18.

Lynch, E., & Hanson, M. (Eds.). (2011). *Developing cross-cultural competence: A guide for working with children and their families* (4th ed.). Baltimore, MD: Brookes.

MacSwan, J., & Rolstad, K. (2006). How language proficiency tests mislead us about ability: Implications for English language learner placement in special education. *Teachers College Record, 108*(11), 2304–2328.

McLaughlin, B. (1984). *Second language acquisition in childhood: Volume 1. Preschool children* (2nd ed.). Hillsdale, NJ: Erlbaum.

Meisel, J. (2004). The bilingual child. In T. K. Bhatia & W. C. Ritchie (Eds.), *The handbook of bilingualism* (pp. 91–113). Malden, MA: Blackwell.

Merino, B. J. (1992). Acquisition of syntactic and phonological features in Spanish. In H. W. Langdon & L. L. Cheng (Eds.), *Hispanic children and adults with communication disorders* (pp. 57–98). Gaithersburg, MD: Aspen.

Nicoladis, E., & Genessee, F. (1996). A longitudinal study of pragmatic differentiation in young bilingual children. *Language Learning, 46,* 439–464.

Paradis, J. (2001). Do bilingual two-year-olds have separate phonological systems? *International Journal of Bilingualism, 5,* 19–39.

Paradis, J. (2005). Grammatical morphology in children learning English as a second language: Implications of similarities with specific language impairment. *Language, Speech and Hearing Services in Schools, 36,* 172–187.

Paradis, J. (2007). Second language acquisition in childhood. In E. Hoff & M. Shatz (Eds.), *Handbook of language development* (pp. 387–406). Oxford, UK: Blackwell.

Paradis, J. (2016). An agenda for knowledge-oriented research on bilingualism in children with developmental disorders. *Journal of Communication Disorders, 63,* 79–84.

Paradis, J., Crago, M., Genesee, F., & Rice, M. (2003). Bilingual children with specific language impairment: How do they compare with their monolingual peers? *Journal of Speech, Language and Hearing Research, 46,* 1–15.

Paradis, J., & Genesee, F. (1996). Syntactic acquisition in bilingual children: Autonomous or interdependent? *Studies in Second Language Acquisition, 18,* 1–25.

Paradis, J., Genesee, F., & Crago, M. (2011). *Dual language development and disorders: A handbook on bilingualism and second language acquisition* (2nd ed.). Baltimore, MD: Brookes.

Peña, E. (1996). Dynamic assessment: The model and language applications. In K. Cole, P. Dale, & D. Thal (Eds.), *Assessment of communication and language* (pp. 281–307). Baltimore, MD: Paul H. Brookes.

Peña, E. (2016). Supporting the home language of bilingual children with developmental disabilities: From knowing to doing. *Journal of Communication Disorders, 63,* 85–92.

Peña, E., Bedore, L. M., & Rappazzo, C. (2003). Comparison of Spanish, English, and bilingual children's performance across semantic tasks. *Language, Speech, and Hearing Services in Schools, 34,* 5–16.

Peña, E., Gillam, R., Bedore, L., & Bohman, T. (2011). Risk for poor performance on a language screening measure for bilingual preschoolers and kindergarteners. *American Journal of Speech-Language Pathology, 20,* 302–314.

Peña, E., Iglesias, A., & Lidz, C. (2001). Reducing test bias through dynamic assessment of children's word learning ability. *American Journal of Speech-Language Pathology, 10,* 138–154.

Peña, E., & Quinn, R. (1997). Task familiarity: Effects on the test performance of Puerto Rican and African American children. *Language, Speech, and Hearing Services in Schools, 28,* 323–332.

Restrepo, M. A. (1998). Identifiers of predominantly Spanish-speaking children with language impairment. *Journal of Speech, Language, and Hearing Research, 41,* 1398–1411.

Restrepo, M. A., & Gray, S. (2012). Professional development practices and content for professionals working with preschool dual language learners. In B. Goldstein (Ed.), *Bilingual language development and disorders in Spanish-English speakers* (2nd ed., pp. 365–378). Baltimore, MD: Brookes.

Roseberry-McKibbin, C. (2002). *Multicultural students with special needs* (2nd ed.). Oceanside, CA: Academic Communication Associates.

Schnitzer, M., & Krasinski, E. (1994). The development of segmental phonological production in a bilingual child. *Journal of Child Language, 21,* 585–622.

Schnitzer, M., & Krasinski, E. (1996). The development of segmental phonological production in a bilingual child: A contrasting second case. *Journal of Child Language, 23,* 547–571.

Swain, M. (1972). *Bilingualism as a first language* (Unpublished doctoral dissertation). University of California, Irvine.

Tabors, P. (1997). *One child, two languages: A guide for preschool educators of children learning English as a second language.* Baltimore, MD: Brookes.

Thordardottir, E., Cloutier, G., Ménard, S., Pelland-Blais, E., & Rvachew, S. (2016). Monolingual or bilingual intervention for primary language impairment? A randomized control trial. *Journal of Speech, Language, and Hearing Research, 58,* 287–300

Tomblin, B. (2000). Perspective on diagnosis. In B. Tomblin, H. Morris, & D. C. Spriestersbach (Eds.), *Diagnosis in speech-language pathology* (pp. 3–33). San Diego, CA: Singular.

Valdés, G., & Figueroa, R. A. (1994). *Bilingualism and testing: A special case of bias.* Norwood, NJ: Ablex.

Vihman, M. (1982). The acquisition of morphology by a bilingual child. *Journal of Child Language, 3,* 141–160.

Vygotsky, L. (1978). *Mind in society.* Cambridge, MA: Harvard University Press.

Williams, A. L. (2003). Target selection and treatment outcomes. *Perspectives on Language Learning and Education, 10(1),* 12–16.

APPENDIX 8–A

Proposed Intervention Process for Bilingual Children

Step 1: Choose Goals

In planning intervention for bilingual children, SLPs often mistakenly begin the process by attempting to determine in which language to provide intervention. Although that is an important step (and is discussed later), it is not the first step. As with anyone who requires services for a speech or language disorder, the first step is to choose the goals based on a comprehensive assessment, as described earlier in the chapter. Goals might be crafted that cut across two intersecting continua (Baker, 2006). The first continuum focuses on goals that are either context embedded or context reduced. That is, goals related to this continuum focus on the amount of contextual support available to the child. A context-embedded goal might be using one- to two-word responses related to an object in the environment. A context-reduced goal might be one where the child describes a television show.

The second continuum focuses on goals that are cognitively demanding or cognitively undemanding. Cognitively undemanding goals are those for which the child has relative mastery of the language skills needed to communicate easily. Cognitively demanding goals are those that are challenging due to the need for rapid processing of information. A cognitively undemanding goal might be one that focuses on the child talking about the weather. In contrast, a cognitively demanding goal is one in which the child is asked to explain and justify an opinion.

Step 2: Choose Targets

Once the goals are chosen, then the specific targets should be identified. For bilingual children, targets might be based on the child's language skills, error patterns, and errors in each of the two languages. For example, errors that are highly occurring in or common to *both* languages might be selected first. Such errors might be deletion of consonant clusters (e.g., /plen/ "plane" → [pen]), omission of the plural marker, and difficulties using the present progressive tense. Then targets that are highly occurring in only one language would be chosen. If the child were a Spanish-English bilingual speaker, the SLP might remediate final consonant deletion in English but flap and trill in Spanish.

Step 3: Choose the Goal Attack Strategy

Fey (1986) outlines three goal attack strategies. Those strategies are adapted here for bilingual speakers. First, utilize a vertical strategy in which one goal at a time is taught until the specified criterion is reached. The bilingual correlate would be to remediate an error that is common to both languages. The error would be remediated in only one language but monitored in the other language. For example, the SLP would target the use of plurals in Language A but monitor their use in Language B. Second, utilize a horizontal strategy in which more than one goal is addressed in a session. The bilingual correlate would be to target the same goal in Language A and in Language B. For example, the SLP would target plurals in Language A for a period, take a break, and then focus on plurals in Language B. Finally, utilize a cyclical strategy in which several goals are addressed over a set time period, although only one goal is remediated within each session. The bilingual correlate would be to rotate not only specific targets but also languages. For example, at time 1, focus on plural -*s* in Language A and present progressive in Language B. At time 2, focus on present progressive in Language A and plural -*s* in Language B.

Step 4: Choose the Approach

Kohnert and Derr (2012) recommend two general approaches to intervention for bilinguals: the bilingual approach and the cross-linguistic approach. The bilingual approach emphasizes skills common to both languages by focusing on the cognitive principles common to all language learning (i.e., efficient processing and quickly attending to changes in form); training aspects of form, content, and use that are shared by both languages; and highlighting interactions between cognition and language or between Language A and Language B (e.g., contrastive analysis; translation). The cross-linguistic approach emphasizes skills that are unique to each constituent language. Such unique skills might relate to aspects such as word order variation, morphology, omission of subjects, word length, syllable types, and orthography, to name a few.

Step 5: Choose the Language of Intervention

It is likely that following the previous four steps will provide insight about the language of intervention. That is, the goals, targets, strategies, and approaches dictate which language should be used for intervention. Initially, language of intervention will depend on a host of factors, including but not limited to:

- Language history (i.e., relative experience with each language)
- Use in each language (i.e., how frequently the child utilizes each of the languages)
- Proficiency in each language (i.e., how well the child understands and produces each language)
- Environment (i.e., where and with whom the child uses each language)
- Family considerations (i.e., the family's goals as part of EBP)
- The child's speech and language skills and errors/error patterns in each of the two languages

Regardless of the approach, it is almost certain that intervention should take place in *both* languages at some time during the course of treatment. Intervention in English only is unlikely to be an option. There is ample research evidence for providing intervention in both languages (see Gutiérrez-Clellen, 1999; Kohnert, 2008; and Kohnert & Derr, 2012, for reviews). Using a bilingual approach has shown to facilitate an increase in speech and language skills in both languages (Kohnert & Derr, 2012). For example, in a group of Spanish-English bilinguals, Lopez and Greenfield (2004) found that English phonological awareness skills were predicted by: (1) English oral proficiency, (2) Spanish oral proficiency, and (3) Spanish phonological awareness skills. That is, skills in Spanish predicted how well the children were performing in English. Research such as this indicates that if the goal of intervention is a bilingual child, then direct intervention in both languages is necessary; that children, even those with impaired language, are capable of acquiring more than one language; and that focusing on Language A will not impede acquisition in Language B, and in some cases, may facilitate it.

Step 6: Monitor Progress

It is imperative to monitor progress during the intervention process by determining **efficiency**, **effects**, and **effectiveness** (after Williams, 2003). Efficiency focuses on determining how long it took for the client to achieve the goals (e.g., number of treatment sessions), determining how much effort was needed to facilitate change by examining the child's response level (e.g., imitation vs. spontaneous production), and determining the hierarchy needed to produce change (e.g., incremental steps vs. a few gradual steps). Effects focuses on determining if the change was significant by charting outcomes throughout the intervention process. Finally, effectiveness measures whether the intervention provided to the child was the agent responsible for the change. To measure effectiveness, the SLP would take baseline data (e.g., measuring skill level before intervention begins), treatment data (e.g., collecting data on the goals and targets), and then withdrawal data (e.g., measuring skill level after intervention ceases). Ideally, follow-up data would be collected as well, that is, weeks or even months after working on a target.

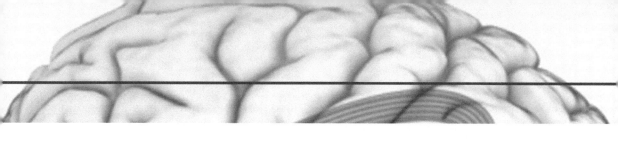

9

Language Development and Hearing

Brian J. Fligor and Sandra Levey

Case Study

You are a speech-language pathologist working in an early intervention program. A 2½-year-old girl on your caseload shows both a receptive and expressive language delay. This child's attention seems limited, and she does not easily respond to verbal directions. She is not easily engaged in language tasks, with little progress in acquiring new consonants. You observe frustration with the inability to express her wants and needs. Eye contact is excellent, as are skills with nonverbal problem-solving tasks. You question if her hearing skills are normal, but she passed the newborn hearing screening. Could this child have a hearing loss? If so, is it medically treatable because it is caused by chronic ear infections? Or is it a permanent hearing loss, requiring audiological intervention? How would you proceed to assist this child?

AN OVERVIEW OF THE ROLE OF HEARING IN LANGUAGE DEVELOPMENT

Children begin their interaction with the world with a fully functioning auditory system, tuned to the sound of their mother's voice. Language learning begins at birth, if not before, when children listen to their mothers' voices in utero. Children with normal hearing abilities possess the ability to perceive the difference between non-speech sounds and spoken language.

In response to their interaction with other language users, children begin producing their own approximations of the language that they are exposed to in the environment. Language abilities develop when children are able to hear spoken language and can attach meaning to the sounds that form words.

Children who do not possess normal hearing need to be identified and given appropriate intervention to provide them with the same language-learning opportunities as children with intact hearing abilities. Children lag behind in language learning, along with a potential delay in the acquisition of literacy, when identification and intervention are not provided. These children also permanently require remediation in order to acquire language and achieve full academic and social potential. Results of a hearing assessment direct the audiologist and speech-language pathologist in methods to provide a child's communication development, along with the opportunity to become a socially, emotionally, and academically equipped adult. Current statistics show that 5.8% of individuals 18 to 44 years of age have hearing difficulties (U.S. Department of Health and Human Services, 2015). Consequently, it is important to be able to recognize the signs of a hearing loss and to provide the support for language and academic progress.

CHAPTER OBJECTIVES

This chapter presents an overview of the impact of hearing loss on communication, along with a review of the methods for determining the type, degree, and configuration of a hearing loss. This chapter also describes audiological interventions for mitigating the negative impact of hearing loss. After reading this chapter, you should understand:

◆ Hearing mechanisms and abilities
◆ The effect of hearing loss on speech and language skills
◆ Methods for the identification of a child with a possible hearing loss
◆ Audiological interventions for a hearing loss

AN EXPLANATION OF HEARING ABILITIES

The human ear consists of three parts: the outer ear, middle ear, and the inner ear (American Speech-Language-Hearing Association, 2017a), as shown in Figure 9–1.

◆ The outer ear consists of the ear canal and eardrum. Sound travels down the ear canal, striking the eardrum and causing it to move or vibrate.
◆ The middle ear is a space behind the eardrum that contains three small bones called **ossicles**. This chain of tiny bones is connected to the eardrum at one end and to an opening to the inner ear at the other end. Vibrations from the eardrum cause the ossicles to vibrate, which in turn creates movement of the fluid in the inner ear.
◆ Movement of the fluid in the inner ear, or **cochlea**, causes changes in tiny structures called **hair cells**. This movement of the hair cells sends electric signals from the inner ear up the auditory nerve (also known as the hearing nerve) to the brain.

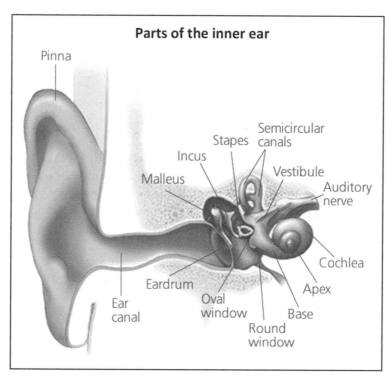

Parts of the inner ear

Pinna

Semicircular
Stapes canals

Incus

Vestibule

Malleus

Auditory
nerve

Cochlea

Eardrum

Apex

Ear
canal

Oval
window

Base

Round
window

Figure 9–1. *Schematic of the structures of the ear. The outer ear comprises the pinna and ear canal and terminates at the eardrum; the middle ear comprises the eardrum, the ossicles (the malleus, incus, and stapes), and the air-filled space and terminates at the oval window; and the inner ear comprises the cochlea (from base to apex) as well as the vestibular system (vestibule and semicircular canals). Signals from the cochlea travel up the auditory nerve to the brain. Reproduced from the National Institute on Deafness and Other Communication Disorders, http://www.nidcd.nih.gov/health/hearing/pages/noise.aspx*

The visible part of the ear is called the **pinna**. The ossicles (also called auditory ossicles) are three bones in the middle ear that transmit sounds to the cochlea: the malleus, incus, and stapes. The cochlea is a snail-shaped tube that contains sensory cells. A sensory cell, when stimulated, conveys nerve impulses. Hair cells are the sensory receptors of the auditory system. The hair cells transfer sound information to the auditory nerve.

Hearing is the ability to receive, process, and interpret sound. Sound vibrations travel through the air in the form of pressure waves. Sound waves are collected by the pinna of the outer ear and funneled down the ear canal toward the eardrum. When a sound wave reaches the eardrum, it causes the eardrum to vibrate. This is the first step in the process of hearing. Sound is amplified in the middle ear due to the lever or pedal action of the bones (ossicles) in the middle ear: the malleus, incus, and stapes (shown in Figure 9–1). The inner ear is the site where hydraulic energy (fluid movement) is converted into chemical energy (hair cell activity) and finally to electrical energy (nerve transmission). Once the signal is transmitted to the nerve, it will travel up to the brain to be interpreted as meaningful sound.

> Sound waves enter the outer ear and are directed to the eardrum (tympanic membrane). Sound vibrations set the eardrum in motion. This leads to movement of the malleus, incus, and stapes (acoustic energy converted into mechanical energy). Mechanical energy is transferred to the cochlea, which contains fluid and hair cells (mechanical energy becomes hydraulic energy). Vibrations in the fluid cause movement of the hair cells. This creates an electrical signal sent to the brain for processing.

TYPES OF HEARING LOSS

Children with hearing loss have been found to have reduced vocabulary skills, difficulty hearing certain sounds, lower reading and mathematical scores, impaired social interaction, and produce shorter and simpler sentences (American Speech-Language-Hearing Association, 2009).

These children also report feeling isolated and having no friends. Hearing loss can affect a child's ability to develop communication, language, and social skills.

Conductive Hearing Loss

Any problem in the outer or middle ear that prevents sound from being conducted properly is known as a **conductive hearing loss**. The most common cause of a conductive hearing loss is **otitis media** (an ear infection). More than one-third of children may experience six or more episodes of otitis media by 7 years of age (Waseem, 2016). Conductive hearing loss is almost always temporary, but hearing sensitivity fluctuates better to worse depending on the health status of the middle ear. Ear infections are most common in children ages 6 months to 2 years and are caused by inflammation (i.e., irritation or infection) of the eustachian tube (Figure 9–2), resulting in eustachian tube dysfunction. Ear infections occur most often in children this age due to their lower immunity to upper respiratory tract infections (common colds), the angle of the eustachian tube (it is more horizontal in children than in adults, thus more difficult to pop open), and length of the eustachian tube (shorter in children than in adults).

Although most common in children under the age of 2 years, conductive hearing loss secondary to fluid in the middle ear is not uncommon in school-age children. This degree of hearing loss has been implicated in reduced academic achievement (Goldberg & McCormick Richburg, 2004). Although an ear infection may sometimes not show obvious symptoms, it frequently results in fever, crankiness, and loss of appetite. This loss results in

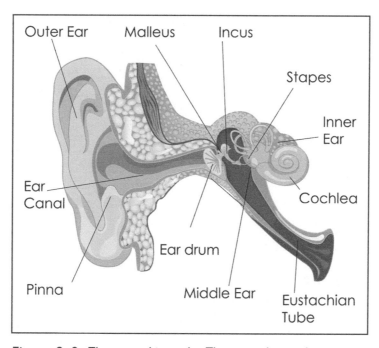

Figure 9–2. *The eustachian tube. The eustachian tube connects the air-filled middle ear to the nasopharynx (top of the back of the throat). At rest the eustachian tube is closed but when yawning, chewing, or swallowing, or under voluntary control, it pops open, recycling air in the middle-ear space. Reproduced with permission from Getty Images.*

decreased hearing sensitivity for as long as the middle-ear fluid is present (Mencher, Gerber, & McCombe, 1997). The degree of hearing loss from otitis media is typically 20 to 30 decibels hearing level (dB HL) (Fria, Cantekin, & Eichler, 1985), which is similar to the hearing of an individual wearing ear plugs. Although this degree of hearing loss is labeled "mild," it can contribute to a delay in the acquisition of spoken language.

Sensorineural Hearing Loss

A **sensorineural hearing loss** results from missing or damaged sensory cells (hair cells) in the cochlea. It is estimated that 3 to 4 of every 1,000 children are born with permanent hearing loss in the United States (Joint Committee on Infant Hearing, 2007), with more children developing hearing loss between infancy and late adolescence. It has been estimated that 19 of every 1,000 high school graduates have a permanent hearing loss (Billings & Kenna, 1999; Shargorodsky, Curhan, Curhan, & Eavey, 2010). Roughly half of the time, a congenital hearing loss is caused by birth complications due to prematurity (resulting from poor oxygenation provided by immature lungs). In the other half of the time, genetic causes are a factor in hearing loss (Billings & Kenna, 1999).

Mixed Hearing Loss

A **mixed hearing loss** is a combination of a sensorineural and conductive hearing loss. This hearing loss results from problems in both the inner and outer or middle ear. There may be damage to the outer or middle ear and in the inner ear (cochlea) or auditory nerve. When this occurs, the hearing loss is referred to as a *mixed* hearing loss.

Minimal Hearing Impairment

A hearing loss of 16 to 25 dB HL has been classified as a **minimal hearing impairment** (**MHI**). Children with a minimal hearing impairment may be missed even with hearing screening, given that hearing screenings are generally placed at 1000, 2000, and 4000 Hz. A minimal hearing impairment may lead to an uncertain grasp of many of the grammatical aspects of spoken language, such as unvoiced fricatives (/f, s, ʃ, h/), stop plosive consonants (/p, t, k/), and morphemes that mark tense (*walked*), possession (*Daddy's hat*), and plurals (*Two cats*). Children with a minimal hearing impairment are frequently not identified as having a hearing loss, as this mild or minimal hearing loss is not as apparent as a more severe hearing loss.

The Centers for Disease Control and Prevention (2011) reported that even a small degree of hearing loss can affect a person's speech, language comprehension, communication, classroom learning, and social interaction. A minimal hearing impairment also leads to difficulty when engaged in conversation, especially within a noisy environment. This may lead to difficulty in communicative interaction with peers within playgrounds, sport activities, and parties. Children with a mild to moderate hearing loss may fall one to four grades below children with normal hearing, with the gap in achievement growing as they progress through school (American Speech-Language-Hearing Association, 2017b).

An early study examined the educational skills of children in third, sixth, and ninth grades and found that 5.4% of children had a minimal hearing loss (MHI) (Bess, Dodd-Murphy, & Parker, 1998). Third graders with MHI had difficulty with reading, language skills, attention, and communication. Children with MHI were significantly more likely to repeat a grade. These findings indicate that a child with even a minimal hearing loss (16 to 25 dB HL) will have difficulty in academic progress.

Noise-Induced Hearing Loss

Another type of hearing loss results from exposure to noise. The onset or early stage of a **noise-induced hearing loss** (**NIHL**) begins with a minimal hearing impairment. Screening may not identify a minimal hearing loss secondary to NIHL, given that the onset of NIHL is prevalent at 6000 Hz (Holmes et al., 2007; Rota-Donahue & Levey, 2016). Consequently, better screening protocols and greater awareness of hearing difficulties are essential factors in supporting children's academic development.

NIHL can be caused by a one-time exposure to an intense sound, such as an explosion, or by continuous exposure to loud sounds over an extended period of time in a noisy environment. Recreational activities (e.g., target shooting and hunting, snowmobile riding, listening to portable music players at high volume through earbuds or headphones, playing in a band, and attending loud concerts) place individuals at risk for NIHL (National Institute on Deafness and Other Communication Disorders, 2017). The onset and the progress of hearing loss may not be apparent. For example, a study of hearing abilities of college-age students (Rota-Donahue & Levey, 2016) found that half of 40 students were found to have NIHL hearing loss, while none were aware that a hearing loss was present. Education on the hazards of noise and the potential effects on hearing is necessary for individuals throughout the lifespan, and early education for children is particularly important (Serpanos & Berg, 2012).

One of the more disquieting sources of a potential NIHL is found in children's toys. Certain children's toys exceed safe listening levels, placing children at risk for NIHL (Axelsson & Jerson, 1985; Nadler, 1995). University of California–Irvine researchers (2007) found that many common children's toys emit sounds at decibel levels high enough to cause permanent hearing damage, with some toys reaching a noise level comparable to that of an ambulance, subway train, or power mower. An investigation of common toys used in play revealed the following volume levels (Cochary, 2009).

◆ Rattles and squeaky toys have been measured at sound levels as high as 110 dB.
◆ Musical toys, drums, and horns can reach sound levels as loud as 120 dB.
◆ Toy phones have been measured between 123 dB and 129 dB.
◆ Toys producing firearm sounds (e.g., toy guns) produce sounds as loud

as 150 dB even if a child is standing a foot away from the source of the noise.

The danger with noisy toys increases when children hold toys close to the ear. A noisy toy exposes the ear to as much as 120 dB of sound (close to the noise level of a jet plane). Safety measures are important when using toys in play with young children (e.g., choosing toys carefully to prevent hearing loss and covering the speakers with tape).

Central Auditory Processing Disorder

Speech perception tests for the assessment of a **central auditory processing disorder (CAPD)** are designed to test the abilities of school-age children who have normal pure-tone audiograms but have difficulty perceiving speech that is affected by background noise, competing signals in the contralateral ear, or rapid rate of presentation. CAPD tests assess binaural integration (how well the two ears work together), auditory memory, and retrieval or recall of auditorily presented information. The child appropriate for CAPD evaluation may present with recurrent complaints from parents, siblings, peers, and classroom teachers of difficulty following directions or reading.

Unilateral Hearing Loss

Current findings show that 25 to 35% of children with a **unilateral hearing loss** may fall behind their peers in academic progress (Packer, 2015). The educational effects appear in difficulty deciphering others' speech productions, such as a teacher's voice, when there is interference from background sounds (e.g., other children, paper rustling, noisy heating/ventilation/air conditioning systems in the classroom). Vocabulary and sentence structure are extremely difficult for a child affected by hearing loss to grasp.

> A unilateral hearing loss or single-sided deafness is a type of hearing loss with normal hearing in one ear and impaired hearing in the other ear. A **bilateral hearing loss** is in both ears.

Children with unilateral hearing loss are not always positioned in such a way that their "good" ear is toward the talker. This results in morpheme and grammatical errors, particularly hearing past tense morphemes (e.g., *waited*), fricatives (e.g., f, v, s, z, h), and stop consonants (e.g., p, t, k).

◆ Unvoiced fricatives consist of /f/ as in fish, /s/ as in soap, /ʃ/ as in shoe, and /h/ as in happy.
◆ Unvoiced stop plosives consist of /p/ as in pin, /t/ as in top, and /k/ as in key.
◆ Morphemes consist of the past verb tense -*ed* morpheme (walked), possessive morpheme -*s* (Mary's book), and the plural -*s* morpheme (two books).

Typically, vowel sounds, which have lower frequency content and greater intensity, are audible to children with mild-to-moderate sensorineural hearing loss, whereas many consonant sounds are not audible (e.g., /k/, /p/, /f/, /s/, and "th"). Functionally, the child would be able to tell that someone is speaking while not being able to understand the content of the spoken message. Understandably, this leads to speech-language delays and social-emotional and behavioral problems that result in frustration, resulting from the child's inability to communicate thoughts, needs, and desires.

NORMAL HEARING SENSITIVITY IN CHILDREN

Normal hearing sensitivity in children is considered to be 15 dB HL or better (Northern & Downs, 2002) because hearing thresholds of 20 to 25 dB HL or poorer are considered to have a significant effect on a child's academic progress. Hearing level is a unit of measurement with zero as its reference point. On occasion, and particularly for younger and developmentally delayed children, 20 dB HL may be considered the limit of normal hearing.

> The term HL means hearing level, which is a scale based on young, normal-hearing individuals with no history of noise exposure or other ear-related problems. Normal hearing is, on average, established as zero decibels at each of the test frequencies (250 Hz, 500 Hz, and so on). So, it is possible to have better than normal hearing (−5 dB HL or −10 dB HL) or poorer than normal hearing (20 dB HL, 30 dB HL, 100 dB HL, and further loss).

HEARING ASSESSMENT

For children with a hearing loss, an **audiogram** describes the type, degree, and configuration of the hearing loss, thus indicating the residual or remaining auditory area (Appendix 9–A). The pure-tone audiogram is a fundamental component of the audiological evaluation. It is the graphical representation of an individual's detection threshold for frequency-specific stimuli in the conventional audiometric range (250–8000 Hz). Descriptions of types of hearing loss can be found in Appendix 9–B.

> A sound is presented by **air conduction** using earphones or a loudspeaker (the sound moves through the air to the ear), and by **bone conduction** using a device (called a bone oscillator) that sends vibration through the skull itself. A bone oscillator can vibrate at different frequencies (e.g., 250 Hz, 500 Hz, 1000 Hz, and so on) and this vibration is carried through the bones of the head to the inner ears (cochlea), since the inner ear is encased in the bones of the skull.

It should be noted that the impact of hearing loss is not fully explained by the audiogram because two individuals with the same audiogram may have different levels of disability, owing in large part to age of onset and differences in the environment in which the individual functions (Yoshinaga-Itano, Sedey, Coulter, & Mehl, 1998). Examples of audiological assessment consist of the following:

Conventional Audiometry (age 4 or 5): The child is asked to raise a hand or push a button every time he or she hears a tone.

Conditioned Play Audiometry (CPA) (ages 2 to 5): The child is shown, nonverbally, how to wait, listen, and perform a repetitive play task, such as placing a peg in a pegboard every time she or he hears a tone.

There are also physiologic measures used in pediatric audiology. One example is **tympanometry**. Tympanometry tests the movement of the eardrum to rule out the presence of an ear infection or another problem in the middle ear. A handheld tool is used to change the air pressure inside the ear and to produce a sound. This tool measures how the eardrum responds to the pressure and the sound.

Following assessment, the degree of hearing loss is classified according to the following list:

Mild hearing loss	21 to 40 dB HL
Moderate hearing loss	41 to 55 dB HL
Moderately severe	56 to 70 dB HL
Severe	71 to 90 dB HL
Profound	91 or greater dB HL

SOUND INTENSITY AND FREQUENCY

Decibels are a unit for expressing the relative intensity (loudness) of sounds. Sound intensity is calculated on a logarithmic scale. Examples of different intensity levels are conversation (60 dB), rock concerts (110 dB), snowmobiles (120 dB), and jet aircraft takeoff (130 dB).

> On a logarithmic scale, sound intensity increases 10-fold for every additional 10 dB. In other words,

each increase of 10 decibels represents a multiplication of the sound intensity by a factor of 10. Consequently, a change from 60 dB (the level of quiet conversation) to 90 dB (the level of heavy traffic) is equivalent to three 10-fold changes, and this change multiplies the intensity by a factor of 10 × 10 × 10 (equal to a 1,000-fold intensity change).

The term Hz (abbreviation of the term **hertz**) is defined as the number of cycles (vibrations) that an object makes when put into motion (Figure 9–3). The number of cycles per unit of time is called the frequency of a sound. The perceived pitch of a sound is the ear or mind's subjective interpretation of its frequency. High-frequency (high-pitched) sounds have waves that are very close together and low-frequency sounds have a greater distance between the peaks of each wave, as shown in the examples in Figure 9–3. High-frequency sounds characterize certain consonant sounds, such as the sound "s" in the word *see*. Low-frequency sounds characterize vowel sounds, such as the sound "oo" in the word *who*.

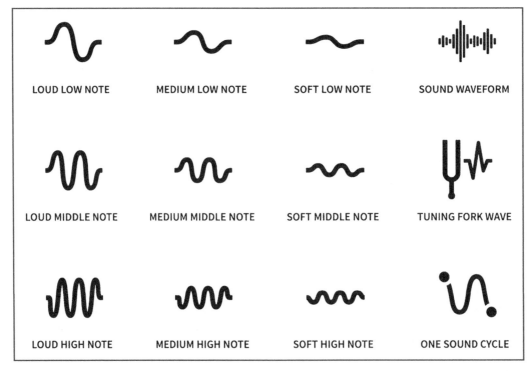

Figure 9–3. *Sound waves. Note the difference between the low note (low-frequency wave) and the high note (high-frequency wave). The frequency of a wave refers to how often the particles of a medium (like air) vibrate when a wave passes through this medium. The higher the frequency, the shorter the distance between each successive compression (i.e., low frequency, medium frequency, and high frequency). In the examples shown in this figure, the intensity (or loudness) is shown in the height of the wave. The higher the wave, the greater the intensity (i.e., loud, medium, and soft). Reproduced with permission from Getty Images.*

THE IMPACT OF A HEARING LOSS ON LANGUAGE DEVELOPMENT

Preliteracy skills (Burgess & Lonigan, 1998) and later reading skills (Parrila, Kirby, & McQuarrie, 2004) depend on **phonological awareness**, which is the ability to hear sounds and to associate these sounds with letters in words. Examples of early phonological awareness skills include the ability to associate spoken speech sounds with written letters (e.g., the speech sound /p/ with the written letter **p**in in the word *pet*) and to recognize words that rhyme (e.g., *hat, bat, cat*). The presence of any hearing loss places a child at risk for impaired phonological awareness, which may lead to an uncertain grasp of many of the grammatical aspects of spoken language. Children who do not develop early phonological awareness, prior to kindergarten, are at risk for literacy difficulties (Goldstein et al., 2017). Phonological awareness skills are essential for developing reading abilities in later grades.

Children with even a "mild" degree of hearing loss possess word-reading and decoding skills that are lower than those with normal hearing sensitivity (Bess et al., 1998). The early identification of children with hearing loss is essential for the prevention of difficulties in their learning and communication skills. The American Speech-Language-Hearing Association (2017b) cites four major ways that hearing loss affects children: delayed receptive and expressive communication skills, learning problems in academic achievement, social isolation, and later vocational choices. A hearing loss causes the following effects on language abilities (Culbertson, 2007; Elfenbein, Hardin-Jones, & Davis, 1994; Tye-Murray, 2007):

Difficulty with the multiple meanings of words that sound alike but have different spellings

- ◆ Write/right
- ◆ Seen/scene
- ◆ Two/to/too

Difficulty with morphemes

- ◆ Auxiliary verbs: *am, is, are, was, were, be, been, have, had*
- ◆ Inflectional morphemes: plural *-s* (*cats*), possessive *'s* (*mommy's*), comparative *-er* (*bigger*), and superlative *-est* (*biggest*)
- ◆ Derivational morphemes: *-er* (*farm/farmer*)
- ◆ Present progressive: *-ing* (*go/going*)
- ◆ Past tense: *-ed* (*wait/waited*)
- ◆ Determiners: *the, a, an*

Speech errors

- ◆ Final consonant omission: *bus* produced as *bu*
- ◆ Voiced consonants (/b, d, g/) produced in place of voiceless consonants (/p, t, k/)
- ◆ Difficulty in the perception of fricatives and stops, especially with unvoiced fricatives (/s, f, h, ʃ, ʒ/, as in **s**un, **f**un, **h**e, **sh**e, trea**s**ure) and unvoiced stops (/p, t, k/, as in **p**et, **t**op, **k**ing).

Academic success and progress can be effected by a child's hearing loss. An early examination of the audiological records of 54,000 school-age children in kindergarten through grade 12 revealed that 106 of these children had hearing loss in one ear (Oyler, Oyler, & Matkin, 1988). Findings were that 24% of these children repeated at least one grade and that 40% of them received special services, such as speech-language pathology intervention.

The earlier children with hearing loss receive services, the more likely they are to reach their full potential (Centers for Disease Control and Prevention, 2017).

AGE OF ONSET OF HEARING LOSS

Children with early, even brief, normal access to spoken language who then adventitiously develop permanent hearing loss are often more prepared for spoken language acquisition than children with congenital onset of hearing loss (Northern & Downs, 2002). The development of the brain's language centers benefits from a greater amount of auditory experience and stimulation. In other words, the more language that is acquired prior to the onset of hearing loss, the greater is the opportunity to lessen the negative impact of the hearing loss on language use. Language centers in the brain are stimulated from the earliest auditory experiences.

Adventitious hearing loss describes individuals who were born with normal hearing. However, at some point in time, these individuals have lost some or all of their hearing through illness or accident. This contrasts with the congenital onset of hearing loss.

Although it is a somewhat artificial distinction, **prelingual** onset requires greater **habilitative** efforts (i.e., the efforts and tools for success) than does **postlingual** onset. A prelingual deaf individual is someone who was born with a hearing loss, or whose hearing loss occurred before he/she began to speak.

Should hearing loss develop adventitiously or unexpectedly, these areas may become dormant or inactive. However, once identification of, and intervention for, the hearing loss occurs, these areas reawaken.

Typically developing children born with normal hearing who lose significant hearing between 18 and 30 months often "catch up" in their language to their normal-hearing peers within 6 to 12 months (Martin & Clark, 1996). Children with congenital (inborn) hearing loss stand an excellent chance of having language on par with their normal-hearing peers. The age of identification and intervention is the principal determinant in the language outcome.

SIGNS OF A HEARING LOSS

Cherry (2011, p. 68) provided a list of signs to help identify a child who may have a hearing loss. Children with a hearing loss may exhibit the following behaviors:

◆ Routinely asks for repetition
◆ Frequently misunderstands what is said
◆ Appears to be inattentive
◆ Has speech problems
◆ Watches others to see what they are doing
◆ Exhibits fatigue at the end of the day
◆ Withdraws from situations that require careful listening

This list is not intended to be all-inclusive of the signs of hearing loss in toddlers and school-age children. In addition, this list should not be used to replace ongoing hearing screening, but if a child exhibits such signs, immediate audiological evaluation would be indicated.

INTERVENTION

Age of Intervention

Prior to 1993, few hospitals provided newborn hearing screening tests except for infants identified as having risk factors (indicators) for hearing loss. The Joint Committee on Infant Hearing (JCIH) was established in 1969. It was composed of members from audiology, otolaryngology, pediatrics, and nursing. The JCIH established recommendations for the early identification of children who had been diagnosed with hearing loss, of children who were at risk for hearing loss, and for newborn hearing screening. In 1993, the National Institutes of Health held a consensus conference (National Institutes of Health, 1993). The result of this conference was a recommendation that all newborns receive a hearing screening within the first 3 months of life. The Joint Committee on Infant Hearing (1994) recommended identification of all infants with hearing impairment by 3 months of age and the onset of habilitative programming by 6 months of age. The seminal work of Yoshinaga-Itano et al. (1998) helped bolster the newborn screening effort with research that found that children with normal cognition, whose hearing losses were identified before 6 months of age, demonstrated significantly better receptive and expressive language scores than children with normal cognition whose hearing losses were identified after 6 months of age. The JCIH (2007) reaffirmed the need for surveillance for adventitious onset of childhood hearing loss. In 2012, JCIH issued a clarification of the interventions, such as requiring that individuals providing services to children who are deaf or hard-of-hearing have expertise in their areas of service. For example, an American Sign Language (ASL) instructor must be fluent in ASL and a therapist providing listening and spoken language stimulation (LSLS) must be a certified LSLS provider.

DEVICES USED FOR HEARING HABILITATION: FM SYSTEMS, HEARING AIDS, AND COCHLEAR IMPLANTS

FM Systems

A child with a unilateral hearing loss (loss in one ear) has difficulty hearing on the affected side and difficulty focusing on spoken language in the presence of competing noises. The most significant effect of unilateral hearing loss is found in classroom performance, given that children with unilateral hearing loss are at significant risk for poor academic performance due to difficulty hearing in a typical (noisy) classroom environment. In fact, it is estimated that children spend approximately 80% of the time listening to spoken language in noise during the school day (Crukley, Scollie, & Parsa, 2011). Even with preferential classroom seating near the teacher and acoustic treatment of the classroom to reduce reverberation of background noise, academic progress should be monitored closely and supports initiated if listening-related difficulties emerge. A hearing aid in the poorer hearing ear may be beneficial, but, typically, it does not improve the child's ability to hear in noise. However, in the classroom, **FM**

educational amplification systems (either ear level or sound field) may be used to improve the amount by which the teacher's voice exceeds the background noise.

> Sound-field systems work by projecting the teacher's voice so that children have a better opportunity to hear clearly the teacher's instructions. These systems do not reduce exposure to external sound sources, but importantly, by raising the level of the teacher's voice, they can increase the level of the speech signal relative to levels of external and internal sound sources (Dockrell & Shield, 2012).

Hearing Aids

As soon as a bilateral hearing loss has been documented and is not felt to be transient, there is no reason for a delay in fitting **hearing aids**, even if the baby is only 1 or 2 months old. With current hearing aid technology, even newborns with severe-to-profound hearing loss can be fitted successfully with hearing aids. Some young children benefit from FM amplification, even during infancy, to provide better hearing of their parents at a distance. The intent of fitting with hearing aids is to amplify speech sounds, giving the child access to speech sounds but not making them uncomfortably loud. The explosion of technology in the area of digital hearing aids and directional microphones enables infants and young children to experience significant benefit from amplification. With appropriately fitted and verified hearing aids, it should be expected that children with up to a severe degree of hearing loss (less than 70 dB HL average

across the speech frequencies) will have significantly better access to the sounds of speech than without using hearing aids.

> If a child with normal cognition and no other concomitant conditions receives an early diagnosis of hearing loss and is fitted with hearing aids, coupled with speech-language therapy, an ear-level FM system in the classroom, and educational and psychosocial support, then speech and language outcomes should be normal to near-normal (Sininger, Grimes, & Christensen, 2010).

Cochlear Implants

Children with severe (71 to 90 dB HL) and profound (greater than 90 dB HL) bilateral hearing loss generally have delayed language development, unless language has been made accessible and habilitation has been well under way by 6 months of age. A **cochlear implant** is a device that includes a magnet and electrode array that is surgically implanted in the inner ear as well as an ear-level externally worn speech processor and microphone.

> Speech sounds picked up by the ear-level microphone are decoded by the speech processor, and this decoded signal is transmitted wirelessly via a coil positioned over the magnet that rests just under the skin in a well drilled out in the temporal bone at the time of the implant surgery. The signal is then transmitted to select electrodes on the array to give the user a sense of "hearing." Historically, patients received only one

cochlear implant, but more recently, a second implant is often used to give patients better access to sound on both sides and perhaps to help hear better in noise.

A cochlear implant provides improved access to spoken language when the child's degree of hearing loss is severe to profound. If the child and family opt for a cochlear implant, these children may still vary in their ability to acquire spoken language and may benefit from the use of one of several forms of visual communication (ASL, signed and spoken English, or Cued Speech). Cued Speech makes all the phonemes (sound-based units) of speech visible by using eight handshapes in four positions near the mouth in combination with the lip shapes and articulation movements of speech (National Cued Speech Association, 2017).

Each child and family presents an individual situation in terms of choice of communication modality and educational setting that ranges all the way from being mainstreamed in regular classes with support services to residential placement at a school for the deaf. Regardless of choice of method and of educational placement, the audiologist, otolaryngologist, speech-language pathologist, teacher of the deaf, and parents work as a team to ensure that the child uses a language to which she has access, that the people in her environment use it effectively with her, that she is making demonstrable progress in that language sufficient to establish a basis for literacy, and that she is developing self-esteem as a successful communicator with her peers as well as with her family. The audiologist and speech-language pathologist have an opportunity to monitor the child's progress, support the parents, and cheer them on in their good work through routine monitoring of hearing and communication success.

SUMMARY

Good auditory access to the cues of speech is necessary to develop phonological awareness. Hearing loss, both transient and permanent, can be undetected without universal newborn hearing screening and close surveillance for hearing loss through childhood. Scientifically valid measures of hearing exist to fully characterize residual hearing function and direct interventions. Interventions, when implemented in a timely, family-centered fashion, are effective at helping children with hearing loss develop language on par with their normal-hearing peers, if cognition is adequate to support such successes.

◆ A team approach among the speech-language pathologist, audiologist, physicians, educators of the deaf, teachers, and family is vital to support the child's development of self-esteem and communication success.

◆ Language abilities develop when children are able to hear spoken language and can attach meaning to the sounds that form words.

◆ Children who do not possess normal hearing need to be identified and provided with appropriate intervention to provide them with the same language-learning opportunities as children with intact hearing abilities.

◆ When such identification and intervention of a hearing loss are not provided, children lag behind in language learning, with a potential delay in the acquisition of literacy.

◆ Permanent hearing loss occurs in 3 to 4 per 1,000 newborns, and the number increases to 19 per 1,000 by high school graduation.

◆ More than one-third of children may experience six or more episodes of otitis media by 7 years of age. Children with transient middle-ear fluid secondary to an ear infection (symptomatic or asymptomatic) have conductive hearing loss that could interfere with normal language development.

◆ Children with prelingual onset of permanent hearing loss stand an excellent chance of having language on par with their normal-hearing peers, with the age of identification and intervention the principal determinants in the language outcome.

◆ The current JCIH position statement (2007) proposes that all newborns have their hearing screened by age 1 month, that those who do not pass and have hearing loss are diagnosed by age 3 months, and that those with hearing loss receive appropriate interventions, including fitting with hearing aids and enrollment in the Individuals with Disabilities Education Act part C Early Intervention.

◆ Children with confirmed permanent bilateral hearing loss should be fitted with hearing aids as soon as the family is ready to pursue this intervention, even if the baby is only 1 to 2 months old.

◆ For children with severe-to-profound hearing loss, cochlear implants are an option to provide access to spoken language should hearing aids provide limited benefit for supporting acquisition of spoken language.

KEY WORDS

Air conduction

Audiogram

Bilateral hearing loss

Bone conduction

Central auditory processing disorder (CAPD)

Cochlea

Cochlear implant

Conductive hearing loss

Decibels

FM educational amplification systems

Habilitative

Hair cells

Hearing aids

Hertz

Masking

Minimal hearing impairment (MHI)

Mixed hearing loss

Noise-induced hearing loss (NIHL)

Ossicles

Otitis media

Phonological awareness

Pinna

Postlingual

Prelingual

Sensorineural hearing loss

Tympanometry

Unilateral hearing loss

STUDY QUESTIONS

1. What is the purpose of universal newborn hearing screening?

2. What are the effects of a hearing loss on children's speech production?

3. A 2-year-old child with speech delay and recurrent ear infections might have what kind of hearing loss that has gone undetected but is contributing to the delays?

4. What are the effects of a hearing loss on a child's academic progress?

5. What are the effects of a hearing loss on children's language abilities?

REFERENCES

American Speech-Language-Hearing Association. (2009). *Noisy toys, dangerous play.* Retrieved from http://www.asha.org/public/hearing/disorders/noisy_toys.htm/noise-center-home/children-and-noise/noisy-toys

American Speech-Language-Hearing Association. (2017a). *Effect of hearing loss on development.* Retrieved from http://www.asha.org/public/hearing/disorders/effects.htm

American Speech-Language-Hearing Association. (2017b). *How we hear.* Retrieved from http://www.asha.org/public/hearing/How-We-Hear/

Axelsson, A., & Jerson, T. (1985). Noisy toys: A possible source of sensorineural hearing loss. *Pediatrics, 76*(4), 574–578.

Bess, F. H., Dodd-Murphy, J., & Parker, R. A. (1998). Children with minimal sensorineural hearing loss: Prevalence, educational performance and functional status. *Ear and Hearing, 19*(5), 339–354.

Billings, K. R., & Kenna, M. A. (1999). Causes of pediatric sensorineural hearing loss. *Archives of Otolaryngology Head Neck Surgery, 125,* 517–521.

Burgess, S. R., & Lonigan, C. J. (1998). Bidirectional relations of phonological sensitivity and prereading abilities: Evidence from a preschool sample. *Journal of Experimental Child Psychology, 70,* 117–141.

Centers for Disease Control and Prevention. (2011). *Noise induced hearing loss.* Retrieved from httpp://www.cdc.gov/healthyyouth/noise

Centers for Disease Control and Prevention. (2015). *Hearing loss in children.* Retrieved from https://www.cdc.gov/ncbddd/hearingloss/index.html

Cherry, R. (2011). Hearing and listening skills. In S. Levey & S. Polirstok (Eds.), *Language development: Understanding language diversity in the classroom* (pp. 59–78). Los Angeles, CA: Sage.

Cochary, J. (2009). *Noisy toys.* Retrieved from http://www.ch-chearing.org/

Crukley, J., Scollie, S., & Parsa, V. (2011). An exploration of non-quiet listening at school. *Journal of Educational Audiology, 17,* 23–35.

Culbertson, D. (2007). Language and speech for the deaf and hard of hearing. In R. L. Schow & M. A. Nerboone (Eds.), *Introduction to audiologic rehabilitation* (pp. 197–244). Boston, MA: Pearson Education.

Dockrell, J. E., & Shield, B. (2012). The impact of sound-field systems on learning and attention in elementary school classrooms. *Journal of Speech, Language, and Hearing Research, 55,* 1163–1176.

Elfenbein, J. L., Hardin-Jones, M. A., & Davis, J. M. (1994). Oral communication skills of children who are hard of hearing. *Journal of Speech and Hearing Research, 37,* 216–226.

Fria, T. J., Cantekin, E. I., & Eichler, J. A. (1985). Hearing acuity of children with otitis media with effusion. *Archives of Otolaryngology, 111,* 10–16.

Goldberg, L. R., & McCormick Richburg, C. (2004). Minimal hearing impairment: Major myths with more than minimal implications.

Communication Disorders Quarterly, 25(3), 152–160.

Goldstein, H., Olszewski, A., Haring, C., Greenwood, C. R., McCune, L., Carta, J., . . . Kelley, E. S. (2017). Efficacy of a supplemental phonemic awareness curriculum to instruct preschoolers with delays in early literacy development. *Journal of Speech, Language, and Hearing Research, 60,* 89–103.

Holmes, A. E., Kaplan, H. S., Phillips, R. M., Kemker, J. F., Weber, F. T., & Isart, F. A. (2007). Screening for hearing loss in adolescents. *Language, Speech, and Hearing Services in Schools, 28,* 70–76.

Joint Committee on Infant Hearing (JCIH). (1994). Position statement. *Pediatrics, 95,* 152–156.

Joint Committee on Infant Hearing (JCIH). (2007). Year 2007 position statement: Principles and guidelines for early hearing detection and intervention programs. *Pediatrics, 120*(4), 898–914.

Martin, F. N., & Clark, J. G. (1996). *Hearing care for children.* Boston, MA: Allyn & Bacon.

Mencher, G. T., Gerber, S. E., & McCombe, A. (1997). Audiology and auditory dysfunction. In G. T. Mencher, S. E. Gerber, & A. McCombe (Eds.), *Anatomy and physiology of the human ear* (pp. 105–232). Needham Heights, MA: Allyn & Bacon.

Nadler, N. B. (1995). Hearing conservation in the vocational classroom. *Hearing Rehabilitation Quarterly, 20*(3), 12–15.

National Cued Speech Association. (2017). *About cued speech.* Retrieved from http://www.cuedspeech.org/cued-speech/about-cued-speech

National Institute on Deafness and Other Communication Disorders. (2017). *Noise-induced hearing loss.* Retrieved from https://www.nidcd.nih.gov/health/noise-induced-hearing-loss

National Institutes of Health. (1993). *Early identification of hearing impairment in infants and young children: Consensus development conference statement.* Retrieved from http://consensus.nih.gov/1993/1993hearinginfantschildren092html.htm

Northern, J. L., & Downs, M. P. (2002). *Hearing in children* (5th ed.). Baltimore, MD: Lippincott Williams & Wilkins.

Oyler, R. F., Oyler, A. L., & Matkin, N. D. (1988). Unilateral hearing loss: Demographics and educational impact. *Language, Speech, and Hearing Services in Schools, 19,* 201–210.

Packer, L. (2015). *How hearing loss affects school performance.* Retrieved from http://www.healthyhearing.com/report/52433-How-hearing-loss-affects-school-performance

Parrila, R., Kirby, J. R., & McQuarrie, L. (2004). Articulation rate, naming speed, verbal short-term memory, and phonological awareness: Longitudinal predictors of early reading development? *Scientific Studies of Reading, 8*(1), 3–26.

Rota-Donahue, C., & Levey, S. (2016). Noise-induced hearing loss in the campus. *Hearing Journal, 69*(6), 38–39.

Serpanos, Y. C., & Berg, A. (2012). Noise exposure and the potential impact on hearing in the pediatric population. In R. Goldfarb (Ed.), *Translational SLP/A: Essays in honor of Dr. Sadanand Singh* (pp. 107–112). San Diego, CA: Plural.

Shargorodsky, J., Curhan, S. G., Curhan, G. C., & Eavey, R. (2010) Change in prevalence of hearing loss in US adolescents. *Journal of the American Medical Association, 304,* 772–778.

Sininger, Y. S., Grimes, A., & Christensen, E. (2010). Auditory development in early amplified children: Factors influencing auditory-based communication outcomes in children with hearing loss. *Ear and Hearing, 31*(2), 166–185.

Tye-Murray, N. (2007). *Foundations of aural rehabilitation* (3rd ed.). Clifton Park, NY: Delmar Cengage Learning.

University of California–Irvine. (2007). *Greater parental guidance suggested for noisy toy use.* Retrieved from http://www.health-care.uci.edu/news_releases.as?filename=07DecToyNoise.Htm

U.S. Department of Health and Human Services. (2015). Retrieved from https://ftp.cdc.gov/pub/Health_Statistics/NCHS/NHIS/SHS/2015_SHS_Table_A-6.pdf

Waseem, M. (2016). *Otitis media.* Retrieved from http://emedicine.medscape.com/article/994656-overview#a2

Yoshinaga-Itano, C., Sedey, A. L., Coulter, D. K., & Mehl, A. L. (1998). Language of early and later-identified children with hearing loss. *Pediatrics, 102,* 1161–1171.

APPENDIX 9–A
Audiogram

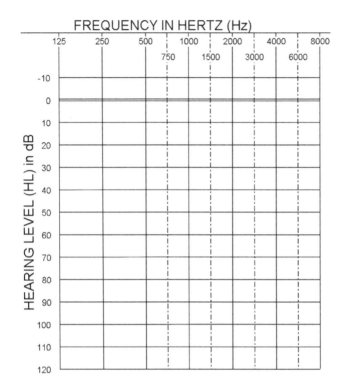

The right ear is graphed with either a circle or a triangle, and the left ear is graphed with an X or a square when headphones are used to represent the air conduction results of the right or left ear.

"S" represents the response of at least one ear or the response of the better hearing ear.

The symbol " [" represents masking the right ear and the symbol "] " represents masking the left ear. **Masking** involves testing one ear while noise is introduced into the other ear. This allows for testing each ear separately.

| | AIR CONDUCTION | | BONE CONDUCTION | | SOUND FIELD | NO |
	UNMASKED	MASKED	UNMASKED	MASKED	(NOT EAR SPECIFIC)	RESPONSE
RIGHT	O	△	<	[		↙
LEFT	X	□	>	]		↘
BOTH			∧		S	↓

Bone conduction testing is represented by the right ear graphed with < or [and the left ear with > or].

Stimulus frequencies, in hertz (Hz), are on the audiogram abscissa. The stimulus intensity, in decibels and hearing level (dB HL), are on the ordinate. The Audiogram Legend is below the audiogram. **Air conduction** testing uses earphones or a loudspeaker (the sound moves through the air to the ear) and **bone conduction** uses a device (bone oscillator) that sends vibration through the skull. A bone oscillator can vibrate at different frequencies (e.g., 250 Hz, 500 Hz, 1000 Hz, and so on) and this vibration is carried through the bones of the head to the inner ear (cochlea).

APPENDIX 9–B
Types of Hearing Loss

Conductive hearing loss	A problem conducting sound waves anywhere along the route through the **outer ear**, tympanic membrane (eardrum), or middle ear (ossicles). Otitis media (inner ear infection) is the most common cause of a conductive hearing loss.
Sensorineural hearing loss	Permanent hearing loss is due to damage or dysfunction in the inner ear.
Mixed hearing loss	A conductive hearing loss that occurs in combination with a sensorineural hearing loss.
Minimal hearing impairment	Some speech sounds may be heard but soft sounds are hard to hear (Centers for Disease Control and Prevention, 2015).
Central auditory processing	Children have normal pure tone audiograms but have difficulty perceiving speech that is degraded by background noise or rapid rate of presentation.
Noise-induced hearing loss	NIHL can be caused by a one-time exposure to an intense sound or by continuous exposure to loud sounds over an extended period of time in a noisy environment. The onset and the progress of NIHL may not be apparent.

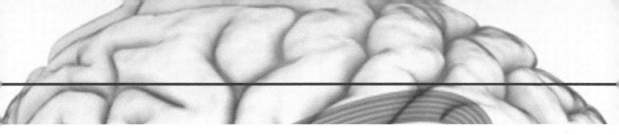

GLOSSARY

Abduct: To move away from midline.

Abduction: Movement from midline.

Abstract thought: Higher level thinking processes characterized by organization and logic.

Acceleration: At certain points in development, bilingual children might demonstrate a faster rate of acquisition than their monolingual peers.

Accommodation: When a new event does not fit into a cognitive schema that already exists (e.g., *penguin*), there is a change in the existing schema (e.g., *birds*) to accommodate the characteristics of this new information.

Acoustic: Relating to the sense or organs of hearing, to sound, or to the science of sounds.

Acoustic resonance: The effect of different vocal tract configurations on the production of speech sounds. Alterations in the cross-sectional area of the vocal tract determine the frequencies at which sound energy will be minimally attenuated or diminished.

Acoustics: Relating to sound, the sense of hearing, or the science of the physics of sounds. Acoustics can also be defined as sound vibration propagating through air or the science of sound.

Action potential: Buildup of electrical current in the neuron.

Adaptation: The tendency of an organism to change in response to the environment.

Adduct: To move toward midline.

Adduction: Movement toward midline.

Afferent fibers: Nerves that carry impulses from the body toward the brain or spinal cord, or blood vessels that carry blood to an organ.

Age of acquisition (AoA): The age that a language is first acquired.

Air–bone gap: The difference, in decibels, between air-conduction and bone-conduction thresholds.

Air conduction: A method of transmitting sound through the outer and middle ear to the inner ear through an earphone delivering sound to the outer ear.

Alveolar ridge: A bony prominence of the hard palate directly behind the upper incisors (teeth) that serves as an important place of articulation for certain speech sounds (e.g., /s/ and /t/).

Alveolar stop: A consonant sound created by bringing the tongue tip in contact with the alveolar ridge, forming a complete closure, then building up pressure behind the point of closure and suddenly releasing the occlusion (e.g., /t/, /d/).

Alveoli: Tiny air sacs within the lungs where the exchange of oxygen and carbon dioxide takes place.

Analogies: Tasks that involve analogical reasoning that uses information from one situation to apply to another situation.

Analogy: Analogical reasoning involves using information from one situation and applying this information to a new situation.

Anaphora: Reference to a word or phrase used earlier by replacing it with a pronoun. An example is the clause *he did so* in the sentence, *I told Paul to close the door and he did so.* The clause *he did so* makes use of anaphora.

Anaphoric term: A linguistic entity which indicates a referential tie to some other linguistic entity in the same text (e.g., *The monkey took the banana and ate it*). "It" is anaphoric as it refers to the banana.

Angular gyrus: A region of the inferior parietal lobe of the brain that is involved in the processing of auditory and visual input and in the comprehension of language. It is involved in processes related to language and cognition.

Approximants: A class of speech sounds produced by bringing one articulator close to another without creating audible noise; the approximation of articulators is critical to the acoustic resonance of these sounds (i.e., /r/, /l/, /w/, /j/).

Apraxia: A neurological disorder that re-sults in difficulty initiating, planning, and/or programming the production of speech sound sequences. Productions are inconsistent.

Arcuate fasciculus: A bundle of nerve fibers that connects Broca's and Wernicke's areas, connecting the speech and language areas in the brain.

Argument: Within grammar, a noun element in a clause that relates directly to the verb, such as the subject or object of the sentence. An argument is an expression that helps complete the meaning of a predicate (the verb). Subject and object phrases are examples of arguments, shown as in the example of the sentence, *John threw the ball*. *John* and *ball* are arguments: *John* the subject argument and *ball* the object argument.

Articulators: Structures in the vocal tract that are used to create speech sounds. There are dynamic (movable) articulators, such as the tongue and lips, and there are static (immovable) articulators, such as the alveolar ridge and teeth, to which the dynamic articulators approximate (make contact) in the production of speech sounds.

Assimilation: 1. In relation to cognition, this term applies to children's exposure to new information or an event. In this case, the new entity can be assimilated or incorporated into a schema that already exists when there is a good fit between the new information and the preexisting schema. 2. In relation to phonetics, this term describes the changing of a speech sound due to the influence of adjacent sounds. The production of a speech sound that is similar to another sound in the same word (e.g., *tat* produced in place of *cat*).

Assimilation processes: Progressive assimilation consists of a speech sound taking on the characteristics of a preceding sound within the word (e.g., *kak* for *cat*). Regressive assimilation consists of a speech sound taking on the characteristics of a succeeding sound (e.g., *tat* for *cat*).

Asymmetrical: A clinically significant difference in the degree of loss between the two ears that may be frequency specific.

Audiogram: A standard graph for representing hearing sensitivity, in decibels hearing level (dB HL) as a function of frequency.

Auditory brainstem response (ABR): The objective, physiologic measure most frequently used for testing infants and children to estimate hearing sensitivity and/or confirm a diagnosis of hearing loss. The ABR is an electroencephalographic (EEG) response that is recorded via three scalp electrodes and represents changes in electrical activity from the auditory nerve to midbrain level as a result of sound presented to the ear.

Auditory cortex: An area of the temporal lobe of the brain that processes auditory information.

Auditory neuropathy spectrum disorder (ANSD): This hearing disorder is characterized by normal outer-, middle-, and inner-ear function at least up to the level of the outer hair cells, but with abnormal function of the inner hair cells or auditory nerve fibers.

Auditory perception: The ability to perceive and understand sounds through the abilities associated with specific organs, such as the human's ear. Sound exists in the form of vibrations that travel through the air or through other substances.

Autism Spectrum Disorder (ASD): Persistent difficulties in the social use of verbal and nonverbal communication for social purposes, the ability to change communication to match context or the needs of a listener, difficulty following rules for conversation and storytelling, difficulty making inferences or interpreting a speaker's meaning, difficulty understanding nonliteral or ambiguous meanings of language (e.g., idioms, and humor).

Autonomic nervous system (ANS): Innervates muscles and glands for involuntary actions (e.g., gland secretions). Responsible for the control of visceral functions (e.g., heart, digestion, and respiration).

Axon: A long fiber of a nerve cell (a neuron) that typically conducts electrical impulses away from the neuron's cell body.

Babbling: The early production of connected sequences of sounds by infants.

Basal ganglia: Structure in the brain responsible for the control of muscle tone and posture, along with organization and guidance of complex motor functions.

Basic sentences: Sentences composed of a subject + verb (e.g., *Susie ran*).

Basilar membrane: The membrane of the cochlea. This is a supporting membrane that aids in translating sound vibrations into electrical signals.

Bilabial stop: Sound produced by approximating the lips (e.g., /b/, /p/).

Bilateral hearing loss: A bilateral hearing loss is a hearing impairment in both ears. When someone has a loss in only one ear, it is known as a unilateral hearing loss.

Bilingual: Describes an individual who has proficiency in two languages. It may also describe individuals who have varying degrees of proficiency in three, four, or even more languages.

Bilingual first language acquisition: Acquiring two first languages from birth.

Bone conduction: A method of transmitting sound to the inner ear by mechanically vibrating the bones of the skull, thereby bypassing the outer and middle ear.

Bootstrapping: A process in which linguistic knowledge is acquired, enabling a child to analyze words or sentences well enough to acquire further knowledge of language. Figuratively, this early knowledge would serve as *bootstraps* by which children can pull themselves up to acquire the language spoken in the surrounding environment.

Bound morpheme: Serves a grammatical purpose and can be attached to a free morpheme.

Brainstem: The lower part of the brain, adjoining and continuous with the spinal cord.

Broca's area: A region in the left frontal lobe of the brain associated with speech that controls movements of the tongue, lips, and vocal cords.

Bronchioles: Tiny air tubes within the lungs that are a continuation of the bronchus. The bronchioles connect to the alveoli (air sacs).

Bronchus: A large air tube that begins at the end of the trachea and branches into the lungs.

Categorical perception: The ability to discriminate (tell the difference between) similar sounding sounds or syllables. Categorical perception tasks ask listeners to discriminate between things that belong to a different category (e.g., ba-ba-ba-ba-da-da-da-da). This task asks listeners to perceive a change.

Causal cognition: Provides children with the understanding of the relationship of cause and effect, such as what object causes another object to move, along with understanding of how desires, emotions, and beliefs are the cause of others' actions.

Causal relationships: Causality connects one process with another process, where the first process is responsible for the second process and the second process is dependent on the first process.

Causality: The principle that everything that happens must have a cause.

Central auditory processing disorder: A disorder in which school-age children have normal pure-tone audiograms but have difficulty perceiving speech that is degraded in any way by background noise, reverberation, competing signals in the contralateral ear, rapid rate of presentation, or filtering.

Central nervous system (CNS): The part of the nervous system that consists of the brain and the spinal cord. The CNS controls motor activities (e.g., walking, sitting, and speech) and movements that are connected to essential body functions (e.g., breathing). The CNS is also responsible for thought processes that emerge from interaction with the environment.

Cerebellum: A region of the brain that plays an important role in motor control. The cerebellum contributes to coordination, precision, and accurate timing of motor skills.

Cerebrum: The largest and uppermost portion of the brain. The cerebrum consists of the right and left cerebral hemispheres and accounts for two-thirds of the total weight of the brain.

Chaining: A narrative form that appears at about 3 years of age, when children talk about events related to a central topic with no particular order of occurrence.

Childhood apraxia of speech (CAS): Childhood apraxia of speech is a motor speech disorder that results in difficulty producing sounds, syllables, and words. CAS is not caused by muscle weakness or paralysis. Instead, the brain has difficulty with planning to move the articulators (e.g., lips, jaw, tongue) needed for speech.

Circumlocution: The use of an unnecessarily large number of words to express an idea, such as saying *I use it to dig a hole in the ground,* instead of saying the word "shovel."

Closed syllable: A syllable that ends in a consonant (e.g., *beet*).

Cochlea: The end organ of hearing; the portion of the inner ear that contains the sensory cells for the auditory system. It is fluid filled and composed of two concentric labyrinths: the outer made of bone and the inner of membrane.

Cochlear: Reference to the spiral-shaped cavity of the inner ear that resembles a snail shell and contains the sensory cells and nerve endings essential for hearing.

Cochlear implant: A device that serves to give a sense of hearing to a person who otherwise does not have access to sound. It includes a magnet and electrode array that is surgically implanted in the inner ear as well as an externally worn ear-level speech processor and microphone.

Code-mixing: A code is a system of signals used for sending messages. Code-mixing or -switching describes changes or mixes from one language or system to another. Speakers use code-switching to shift from a native language to a second language. Code-mixing can also be used to mark oneself as part of a particular ethnic group.

Cognition: The mental processes that consist of knowledge, along with the mechanisms to acquire knowledge. Cognitive skills consist of attention, working memory, reasoning, intuition, judgment, and perception.

Cognitive theory: Language emerges through cognitive skills, such as object permanence (the ability to produce words for entities or things that are absent) and through schema formation (the psychological structures that allow children to attach meaning to experiences and entities).

Coherence: Involves interpreting the meaning of a context or situation by considering all aspects of a situation, along with any previous knowledge that relates to an event.

Cohesion: The use of transitional expressions and other devices to guide readers and show how the parts of a text (written or spoken) relate to one other.

Cohesive devices: Linking words and phrases to make an organized thought. In narrative, the use of words to connect the text (e.g., *and then . . .*).

Communication: 1. The exchange of information between people through speaking, writing, or using a common system of signs or behavior. 2. The vehicle for social interaction, consisting of both verbal (words, sentences, narratives, and conversations) and nonverbal acts (eye gaze, gesture, turn-taking in conversation, and facial expressions).

Communicative competence: A person's knowledge of grammar, syntax, morphology, and phonology, along with an understanding of how and when to use this knowledge appropriately.

Communicative unit (C-unit): A method of separating spoken utterances or written sentences into distinct independent clauses (simple sentence) and any dependent or subordinating clauses, often used to measure growth in language abilities.

Competition model: The competition model views language processing as a series of competitions between lexical items, phonological forms, and syntactic patterns. The learning of language forms is based on the accurate recording of many exposures to words and patterns in different contexts.

Complex: When used to describe a sentence, complexity consists of the presence of an independent clause and at least one other independent or dependent clause. When used to describe language, complexity can consist of lengthy and complex utterances or reference to events not present in the current context.

Complex sentence: A sentence that contains an independent clause with one or more dependent clauses. A complex sentence always has a subordinator, such as *because, since, after, although,* or *when,* or a relative pronoun, such as *that, who,* or *which.*

Compound-complex sentence: A sentence made up of more than one main clause and at least one subordinate clause. It is the combining of a compound sentence with a complex sentence.

Compound sentence: A sentence that contains two independent clauses joined by a coordinator, such as *for, and, nor, but, or, yet,* or *so.*

Concepts: Abstract ideas, thoughts, or notions that are formed by experiences or occurrences. Children's conceptual development is supplied by the environment and the cognitive ability to form concepts about spatial (location), temporal (time), quantitative (number), qualitative (description), or social-emotional (feelings) knowledge.

Concrete operations stage: Stage of development that emerges at 6 years of age and continues until age 12. At this stage, children form ideas based on reasoning and are able to employ abstract thought.

Concrete (words): A concrete noun is one which can be experienced by our senses as we can touch it, see it, or hear it (e.g., table, apple, and dogs). An abstract noun cannot be experienced by our senses, as these nouns express a concept (e.g., truth).

Conductive: Something that can **conduct** or transfer heat, sound, or electricity.

Conductive hearing loss: A conductive hearing loss occurs when there is a loss of sound energy being transmitted through the outer ear or middle ear (tympanic membrane and/or ossicles). Conductive hearing loss decreases the sound energy reaching the cochlea for sounds of all intensity levels, thus making all sound perceived at levels more softly than would be perceived by a person with normal hearing sensitivity.

Confidence intervals: A confidence interval gives an estimated range of values, which is likely to include an unknown population parameter or the estimated range being calculated from a given set of sample data.

Congenital: Refers to a defect or condition in a fetus, present at birth.

Conjoined sentences: Composed of two main clauses that are conjoined by conjunctions (e.g., *and, or, but,* and *because*).

Conjunctions: Words that connect words, phrases, and clauses.

Content: The meaning of an expression.

Content word: A word that conveys meaning, such as a noun, verb, or adjective,

Context clues: Context clues help a reader to define a difficult or unusual word. Clues may appear within the same sentence or in the sentences that are contained in the text.

Contextualized language: Talk about the here and now, by referencing people, objects, and action that are present in the immediate context.

Contextualized narratives: Descriptions of people, things, or events present in the immediate environment.

Continuity: The hypothesis that there is continuity between children's preverbal behaviors (e.g., gestures, eye contact, prelinguistic vocalizations) and later language skills.

Conversational postulates: Conversation contains the conversational postulate or the assumption that a speaker is telling the truth, is offering information that is new and relevant to the conversation, and is offering information that the listener genuinely wants to hear.

Cooing: A stage in infants' prelinguistic speech development that consists of the production of single-syllable, vowel-like sounds.

Copula: In grammar, a linking verb, which links the subject of a sentence with an adjective or noun-phrase complement relating to it (e.g., *to be*, or *to seem*).

Corpus callosum: A structure of the brain in the longitudinal fissure that connects the left and right cerebral hemispheres. This is the structure that facilitates communication between the two hemispheres.

Counterfactual reasoning: Thoughts about events that did not actually occur, based on the condition of *what might* have happened.

Cranial nerves: These are nerves that emerge from the brain and brainstem. Ten of the 12 emerge from the brainstem. Cranial nerves relay information between the brain and body.

Critical thinking: Analysis of an action or event for accuracy and logic.

Cross-linguistic effects: The bi-directional influence of one language on the other in bilingual speech and language production.

Cultural broker: An individual, usually sharing the family's cultural background, who can provide an insider's information on that culture and aid in the interpretation of the family's linguistic and non-linguistic characteristics.

Culturally and linguistically diverse: Denotes not only those who are acquiring more than one language but also those who might be using more than one dialect (i.e., a rule-governed variant of a language, such as Appalachian English).

Deceleration: At certain points in development, bilingual children might demon-strate a slower rate of acquisition than their monolingual peers.

Decentration: Children are able to consider multiple multiple attributes of an object or situation (e.g., height and width of an object).

Decibels (dB): A mathematically derived ratio of sound level based upon the pressure exerted by a particular vibration relative to some reference pressure. Decibels hearing level (dB HL) refers to hearing sensitivity relative to normative data of sound pressure as a function of frequency.

Declarative sentences: Statements that provide information.

Decode: 1. Decoding is the ability to read something that has been written. 2. An individual is able to comprehend or understand information from another source.

Decontextualized language: Consists of language that is understandable without contextual support (e.g., things that support the meaning of the utterance). Meaning is conveyed only via linguistic cues.

Decontextualized narrative: Refers to descriptions of people, objects, and events that are not present in the immediate environment.

Deep structure: In transformational grammar, the deep structure is an abstract representation of a sentence, while surface structure corresponds to the version of the sentence that can be spoken and heard. Surface structures are derived from deep structures by a series of transformations.

Deferred imitation: Imitation of an event after a period of delay, showing that the child understands an expression. The child's imitative response may change or expand the original utterance.

Deictic terms: The phenomenon wherein understanding the meaning of certain words and phrases in an utterance requires contextual information (e.g., *that one, over there, here, he, she*). Words are deictic if their semantic meaning is fixed but their specific reference varies depending on time and/or place.

Deixis: An aspect of a communicative utterance whose full interpretation depends on knowledge of the context in which the communication occurs (e.g., the use of a word or expression such as *he, that, now,* or *here*).

Dendrites: Projections of the neuron that conduct stimulation received from other neurons to the cell body (soma) of a neuron.

Denial: Unwillingness to believe in something or admit that something exists.

Derivational morphemes: Prefixes and suffixes that are added to a root word to create additional meaning. This often changes the part of speech of the root word, as in adding the suffix *-er* to the verb *teach* to create the noun *teacher.*

Dialect: A rule-governed variant of a language.

Dialogic reading: A method to support a child's literacy and language skills through asking questions during a reading task.

Digraphs: A pair of written letters that represent a single speech sound (e.g., *th, sh, ch*).

Diphthongs: Vowel-like sounds that are produced with a gradually changing articulation (e.g., *how, boy,* and *sky*).

Discourse: The exchange of information or conversation between people consists of the transmission of information, opinions, ideas, or feelings.

Disinhibited: Lacking the ability to restrain from impulsive actions.

Divergent thinking: The ability to explore and provide multiple solutions to a problem.

Domain-specific vocabulary: Words that are specific to a specific domain (area or field) of study.

Dual language learners: Individuals acquiring two or more languages simultaneously while continuing to develop their first language.

Duration: The length of a syllable.

Dynamic assessment: An interactive approach to assessment that embeds intervention within the assessment process. This begins with a pretest, followed by intervention, and ending with a posttest. The goal is to determine the child's response to intervention.

Dysarthria: A motor speech disorder that affects the muscles of the mouth, face, pharynx, larynx, and respiratory system.

Dyslexia: A specific learning disability that affects reading. This disorder affects reading accurately and fluently. Dyslexia may also impact on reading comprehension, spelling, and writing.

Effectiveness: A measure to determine whether intervention was responsible for a change.

Effects: Focuses on determining if change occurred as a result of intervention. Change can be measured by charting outcomes throughout the intervention process.

Efferent fibers: Carrying information away from the central nervous system.

Efficiency: Determining how long it took the client to achieve the goals, how much effort was needed to facilitate change, and the hierarchy needed to produce a change.

Egocentric, egocentrism: Characterized by preoccupation with one's own internal world. The belief that you are the center of the universe and everything revolves around you.

Egocentric speech: The type of speech typically observed in young children which is not addressed to another person.

Electromotility: The movement, resulting from change in shape, of the cochlear outer hair cells in response to electrical changes within the outer hair cells.

Ellipsis: The omission of one or more words from a sentence, especially when the word that is omitted can be understood from the context. In the sentence, *I went but my wife didn't,* the omission of "go" at the end of the sentence (*I went but my wife didn't go*) is an example of ellipsis.

Embedding: A process by which one clause is included (**embedded**) in another.

Embodied cognition: A theory that the body influences cognition through the motor system, the perceptual system, and the body's interaction with the environment. In this view, the motor system influences the body and the mind influences body actions. Children's cognitive skills develop through the relationship between the infant's mind and physical body.

Emergent literacy: The period when preschoolers learn about print, before they actually learn to read. The skills and knowledge about literacy that a child acquires before learning to read, such as knowing that the print on a page contains information about the story.

Emergentism: The theory that language acquisition emerges from the interaction of biological forces and the environment. According to this theory, neither nature nor nurture alone is sufficient to prompt language learning and both of these influences must work in tandem to allow a child to acquire a language.

Encode: Encoding involves converting incoming information into meaning, such as spoken speech sounds into words. A sender transmits information (**encodes**) that a receiver comprehends or understands (decodes).

English language learners: Individuals who are learning English as another language.

Environment: The external factors influencing the life and activities of people, plants, and animals. Reference to the entities, things, and events that play a role in learning language.

Environmental: Relating to, or caused by, a person's interactions and surroundings.

Environmental theory: Environmental theory posits that the external environment provides the essential information to support language development.

Equilibrium: The process of fitting new information or input into an existing cognitive schema.

Eustachian tube: A slender tube that connects the middle ear cavity with the nasal part of the pharynx and serves to equalize air pressure on either side of the eardrum.

Evidence-based practice: The integration of clinical expertise, expert opinion, external scientific evidence, and client/patient/caregiver perspectives to provide high-quality services reflecting the interests, values, needs, and choices of the individuals we serve.

Executive function(s): The cognitive processes of planning, problem solving, working memory, inhibition, and multitasking.

Expansions: An adult's more mature version of a child's utterance that preserves the word order of the child's utterance (e.g., child says *Doggie eat*, adult might say, *The doggie is eating*).

Experience dependent development: The abilities that a human must acquire during development or adulthood that are unique to its own particular environment, such as information about the physical characteristics of the surroundings, the details of one's language, and other cognitive capacities. These are experiences that the brain does not expect (such as the ability and the skills to care for animals on a farm).

Experience expectant development: The brain is prepared for exposure to environmental experiences that result in the establishment of neural pathways that result in learning. For example, the brain expects to be exposed to visual images and spoken sounds to allow the development of visual and auditory systems.

Expository: A type of writing where the purpose is to describe, inform, explain, or define the author's subject to the reader.

Expository discourse: Language that is typically found in textbooks, classroom lectures, and technical papers.

Expressive language: The language an individual produces spontaneously. Expressive language skills consist of a variety of expressive skills, such as expressing words, ideas, and information.

Exuberant synaptogenesis: Tremendous growth in the number of synapses in the brain at about week 12 of development.

Fast mapping: A hypothesized mental process whereby a new concept can be learned based only on a single exposure to a given unit of information. Fast mapping is thought by some researchers to be particularly important during language acquisition in young children.

Fictional narrative: A story drawn from a child's imagination and in which the content is invented.

Figurative language: Non-literal phrases consisting of idioms, metaphors, similes, and proverbs.

Fissures: A series of valleys or depressions on the surface of the cerebrum.

Fluency: 1. The ability to read a text quickly, accurately, and with proper expression. This involves the ability to read with little effort and without conscious attention to the mechanics of reading. 2. The ability to speak, read, and/or write without difficulty.

FM educational amplification systems: A sound system used in the classroom to improve the degree to which the teacher's voice exceeds the background noise at the location of the receiver, thereby improving signal-to-noise ratio.

Form: The components of language that include syntax, morphology, and phonology.

Formal operations: The formal operational stage begins at approximately age 12 and lasts into adulthood. During this time, children develop the ability to think about abstract concepts with the use of logical thought, deductive reasoning, and systematic planning.

Free morphemes: A morpheme that can stand alone as a word. A free morpheme is also termed an unbound morpheme or a free-standing morpheme.

Frequency: Language processing is connected to input frequency in the frequency effects in the processing of phonology, phonotactics, reading, morphosyntax, formulaic language, language comprehension, grammaticality, sentence production, and syntax.

Function words: These express a grammatical or structural relationship with other words in a sentence. Function words include determiners (for example, *the, that*), conjunctions (*and, but*), prepositions (*in, of*), pronouns (*she, they*), auxiliary verbs (*be, have*), modals (*may, could*), and quantifiers (*some, both*).

Functional magnetic resonance imaging (fMRI): This is a functional neuroimaging procedure using MRI technology. This procedure measures brain activity by detecting changes associated with blood flow. When an area of the brain is in use, blood flow to that region also increases. In this way, brain activity during different tasks or activities can be determined.

Generative: A speaker's ability to generate many types of sentences (to generate or to produce).

Generative grammar: A finite set of rules that can be applied to generate sentences that are grammatical in a given language. These rules are derived from a speaker's tacit grammatical knowledge of the system of that language.

Gestation: The period of development before birth.

Glides: Often referred to as semi-vowels, these are vowel-like sounds that do not make up the nucleus of a syllable (i.e., /j/ and /w/).

Glottis: The space between the vocal folds.

Grammar: The rules that govern the composition of sentences, phrases, and words in any given language.

Graphemes: Written symbols, letters, or combinations of letters that represent a single sound. For example, the phoneme /f/ can be represented as *f* in the word *fast*, as *ph-* in *phone*, and as *-gh* in *laugh*.

Gray matter: The gray matter of the brain is mainly composed of neuronal cell bodies and unmyelinated axons. Axons are the processes that extend from neuronal cell bodies, carrying signals between those bodies. In the gray matter, these axons are mainly unmyelinated, meaning they are not covered by a whitish-colored, fatty protein called myelin. The gray matter serves to process information in the brain.

Guided distributional learning: This theory is part of emergentism, stating that language acquisition emerges from the interaction of biological forces and the environment. In this view, neither nature nor nurture alone is sufficient to prompt language learning.

Gyri: A series of elevations or ridges on the surface of the cerebral and cerebellar cortices.

Habilitative: Adjectival form of *habilitate*, meaning to make able to do something.

Hair cells: The sensory receptors of the auditory system. The hair cells transfer sound information to the auditory nerve.

Heaps: A stage in a child's pre-narrative development. The child expresses an assortment of unrelated ideas rather than connected information. For example, a child might just label objects or actions with no connection among these pieces of information.

Hearing aids: An electroacoustic device which typically fits in or behind the user's ear and is designed to selectively amplify sound based on the user's hearing loss for the sake of giving improved access to speech sounds.

Hertz: The term hertz (abbreviation Hz) is defined as the number of cycles (vibrations) that an object makes when put into motion). The number of cycles per unit of time is called the frequency of a sound. The perceived pitch of a sound is the ear's or mind's subjective interpretation of its frequency.

Heschl's gyrus: Gyri (prominent, rounded, elevated convolutions on the surfaces of the cerebral hemispheres) located on the upper surface of the temporal area of the cortex that are involved in the processing of auditory stimuli.

Homorganic: Having the same place of articulation in the vocal tract (e.g., /t/, /n/, and /d/).

Hypothalamus: A region of the brain located between the thalamus and the midbrain that controls the autonomic nervous system. For example, the hypothalamus regulates sleeping cycles, body temperature, and appetite.

Idioms: Expressions with meanings that cannot be predicted from the usual meaning of its constituent elements or words (e.g., kick the bucket).

Imperative sentences: Consist of a demand or request.

Incidental learning: The type of learning that occurs without direct teaching. Incidental learning describes children's learning of new words.

Incus: The middle bone of the ossicular chain in the middle ear. It articulates with the malleus at the top and has a projection that is joined to the stapes at the bottom.

Indirect speech act: An utterance whose linguistic form (a question) does not directly refer to its communicative purpose (a request for action).

Infant-directed speech: Patterns that consist of slowed rate and exaggerated intonational patterns. This type of speech has been termed "motherese."

Inferior frontal gyrus (IFG): Known as Broca's area and important for the motor programming and the expression of spoken language.

Inflectional morphemes: Maintain the word's grammatical category (e.g., noun, verb) and add a grammatical feature to that word (e.g., possession, or tense).

Inhibition: When an activity, impulse, desire, or a response is restrained or prevented.

Innate: Qualities or abilities that are inborn.

Innateness theory: A theory of language acquisition which states that at least some linguistic knowledge exists in humans at birth.

Inner hair cells: Transform the sound vibrations in the fluids of the cochlea into electrical signals that are then relayed via the auditory nerve and the auditory brainstem to the auditory cortex.

Input: Sensory information that is processed from an outside influence and is then acted upon or integrated.

Instrumental function: Playing a part in achieving a result or accomplishing a purpose.

Intelligibility: Refers to how clear and easily understood the speaker's speech is to a listener.

Intention: The meaning conveyed by a speaker. A listener must understand the speaker's intent or intention to understand the meaning of an utterance.

Intentional: The use of communication to indicate specific wants, desires, or needs.

Interaction function: Communication or joint activity involving two or more people.

Interactional dual systems model: A theory of bilingual language acquisition stating that bilingual children develop distinct linguistic systems for each language.

Interneurons: Interneurons are located in the CNS (brain and spinal cord). These are neurons that act as a link between sensory and motor neurons (sensation and movement). They transmit signals through the use of neurotransmitters, the chemicals that allow the transmission of signals from one neuron to the next.

Interpreter: One who conveys information from one language to another.

Interrogative sentences: These sentences ask a question. These sentences require an inversion of the subjects and auxiliary verbs (e.g., *am, is, are, was, were*).

Intonation: The rising or falling pitch of the voice when a word or syllable is produced.

Intrasentential growth: Refers to the advances in syntactic knowledge and use seen within the length of a sentence. This is a term meant to capture syntactic changes.

Item-based: A usage-based model in which children imitatively learn concrete linguistic expressions from the language they hear around them. Children use their general cognitive and social-cognitive skills to combine these individually learned expressions and structures to develop language.

Jargon: 1. Sequences of variegated babbling that have the intonation shape of the child's native language. 2. The language and vocabulary associated with a particular discipline, often confusing to novices and persons not familiar with that discipline.

Joint action: The shared action of two individuals on a single object or a collective activity.

Joint attention: The process by which young children focus their attention on an object or event with a social partner through nonverbal communication. This may include joint gaze and pointing.

Labio-dental: Produced at a place of articulation involving the lower lip and upper teeth (e.g., /f/ and /v/).

Language: A system of arbitrary symbols which is rule based, dynamic, generative, and used as a social tool in communication.

Language acquisition device (LAD): The concept that infants have an instinctive mental capacity which enables them to acquire and produce language. This theory asserts that humans are born with the instinct or innate facility for acquiring language. It is believed that without this innate knowledge of grammar, children would be unable to learn language as quickly as they do.

Language content: Semantics, or the meaning of words, phrases, sentences, and longer spoken utterances or written language.

Language dominance: When bilinguals are said to have greater skills in one language than in the other.

Language exposure: The amount of time an individual is exposed to a particular language.

Language form: The language areas that define the structure and rules of language: phonology, morphology, and syntax.

Language loss: This process occurs, over time, when the speech and language features of the first language are no longer utilized by the speaker, possibly due to less exposure or use of the speaker's first language.

Language processing: The way words are used to communicate ideas and feelings and how communication is understood.

Language proficiency: How well a language is spoken.

Language status: The degree of admiration or respect for a particular language.

Language use: How often and with whom each language is used.

Laryngeal system: The vocal folds are housed within the laryngeal system. The vocal folds are energized by air from the lungs and vibrate to produce phonation (sound produced by the vibration of the vocal folds).

Larynx: A set of structures that house the vocal folds.

Lexicon: A lexicon is the vocabulary of a person or a language.

Limbic system: A part of the brain that supports many functions, including emotions, long-term memory, self-preservation, and sensory processing (e.g., smells or scents).

Limited English proficient (LEP): This is a term used to describe a student who is limited in English proficiency and has not yet mastered English in the four domains of reading, writing, listening, and speaking.

Lingua-alveolar: Sounds produced at a place of articulation in which the tongue completely or nearly closes against the alveolar ridge (e.g., /s/, /t/, and /d/).

Lingua-dental: Sounds produced at a place of articulation involving the tongue and teeth, such as the sound "th."

Lingua-palatal: Sounds produced when the tongue articulates with the hard palate, such as the sound "sh."

Lingua-velar: Sound produced at a place of articulation involving the tongue and velum or the soft palate (e.g., /k/, and /g/).

Linguistic competence: Linguistic knowledge possessed by native speakers of a language. It is distinguished from linguistic performance, which is the way a language system is used in communication.

Linguistic individualism: The language experiences of children and adolescents outside of the family or traditional academic setting, consisting of unique vocabulary or concepts that allow a child or adolescent to acquire an individualized personal vocabulary or a different way of talking.

Liquids: A class of speech sounds also known as approximants (e.g., /l/, /r/).

Magical thinking: Magical thinking is most present in younger children, when children believe that their personal thought has a direct effect on the rest of the world.

Majority language: A language spoken by the majority of speakers in a region or in a country.

Main verb: The verb that conveys meaning in a sentence.

Malleus: This is the largest of the ossicles. It is continuous with the eardrum and articulates with the incus, the next bone in the chain in the middle ear.

Mandible: The bone making up the lower jaw of the face.

Marked sounds: Less natural occurring sounds in most languages (see *unmarked*).

Masked: The use of a noise applied to the non-test ear while testing the hearing sensitivity of the other ear; used when hearing sensitivity of the non-test ear is possibly better than the test ear, for the sake of determining true hearing sensitivity of the test ear.

Masking: Involves testing one ear while noise is introduced into the other ear. This allows for testing each ear separately.

Mean length of utterance (MLU): The average number of morphemes (basic units of meaning) a child produces. For example, *jump* is one morpheme, whereas *jumps* (*jump + s*) is two.

Means-end: This is a process in which the problem solver begins by envisioning the end, or ultimate goal, and then determines the best strategy for attaining the goal in his/her current situation.

Means-end behavior: Children's anticipation of an outcome allows them to achieve a goal.

Mental lexicon: A mental dictionary that contains information regarding a word's meaning, pronunciation, and syntactic characteristics.

Mental state verbs: These are verbs that refer to a person's mental state, e.g., *frighten, like, disappoint, think, believe,* and *remember*. These verbs are sometimes called mental verbs.

Metacognition: Knowledge of one's own thoughts and the aspects that influence thinking. Metacognition involves self-reflection, self-responsibility, initiative, goal setting, and time management.

Metalinguistic abilities: Allow a child to think and talk about language, along with the ability to use language to talk about language

Metalinguistic awareness: Refers to the ability to objectify language as a process as well as a thing and to consciously reflect on the nature of language.

Metalinguistic competence: Involves the awareness that language is composed of syntactic, semantic, morphological, phonological, and pragmatic domains that can be synthesized, analyzed, and reorganized.

Metalinguistic knowledge: The ability to think about language in a conscious manner.

Metalinguistic strategies: Allow children to reflect on and knowingly consider oral and written language and how it is used. The strategies that support vocabulary knowledge are semantic mapping, semantic feature analysis, and context clues.

Metaphor: A figure in which a word or phrase literally denoting one kind of object or idea is used in place of another to suggest a likeness between them (e.g., *drowning in money*).

Minority language: A language spoken by a minority or a smaller number of speakers in the region of a country.

Mirror neurons: These are neurons in the brain that fire when we undertake an action or perceive the actions of others. They provide an inner simulation or mirror of the actions that we observe, allowing the viewer's brain to symbolize and understand the actions of others.

Mixed hearing loss: When bone-conduction thresholds are poorer than 20 dB HL and air-conduction thresholds are elevated by another 10 dB or more (an air–bone gap is present).

Modal auxiliaries: Verbs that express mood (e.g., feeling, or intention), such as *can, could, shall, should, will,* and *would*.

Modal auxiliary verbs: A verb that combines with another verb to express mood or tense (e.g., *can, could, would,* and *should*).

Models: Examples of more mature language that can be imitated by a child. These consist of scaffolds that support language development.

Modifiability: This describes a child's responsiveness to intervention. This information consists of how the child responds to and uses new information, the quantity and quality of effort needed to make a change, the transfer of goals, or the generalization of new skills.

Morphemes: The minimal, meaningful, and distinctive components of grammar. Morphemes are commonly classified into free (morphemes which can occur as separate words) or bound forms (morphemes that cannot occur by themselves, such as affixes).

Morphology: A study of the system of rules for combining the smallest units of language into words.

Morphophonemic: Referring to the changes in pronunciation undergone by allomorphs of morphemes as they are modified by neighboring sounds, such as the change in the plural morpheme *-s* (i.e., /s/ to /z/) when following a voiced sound (e.g., cats vs. dogs).

Morphophonology: The study of the interaction between a language's morphemes and its phonological processes, focusing on the sound changes that occur when morphemes (minimal meaningful units) combine to form words.

Morphosyntactic development: The addition of morphemes that expand a child's syntax or sentence length. Examples consist of the production of determiners (*the*) and inflectional morphemes (e.g., the present progressive morph *-ing* and the plural morpheme *-s*).

Motherese: A form of speech that differs from typical adult speech, usually delivered with a "cooing" pattern of intonation, slowed production, a higher pitch, and greater intonation changes.

Motility: Capable of or demonstrating movement.

Motor: Activities such as walking, sitting, and speech that are controlled by the central nervous system.

Motor cortex: The part of the cerebral cortex in the brain where the nerve impulses originate that initiate voluntary muscular activity.

Motor neurons: Transmit "directions" to muscles for active movement.

Multilingual: The use of more than two languages.

Multilingualism: The knowledge or use of more than two languages.

Mutual exclusivity bias: Children's assumption that every object has only one label or name (e.g., *Mommy* cannot be called

Marissa). This bias is often held until children learn that an entity or an object can have more than one name.

Myelin: A sheath that covers many axons in the central nervous system, critical to neural transmission and normal muscle function by facilitating the rapid transmission of electrical impulses.

Myths: Traditional stories that consist of events that serve to explain a practice, belief, or natural phenomenon.

Nares: Nostrils.

Narrative: A verbal description of events which is longer than a single utterance. Narratives possess a structure that aids children's understanding of stories.

Nasal cavity: A cavity of the vocal tract that is important for the resonance of nasal sounds (i.e., /m/, /n/, and /ŋ/).

Nasals: Sounds produced by vocal fold vibration with the resonance of the nasal cavity added to the pharynx and oral cavity (e.g., /m/, and /n/).

National Institutes of Health: An agency of the U.S. Department of Health and Human Services that supports much of medical research.

Negative sentences: Sentences in which the child demonstrates a rejection or protest.

Nerve fibers: A process, axon, or dendrite of a nerve cell.

Nerves: These fibers form a network of pathways for conducting information throughout the body. Sensory (afferent) nerves carry information into the central nervous system about sensations (e.g., touch, temperature, and pain), and motor (efferent) nerves carry information away from the central nervous system for muscle control.

Nervous system: This system consists of nerve tissues and structures of the central and peripheral nervous systems that are responsible for thought, muscle control, and sensory functions.

Neural tube: Formed by the closure of ectodermal tissue in the early vertebrate embryo that later develops into the brain, spinal cord, nerves, and ganglia.

Neuron: A nerve cell.

Neuroplasticity: The lifelong ability of the brain to reorganize neural pathways based on novel or new experiences, along with anatomical or physiological changes due to injury.

Neurotransmitters: Chemicals which facilitate the transmission of signals from one neuron to the next across synapses. This chemical substance is released from the axon terminal that travels along the synapse to transfer an impulse to another cell.

Non-English proficient: Having minimal or no English proficiency.

Nonexistence: Children at the one- and two-word utterance stage express nonexistence to indicate disappearance (e.g., *All gone cookie*).

Noun phrase: The noun phrase is a part of a sentence that consists of a noun and its modifiers, including a noun clause, a word, or a pronoun that can function as the subject or object of a verb.

Nucleus: The nucleus of neurons contains genetic material (chromosomes) including information for cell development and synthesis of proteins necessary for cell maintenance and survival.

Object constancy: The understanding that objects remain the same even when viewed from a different perspective.

Object permanence: 1. The knowledge that objects have an existence in time and space, independent of whether or not they can be seen or touched. 2. The ability to remember that an object exists even when removed from sight.

Obligatory: An obligatory context is when a morpheme is required to make an equivalent grammatical sentence in adult speech, whether for linguistic or contextual reasons.

Onset: An onset is the part of the syllable that precedes the vowel of the syllable (e.g., /s/ from the word *sit*).

Open syllable: An open syllable is one in which the final sound in the syllable is a vowel (e.g., *bee*).

Operant conditioning: Modification of voluntary behavior through reward/positive reinforcement (a consequence that increases the likelihood of a behavior) or through punishment/negative reinforcement (a consequence that decreases the likelihood of a behavior).

Oral cavity: An air-filled cavity of the vocal tract (the mouth) that contains the tongue, teeth, hard palate, and the velum.

Orthography: Written system of a language, such as letters that compose written words.

Ossicles: Small bones within the middle ear that consist of the malleus, incus, and stapes.

Otitis media: An inflammation or infection of the middle ear, with or without the presence of effusion (fluid), that occurs in the area between the eardrum (the end of the outer ear) and the inner ear, including the eustachian tube.

Otoacoustic emissions (OAEs): Tiny sounds present in the ear canal that are thought to be generated by the electromotility of the outer hair cells of the cochlea.

Outer hair cells: Outer hair cells help amplify sound vibrations entering the inner ear from the middle ear. When hearing is working normally, the inner hair cells convert these vibrations into electrical signals that travel as nerve impulses to the brain, where the impulses are interpreted as sound.

Overextension: The process in which a child applies a word meaning to more exemplars than an adult would. A type of error in a child's early word usage that reflects overly inclusive definitions that are beyond acceptable adult usage. For example, a child may perceive similarities in the characteristics of entities and call them all the same name (e.g., all four-legged animals would be called *doggie*).

Overgeneralization: A typical process of extending the features of an entity to another entity (e.g., all four-legged animals called *doggie*). This process also applies to use of a rule, such as the use of the morpheme *-ed* to form the past tense form of a verb (e.g., *throwed, eated, goed*).

Overgeneralize: A process whereby children extend their use of grammatical features beyond the context of those in adult language, e.g., use of *-ed, walk + ed* to signify past tense of all verbs, *eat + ed* as opposed to *ate*). The term *overgeneralization* refers to this typical developmental process.

Paradigmatic: A response in a word association task from the same class (e.g., *hot-cold*). This response appears around age 9 when children possess a more developed semantic system. See **syntagmatic**.

Paralinguistic: The non-verbal elements of communication that modify meanings and convey emotion, including the pitch, volume, and intonation of speech.

Parallel distributed processing: The theory views the mind as composed of a great number of elementary units connected in a neural network. Mental processes are interactions between these units which excite and inhibit each other in parallel rather than sequential operations.

Parameters: Language-specific rules that apply to the specific syntactic rules for languages, such as word-order rules for sentence construction that differ across languages.

Paraphasias: The incorrect production of the wrong word or words.

Parasympathetic: The parasympathetic nervous system plays a role in the processes of the body, such as digestion, control of the heart rate, and contraction of the pupils. In contrast, the sympathetic nervous system increases the heart rate and dilates the pupils.

Pattern finding: Children's sensitivity to regularities in the patterns of the adult's utterances.

Perception: The use of senses (e.g., visual and auditory perception) and one's own concepts to acquire information about the environment.

Perceptual: Relating to or involving sensory perception.

Performatives: Speech acts that constitute an act of some kind, such as promising, threatening, or requesting.

Peripheral nervous system (PNS): The PNS consists of two parts: the somatic nervous system and the autonomic nervous system.

Perseveration: The excessive repetition of a word, phrase, or longer utterance.

Personal function: When a child attempts to communicate to express his/her feelings or attitudes.

Personal narrative: A narrative that describes past events experienced by the narrator or someone familiar to the narrator.

Perspective-taking: The perception of physical, social, or emotional situations from a point of view other than one's own.

Pharyngeal cavity: The cavity of the pharynx that consists of a part continuous anteriorly with the nasal cavity by way of the nasopharynx, a part opening into the oral cavity, and a part continuous posteriorly with the esophagus and opening into the larynx. Its anterior boundary is the root of the tongue and its posterior boundary is the pharyngeal wall.

Phonation: The process of setting the vocal folds into vibration to produce sound.

Phonemes: The smallest units of the sounds of a language that act to differentiate the meaning of words (e.g., /b/ in *bat* vs. /k/ in *cat*).

Phonemic awareness: A subset of phonological awareness that allows children to hear, identify, and manipulate phonemes.

Phonemic representations: A system for using letters or symbols to represent sounds in speech. The basis of phonetic and phonemic transcription is the phoneme, the smallest part of a word's sounds that can be clearly defined as a separate sound that affects meaning.

Phonetically consistent forms: Expressions used to convey consistent meaning, such as *doggy* used only to label dogs.

Phonetics: The study of the perception and production of speech sounds.

Phonics: Sound-letter or phoneme-grapheme correspondence.

Phonological awareness: Defined as children's awareness of the sound structure of words. This awareness consists of the ability to notice and manipulate the sounds of a language, separately from the meaning of the word.

Phonological processes: Children's simplification of words. These processes are predictable and consistent with typical development (e.g., "nana" produced in place of the word *banana*).

Phonology: Rules for the combination of sounds to form words in a language.

Phonotactics: A branch of phonology that deals with restrictions in a language on the permissible combinations of phonemes.

Phrase structure rules: Describe a language's syntax and sentence structure.

Pinna: The visible part of the ear.

Plasticity: Plasticity, also known as neuroplasticity, is a term that refers to the brain's ability to change and adapt as a result of experience.

Positron emission tomography (PET): A nuclear functional imaging technique used to observe metabolic processes in the body. PET provides the opportunity to study the organization of cognitive functions and language processing in the working brain.

Postlingual: After the development of speech and/or language.

Practical intelligence: The knowledge, not explicitly taught, needed to achieve or accomplish a goal. The skills involved with practical intelligence can be thought of as applied to practical skills (e.g., what an infant must do to obtain a goal or solve a problem).

Pragmatic: Relating to the rules for appropriate social interaction.

Pragmatics: 1. The branch of linguistics that studies language use rather than language structure. 2. The connection between language development and the environment or the context in which the communication occurs.

Predicate: The part of a sentence that provides information about the subject of the sentence, such as what the subject is doing or how the subject is affected. A sentence contains a subject (what or whom the sentence is about) and a predicate (which tells us something about the subject).

Prelingual: The period between birth and 13 months of age when an infant employs sounds and gestures to communicate wants and needs before recognizable speech develops.

Preoperational stage: This stage begins at approximately 18 months and ends at 6 years of age. During this period of development, children form ideas based on their own perception of events. This derives from egocentrism, with children centered on themselves, their own experience, and their own desires.

Presuppositions: Beliefs that a particular state of affairs is true or false without the provision of evidence.

Primary auditory cortex: The part of the temporal lobe that processes auditory information.

Principles: Innate language-general rules or general principles that apply to all languages, such as the principle that a sentence must contain a subject.

Principles and parameters theory: An innate language acquisition device that consists of language principles common to all languages and parameters that can be set for the grammatical rules for a particular language.

Print awareness: Knowledge that the printed word carries a message, including but not limited to the meaning and function of the printed word, recognition of words and letters, and terminology.

Private speech: This type of speech is often called egocentric speech, with children's speech not adapted to a listener's understanding or needs.

Processing: Involves the functions performed in the brain that allow us to perceive and understand spoken language, along with a speaker's ideas and feelings.

Propositions: A statement claiming that something is true or false.

Prosody: The suprasegmental aspects of speech, including intonation, stress pattern, word juncture, loudness, pausing, and rhythm. Prosody extends over syllables, words, or phrases.

Prospective mental development: What a child needs to learn with guidance from an adult or more experienced peer, in relation to the child's *zone of proximal development*.

Proverb: Expressions that express a thought or truth.

Proximity: Closeness in time and/or space.

Real-time functional magnetic resonance imaging (rtfMRI): Allows for brain–computer interface with a high spatial and temporal resolution and whole-brain coverage.

Recasts: An adult's correction or modifications of a child's utterances.

Receptive language: The language that people comprehend or understand.

Recurrence: A semantic relation produced by children to indicate the request of repetition (e.g., *More juice*).

Reduplicated babbling: Repeated sequences of repeated consonant-vowel pairs (e.g., *babababababa*).

Referent absent: Reference to a person, thing, or event absent from the current environment.

Referent present: Reference to a person, thing, or event when these elements are present within the current environment to which a linguistic expression refers.

Reflexive pronouns: Refer to the subject of the sentence compounded with *-self* (e.g., *myself, herself,* and *himself*).

Register: Modifications of language influenced by the current situation (e.g., conversation with close friends as compared with conversation with professors).

Regulatory function: Language used specifically to convey or to establish social dynamics between individuals. In child language, the attempt to regulate the behavior of another.

Rejection: The semantic relation used to reject (e.g., *no bed*).

Relational terms: These terms express a syntactic relationship between elements in a phrase or a sentence (e.g., *less, more, longer,* *because,* and *between*). The understanding of relational terms that develop as children develop the concepts that label these relationships.

Representational thought: The ability to picture something in your head.

Resonance: A phenomenon in which a body of air, having a natural tendency to vibrate at a particular frequency or frequencies, is set into vibration by another structure vibrating at or near those frequencies.

Retrospective mental development: The current skills that a child has mastered in relation to the child's *zone of proximal development.*

Reversibility: The capacity to be reversed or undone.

Rhotic diphthongs: These are r-colored or rhotic vowels (also called retroflex vowels, vocalic /r/, or rhotacized vowels) that can be articulated in various ways: The tip or blade of the tongue may be turned up during at least part of the articulation of the vowel (a retroflex articulation) or the back of the tongue may be bunched. Examples are found in the following words: *car, bear, ear,* and *four.*

Rhythm: The pattern formed by a sequence of stressed and unstressed syllables.

Rime: The part of a syllable which consists of its vowel and any consonant sounds that come after it (e.g., "it" from the word *sit*).

Scaffolding: The use of a model which consists of the input from more experienced language users to younger children to correct word use, sentence structure, and other forms of language.

Scaffolds: Input from adults that provide children with cues and supports that allow them to acquire language. Scaffolds are used when children produce words or sentences that are not consistent with adults' productions (e.g., *eated/ate, goed/went, I eating/I am eating*).

Schemas: 1. According to Piaget, the basic psychological structures for organizing information. 2. Organizational or conceptual patterns in the mind used to catagorize objects or ideas.

Scripts: A sequence of familiar comments, narratives, and events that have been routinized with familiarity to a situation or event.

Selection restrictions: Constraints on particular word meanings that govern potential word combinations.

Semantic features: The perceptual or functional aspects of meaning that characterize a word. Semantic processing occurs when we hear a word and encode its meaning, which involves understanding.

Semantic relations: The relationship between the concepts or meanings (e.g., agent + action = *Dogs bark*).

Semantic roles: A semantic role is the underlying relationship that a word has with the main verb in a clause, as shown in the relation of the semantic role of the agent (*boy*) to the verb *left* in the sentence, *The boy left yesterday.*

Semantics: 1. The study of *meaning* in a language, as it is expressed in words, phrases, sentences, and longer spoken, written, or signed utterances. 2. The component of language that refers to meaning, and the rules that govern the assignment of meaning to entities (people, animals, and things) along with activities or events. 3. A subdivision of linguistics devoted to the study of meaning in language and how the meanings in language are formed by the use and interrelationships of words, phrases, and sentences.

Semiotic function: How words or signs create *meaning* as elements of communicative behavior, such as signs that take the form of words, images, sounds, gestures, and objects.

Sensitivity: 1. The ability to detect the presence of a signal; e.g., hearing loss exists when there is diminished sensitivity to the sounds heard at intensity levels consistent with normal hearing. 2. The percentage of individuals correctly identified with a disorder.

Sensorineural: A hearing loss is caused by the inner ear.

Sensorineural hearing loss: Occurs when there is dysfunction in the cochlea or the nerve pathways from the inner ear to the brain, resulting in loss of hearing sensitivity. This is the most common type of hearing loss and generally cannot be medically or surgically corrected.

Sensory cells: Detect information (e.g., sounds, light, touch, smell, taste, and temperature) through receptors on their surface. This information travels through nerves from the sensory cells to the brain.

Sensory information: Sensory acuity is the actual physical ability of the sensory organs to receive input, while sensory processing is the ability to interpret the information the brain has received. The processing of sensory information consists of tactile perception (touch), visual perception (vision), gustatory perception (taste), auditory perception (hearing), and olfactory perception (smell). Additional sensory information consists of the perception of pain, touch, temperature sense, and limb proprioception or limb position.

Sensory neurons: Nerve cells that transmit sensory information (e.g., sight, sound, touch, or feeling). This sensory input sends this information to other elements of the nervous system, with final transmission of the sensory information to the brain or spinal cord.

Sequential bilinguals: Those who acquire a second language after establishing a foundation in their first language.

Simile: A figure of speech in which two unlike things are explicitly compared, as in, "she is like a rose."

Simple sentence: A sentence that contains only a subject and a verb (e.g., *Dogs bark*).

Simultaneous bilinguals: Those who acquire at least two languages before the age of about 5 years.

Social cognition: The psychological processes that enable individuals to take advantage of social signals that include facial expressions, such as fear and disgust, which warn us of danger, and eye gaze direction, which indicate where interesting things can be found.

Social competence: The emotional and cognitive skills and behaviors that children need for successful social adaptation and social interaction.

Social information processing: The way in which people think about themselves and the social world, including how they select, interpret, remember, and use social information gained in interaction.

Social interaction: Any action that is shared with others and contains a shared symbolic system.

Social-interaction theory: Children's language acquisition emerges through social interaction and experience with language used in the external environment. Children possess the innate desire for social interaction.

Socio-interactional: Relating to social relations or social interaction as a factor in language development.

Soma: The main part of the neuron that contains the nucleus of the cell.

Somatic nervous system: Relating to the nerves that carry motor (movement) and sensory (e.g., hearing, touch, and sight) information to and from the central nervous system. These nerves are responsible for voluntary muscle movements and for processing sensory information.

Specificity: Measures the proportion of positives that are correctly identified as such and the proportion of negatives that are correctly identified as such. For example, the percentage of individuals correctly identified as typically developing.

Speech: The neuromuscular process by which humans create a meaningful sound signal that is transmitted through the air (or another medium, such as a telephone line) to a receiver.

Speech acts: A method of categorizing a speakers's intent or meaning (e.g., request, comment, promise). These spoken utterances are called *acts* because many types are intended to result in action (e.g., *Can you pass the salt?*).

Speech awareness threshold (SAT): The weakest intensity at which the child demonstrates awareness of the presence of sound, when a speech stimulus is presented through the audiometer using a developmentally appropriate test method.

Speech reception threshold (SRT): The weakest intensity at which the child can identify 50% of spondee words from a closed set of familiar items. A spondee word has two syllables with equal stress, such as *baseball* or *toothbrush*.

Stapes: The third and smallest of the ossicles in the middle ear.

Stereocilia: Small, hair-like projections situated on the top of the hair cells that are located in the inner ear.

Stop-plosive: A class of speech sounds produced by forming a complete closure in the oral cavity, building up pressure behind that closure, and suddenly releasing the closure to produce a brief noise burst.

Strategies: Chosen plans to bring about a desired future, such as achievement of a goal or solution to a problem.

Stroke: A stroke is the sudden death of brain cells in a localized area due to inadequate blood flow.

Subordinate clause: A subordinate clause, sometimes called a dependent clause, usually introduced by a subordinating element such as a subordinating conjunction or relative pronoun.

Subordinate dependent clause: A subordinate clause, sometimes called a dependent clause, usually introduced by a subordinating element such as a subordinating conjunction or relative pronoun. The subordinate dependent clause must always be attached to a main clause, as it completes the meaning of the sentence (e.g., *After Mary ate the sandwich, she cleaned the table*).

Subordinating conjunctions: Words that join a subordinate clause to a main clause, such as *after, although, because, until,* and *when*.

Subordination: This is a concept of syntactic formation, with one clause subordinate to another. A dependent clause is called the subordinate clause and the independent clause is called the main clause. The subordinate clause is introduced with subordinate conjunctions, such as *after, because,*

before, while, and *when* (e.g., **Before we eat**, *we wash our hands*).

Substitution processes: Consist of the substitution of one phonemic class (e.g., stops) for another (e.g., fricatives).

Sulci: A series of valleys or depressions on the surface of the cerebrum.

Superior frontal gyrus: Contributes to higher cognitive functions and working memory.

Superior temporal gyrus (STG): This area of the brain consists of the primary auditory cortex, responsible for processing sounds. It also comprises Wernicke's area, which is involved in language comprehension.

Supralaryngeal vocal tract: Consists of the oral, pharyngeal, and nasal cavities.

Surface structure: Structural characteristics of the actual spoken message. The surface structure derives from the deep structure through the utilization of phrase structure and transformational rules.

Syllable structure processes: Refers to the composition and sequencing of consonants and syllables within a word.

Syllogism: Involves a deductive process. A formal argument consisting of a major and minor premise and a conclusion.

Symbolic functions: A word used to represent an entity or activity not present in the current context. Children's ability to think or label a person, thing, or event even when not present.

Symmetrical: Similar degree of hearing loss in both ears across frequencies.

Sympathetic: The part of the nervous system that plays an excitatory role, such as preparing the body for a fight or flight response.

Synapse: Connection between neurons through which signals flow from one neuron to another.

Synaptic cleft: The space between neurons at a nerve synapse, across which a nerve impulse is transmitted by a neurotransmitter.

Syntagmatic: Relating to the function and behavior of a word or phrase within a syntactic unit. Within a word association task, a child's response that follows in a syntactic sequence (e.g., *big-ball*). By age 9, children respond with a word from the same class (a paradigmatic response).

Syntagmatic-paradigmatic shift: Refers to the change that occurs when children provide a response that is in the same grammatical class as the stimulus word (e.g., *table-chair*). Younger children provide a response that represents a syntactic form (e.g., *table-eat*).

Syntax: 1. Rules that govern the way words combine to form phrases, clauses, and sentences. 2. The order or arrangement of words in a sentence.

Tectorial membrane: The gelatinous structure that extends along the longitudinal length of the cochlea parallel to the basilar membrane. The tectorial membrane moves along with the pressure variations of the cochlear fluid, with movement encoded into electrical digital signals to the brain through the cochlear nerve.

Temporal-parietal cortex: Incorporates information from the thalamus and the limbic system, as well as from the visual, auditory, and somatosensory systems. This area of the brain also integrates information from both the external environment as well as from within the body.

Text structure: The way written text is organized. Knowledge of text structure supports comprehension of the text.

Thalamus: A part of the brain associated with basic functions, such as sleep and attention. The thalamus also relays information from eyes, ears, and spinal cord to the cerebral cortex.

Thematic roles: These terms (e.g., *agent, patient,* and *location*) label the semantic relationship between the verb and noun phrases of sentences (e.g., *agent + action = daddy go*).

Theory of mind (TOM): The ability to understand others' mental states, such as individuals' beliefs, intents, wishes, beliefs, and knowledge.

Total vocabulary size: The vocabulary knowledge of an individual, based on vocabulary for all languages spoken.

Transfer: The generalization of new skills.

Transformation: The rules for transforming one type of sentence into another, such as the transformation of an active sentence (*John kicked the ball*) into a passive sentence (*The ball was kicked by John*).

Transformational rules: Rules that operate on strings of symbols, rearranging phrase-structure elements to form an acceptable sentence for output.

Translation equivalents: Words that have an identical or functional meaning across languages.

Translator: Conveys information from one language to another.

Traumatic brain injury: Traumatic brain injury occurs when an external mechanical force causes brain dysfunction. Traumatic brain injury usually results from a violent blow or jolt to the head or body. An object penetrating the skull, such as a bullet or shattered piece of skull, also can cause traumatic brain injury.

T-units: Measurements used to determine average sentence length in the spoken or written language of school-age children and adolescents. T-units include only full, independent clauses (e.g., basic sentences) and any dependent clauses.

Tympanometry: A procedure conducted principally to assess middle-ear function (how well sound is conducted through the eardrum and ossicles), rather than a test of hearing.

Underextension: The use of a general word to mean one very specific thing, (e.g., "baba" may mean MY bottle and my bottle only). This constitutes a restricted understanding of the meaning of a term.

Unilateral hearing loss: Refers to a hearing loss in only one ear, while a bilateral hearing loss is a hearing impairment in both ears.

Unmarked: A sound that appears to be naturally occurring and is acquired earlier. Unmarked sounds tend to occur more frequently across languages than marked sounds.

Unmasked: The unmasked threshold is the quietest level of a signal that can be perceived without a masking signal present when testing hearing sensitivity. The masked threshold is the quietest level of the signal perceived when combined with a specific masking noise.

Usage-based theory: A theory of language development in which children begin with a concrete understanding of language, beginning with imitation.

Use: A linguistic term that defines the pragmatics of language, or rules for using language in interaction.

Variegated babbling: A stage in babbling characterized by varied sequences of sounds in syllables. (e.g., *babigoogi*).

Velar stop: A sound produced when the dorsum of the tongue articulates against the velum (soft palate) (e.g., /k/, /g/).

Velum: A muscular extension of the hard palate also known as the soft palate. The velum is lowered during production of nasal sounds (e.g., /m/, and /n/) and is raised during production of all other English speech sounds.

Velopharyngeal closure: The closing of the nasal cavity from the oral and pharyngeal cavities.

Verbal reasoning: Involves the ability to draw conclusions, solve problems, and make decisions.

Verb phrase: The predicate of a sentence provides information about the subject (e.g., The car *was stolen*). The verb phrase (*was stolen*) consists of the information about the subject (*The car*).

Visual language: A part of the reading process that is considered a secondary system, based on the use of visual skills to successfully recognize words and gather meaning from the written text.

Vocables: Word-like productions that emerge at about 10 to 12 months. These words lack precise meaning but are perceived to sound like a real word.

Vocal folds: A pair of muscular tissues in the larynx that are separated during inhalation and achieve closure to be set into rapid vibration to produce sound (phonation). The vocal folds are also known as vocal cords.

Voiced fricatives: Produced by forming a significant constriction, building up pressure behind the constriction, and forcing air through the constriction. Voiced fricatives are produced while the vocal folds are set into vibration (e.g., /v/, /ð/, /z/, and /ʒ/).

Voiced stops: A class of speech sounds produced by forming a complete closure in the oral cavity, building up pressure behind that closure, and suddenly releasing the closure to produce a brief noise burst. Voiced stops are produced when the vocal folds are set into vibration (e.g., /b/, /d/, and /g/).

Voiceless fricatives: Sounds produced by forming a significant constriction, building up pressure behind the constriction, and forcing air through the constriction. Voiceless fricatives are produced without vibration of the vocal folds. All fricatives, with the exception of /h/, a glottal fricative, are created in the oral cavity.

Voiceless stops: A class of speech sounds produced by forming a complete closure in the oral cavity, building up pressure behind that closure, and suddenly releasing the closure to produce a brief noise burst. Voiceless stops are produced without vibration of the vocal folds (e.g., /p/, /t/, and /k/).

Vowels: Speech sounds that are formed without a significant constriction of the oral and pharyngeal cavities and that serve as a syllable nucleus.

Wernicke's area: A region of the brain that is important in language development. Wernicke's area is located on the temporal lobe on the left side of the brain and is responsible for the comprehension of speech (Broca's area is related to the production of speech).

Word: A meaningful sound or combination of sounds that is a unit of language or its representation in a text.

Word recognition: How well the individual understands speech stimuli.

Working memory: A type of memory in which information is held while being processed. Working memory allows a child to understand and remember a series of directions.

Zone of proximal development: The distance between the actual developmental level, which is determined by autonomous problem solving, and the level of potential development, determined through problem solving under adult guidance or in collaboration with more proficient peers.

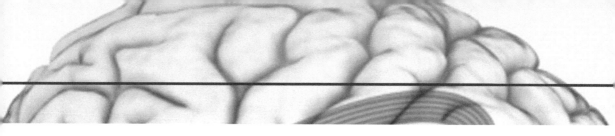

INDEX

Note: Page numbers in **bold** reference non-text material

A

Abstract concepts, 153
Abstract lexical terms, 132
Abstract thought, 61, 81, 150, 152
Acceleration, of language acquisition in
bilingual children, 211
Accommodation, 80
Active engagement, 41
Adaptation, 80
Additive chains, 136
Additive conjunctions, 138
Adjectives, 12, **14**
Adolescence
abstract thought in, 150
critical-thinking skills in, 154
figurative language in, **151**, 157
genre comprehension in, 197–198
language development in, 149–150,
172–173
language skills in, 150
linguistic attainments in, **151**
literacy development in, 197–200
literacy skills in, 170–171, **171–173**
metalinguistic awareness in, 150, 152
metalinguistic competence in, 152–153
metalinguistic knowledge in, **152**,
152–153
metalinguistic strategies used in, 156,
156
morphological development in, 164,
166–167, **166–167**
pragmatic development in, **151**, 167, **169**,
169–170

reading comprehension in, 197–198
reading fluency in, 199
self-esteem in, 200
semantic development in
conversation, 160
expository discourse, 160–161, **161**
figurative language, **151**, 157
idiom, 157–158
metaphor, 158
narratives, 159–160
persuasion, 161
proverbs, 158–159
riddles, 159
similes, 158
vocabulary, 155–157
sentence development in, 167, **168**
syntactic complexity analysis in, 164,
164–165
syntactic development in, 162–164
syntactic elaboration in, 162–163
verbal reasoning in, 153–155
vocabulary comprehension in, 197–198
writing in, 199
Adventitious hearing loss, 238–239
Adverbial clause, 164, **164**
Adverbial conjunct terms, 163
Adverbs, 13, **14**
Affect, **3**
Affix, 192
African American English, Mainstream
American English versus, 87, **88–90**,
167
Air conduction testing, 235, **246**
American Sign Language, 239